Forest Management and Water Resources in the Anthropocene

Special Issue Editors

Ge Sun

James M. Vose

MDPI • Basel • Beijing • Wuhan • Barcelona • Belgrade

MDPI

Special Issue Editors

Ge Sun
United States Department of
Agriculture
Forest Services
USA

James M. Vose
United States Department of
Agriculture
Forest Services
USA

Editorial Office
MDPI AG
St. Alban-Anlage 66
Basel, Switzerland

This edition is a reprint of the Special Issue published online in the open access journal *Forests* (ISSN 1999-4907) from 2015–2016 (available at: http://www.mdpi.com/journal/forests/special_issues/forest_water).

For citation purposes, cite each article independently as indicated on the article page online and as indicated below:

Author 1; Author 2. Article title. *Journal Name* **Year**, *Article number*, page range.

First Edition 2017

ISBN 978-3-03842-575-5 (Pbk)
ISBN 978-3-03842-576-2 (PDF)

Cover photo courtesy of Victor T. Sun

Table of Contents

About the Special Issue Editors

Ge Sun is a Research Hydrologist with the Eastern Forest Environmental Threat Assessment Center, USDA Forest Service Southern Research Station, and an adjunct professor at North Carolina State University. Dr. Sun conducted forest hydrological research on various ecosystems from Florida's cypress swamps in the humid southeastern United States to northern China's Loess Plateau dry lands. Currently Dr. Sun's research focuses on the effects of climate change, land use change, and wildland fires on water and carbon resources at multiple scales. Dr. Sun has authored more than 200 journal articles and book chapters. Dr. Sun received several distinguished awards including Fellow of the American Water Resources Association and the Southern Research Station Director's Distinguished Science Award. He was the co-founder of the US-China Carbon Consortium and served as a forestry expert for the Forest Service International Programs mission in Asia, Africa, and Mexico. He received degrees in forest hydrology from Beijing Forestry University (BS in 1985 and MS in 1988) and the University of Florida (Ph.D. in 1995).

James M. Vose is a Senior Research Ecologist with the Center for Integrated Forest Science, USDA Forest Service, Southern Research Station and in partnership with the North Carolina State University, Department of Forestry and Environmental Resources, where he is also Adjunct Professor. Prior to becoming co-founder of CIFS in 2012, Dr. Vose conducted and led cutting-edge research in forest ecosystem science at the Coweeta Hydrologic Laboratory for 25 years, including interdisciplinary studies investigating ecosystem responses to fire, evaluating the effectiveness of riparian zone restoration and buffer widths, and quantifying ecosystem responses to climate change, forest management activities, and insect outbreaks. His current research is focused on science synthesis and understanding the complex interactions among climate, land use, and water resources at multiple scales. He has received numerous awards for his scientific accomplishments and has authored over 250 scientific papers and book chapters. He received degrees in forestry and forest ecology from Southern Illinois University (BS in 1982), Northern Arizona University (MS in 1984), and North Carolina State University (PhD in 1987).

Preface to "Forest Management and Water Resources in the Anthropocene"

The Earth has entered the Anthropocene epoch that is dominated by humans. Forests are widely recognized for their capacity to provide an array of ecosystem services. Decades of forest hydrological research around the world has provided a depth of understanding on the relationships among forests and water, and how these relationships change in response to climate variability, disturbance, and forest management. This understanding has facilitated a strong predictive capacity and the development of best management practices to protect water resources while sustaining other natural resources. Despite the advancement in ecohydrological science and understanding of forest and water interactions, the rapid pace of changes in climate, disturbance regimes, wildlands, invasive species, human population growth, and land use expected in the 21st century is likely to create substantial challenges for watershed management. These challenges are likely to be complex and large scale, involving a combination of direct effects and indirect biophysical watershed responses, as well as socioeconomic impacts and feedbacks. New approaches, models, and best management practices may be required to ensure resiliency of forest watersheds to future conditions.

This book represents a collection of 13 papers published as a Special Issue in Forests during 2015-2016. These studies explore the complex relationships between forests and water in a rapidly changing environment, examine the trade-offs and conflicts between water quantity and other ecosystem services such as soil erosion control and water quality improvement, and propose new management approaches for sustaining water resources in the Anthropocene. We organize the 13 papers in four major themes that address emerging issues about forest water management in several unique regions.

The first theme examines the complex interactions among climate, water, forests, and humans. It provides an overview of the grand challenges and opportunities facing the forest land managers in sustaining water resources as one of the key ecosystem services under a rapid changing environment. Long term forest hydrological studies from North America (i.e., Canada, U.S.) and the arid Loess Plateau region of northern China are summarized to demonstrate the importance of forests in sustaining water resources [1–3]. The second theme presents process-based studies on the effects of land use changes on ecohydrological processes including baseflow [4], coefficient of flow immoderation and variation [5], and evapotranspiration in the humid Amazon [6] and semi-arid alpine regions in western China [7]. The third theme includes studies on the impacts of climate change and variability on soil moisture [8], and water supply and quality [9], and presents a case study to demonstrate the combined effects of changes in land cover and climate on streamflow and sediment loading in Vietnam [10]. The fourth and last theme covers studies that focus on innovative research methodology and models that are being used in addressing emerging forest water issues such as 'paired watershed', understanding small watershed to landscape-level hydrological processes [11], evaluating impacts of wildland fires [12], and mapping stream network for riparian forest management [13]. In summary, these studies clearly show that the science of ecohydrology and watershed management are evolving rapidly amid global environmental changes.

Forest managers are facing unprecedented demands to provide multiple ecosystem services in the Anthropocene. We hope that the information provided by this book is timely and helpful for land managers and policy makers to better understand and undertake the future challenges in forest and water management. We would also like to thank the authors for sharing their research and the reviewers and editors for their dedication that made this Forests Special Issue a success.

Ge Sun and James M. Vose

Special Issue Editors

References

1. Sun, G.; Vose, J. Forest Management Challenges for Sustaining Water Resources in the Anthropocene. *Forests* **2016**, *7*, 68, doi:10.3390/f7030068.
2. Creed, I.; Weber, M.; Accatino, F.; Kreutzweiser, D. Managing Forests for Water in the Anthropocene—The Best Kept Secret Services of Forest Ecosystems. *Forests* **2016**, *7*, 60, doi:10.3390/f7030060.
3. Zhang, J.; Zhang, T.; Lei, Y.; Zhang, X.; Li, R. Streamflow Regime Variations Following Ecological Management on the Loess Plateau, China. *Forests* **2016**, *7*, 6, doi:10.3390/f7010006.
4. Huang, X.; Shi, Z.; Fang, N.; Li, X. Influences of Land Use Change on Baseflow in Mountainous Watersheds. *Forests* **2016**, *7*, 16, doi:10.3390/f7010016.
5. Assani, A.; Delisle, F.; Landry, R.; Muma, M. Effects of Land Use on Flow Rate Change Indices. *Forests* **2015**, *6*, 4349–4359, doi:10.3390/f6114349.
6. Kunert, N.; Aparecido, L.; Barros, P.; Higuchi, N. Modeling Potential Impacts of Planting Palms or Tree in Small Holder Fruit Plantations on Ecohydrological Processes in the Central Amazon. *Forests* **2015**, *6*, 2530–2544, doi:10.3390/f6082530.
7. Gao, B.; Qin, Y.; Wang, Y.; Yang, D.; Zheng, Y. Modeling Ecohydrological Processes and Spatial Patterns in the Upper Heihe Basin in China. *Forests* **2016**, *7*, 10, doi:10.3390/f7010010.
8. Liu, Y.; Zhao, W.; Wang, L.; Zhang, X.; Daryanto, S.; Fang, X. Spatial Variations of Soil Moisture under Caragana korshinskii Kom. from Different Precipitation Zones: Field Based Analysis in the Loess Plateau, China. *Forests* **2016**, *7*, 31, doi:10.3390/f7020031.
9. Elias, E.; Rodriguez, H.; Srivastava, P.; Dougherty, M.; James, D.; Smith, R. Impacts of Forest to Urban Land Conversion and ENSO Phase on Water Quality of a Public Water Supply Reservoir. *Forests* **2016**, *7*, 29, doi:10.3390/f7020029.
10. Wang, J.; Hiroshi, I.; Ning, S.; Khujanazarov, T.; Yin, G.; Guo, L. Attribution Analyses of Impacts of Environmental Changes on Streamflow and Sediment Load in a Mountainous Basin, Vietnam. *Forests* **2016**, *7*, 30, doi:10.3390/f7020030.
11. Neary, D. Long-Term Forest Paired Catchment Studies: What Do They Tell Us That Landscape-Level Monitoring Does Not?. *Forests* **2016**, *7*, 164, doi:10.3390/f7080164.
12. Robinne, F.; Miller, C.; Parisien, M.; Emelko, M.; Bladon, K.; Silins, U.; Flannigan, M. A Global Index for Mapping the Exposure of Water Resources to Wildfire. *Forests* **2016**, *7*, 22, doi:10.3390/f7010022.
13. Ågren, A.; Lidberg, W.; Ring, E. Mapping Temporal Dynamics in a Forest Stream Network—Implications for Riparian Forest Management. *Forests* **2015**, *6*, 2982–3001, doi:10.3390/f6092982.

![forests logo] *forests*

MDPI

Communication

Forest Management Challenges for Sustaining Water Resources in the Anthropocene

Ge Sun [1,*] and James M. Vose [2]

[1] U.S. Department of Agriculture, Forest Service, Southern Research Station, Eastern Forest Environmental Threat Assessment Center, Raleigh, NC 27606, USA
[2] U.S. Department of Agriculture, Forest Service, Southern Research Station, Center for Integrated Forest Science, Department of Forestry and Environmental Resources, Raleigh, NC 27695, USA; jvose@fs.fed.us
* Correspondence: gesun@fs.fed.us; Tel.: +1-919-515-9498; Fax: +1-919-513-2978

Academic Editor: Timothy A. Martin
Received: 19 January 2016; Accepted: 10 March 2016; Published: 15 March 2016

Abstract: The Earth has entered the Anthropocene epoch that is dominated by humans who demand unprecedented quantities of goods and services from forests. The science of forest hydrology and watershed management generated during the past century provides a basic understanding of relationships among forests and water and offers management principles that maximize the benefits of forests for people while sustaining watershed ecosystems. However, the rapid pace of changes in climate, disturbance regimes, invasive species, human population growth, and land use expected in the 21st century is likely to create substantial challenges for watershed management that may require new approaches, models, and best management practices. These challenges are likely to be complex and large scale, involving a combination of direct and indirect biophysical watershed responses, as well as socioeconomic impacts and feedbacks. We discuss the complex relationships between forests and water in a rapidly changing environment, examine the trade-offs and conflicts between water and other resources, and propose new management approaches for sustaining water resources in the Anthropocene.

Keywords: climate change; disturbance; drought; forest hydrology; modeling; urbanization; watershed management

1. Introduction

According to the International Union of Geological Sciences (IUGS), we are officially in the Holocene ("entirely recent") epoch, which began 11,700 years ago after the last major ice age. However, since the 1990s, some scientists have argued that the Earth entered an "Anthropocene" epoch beginning from the industrialization in the 1800s [1,2]. Anthropocene represents anthropo, for "man", and cene, for "new". The Anthropocene epoch is dominated by humans and is characterized by mass extinctions of plant and animal species, water and soil pollution, and an altered atmosphere. We are living in an environment which is significantly different from the Holocene [1,2]. For example, the concentration of atmospheric CO_2 during the preindustrial period was 270–275 ppm, but it has exceeded 400 ppm today [3]. The world population has reached to 7.3 billion in contrast to merely 1.0 billion in 1800. The world's urban population (3.9 Billion) has grown more than four times during the past 60 years. Global cropland area expanded from about 4 million km^2 in the 1800s to 15 million km^2 in the 1990s at the expense of forest, shrub, and grasslands.

Today about 31% of the land surface or 4 billion ha is covered by forests [4]. About one half of the primary forests on Earth have disappeared from land conversion, and 16 million hectares of the remaining forests are lost each year. At the same time, forests have been increasingly recognized for their important services, such as water supply and provision of food, medicinal, and forest products, as well as other recreational, cultural, aesthetic, and spiritual benefits [5]. For example, on a global scale, forests contribute ~50% of terrestrial net primary production and store ~45% of terrestrial carbon [5]. Over half of the water supply in the U.S. flows from forestlands [6,7]. It is estimated that tropical and temperate forests worldwide provide ecosystem goods and services of $23.32 trillion per year [8].

Great progress has been made in understanding the complex interactions among forests, water, climate change and humans during the past century (Figure 1). Forest conservation and sustainable forest management practices around the world have slowed forest losses [9]; however, serious future challenges are emerging in the Anthropocene. For example, forest managers face global environmental threats from a warming climate [10,11], and rapid urbanization and demographic changes are increasing the demands of forest ecosystem services such as timber supply, clean water [12], and recreation opportunities. To meet these unprecedented challenges, we propose that land managers will require new thinking and innovative approaches for sustainable forest management in the 21st century [13]. Based on many past successes, there is an expectation by land managers and the public that we have sufficient knowledge and tools to keep watersheds functioning and capable of providing and sustaining ecosystem services into the future [10]. Recent research suggests rapid and substantial progress in our knowledge of watershed sensitivity to rapidly changing conditions [13,14]; however, critical knowledge gaps exist in applying forest watershed sciences to sustain ecosystem services in a new environment [10]. In particular, we lack a mechanistic understanding of hydrological responses to the combined effects of climate change (especially climate extremes) and human disturbances such as urbanization and land use change. Without a mechanistic understanding, our modeling tools and management approaches developed in the past may not fit the future environment.

In this communication, we examine how new emerging global environmental threats interact with forest water resources and ecosystem functions in the Anthropocene. We discuss how watershed ecohydrological science [13], the study of interactions between hydrological processes (*i.e.*, water quantity and quantity) and ecological processes (*i.e.*, vegetation dynamics) under a changing environment, can help forest managers achieve forest sustainability for the benefits of current and future generations.

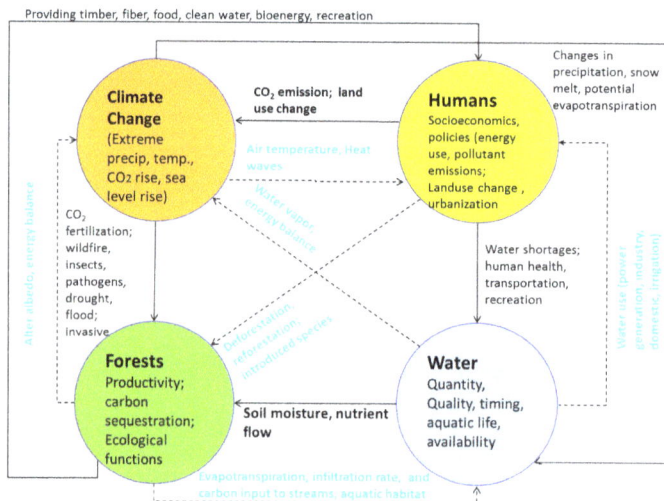

Figure 1. Complex interactions among forests, water resources, climate change, and humans in the Anthropocene. The solid lines represent impacts of stressors while the dotted lines represent feedbacks.

2. Emerging Global Environmental Threats to Forest Water Resources

2.1. Climate Change: Warming Temperature, Increasing Storms, and Sea Level Rise

Anthropogenic climate change refers to the changes of meteorological variables such as air temperature and precipitation over an extended period in terms of their average and/or variability. Elevated concentrations of atmospheric carbon dioxide (CO_2) concentrations and other greenhouse gases are the causes of climate change [3,15]. Since 1750, atmospheric concentrations of CO_2 have increased by about 40%, nitrous oxide by 20%, and methane by about 150%. The global average temperatures increased by 0.85 °C (about 1.6 °F) between 1880 and 2012 [15]. Annual precipitation has increased over the mid-latitude terrestrial areas of the Northern Hemisphere at a rate from 1.44 to 3.82 mm per decade. While annual precipitation trends over other areas have been less significant, the temporal variability of precipitation has increased. Increased ocean temperatures along with the melting of glaciers and ice caps have contributed to an observed rise in global sea level of approximately 0.2 m between 1901 and 2010 [15].

Climate change is hydrological change, thus it has direct and indirect impacts on forest ecosystems [16] through altering the amount and timing of water and energy movement and availability [13,17,18]. One of the most observable changes is hydrologic intensification: the increased frequency of hydrologic extremes such as low and high flows. For example, studies have detected both decreasing and increasing flows in the southern U.S. and the changes were attributed, at least in part, to greater precipitation variability [19]. While changes in annual mean (or totals) values in metrics such as streamflow and groundwater recharge are important, a greater challenge is posed by changes in hydrologic extremes. Climate change implies that the stationarity of ecosystem functions is a false assumption. The lack of stationarity amplifies the challenges because our reference points for developing and applying management responses may no longer be appropriate. The past no longer serves as an appropriate analog for the future and this non-stationarity is likely to amplify in the future. Many of the tools (e.g., models), guidelines, and best management practices have been developed based on historical (and soon to be obsolete) hydrologic conditions and disturbance regimes. A key question is whether existing approaches and tools for protecting and enhancing water resources will be sufficient to mitigate or adapt to future conditions.

2.2. Population Growth, Urbanization, Land Use Change, and Demographic Change

Population growth is a strong driver of urbanization, land use change, and water supply stress. By 2050, the world population is projected to be 9.6 billion [20] and majority of the total population is expected to live in urban areas. For example, 80% of the population lives in urban areas in the United States and urban population has exceeded 50% in China. In 1950 there were fewer than a dozen Mega (population >10 million) cities worldwide. Today, there were almost 40 Mega Cities (population >10 million) [21].

Population expansion over the next century is expected to occur primarily in less-developed regions placing more pressure on forest ecosystems to provide essential ecosystem services. By 2025 it is projected that there will be 50 Mega Cities with the fastest growth occurring in Africa and Asia. Urban expansion is usually characterized as increasing impervious surface areas and losing agricultural and forest lands bring many well-recognized environmental consequences such as water shortages [21,22], water and air pollution [23], and urban heat island [24]. In particular, urbanization affects watershed microclimate, surface water dynamics, groundwater recharge, stream geomorphology, biogeochemistry, and stream ecology [23,25]. We lack knowledge of the impacts of urbanization on ecosystem structure and function, society, and culture under future climate change [22] and how forest management can play a role in an urbanizing world to reduce the negative aspects of urbanization [26].

Securing adequate and reliable water resources for large cities has become one of top priorities for policy makers, city planners, and land managers worldwide [27]. Forested watersheds are often the most important sources of clean water for city inhabitants. As noted previously, there is an expectation that we have sufficient knowledge and tools to keep watersheds functioning and capable of providing and sustaining ecosystem services into the future [21]. While substantial progress has been made in research approaches and our understanding of watershed sensitivity to rapidly changing environmental conditions [28], it is largely unknown whether this new knowledge will be sufficient or effective in changing management practices because linking this new knowledge to existing modeling tools, Best Management Practices (BMPs), and guidelines is not straightforward and often requires challenging existing dogma and revising long-standing approaches [29].

3. Challenges to Forest Water Management

3.1. Rapid and Complex Environmental Changes Are Difficult to Understand

The Anthropocene represents a relatively recent period in the earth's history where human-caused changes are dramatically altering the structure and functions of natural and social systems [1]. Over the past few decades, these changes have accelerated and are expected to accelerate even more rapidly in the future [1]. Changes in the earth's climate have significant impacts on forest water resources by altering the ecohydrological processes [30] such as plant growth rate and water use efficiency and consequently water balances [28]. Direct effects include the influences of altered precipitation amount, timing, and variation, and changes in temperature and elevated atmospheric CO_2 concentration [31,32]. Indirect effects include vegetation responses to these direct changes and other disturbances and stressors, such as fire, insect outbreaks, tree mortality [33,34] and sea level rise that are indirectly altered by direct effects. These changes are complex and often occur in combination. An even greater challenge will be new combinations and interactions that we have not observed. Changing conditions may favor (or tolerate) new invasive species that may increase wildfire risk and/or permanently alter hydrologic processes. For example, wetter conditions, fire suppression, and the maturation of much of the forest following widespread harvests during the 20th century in the southern U.S. have resulting in forest "mesophication", a process of shifting species dominance to more xeric conditions. Mesophication caused an increase in evapotranspiration and an decrease in water yield [19].

It is difficult to predict how forest ecosystems will respond to traditional forest management practices in a novel environment. For example, fertilization under drought may do harm to plantation forests and increase vulnerability to drought [35,36]. The traditional practices of ditching to grow trees in coastal lowlands may need to be revisited under sea level rise to maximize economic and ecological benefits of intensively managed plantation forests [37,38]. At the large watershed scale, climate change impacts may be masked by management effects. For example, deforestation (deforestation) generally increases (decreases) streamflow, but the influences of this management practice could be offset by increasing or decreasing precipitation and greater evapotranspiration due to climate warming [39,40].

3.2. Extreme Events Challenge Existing Modeling Tools

Sophisticated simulation models have been widely used in forest ecohydrological research and watershed management since the 1990s when personal computers became available [41–44]. However, the ability to predict the impacts of extreme events presents considerable challenges to existing models [45]. Performance of watershed-scale models, lumped models in particular, is often evaluated on data that have been averaged in space and time [41] and this precludes evaluation of performance of extreme events [46–48] such as drought and flooding events. Where finer resolution evaluations have been conducted, model performance of most hydrologic models is often poor, especially for drought conditions. The impacts of high rainfall events on streamflow are easier to model because once soils are saturated, hydrologic responses are driven primarily by physical features of the watershed. If these characteristics are well defined, then flood characteristics (amount, timing, location, *etc.*) can be predicted with relative certainty. However, in mountainous terrain, large storms may increase landslide risk and understanding and modeling the biophysical controls on landslide risk in space and time are difficult [49].

Predicting the impacts of drought on streamflow is especially challenging for a variety of reasons. First, there is often a temporal disconnect between meteorological drought and hydrologic drought that varies based on physical properties (e.g., soil depth, soil water holding capacity, topography, *etc.*) [50,51]. Secondly, physical responses interact with chemical and biological responses [52]. For example, recent warming trends and more prolonged and frequent droughts have increased wildfire frequency and intensity in the western U.S. [53]. Wildfire events can have short term (e.g., peakflow, flooding, landslide) and long term (e.g., geomorphology, land cover shift) consequences to watershed hydrology [54,55]. Droughts have also accelerated the spread and intensity of insect (*i.e.*, Mountain Pine Beetles) attacks and tree die-off [56] in the western U.S. that kill canopy trees, altering stand structure, changing the energy balance of the land surface and affecting many hydrologic processes [57–59]. Consequently, predicting the future impacts of climate warming and hydrologic drought on watershed hydrology is difficult. While there is growing information about how drought interacts with hydraulic architecture and stomatal responses [60–62], we know very little (and hence, can't model) about how drought impacts root structure and function. Furthermore, in mixed species stands drought does not affect trees equally. Some tree species may be more or less affected by drought through better resistance to drought relative to other species, or through enhanced competitive ability during or after drought (*i.e.*, resilience) [63].

Hydrologic models will need to be able to account for these interactions and responses at the species-level. This expectation requires models that couple leaf-level physiology, above- and belowground whole-tree responses, root dynamics and soil water access, stand level responses, and physical hydrology [64]. Generalized empirical models will have limited utility, as conditions are likely to exceed the data used to develop empirical relationships and non-linearity should be expected [65,66]. Unfortunately, process-based models require a large amount of parameters and input variables and can be only applied at intensively studied research sites, and thus have limited use to answer regional questions [44].

3.3. Challenges to Existing Best Management Practices (BMPs) and Modeling Tools

Extreme climates, such as drought, ice storms, heat waves, are often large scale (*i.e.*, region, continental, global) environmental stressors [67], but their impacts are observable at a range of spatial scales (*i.e.*, tree, stand, basin). In contrast, management responses are typically focused on a limited area, especially in areas with mixed ownership, and usually at the stand scale. For example, climate change, movement of invasive species, water withdrawals, wildfires are global or regional in scale, and cross ecosystem and geographic and political boundaries. Dealing with these large scale issues requires management responses that are also large scale [10]. However, coordinated and large scale management activities are rare. This is especially true where private land is predominant and coordination is especially difficult. Forest BMPs must be designed site specific to suit local watershed physical conditions such as topography, geology and soils, drainage patterns, but they also should consider future climate and hydrologic conditions [29].

Many of models available are not capable of providing the information needed to assist water managers [68]. For example, water managers need information on streamflow amount and quality at a weekly resolution at a spatial scale specific to the water intake or storage reservoir for the water treatment facility. However, models are usually generic and need specific parameters for a certain watershed with unique characteristics and management conditions. Watershed managers also need to know how changing landscape conditions, forest type, and climate interact to determine risks and vulnerabilities, and evaluate management actions to offset them. Hence, models and tools need to be dynamic and account for varying land uses, species and structure [69], and disturbances at fine spatial (e.g., tree) and temporal (e.g., storm event) scales. Empirical rainfall-runoff models built from historical data may not be applicable under future climate change conditions when plant growing season length, forest structure and species composition, and plant water use efficiency [70] have changed over time.

The ability of current models to provide this type of information is extremely limited and the models do not match the needs of water managers in space and time.

4. What Is Needed to Meet the Challenges of Increasing Demand for Forest Water Resources?

4.1. Anticipate and Manage for Extreme Stressors

As discussed in the above section, anticipating and managing for extreme stressors poses a great challenge for land managers [71] due to high uncertainty and the lack of effective tools to manage forests at the appropriate scales. Recent mega-droughts, heat waves, and large wildfires portend a future with large-scale changes to ecohydrologic processes and forest functions [72]. In some cases, management activities such as thinning and tree species conversion can increase resilience to these extreme events [11], but increasing resistance on a small subset of stands may be futile unless management occurs at the scale and intensity that will be required. Recognizing that extreme events will alter forests ecosystems, land managers may need to consider management actions that can help facilitate transitions to new and perhaps novel conditions.

4.2. Develop Flexible Modeling Tools in Anticipating Novel Conditions

Modeling tools must be able to account for complexity at the correct spatial and temporal scales [73] and they must include variables required to evaluate management options such as fertilization [74], prescribed burning, and thinning [75]. We should also expect that watershed ecosystems will continue to respond to global change in complex ways characterized as nonlinear and threshold response, some of which may be novel and unprecedented. For example, climate warming may increase evaporation potential but the rise of atmospheric CO_2 concentration may increase water use efficiency thus reduce water use by trees at the leaf level for some species [76]. The end results on hydrology and ecosystem dynamics at the scale of a watershed with mixed land use and variable precipitation patterns can be unpredictable [31]. As these changes occur, it is uncertain whether existing models will be capable of predicting hydrologic responses at the appropriate spatial and temporal resolution. This is especially true for empirical models, as many of the changes will likely be outside the range of data used to generate relationships. Hydrologic "process-based models" usually also include a high level of empirical simplifications and calibrations that will also challenge the performance of existing models.

Forest ecosystem functions and forest uses by people are changing in Anthropocene. Land managers require new tools to detect change using updated knowledge and adjust management approaches accordingly. The rapid pace of change will amplify the need to detect ecosystem responses over wide spatial scales in both natural and managed forests. Significant advances in remote sensing-based change recognition [77] and tracking system holds promise for monitoring some forest conditions in near real time (*i.e.*, ForWarn) [78]; however, it is unclear if this technology will be appropriate for quantifying and analyzing the effectiveness of management actions. Hence, a combination of remote sensing and "on-the-ground" management platforms such as FIA [79], NEON, and other large-scale networks will be critical for change detection. In addition, new knowledge needs to be rapidly incorporated into management actions and user friendly predictive models, such as the Water Supply Stress Index (WaSSI) model (http://www.wassiweb.sgcp.ncsu.edu/), a water and carbon accounting model that has been used to project climate change impacts on water and carbon resources across the United States [7,12,80]. Climate change mitigation and adaptation management guides such as the Template for Assessing Climate Change Impacts and Management Options (TACCIMO) (www.forestthreats.org/taccimo) provide rapid updates to the "state-of-the-science" from the published literature thus connects forest planning to peer-reviewed climate change science; Such a system delivers information from peer-reviewed publication findings describing effects and management options and interactive maps of climate projections and models that provide insight into climate influences on natural resources. Additional information could be provided from land managers as they observe changes in the forests that they manage. New approaches to collecting and disseminating information such as citizen science networks and "crowd sourcing" approaches could accelerate the pace of experiential knowledge, observations, and data collection to supplement information from the published literature. Finally, improvements in data collection, storage, and access systems over the past few decades has created massive amounts of readily available data that has facilitated large scale "big data" analyses of hydrologic trends [81]. These new approaches are likely to provide significant insight into the interactions between large scale drivers such as climate change, and smaller scale controls such as land use and management intensity. We also recommend that models be available as open source that can be modified as new data and understanding become available.

4.3. Be Realistic about Forest Management Options

Active management including implementing Best Management Practices (BMPs) is critical to offset increasing environmental threats to forest ecosystem services [82]. In the past, improvement in forest condition with forest management in many parts of the world has been tremendously successful [9]. Among the best examples, is the recovery of heavily cutover lands in the eastern U.S. Reforestation and the implementation of best management practices has restored these forests and associated ecosystem services [82,83]. Forest coverage in China has been increasing thanks to large scale reforestation campaigns that aims at reducing soil erosion and protecting remaining forests in the last three decades [84]. The socioeconomic (*i.e.*, poverty reduction through food subsidies through the Grain for Green Project) and ecological benefits (*i.e.*, soil erosion control, carbon sequestration) of these policy-driven ecological restoration efforts are well documented [85]. However, tradeoffs of ecosystem services of reforestation and unintended environmental consequences such as decline in deep soil moisture (*i.e.*, soil desiccation) and water yield reduction in some arid regions [86,87] are emerging.

Can we manage forests in the face of future threats to continue to provide the level of existing ecosystem services? Or, more importantly, can we provide and sustain ecosystem services required in the future? We contend that large scale and extreme changes in social-economic and biophysical conditions will preclude the ability to sustain many ecosystem services. We contend that it will be difficult to "manage" our way out of future threats due to the large uncertainty of environmental conditions. Traditional approaches to forest conservation and management that assume a constant climate; stable forest dynamics, and socioeconomic, and demographic conditions; and rely heavily on historical reference conditions will be inadequate [88] to meet future demand on forest ecosystem services. Instead, new approaches that focus on anticipating and guiding ecological responses to change, are urgently needed to ensure the full value of forest ecosystem services for future generations. For example, warmer and drier conditions are increasing the frequency and size of wildfires throughout many areas of the world [89]. How to manage the threats from large area of wildfires is debatable although comprehensive strategies have been proposed [90–92]. There are proposed management options that may be implemented to minimize the impacts of drought on water quantity and quality [10]. For example, reducing leaf area by thinning and regenerating cut or planting native tree species that use less water than exotic species may help reduce water stress and increase water availability to tree growth [93], aquatic systems in forest streams, and downstream water supply for people. However, as with other natural disturbances, droughts are difficult to prepare for because they are unpredictable. Management actions such as thinning [75] and prescribed burning [94] are typically not implemented at a scale or intensity to offset climatic driving forces. Similarly, the growing conflict between managing for carbon *vs.* managing for water [95] will only increase as efforts to mitigate CO_2 emissions using bioenergy promote management of fast growing species [96,97]. In short, managers should prepare for growing conflicts among management priorities and the need to articulate the limitations of forest management for providing ecosystem services in the future. The disparity between winners and losers will widen, and trade-offs will need to be carefully evaluated.

5. Summary

In the remainder of the twenty-first century, humans will likely be impacted by the degradation of ecosystem services, and the potential loss of the planet's ability to recover [98]. The forestry community is facing large global environmental and socioeconomic challenges, such as climate change and urbanization, to meet the ever increasing demand for ecosystem services from forest ecosystems. Traditional watershed management is facing new challenges as rapid and compounded environmental, economic, and social change contribute to an increasingly uncertain future [19]. Our knowledge of ecohydrological response to extreme stressors (e.g., drought) is lacking, so current modeling tools may be insufficient to project the impacts of climate change on ecosystem functions at the scales needed in forest management. Future forest water resource management must consider the trade-offs of forest ecosystem services and coupled nature–human systems. Existing forest Best Management Practices (BMPs) [82] should be revisited to mitigate and adapt to the negative impacts of natural and anthropogenic disturbances that are expected to increase in the Anthropocene.

Conflicts of Interest: The authors declare no conflict of interest.

References

1. Steffen, W.; Grinevald, J.; Crutzen, P.; McNeill, J. The Anthropocene: Conceptual and historical perspectives. *Philos. Trans. R. Soc. A* **2011**, *369*, 842–867. [CrossRef]
2. Steffen, W.; Crutzen, P.J.; McNeill, J.R. The Anthropocene: Are humans now overwhelming the great forces of nature. *Ambio* **2007**, *36*, 614–621. [CrossRef]
3. IPCC. Summary for policymakers. In *Climate Change 2014: Impacts, Adaptation, and Vulnerability. Part A: Global and Sectoral Aspects*; Contribution of Working Group ii to the Fifth Assessment Report of the Intergovernmental Panel on Climate Change; Field, C.B., Barros, V.R., Dokken, D.J., Mach, K.J., Mastrandrea, M.D., Bilir, T.E., Chatterjee, M., Ebi, K.L., Estrada, Y.O., Genova, R.C., *et al*, Eds.; Cambridge University Press: Cambridge, UK; New York, NY, USA, 2014; p. 32.
4. FAO. *Global Forest Resources Assessment 2015: How Have the World's Forests Changed?*; FAO: Rome, Italy, 2015.
5. Bonan, G.B. Forests and climate change: Forcings, feedbacks, and the climate benefits of forests. *Science* **2008**, *320*, 1444–1449. [CrossRef] [PubMed]
6. Brown, T.C.; Hobbins, M.T.; Ramirez, J.A. Spatial distribution of water supply in the coterminous United States. *J. Am. Water Resour. Assoc.* **2008**, *44*, 1474–1487. [CrossRef]
7. Sun, G.; Caldwell, P.; Noormets, A.; McNulty, S.G.; Cohen, E.; Myers, J.M.; Domec, J.C.; Treasure, E.; Mu, Q.Z.; Xiao, J.F.; *et al.* Upscaling key ecosystem functions across the conterminous United States by a water-centric ecosystem model. *J. Geophys. Res. Biogeosci.* **2011**, *116*. [CrossRef]
8. De Groot, R.; Brander, L.; van der Ploeg, S.; Costanza, R.; Bernard, F.; Braat, L.; Christie, M.; Crossman, N.; Ghermandi, A.; Hein, L.; *et al.* Global estimates of the value of ecosystems and their services in monetary units. *Ecosyst. Serv.* **2012**, *1*, 50–61. [CrossRef]
9. MacDicken, K.G. Global forest resources assessment 2015: What, why and how? *For. Ecol. Manag.* **2015**, *352*, 3–8. [CrossRef]
10. Vose, J.M.; Klepzig, K.D. *Climate Change Adaptation and Mitigation Management Options: A Guide for Natural Resource Managers in Southern Forest Ecosystems*; CRC Press: Boca Raton, FL, USA, 2014; p. 476.
11. Ford, C.R.; Laseter, S.H.; Swank, W.T.; Vose, J.M. Can forest management be used to sustain water-based ecosystem services in the face of climate change? *Ecol. Appl.* **2011**, *21*, 2049–2067. [CrossRef] [PubMed]
12. Sun, G.; McNulty, S.G.; Myers, J.A.M.; Cohen, E.C. Impacts of multiple stresses on water demand and supply across the southeastern United States. *J. Am. Water Resour. Assoc.* **2008**, *44*, 1441–1457. [CrossRef]
13. Vose, J.M.; Sun, G.; Ford, C.R.; Bredemeier, M.; Otsuki, K.; Wei, X.H.; Zhang, Z.Q.; Zhang, L. Forest ecohydrological research in the 21st century: What are the critical needs? *Ecohydrology* **2011**, *4*, 146–158. [CrossRef]
14. Vogel, R.M.; Lall, U.; Cai, X.M.; Rajagopalan, B.; Weiskel, P.K.; Hooper, R.P.; Matalas, N.C. Hydrology: The interdisciplinary science of water. *Water. Resour. Res.* **2015**, *51*, 4409–4430. [CrossRef]

15. Stocker, B.D.; Roth, R.; Joos, F.; Spahni, R.; Steinacher, M.; Zaehle, S.; Bouwman, L.; Xu-Ri; Prentice, I.C. Multiple greenhouse-gas feedbacks from the land biosphere under future climate change scenarios. *Nat. Clim. Chang.* **2013**, *3*, 666–672. [CrossRef]

16. Melillo, J.M.; Richmond, T.; Yohe, G.W. *Climate Change Impacts in the United States: The Third National Climate Assessment*; Global Change Research Program: Washington, DC, USA, 2014.

17. Felzer, B.; Sahagian, D. Climate impacts on regional ecosystem services in the United States from cmip3-based multimodel comparisons. *Clim. Res.* **2014**, *61*, 133–155. [CrossRef]

18. Sun, S.L.; Sun, G.; Caldwell, P.; McNulty, S.; Cohen, E.; Xiao, J.F.; Zhang, Y. Drought impacts on ecosystem functions of the us national forests and grasslands: Part ii assessment results and management implications. *For. Ecol. Manag.* **2015**, *353*, 269–279. [CrossRef]

19. Vose, J.M.; Martin, K.L.; Barten, P.K. Applications of forest hydrologic science to watershed management in the 21st century. In *Forest Hydrology*; Amatya, T., Williams, L., de Jong, C., Eds.; CABI: Cambridge, UK, in press.

20. UN. *World Urbanization Prospects*; the 2014 Revision; UN: New York, NY, USA, 2014.

21. Li, E.J.; Endter-Wada, J.; Li, S.J. Characterizing and contextualizing the water challenges of megacities. *J. Am. Water. Resour. Assoc.* **2015**, *51*, 589–613. [CrossRef]

22. McDonald, R.I.; Green, P.; Balk, D.; Fekete, B.M.; Revenga, C.; Todd, M.; Montgomery, M. Urban growth, climate change, and freshwater availability. *Proc. Natl. Acad. Sci. USA* **2011**, *108*, 6312–6317. [CrossRef] [PubMed]

23. O'Driscoll, M.; Clinton, S.; Jefferson, A.; Manda, A.; McMillan, S. Urbanization effects on watershed hydrology and in-stream processes in the southern United States. *Water-Sui* **2010**, *2*, 605–648. [CrossRef]

24. Zhou, D.C.; Zhao, S.Q.; Zhang, L.X.; Sun, G.; Liu, Y.Q. The footprint of urban heat island effect in China. *Sci. Rep.* **2015**, *5*. [CrossRef] [PubMed]

25. Paul, M.J.; Meyer, J.L. Streams in the urban landscape. *Annu. Rev. Ecol. Syst.* **2001**, *32*, 333–365. [CrossRef]

26. Sun, G.; Lockaby, B.G. Water quantity and quality at the urban-rural interface. *Urban Rural Interfaces Link. People Nat.* **2012**, 29–48.

27. Sun, G.; Michelsen, A.M.; Sheng, Z.P.; Fang, A.F.; Shang, Y.Z.; Zhang, H.L. Featured collection introduction: Water for megacities challenges and solutions. *J. Am. Water Resour. Assoc.* **2015**, *51*, 585–588. [CrossRef]

28. Vose, J.M.; Miniat, C.F.; Luce, C.H.; Asbjornsen, H.; Caldwell, P.V.; Campbell, J.L.; Grant, G.E.; Isaak, D.J.; Loheide, S.P.L., II; Sun, G. Ecohydrological implications of drought for forests in the United States. *For. Ecol. Manag.* **2016**, in press.

29. Marion, D.A.; Sun, G.; Caldwell, P.V.; Miniat, C.F.; Ouyang, Y.; Amatya, D.M.; Clinton, B.D.; Conrads, P.A.; Gull Laird, S.; Dai, Z.; *et al.* Managing forest water quantity and quality under climate change. In *Climate Change Adaption and Mitigation Management Optionsa Guide for Natural Resource Managers in Southern Forest Ecosystems*; Vose, J.M., Klepzig, K.D., Eds.; CRC Press/Taylor and Francis: Boca Raton, FL, USA, 2014; pp. 249–306, p. 58.

30. Parolari, A.J.; Katul, G.G.; Porporato, A. An ecohydrological perspective on drought-induced forest mortality. *J. Geophys. Res. Biogeosci.* **2014**, *119*, 965–981. [CrossRef]

31. Tor-Ngern, P.; Oren, R.; Ward, E.J.; Palmroth, S.; McCarthy, H.R.; Domec, J.C. Increases in atmosphericco(2) have little influence on transpiration of a temperate forest canopy. *New Phytol.* **2015**, *205*, 518–525. [CrossRef] [PubMed]

32. Hanson, P.J.; Wullschleger, S.D.; Norby, R.J.; Tschaplinski, T.J.; Gunderson, C.A. Importance of changing CO_2, temperature, precipitation, and ozone on carbon and water cycles of an upland-oak forest: Incorporating experimental results into model simulations. *Glob. Chang. Biol.* **2005**, *11*, 1402–1423. [CrossRef]

33. Allen, C.D.; Breshears, D.D.; McDowell, N.G. On underestimation of global vulnerability to tree mortality and forest die-off from hotter drought in the anthropocene. *Ecosphere* **2015**, *6*, 1–55. [CrossRef]

34. Allen, C.D.; Macalady, A.K.; Chenchouni, H.; Bachelet, D.; McDowell, N.; Vennetier, M.; Kitzberger, T.; Rigling, A.; Breshears, D.D.; Hogg, E.H.; *et al.* A global overview of drought and heat-induced tree mortality reveals emerging climate change risks for forests. *For. Ecol. Manag.* **2010**, *259*, 660–684. [CrossRef]

35. Ward, E.J.; Domec, J.C.; Laviner, M.A.; Fox, T.R.; Sun, G.; McNulty, S.; King, J.; Noormets, A. Fertilization intensifies drought stress: Water use and stomatal conductance of pinus taeda in a midrotation fertilization and throughfall reduction experiment. *For. Ecol. Manag.* **2015**, *355*, 72–82. [CrossRef]

36. Bartkowiak, S.M.; Samuelson, L.J.; McGuire, M.A.; Teskey, R.O. Fertilization increases sensitivity of canopy stomatal conductance and transpiration to throughfall reduction in an 8-year-old loblolly pine plantation. *For. Ecol. Manag.* **2015**, *354*, 87–96. [CrossRef]

37. Lohmus, A.; Remm, L.; Rannap, R. Just a ditch in forest? Reconsidering draining in the context of sustainable forest management. *Bioscience* **2015**, *65*, 1066–1076. [CrossRef]

38. Amatya, D.M.; Gregory, J.D.; Skaggs, R.W. Effects of controlled drainage on storm event hydrology in a loblolly pine plantation. *J. Am. Water Resour. Assoc.* **2000**, *36*, 175–190. [CrossRef]

39. Wei, X.H.; Liu, W.F.; Zhou, P.C. Quantifying the relative contributions of forest change and climatic variability to hydrology in large watersheds: A critical review of research methods. *Water-Sui* **2013**, *5*, 728–746. [CrossRef]

40. Liu, W.F.; Wei, X.H.; Liu, S.R.; Liu, Y.Q.; Fan, H.B.; Zhang, M.F.; Yin, J.M.; Zhan, M.J. How do climate and forest changes affect long-term streamflow dynamics? A case study in the upper reach of poyang river basin. *Ecohydrology* **2015**, *8*, 46–57. [CrossRef]

41. Sun, S.L.; Sun, G.; Caldwell, P.; McNulty, S.G.; Cohen, E.; Xiao, J.F.; Zhang, Y. Drought impacts on ecosystem functions of the us national forests and grasslands: Part i evaluation of a water and carbon balance model. *For. Ecol. Manag.* **2015**, *353*, 260–268. [CrossRef]

42. Tian, S.Y.; Youssef, M.A.; Sun, G.; Chescheir, G.M.; Noormets, A.; Amatya, D.M.; Skaggs, R.W.; King, J.S.; McNulty, S.; Gavazzi, M.; *et al.* Testing drainmod-forest for predicting evapotranspiration in a mid-rotation pine plantation. *For. Ecol. Manag.* **2015**, *355*, 37–47. [CrossRef]

43. Sun, G.; Riekerk, H.; Comerford, N.B. Modeling the hydrologic impacts of forest harvesting on florida flatwoods. *J. Am. Water Resour. Assoc.* **1998**, *34*, 843–854. [CrossRef]

44. Ollinger, S.V.; Aber, J.D.; Federer, C.A. Estimating regional forest productivity and water yield using an ecosystem model linked to a gis. *Landsc. Ecol.* **1998**, *13*, 323–334. [CrossRef]

45. Amatya, D.M.; Sun, G.; Rossi, C.G.; Ssegane, H.S.; Nettles, J.E.; Panda, S. Forests, land use change, and water. In *Impact of Climate Change on Water Resources in Agriculture*; Rodrigues, R., Ed.; CRC Press/Taylor & Francis Group: Boca Raton, FL, USA, 2015.

46. Sun, S.L.; Chen, H.S.; Ju, W.M.; Yu, M.; Hua, W.J.; Yin, Y. On the attribution of the changing hydrological cycle in poyang lake basin, China. *J. Hydrol.* **2014**, *514*, 214–225. [CrossRef]

47. Hao, L.; Zhang, X.Y.; Gao, J.M. Simulating human-induced changes of water resources in the upper xiliaohe river basin, China. *Environ. Eng. Manag. J.* **2011**, *10*, 787–792.

48. Hao, L.; Sun, G.; Liu, Y.Q.; Qian, H. Integrated modeling of water supply and demand under management options and climate change scenarios in Chifeng city, China. *J. Am. Water Resour. Assoc.* **2015**, *51*, 655–671. [CrossRef]

49. Band, L.E.; Hwang, T.; Hales, T.C.; Vose, J.; Ford, C. Ecosystem processes at the watershed scale: Mapping and modeling ecohydrological controls of landslides. *Geomorphology* **2012**, *137*, 159–167. [CrossRef]

50. Geris, J.; Tetzlaff, D.; McDonnell, J.; Soulsby, C. The relative role of soil type and tree cover on water storage and transmission in northern headwater catchments. *Hydrol. Process.* **2015**, *29*, 1844–1860. [CrossRef]

51. Adams, H.R.; Barnard, H.R.; Loomis, A.K. Topography alters tree growth-climate relationships in a semi-arid forested catchment. *Ecosphere* **2014**, *5*, 1–16. [CrossRef]

52. Hanson, P.J.; Amthor, J.S.; Wullschleger, S.D.; Wilson, K.B.; Grant, R.F.; Hartley, A.; Hui, D.; Hunt, E.R.; Johnson, D.W.; Kimball, J.S.; *et al.* Oak forest carbon and water simulations: Model intercomparisons and evaluations against independent data. *Ecol. Monogr.* **2004**, *74*, 443–489. [CrossRef]

53. Flannigan, M.D.; Krawchuk, M.A.; de Groot, W.J.; Wotton, B.M.; Gowman, L.M. Implications of changing climate for global wildland fire. *Int. J. Wildland Fire* **2009**, *18*, 483–507. [CrossRef]

54. Bladon, K.D.; Emelko, M.B.; Silins, U.; Stone, M. Wildfire and the future of water supply. *Environ. Sci. Technol.* **2014**, *48*, 8936–8943. [CrossRef] [PubMed]

55. Ice, G.G.; Neary, D.G.; Adams, P.W. Effects of wildfire on soils and watershed processes. *J. For.* **2004**, *102*, 16–20.

56. Adams, H.D.; Luce, C.H.; Breshears, D.D.; Allen, C.D.; Weiler, M.; Hale, V.C.; Smith, A.M.S.; Huxman, T.E. Ecohydrological consequences of drought- and infestation-triggered tree die-off: Insights and hypotheses. *Ecohydrology* **2012**, *5*, 145–159. [CrossRef]

57. Bearup, L.A.; Maxwell, R.M.; Clow, D.; McCray, J.E. Hydrological effects of forest transpiration loss in bark beetle-impacted watersheds. *Nat. Clim. Chang.* **2014**, *4*, 481–486. [CrossRef]
58. Langhammer, J.; Su, Y.; Bernsteinova, J. Runoff response to climate warming and forest disturbance in a mid-mountain basin. *Water-Sui* **2015**, *7*, 3320–3342. [CrossRef]
59. Pugh, E.; Gordon, E. A conceptual model of water yield effects from beetle-induced tree death in snow-dominated lodgepole pine forests. *Hydrol. Process.* **2013**, *27*, 2048–2060. [CrossRef]
60. Domec, J.C.; Noormets, A.; King, J.S.; Sun, G.; McNulty, S.G.; Gavazzi, M.J.; Boggs, J.L.; Treasure, E.A. Decoupling the influence of leaf and root hydraulic conductances on stomatal conductance and its sensitivity to vapour pressure deficit as soil dries in a drained loblolly pine plantation. *Plant Cell Environ.* **2009**, *32*, 980–991. [CrossRef] [PubMed]
61. Noormets, A.; McNulty, S.G.; DeForest, J.L.; Sun, G.; Li, Q.; Chen, J. Drought during canopy development has lasting effect on annual carbon balance in a deciduous temperate forest. *New Phytol.* **2008**, *179*, 818–828. [CrossRef] [PubMed]
62. Domec, J.C.; Palmroth, S.; Ward, E.; Maier, C.A.; Therezien, M.; Oren, R. Acclimation of leaf hydraulic conductance and stomatal conductance of pinus taeda (loblolly pine) to long-term growth in elevated CO_2 (free-air CO_2 enrichment) and n-fertilization. *Plant Cell Environ.* **2009**, *32*, 1500–1512. [CrossRef] [PubMed]
63. Ford, C.R.; Hubbard, R.M.; Vose, J.M. Quantifying structural and physiological controls on variation in canopy transpiration among planted pine and hardwood species in the southern appalachians. *Ecohydrology* **2011**, *4*, 183–195. [CrossRef]
64. Tague, C.L.; McDowell, N.G.; Allen, C.D. An integrated model of environmental effects on growth, carbohydrate balance, and mortality of pinus ponderosa forests in the southern rocky mountains. *PLoS ONE* **2013**, *8*, e80286. [CrossRef] [PubMed]
65. Zhou, G.; Wei, X.; Chen, X.; Zhou, P.; Liu, X.; Xiao, Y.; Sun, G.; Scott, D.F.; Zhou, S.; Han, L.; *et al.* Global pattern for the effect of climate and land cover on water yield. *Nat. Commun.* **2015**, *6*. [CrossRef] [PubMed]
66. Sun, G.; Alstad, K.; Chen, J.Q.; Chen, S.P.; Ford, C.R.; Lin, G.H.; Liu, C.F.; Lu, N.; McNulty, S.G.; Miao, H.X.; *et al.* A general predictive model for estimating monthly ecosystem evapotranspiration. *Ecohydrology* **2011**, *4*, 245–255. [CrossRef]
67. Sun, G.; Caldwell, P.V.; McNulty, S.G.; Georgakakos, A.P.; Arumugam, S.; Cruise, J.; McNider, R.T.; Terando, A.; Conrads, P.A.; Feldt, J.; *et al.* Impacts of climate change and variability on water resources in the southeast USA. In *Climate of the Southeast United States: Variability, Change, Impacts, and Vulnerability, NCA Southeast Technical Report*; Ingram, K.T., Dow, K., Carter, L., Anderson, J., Eds.; Island Press: Washington, DC, USA, 2013; p. 31.
68. Amatya, D.M.; Douglas-Mankin, K.R.; Williams, T.M.; Skaggs, R.W.; Nettles, J.E. Advances in forest hydrology: Challenges and opportunities. *Trans. ASABE* **2011**, *54*, 2049–2056. [CrossRef]
69. Brantley, S.T.; Miniat, C.F.; Elliott, K.J.; Laseter, S.H.; Vose, J.M. Changes to southern appalachian water yield and stormflow after loss of a foundation species. *Ecohydrology* **2015**, *8*, 518–528. [CrossRef]
70. Liu, Y.B.; Xiao, J.F.; Ju, W.M.; Zhou, Y.L.; Wang, S.Q.; Wu, X.C. Water use efficiency of China's terrestrial ecosystems and responses to drought. *Sci. Rep.* **2015**, *5*. [CrossRef]
71. Patel-Weynand, T.; Peterson, D.L.; Vose, J.M. *Effects of Climatic Variability and Change on Forest Ecosystems: A Comprehensive Science Synthesis for the U.S.*; USDA Forest Service Pacific Northwest Research Station: Portland, OR, USA, 2012; p. 265.
72. Matyas, C.; Sun, G. Forests in a water limited world under climate change. *Environ. Res. Lett.* **2014**, *9*. [CrossRef]
73. Porporato, A.; Feng, X.; Manzoni, S.; Mau, Y.; Parolari, A.J.; Vico, G. Ecohydrological modeling in agroecosystems: Examples and challenges. *Water. Resour. Res.* **2015**, *51*, 5081–5099. [CrossRef]
74. Amatya, D.M.; Rossi, C.G.; Saleh, A.; Dai, Z.; Youssef, M.A.; Williams, R.G.; Bosch, D.D.; Chescheir, G.M.; Sun, G.; Skaggs, R.W.; *et al.* Review of nitrogen fate models applicable to forest landscapes in the southern US. *Trans. ASABE* **2013**, *56*, 1731–1757.
75. Sun, G.; Caldwell, P.V.; McNulty, S.G. Modelling the potential role of forest thinning in maintaining water supplies under a changing climate across the conterminous United States. *Hydrol. Process.* **2015**. [CrossRef]

76. Cheng, L.; Zhang, L.; Wang, Y.P.; Yu, Q.; Eamus, D.; O'Grady, A. Impacts of elevated CO_2, climate change and their interactions on water budgets in four different catchments in Australia. *J. Hydrol.* **2014**, *519*, 1350–1361. [CrossRef]

77. Hansen, M.C.; Potapov, P.V.; Moore, R.; Hancher, M.; Turubanova, S.A.; Tyukavina, A.; Thau, D.; Stehman, S.V.; Goetz, S.J.; Loveland, T.R.; *et al.* High-resolution global maps of 21st-century forest cover change. *Science* **2013**, *342*, 850–853. [CrossRef] [PubMed]

78. Norman, S.P. *Highlights of Satellite-Based Forest Change Recognition and Tracking Using the Forwarn System*; U.S. Department of Agriculture, Forest Service, Research & Development, Southern Research Station: Asheville, NC, USA, 2013; p. 30.

79. Coulston, J.W.; Wear, D.N.; Vose, J.M. Complex forest dynamics indicate potential for slowing carbon accumulation in the southeastern United States. *Sci. Rep.* **2015**, *5*. [CrossRef] [PubMed]

80. Caldwell, P.V.; Sun, G.; McNulty, S.G.; Cohen, E.C.; Myers, J.A.M. Impacts of impervious cover, water withdrawals, and climate change on river flows in the conterminous US. *Hydrol. Earth Syst. Sci.* **2012**, *16*, 2839–2857. [CrossRef]

81. Rice, J.S.; Emanuel, R.E.; Vose, J.M.; Nelson, S.A.C. Continental U.S. Streamflow trends from 1940 to 2009 and their relationships with watershed spatial characteristics. *Water Resour. Res.* **2015**, *51*, 6262–6275. [CrossRef]

82. Cristan, R.; Aust, W.M.; Bolding, M.C.; Barrett, S.M.; Munsell, J.F.; Schilling, E. Effectiveness of forestry best management practices in the United States: Literature review. *For. Ecol. Manag.* **2016**, *360*, 133–151. [CrossRef]

83. Boggs, J.; Sun, G.; McNUlty, S.G. Effects of timber harvest on water quantity and quality in small watersheds in the piedmont of North Carolina. *J. For.* **2015**, *114*, 27–40. [CrossRef]

84. Sun, G.; Zhou, G.Y.; Zhang, Z.Q.; Wei, X.H.; McNulty, S.G.; Vose, J.M. Potential water yield reduction due to forestation across China. *J. Hydrol.* **2006**, *328*, 548–558. [CrossRef]

85. Lu, Y.H.; Fu, B.J.; Feng, X.M.; Zeng, Y.; Liu, Y.; Chang, R.Y.; Sun, G.; Wu, B.F. A policy-driven large scale ecological restoration: Quantifying ecosystem services changes in the loess plateau of China. *PLoS ONE* **2012**, *7*, e31782. [CrossRef] [PubMed]

86. Cao, S.X.; Sun, G.; Zhang, Z.Q.; Chen, L.D.; Feng, Q.; Fu, B.J.; McNulty, S.; Shankman, D.; Tang, J.W.; Wang, Y.H.; *et al.* Greening China naturally. *Ambio* **2011**, *40*, 828–831. [CrossRef] [PubMed]

87. Liang, W.; Bai, D.; Wang, F.Y.; Fu, B.J.; Yan, J.P.; Wang, S.; Yang, Y.T.; Long, D.; Feng, M.Q. Quantifying the impacts of climate change and ecological restoration on streamflow changes based on a budyko hydrological model in China's Loess Plateau. *Water Resour. Res.* **2015**, *51*, 6500–6519. [CrossRef]

88. Golladay, S.W.; Martin, K.L.; Vose, J.M.; Wear, D.N.; Covich, A.P.; Hobbs, R.J.; Klepzig, K.D.; Likens, G.E.; Naiman, R.J.; Shearer, A.W. Achievable future conditions as a framework for guiding forest conservation and management. *For. Ecol. Manag.* **2016**, *360*, 80–96. [CrossRef]

89. Liu, Y.Q.; Stanturf, J.; Goodrick, S. Trends in global wildfire potential in a changing climate. *For. Ecol. Manag.* **2010**, *259*, 685–697. [CrossRef]

90. Moritz, M.A.; Batllori, E.; Bradstock, R.A.; Gill, A.M.; Handmer, J.; Hessburg, P.F.; Leonard, J.; McCaffrey, S.; Odion, D.C.; Schoennagel, T.; *et al.* Learning to coexist with wildfire. *Nature* **2014**, *515*, 58–66. [CrossRef] [PubMed]

91. Stephens, S.L.; Agee, J.K.; Fule, P.Z.; North, M.P.; Romme, W.H.; Swetnam, T.W.; Turner, M.G. Managing forests and fire in changing climates. *Science* **2013**, *342*, 41–42. [CrossRef] [PubMed]

92. North, M.P.; Stephens, S.L.; Collins, B.M.; Agee, J.K.; Aplet, G.; Franklin, J.F.; Fule, P.Z. Reform forest fire management. *Science* **2015**, *349*, 1280–1281. [CrossRef] [PubMed]

93. Grant, G.E.; Tague, C.L.; Allen, C.D. Watering the forest for the trees: An emerging priority for managing water in forest landscapes. *Front. Ecol. Environ.* **2013**, *11*, 314–321. [CrossRef]

94. Vose, J.M.; Elliott, K.J. Oak, fire, and global change: What might the future hold? *Fire Ecol.* **2016**. in prerss.

95. Jackson, R.B.; Jobbagy, E.G.; Avissar, R.; Roy, S.B.; Barrett, D.J.; Cook, C.W.; Farley, K.A.; le Maitre, D.C.; McCarl, B.A.; Murray, B.C. Trading water for carbon with biological sequestration. *Science* **2005**, *310*, 1944–1947. [CrossRef] [PubMed]

96. King, J.S.; Ceulemans, R.; Albaugh, J.M.; Dillen, S.Y.; Domec, J.C.; Fichot, R.; Fischer, M.; Leggett, Z.; Sucre, E.; Trnka, M.; *et al.* The challenge of lignocellulosic bioenergy in a water-limited world. *Bioscience* **2013**, *63*, 102–117.

97. Vose, J.M.; Miniat, C.F.; Sun, G.; Caldwell, P.V. Potential implications for expansion of freeze-tolerant eucalyptus plantations on water resources in the southern United States. *For. Sci.* **2015**, *61*, 509–521. [CrossRef]
98. Steffen, W.; Persson, A.; Deutsch, L.; Zalasiewicz, J.; Williams, M.; Richardson, K.; Crumley, C.; Crutzen, P.; Folke, C.; Gordon, L.; *et al.* The anthropocene: From global change to planetary stewardship. *Ambio* **2011**, *40*, 739–761. [CrossRef] [PubMed]

© 2016 by the authors. Licensee MDPI, Basel, Switzerland. This article is an open access article distributed under the terms and conditions of the Creative Commons Attribution (CC BY) license (http://creativecommons.org/licenses/by/4.0/).

forests

MDPI

Review

Managing Forests for Water in the Anthropocene—The Best Kept Secret Services of Forest Ecosystems

Irena F. Creed [1,*], Marian Weber [2], Francesco Accatino [1] and David P. Kreutzweiser [3]

[1] Department of Biology, Western University, 1151 Richmond St., London, ON N6A 5B7, Canada; faccatin@uwo.ca
[2] Alberta Innovates, 250 Karl Clark Road, Edmonton, AB T6N 1E4, Canada; marian.weber@albertainnovates.ca
[3] Natural Resources Canada, Canadian Forest Service, 1219 Queen St. East, Sault Ste. Marie, ON P6A 2E5, Canada; Dave.Kreutzweiser@canada.ca
*   Correspondence: icreed@uwo.ca; Tel.: +1-519-661-4265

Academic Editors: Ge Sun and James M. Vose
Received: 18 December 2015; Accepted: 3 March 2016; Published: 8 March 2016

Abstract: Water and forests are inextricably linked. Pressures on forests from population growth and climate change are increasing risks to forests and their aquatic ecosystem services (AES). There is a need to incorporate AES in forest management but there is considerable uncertainty about how to do so. Approaches that manage forest ecosystem services such as fiber, water and carbon sequestration independently ignore the inherent complexities of ecosystem services and their responses to management actions, with the potential for unintended consequences that are difficult to predict. The ISO 31000 Risk Management Standard is a standardized framework to assess risks to forest AES and to prioritize management strategies to manage risks within tolerable ranges. The framework consists of five steps: establishing the management context, identifying, analyzing, evaluating and treating the risks. Challenges to implementing the framework include the need for novel models and indicators to assess forest change and resilience, quantification of linkages between forest practice and AES, and the need for an integrated systems approach to assess cumulative effects and stressors on forest ecosystems and AES. In the face of recent international agreements to protect forests, there are emerging opportunities for international leadership to address these challenges in order to protect both forests and AES.

Keywords: forest management; aquatic ecosystem services; cumulative effects; risk management; scenario analysis; bowtie analysis

1. Introduction

We believe that forests are important for the water supply of humanity—Statement by participants of the Kunming Expert Meeting on forests and water, March 2014.

Forests are critical to human well-being, yet the loss of forest to other land uses has been extensive and much of the world's remaining forest is unprotected or degraded [1]. Globally, forest health continues to be at risk due to unrelenting pressures from growing populations for food, fiber and energy [2]. There have been substantial changes to forest management and other land use practices over the past 25 years that have had positive effects on forest ecosystems. Generally, the conversion of forested land to other land uses has decreased, but in some parts of the world, particularly in developing countries, conversion of forests to agriculture continues to be a problem (Figure 1; [3,4]). Where forest conversion is not an issue, fragmentation from forest harvest in combination with other temporary land uses is occurring under the overarching effect of climate change, leading to increased frequency and intensity of other natural stressors such as fire and pest outbreaks (e.g., [4–8]). Together, the effects of natural and anthropogenic stressors place the sustainability of forest ecosystems at risk (e.g., [9–11]).

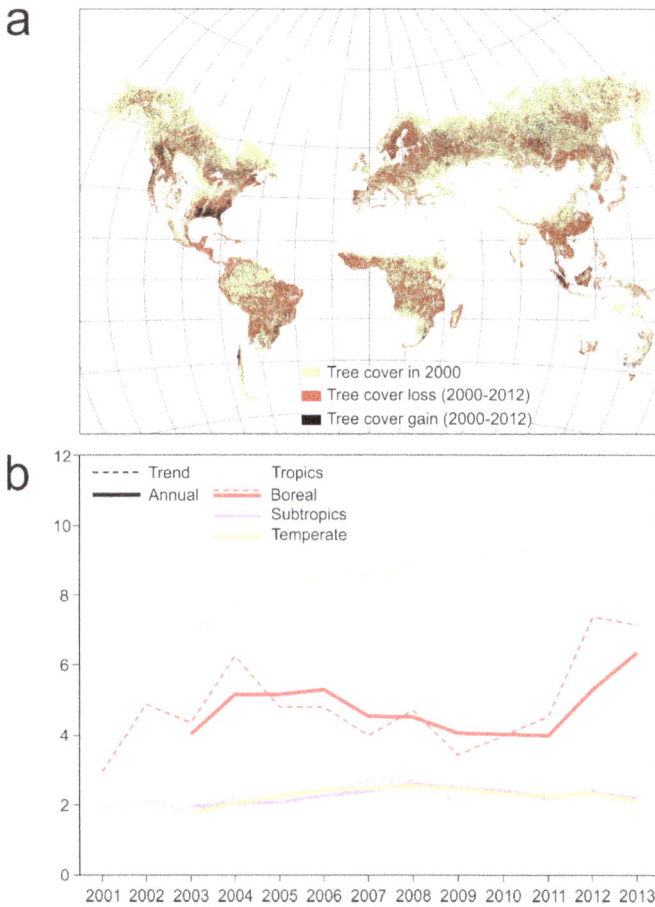

Figure 1. (**a**) Global forest loss; and (**b**) biome specific rates of forest loss (modified from [3]). Data for both (**a**) and (**b**) from [4].

Ecosystem services (ES) are the benefits to people from healthy functioning ecosystems. The Millennium Ecosystem Assessment (MEA) [12] classifies ES as: provisioning (the products obtained from ecosystems such as food, fiber and fresh water); regulating (the benefits obtained from the regulation of ecosystem processes such as climate and nutrient cycling); cultural (the non-material benefits people obtain from ecosystems such as recreation and aesthetic experiences); and supporting (the indirect benefits that facilitate all other ES such as biodiversity). Over 25% of the total global forest area is managed for ES, with only minor variations over the last 25 years [13].

Forests provide a wide array of ES [14–16]. Among the most valuable services produced by forests are aquatic ecosystem services (AES). Forests are source areas for clean water. In the U.S., national forests are the largest source of drinking water [17]. Forests regulate flow patterns and maintain water quality by filtering sediments, nutrients and other contaminants from runoff, reducing the need for water treatment infrastructure [8,18–20]. Forests also provide water for irrigation, hydropower, recreation and fisheries [21,22]. Forest vegetation absorbs snowmelt and rainfall, controlling runoff and erosion and regulating groundwater recharge and discharge [23,24]. These processes maintain human and natural assets by reducing the frequency and intensity of flooding and drought [25]. Forest vegetation is also important for maintaining high quality aquatic habitat for biodiversity. In 2008, the U.S. Chief Forester remarked that AES are among the most valuable products produced by forests, largely due to the high costs of flood damage and the need to replace forest ecosystems with human infrastructure [26]. More recently, the U.S. Deputy Chief Forester stated that the U.S. Forest Service is the "nation's largest water company" [27].

Since the release of the MEA, there have been numerous efforts to mainstream AES in public policy, both in Europe [28] and North America [29,30]. In spite of these initiatives and the growing public awareness of the importance of forests for AES, a systematic integration of AES in forest resource assessment and management is lacking in both science and policy. As the interconnections between forests and the hydrologic cycle become more apparent, the urgent need to understand the role of forests and water has emerged as an international priority. Of particular note is the 2002 *Shiga Declaration on Forests and Water*, stating that governments and stakeholders should adopt holistic, multidisciplinary and multi-stakeholder approaches to improve understanding of forest and water relationships and effective implementation of policies, planning and management initiatives worldwide related to forests and water (Table 1; [31]).

Table 1. Principles for forest and water management in the Anthropocene (Recommendations for decision makers stated in the Shiga Declaration (Final): Adopted on 22 November 2002, Shiga, Japan [31]).

Principle	Description
Principle 1	Move from a sectoral to an integrated cross-sectoral approach to economic, social and environmental planning at local, national and international levels.
Principle 2	Capture the total economic value of forest and water resources and evaluate trade-offs and distributional and equity effects of policies to maintain AES.
Principle 3	Put in place appropriate incentives to support the sustainable management of forest and water services to ensure that those who use resources pay the full cost of their exploitation and those who bear the costs of conservation are equitably compensated.
Principle 4	Promote effective and equitable collaborative arrangements and partnerships among governments and stakeholders to develop new tools for managing AES.

Since the Shiga Declaration, many events on forests and water have been organized by the Food and Agricultural Organization (FAO) of the United Nations (UN) and other institutions to provide insight into the topic as well as important recommendations for moving forward. The FAO synthesized the main outcomes and recommendations resulting from these processes to develop a comprehensive and practical international *Forests and Water Agenda* [32] to guide future action. The Agenda is a 20-point program to advocate for the "recognition of forest-water interactions and the role trees and forests play in maintaining resilient landscapes and providing high-quality water resources, taking into account forest-water interactions for different climatic zones, forest ecosystems and at different landscape scales." The FAO then launched a five-year *Forests and Water Action Plan* at the World Forestry Congress that was held in September 2015 in Durban, South Africa. The Action Plan aims to balance trade-offs and maximize synergies between forests and water management [33]. Coinciding with the launch of the Action Plan was the release of the *UN Sustainable Development Goals* [2], where the status of forests and their benefits were given prominent consideration. In particular, Goals 6 (recognizing the role of forests in ensuring sustainable and secure water supplies) and 15 (protecting, restoring and promoting sustainable use of forests and ecosystems and their services) highlight the importance of managing forests for water and other ES to promote resilient landscapes and communities [2].

Despite these initiatives, a systematic integration of forest AES into management decisions remains lacking. A key barrier to managing AES is that we have not developed the scientific basis, nor the policy and finance mechanisms, to systematically incorporate AES into forest management decisions. Specifically, we need a better understanding of: (1) how human activities affect the ecosystem and the production of AES; (2) how the supply and demand for AES interact at different scales and how this information can be integrated into decision-making; (3) how to quantify the magnitude of AES benefits so that the trade-offs of alternative forest management strategies can be understood and ranked; and (4) how to turn AES values into effective incentive and finance mechanisms at a large enough scale to have an impact [34].

To overcome this barrier, we need a paradigm shift. The concept of ES was originally introduced as a metaphor to illustrate the dependence of humans on healthy functioning ecosystems; however, the risks to global atmospheric and hydrologic cycles from forest degradation and deforestation illustrate the peril of viewing forests as simply a stream of human benefits that can be unbundled and severed from each other in the design of policies and incentives (e.g., [35]). Ecosystems are characterized by complexity that operates at multiple scales, resulting in unavoidable trade-offs and risks in the face of changing human behavior and preferences. Our limited understanding about how particular forest management strategies affect AES means that policies to enhance particular services can have unintended consequences. We need to consider the connection between forests and people more holistically to reflect a broader set of values in forest management decisions [36]. We must move from an optimization approach that treats AES as a suite of independent benefit streams that can be unbundled from landscapes and maximized across human endpoints, to a risk-based approach that maintains the regulating and supporting services that underpin all other services, and develop policies and incentives that reconcile social and economic behaviors within these ecological constraints.

Now is the time to act to ensure that we develop appropriate strategies and supporting science to integrate AES in forest management policies and practices. The formal integration of AES into forest management would benefit from an internationally recognized standard and credible framework that addresses the risks inherent in uncertain and complex systems. The International Organization for Standardization (ISO) 31000 Risk Management Standard [37] is an internationally recognized standard used across sectors to analyze policy effectiveness and manage risks of management actions. The purpose of this paper is to present the ISO framework and show how it could be used to analyze the main characteristics of the integrated forest-AES system. We also identify conceptual challenges associated with developing management goals for AES and propose new approaches to reduce risk and ensure sustainable forest management for AES.

2. Managing Forests to Reduce Risk

The ISO 31000 [37] and its Bowtie analysis tool [38] provide a credible framework and approach to reduce complexity and can enable the integration of desired ES into management systems (Figure 2). The standard can be used to address the uncertainties associated with ecosystem processes and with human and ecological responses to management interventions. Complexities include non-linear responses, interactive effects, and feedbacks that operate at multiple scales, resulting in unavoidable trade-offs and risks in the face of changing human behavior and preferences.

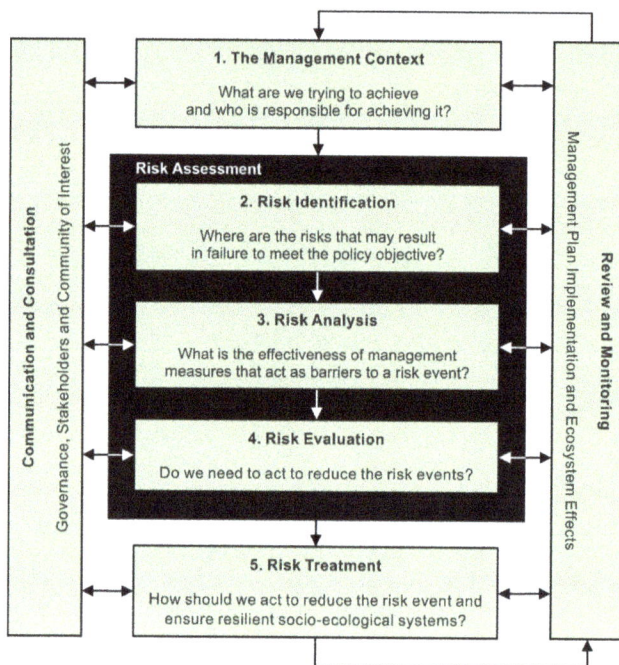

Figure 2. International Organization for Standardization (ISO) 31000 Risk Management Framework for the management of forest-ecosystem risk. Modified from [39,40].

Applying the ISO 31000 risk management framework to forest ecosystems and their AES simplifies and streamlines the analysis of the risks of alternative management strategies in the following ways: it helps identify the most relevant characteristics of the system that make it susceptible to risk; it helps identify the main risks rising from failing to meet management goals; and it informs new and innovative solutions. The ISO 31000 risk management framework in our context consists of five steps (Figure 2): (1) defining forest AES management objectives (goals) and context (boundaries); (2) identifying risk; (3) analyzing risks by looking at pressures-effects-impacts within the system; (4) evaluating the severity and distribution of risk and identifying risk limits to avoid strategies that lead to intolerable or catastrophic outcomes; and (5) developing and implementing management strategies to treat the risk.

In the remainder of this paper, we outline the steps and explore conceptual considerations and challenges in applying the ISO 31000 risk management framework to managing forest-derived AES. We conclude by suggesting a plan of action to develop tools and the capacity to enable governments to address these challenges.

2.1. Step 1. The Management Context: What Are We Trying to Achieve, and Who Is Responsible for Achieving It?

The first step requires defining a realistic boundary for describing the management context for AES. Forests and AES are part of a broader system in which the social and the ecological components are strongly interrelated as in Figure 3 [41,42]. The characteristics of forest ecological and social systems are defined by larger scale external ecological drivers, such as climate, disturbance and succession regimes, and social drivers, such as value systems and legal institutions, which lie outside the management context for AES. The management context is defined by forest ecosystem and social system characteristics as well the forest management context, which translates forest characteristics into AES and their relationship to people. The forest ecosystem is defined by forest structures (e.g., nutrient pools) and functions (e.g., nutrient cycling) which individually or in combination produce AES (e.g., clean water supply). The forest social system is similarly defined by structures (e.g., decision makers, communities, property rights) and processes (e.g., consultation, legal). Together these systems combine to set up the rules for forest management and determine how forest management decisions (*i.e.*, forest plans, harvest rates and locations) based on tenures, forest regulations, and market conditions translate into forest AES and human benefits.

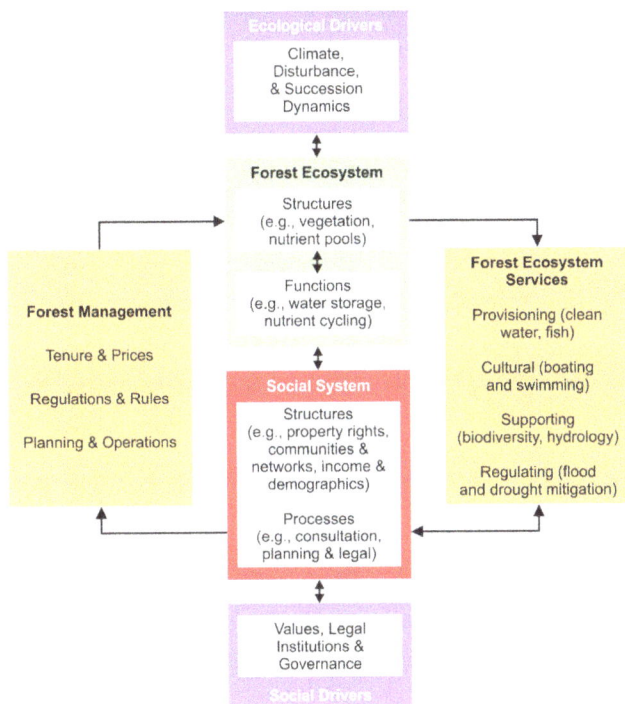

Figure 3. Forest aquatic ecosystem services are part of a socio-ecological system. Modified from [41].

The boundary of the management context is fuzzy, due to the dynamics and feedbacks within and between the ecological and social systems [43]. There are multiple pathways from forest ecosystems to AES and their beneficiaries that are contingent on cross-scale interactions. Therefore, forest management decisions can have consequences far from and long after the fact (Figure 4; [44]). For example, there are numerous relationships between AES supply areas and beneficiary areas [45]. Services can be produced and consumed at the same location, or benefits can be detached from service areas, either with distinct directional patterns (e.g., downstream or downwind from service areas) or multiple directional patterns. This means that for some AES, the management context can extend across regional, national and transnational boundaries and that forest management decisions can have time lags that affect benefits of future generations. The choice of which benefits and beneficiaries to include in the risk management assessment is critical since choices can lead to a biased evaluation of the risks and have a significant effect on whether or not an intervention is beneficial (e.g., [46]). Limiting the scope of benefit assessment to the supply area can significantly underestimate the value of AES (e.g., [18,47,48]). This is particularly important for countries such as Canada and Russia where populations benefitting from forest AES largely reside outside of forest areas.

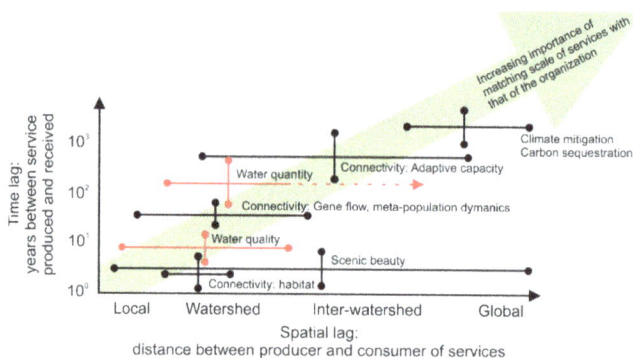

Figure 4. Forest aquatic ecosystem services affect people long after and far from where forest management decisions are made. The vertical axis shows the time lag in terms of multi-decadal recovery, and scale of impacts ranging from local to national and global. Modified from [44].

The impacts of forest management decisions on beneficiaries and their values can create feedbacks within the social system, resulting in changes in regulations and planning processes governing forest management, which over time may drive a redistribution of AES. A realistic boundary for the management context must, therefore, include multiple interacting spatial and temporal scales and feedbacks between the distribution of AES and forest management rules.

Challenges

1. Decision makers need to identify the linkages between the forest AES and people and be cognizant of the spatial and temporal mismatches between ecosystem functions, services, and beneficiaries. Mapping service areas helps us understand who the decision makers are that affect services and where management interventions should be concentrated while beneficiary mapping helps us understand who is affected by decisions, and from a financing perspective who might be willing to pay or need to be compensated for practice changes.
2. We need to understand the full scope for trade-offs and externalities. Ecosystems are multi-functional with ecosystem functions that contribute to multiple AES in potentially conflicting ways. To avoid inconsistencies, we need to develop a conceptual map that shows the causal chain from forest management decisions to ecosystem services and benefits (e.g., [49]).
3. We need to understand what incentives currently link AES to people and where there are policy gaps and opportunities. For commodities such as timber, the demand is global with supply linked to demand through global commodity markets [50]. In contrast, the demand for flood protection/water purification or other AES is local or regional and linked to supply through forest watershed management or water treatment facilities. We need to identify where current incentives create vulnerabilities and feedbacks between beneficiaries and the capacity of ecosystems to supply AES.

2.2. Step 2. Risk Identification: Where Are the Risks That May Result in Failure to Meet the Policy Objective?

The period since the 1950s has been termed the Great Acceleration, or the Anthropocene. It is characterized by accelerated demographic, industrial and technological changes caused by an unprecedented growth in population, which is expected to surpass 8 billion by 2030 [51]. These accelerated changes are reflected in numerous ecological and socio-economic indicators that suggest that ecological systems may have moved outside of the natural range of variation, a concept that has traditionally been used to identify limits of acceptable change [52]. By moving beyond the historical range of natural variation we are in uncharted territory with increased risk of passing a threshold or tipping point resulting in regime shift [53] and irreversible consequences for forest water resources (e.g., [54,55]).

Cumulative effects are changes to the environment that are caused by the combination of past, present and future human actions, which individually are insignificant but collectively have large and potentially destabilizing effects [56]. For example, cumulative effects of even minor modifications to forest management practices distributed across numerous headwater reaches might be significant for key downstream AES at the scale of regional drainage basins (e.g., [57–59]). Furthermore, legacy cumulative effects may be exacerbated by emerging forest management practices like those based on emulating natural disturbance regimes [60,61], increasing industrial encroachment on previously unmanaged landscapes [7], and a growing forest biomass removal industry to provide biofuel feedstock [62].

Forest managers need standardized methods for quantifying and predicting cumulative effects of forest management strategies (e.g., [55]). The methods need to include interactions and feedbacks and distinguish the effects of management from the underlying consequences of climate change. Furthermore, the methods must be robust enough to capture not only the range of natural variability but also thresholds, tipping points and regime shifts (Figure 5). Scenario analyses can be used to identify and address the risks from cumulative effects. The merit of future scenario analysis is recognized globally; the users of the Global Forest Resources Assessment indicated interest in scenario analysis to better understand the drivers and pressures affecting future forests, and to gain an understanding of forest dynamics in the face of predicted stressors, in order to design more effective policies [63]. Scenarios, together with models and indicators of the cumulative effects associated with these land use/land cover scenarios, are necessary to explore alternative assumptions of socioeconomic and environmental conditions that can be used to communicate key risks and uncertainties to the public and decision makers (e.g., [64]).

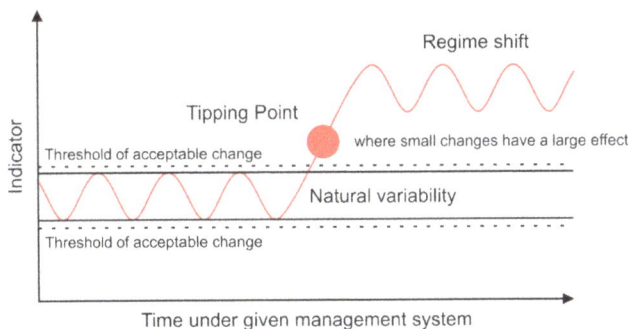

Figure 5. Concepts of thresholds, tipping points and regimes shifts into forest management strategies.

In conducting scenario analyses, either quantitative or qualitative approaches can be used (Figure 6). For quantitative scenario analysis, high quality modeling of future forest land use/land cover changes needs to be coupled with spatial databases of socio-economic and biophysical variables linking underlying drivers and pressures to forest loss and gain (e.g., [49]). The models provide a starting point for informing a future vision of the forest. Underlying assumptions can be drawn from a set of internally consistent global narratives of future social and ecological drivers to assess land use and land cover change and implications for forest AES (e.g., [63]). Land use/land cover scenarios are key to exploring scientific uncertainties related to interacting changes in the carbon cycle, hydrologic processes, and climate (e.g., [65]), or those prepared for the MEA [64,66]. Multi-scale (national, regional and spatially explicit) land use/land cover scenarios are used to link projections of future climate and socio-economic changes to regional and local decision-making (e.g., [64]). Downscaled and spatially explicit scenarios are particularly important for understanding forest AES since place matters both in terms of forest management as well as the spatial and temporal relationships between the supply and demand for AES. For example, the relative amounts of precipitation, forest evapotranspiration, runoff and streamflow at a particular site can be used by forest managers to decide if a forested landscape could be used for source water, forest products or soil water conservation [67]. The physical, chemical and biological properties of water flowing through forested landscapes will be influenced by the balance between precipitation *versus* evaporation and surface *versus* subsurface flow paths, and the contributions of local, intermediate and regional flow systems to the surface waters. Therefore, indicators that are used to monitor AES must reflect the ecological and hydrological diversity at local, watershed, region and inter-regional scales.

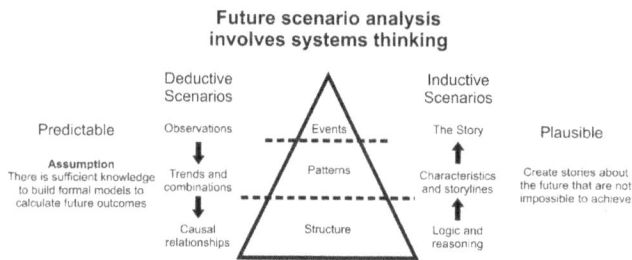

Figure 6. Quantitative (deductive) *versus* qualitative (inductive) scenario analyses.

Qualitative scenario analysis is an alternative approach to quantitative analysis, which can reveal hidden assumptions, risks and uncertainties in our understanding of a system's behavior [68]. Qualitative approaches use logic and intuition to build internally consistent and flexible scenarios free from the restrictions of mathematical algorithms, creating a space where alternative futures as a function of known uncertainties can be considered [69–71]. By engaging diverse sets of stakeholders (including experts, decision makers, and others with valuable perspectives and backgrounds) and considering system drivers of change across disciplines, qualitative approaches can foster interdisciplinary, integrative and innovative problem solving for complex environmental challenges [72,73]. By embracing uncertainty, qualitative scenario analysis can build strategic decision-making capacity rather than cripple it, because participants learn to anticipate perceived uncertainty [73,74]. Furthermore, this approach fosters genuine conversations about the future captured by the scenario narratives [73,75]. Important qualitative factors can be revealed and incorporated into the process when scenarios are developed as narratives, including values, behaviors and institutions, all of which encourage broad thinking and add depth to future scenario narratives when compared to those generated by mathematical modelling alone [76].

Challenges

1. We need spatial and temporal data that are consistent and comparable at different scales. Both traditional but also contemporary data-capture methods such as airborne and satellite imagery will be vital.
2. We need multi-temporal and multi-spatial scale models to understand better the risks to AES from drivers of changing forest landscapes (both retrospectively and prospectively) and to create narratives for exploring management options under different scenarios.
3. We need models that can represent interacting pressures on forest ecosystems that are poorly understood but may further threaten the sustainability of AES and that link forest and social system behaviors.
4. We need to represent uncertainties at national, regional and local scales.

2.3. Step 3. Risk Analysis: What Is the Effectiveness of Management Measures That Act as Barriers to a Risk Event?

Risk analysis is based on the following logic: "*if* cumulative effects are the result of the residual pressures after implementing existing management measures, *then* we need to enhance the system of management measures to reduce pressures below detectable effects (prevention), or reduce the effects to minimize impacts (mitigation)" [40].

Step 3 begins with identifying risk drivers (human activities that are considered the sources of pressures) that influence the pressures-effects-impacts cycle. *Pressures* are the physical, chemical or biological agents that are introduced to the ecosystem as the result of the risk drivers that trigger an undesirable effect, and *impacts* are the result of the undesirable effect (Figure 7). The risk analysis step analyzes the performance of the management system that is put in place to reduce pressures. The management system includes hard controls, which are actions or structures that prevent or reduce the pressure. These hard controls are based on design criteria (set by science and engineering) that *contribute to the effectiveness* of the management measure. The management system also includes soft controls, which are enabling, facilitating and tracking activities that *contribute to the compliance* of the management measure. The performance of the management system is analyzed in terms of the effectiveness of the management controls, as well as their compliance (regulatory) or adoption (voluntary), and must consider both preventive (pressures-to-effects) and mitigation (effects-to-impacts) measures (Table 2).

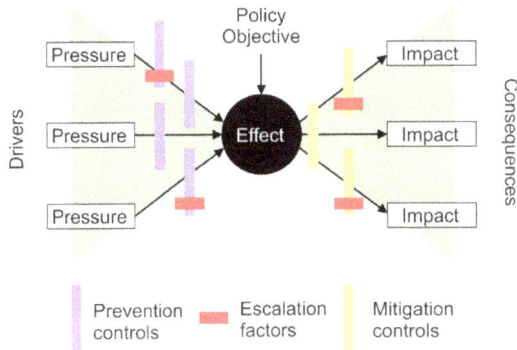

Figure 7. ISO 31010 Bowtie Analysis Tool to analyze the performance of the management system. *Prevention controls* act to reduce the effect. *Mitigation controls* act to decrease the severity of the impacts as a result of the effect. *Escalation factors* are outside influences (e.g., climate change) that undermine the performance of prevention or mitigation controls. Modified from [77].

Table 2. System of management measures (adapted from [78] and illustrated in [40]).

		Management Measures
Hard Controls	Avoid	Where and when is the human activity allowed to occur?
	Prevent	What is the amount of human activity permitted?
	Mitigate	What is the degree of impact?
Soft Controls	Enable	What is the allocation and coordination of authority?
	Facilitate	How can we make the public care that we can meet the policy objectives?
	Track	What is the target, and how can we track compliance and conformity to reach the target?

The way we evaluate the performance of the forest management system is a product of our forest management philosophy. Over the past century, forest management paradigms have shifted from the principle of maximum sustained yield (mid-1900s to 1980s), to ecosystem-based management (1980s to present). Ecosystem-based management is largely focused on the emulation of natural disturbance and uses the natural range of variation in ecosystem attributes as a reference condition against which to evaluate the performance of the management system [79].

To track the performance of the management system we need indicators and models that provide information on changing "baseline" conditions as well as the human activities that cause deviations from baseline conditions. Models enable us to answer "what-if" questions and different model scenarios provide an estimate of the risks of effects arising from the adoption of different management measures. Linking models with management in this manner allows governments to identify potential weaknesses and strengths in the performance of the management system, as well as to identify threats and opportunities for enhancing the performance. A system in baseline condition expresses attributes within the range of natural variation in the absence of human activity. However, as climate change intensifies and systems evolve beyond historic analogues, the concepts of baseline condition and natural range of variation are no longer useful or even desirable as management objectives (e.g., [80,81]). With accelerated anthropogenic and global stressors, we are increasingly moving our ecosystems outside of the range of natural variation. Equilibrium-based modeling approaches are not very good at predicting outcomes in natural systems that exhibit non-linear dynamics. Similarly, parametric approaches may fit well to existing data but lack out-of-sample predictive skill and misidentify key driving variables in nonlinear systems [82].

We need new ways to evaluate performance and bring the concepts of resilience including resistance, recovery, thresholds and regime shift into forest management [83–85]. Resilience is often suggested as a policy goal and a performance measure for the stability of social and ecological systems; however, there is significant debate on what resilience means and how to measure and manage for it [86]. Ecological definitions focus on concepts of *resistance* (related to the risk and severity of impact from exposure to disturbance), *recovery* (ability to return to the prior functioning state) and *proximity to thresholds or tipping points* [83,85,86]. While some efforts to measure resilience are underway, the development of modeling approaches and indicators to assess resilience remains a challenging field of research.

We also need ways to evaluate the complexity of interacting stressors that lead to changes in ecosystem states. For example, models have been developed that use changes in variance as a basis for predicting impending changes in ecosystems (e.g., regime shifts) due to anthropogenic stress [87–89]. The approach is based on the premise that ecosystem dynamics may become more variable before a regime shift and that this variance can be used as an indicator of the impending change [87]. An interesting characteristic of this approach from a management standpoint is that variance can be modeled even when there is no clear understanding of the underlying (typically non-linear) mechanisms of the impending change in ecosystem state. This suggests that detection may be possible using only routine monitoring data [87,89]. These measures of resilience are primarily used to measure how close systems are to thresholds and regime shift—the regime shift itself is seen as neither good nor bad, which makes a focus on measuring resistance, recovery and regime shift *per se* incomplete and unsatisfying for understanding resilience.

New approaches are being developed to understand the stability of systems and feedbacks between multiple systems. The best analogy for these indicators is that they are related to concepts of redundancy and adaptation/mutation. One promising approach focuses on entropy indicators [90]. Entropy indicators are based on the assumption that the more processes, interactions, and feedbacks that are present in a system, the more likely the system is to persist and adapt to changes [91,92]. Similarly, indicators based on information theory express the degree of predictability and self-organization of a system [90,93]. For evaluating these indicators, the feedbacks in the socio-ecological system must be carefully identified at multiple scales and across different components [93].

Challenges

1. We need to build and share databases of regulatory and voluntary management measures.
2. We need to evaluate the performance of the system of management measures that are put in place to reduce the risk of cumulative effects in the face of changing global conditions, including their effectiveness as well as the compliance of regulatory measures and the adoption of voluntary measures.
3. We need to bring the concepts of thresholds, tipping points and regimes shifts, and their appropriate indicators, into forest management strategies.
4. We need to create new indicators and methods for modeling resilience that reveal the pathways between pressures-effects-impacts, and that incorporate synergistic/antagonistic interactions and feedbacks within the managed system.

2.4. Step 4. Risk Evaluation: Do We Need to Act to Reduce the Risk Events?

Where Step 3 identifies deficiencies in the management system, either through inadequate effectiveness, compliance or adoption, Step 4 evaluates the likelihood of undesired consequences and assesses them in terms of exceeding risk tolerance levels or acceptable bounds. Risk evaluation is a normative process that matches the severity of ecological, social and economic impacts under different scenarios to tolerances expressed by stakeholders in order to define a safe operating space. The application of the concept of AES can assist in this process because it links consequences of forest management that affect AES to human benefits, thereby framing risks from forest-water interactions in terms that people can understand.

Risk evaluation may be based on probability impact graphs developed either qualitatively or quantitatively [94,95]. Risk tolerance curves (e.g., Figure 8) show that limits of acceptable and tolerable risk are based on underlying assumptions about: (1) adaptive capacity including the ability and limits of current technologies to mitigate risk; (2) feasibility of adaptation which is determined in part by social context and financial capacity; and (3) societal preferences about the amount and distribution of risk across different assets and communities [96]. Framing risk tolerance regarding adaptation incorporates institutional and social responses in defining limits [94]. Risks are then delineated according to whether they are tolerable (impacts that can be avoided and mitigated with adaptation), or intolerable (impacts that are unacceptable and unavoidable through adaptation). Tolerable risks would include adapting to soil moisture deficits through irrigation. Intolerable risks would include those that have a low probability but catastrophic consequences, such as the cascading effects of drought and famine from changes in atmospheric moisture patterns, as well as those that have a relatively low impact but are sufficiently frequent to be disruptive and impose unacceptable cost over time, such as recurring extreme flood events.

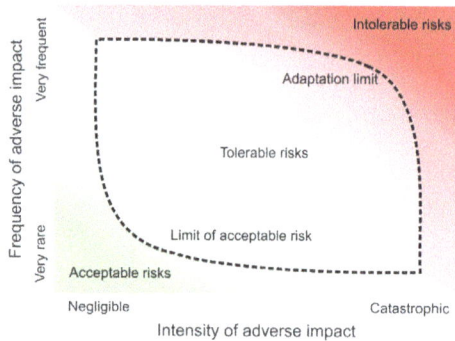

Figure 8. Risk tolerance curve is based on acceptable risks (there is no need to act), tolerable risks (risks can be managed by adaptation), and intolerable risks (risks that cannot be managed with adaptation). Modified from [94] based on [95].

Risk perceptions are subjective and individuals have different tolerances for risk. Therefore, the process for deriving societal risk tolerances must be transparent (Figure 9; [77]). It is important to ensure that all affected communities are involved in evaluating risks and in developing adaptation strategies. Typically, forest planning and operation take place at watershed or sub-watershed scales where stakeholder representation is limited to local and regional interests. This can result in a biased prioritization of risks, focusing on those that are local and decisions that have short-term payoffs with relatively certain costs and benefits. This leaves a gap in representation of potential broader risks to AES, which are more uncertain but may underpin the productivity of the system overall. To address risks to AES at an appropriate scale, it will be necessary to increase the scope of forest planning processes and tools to broader regional strategic assessment that can represent cross-sector (e.g., agricultural) impacts and longer-term perspectives.

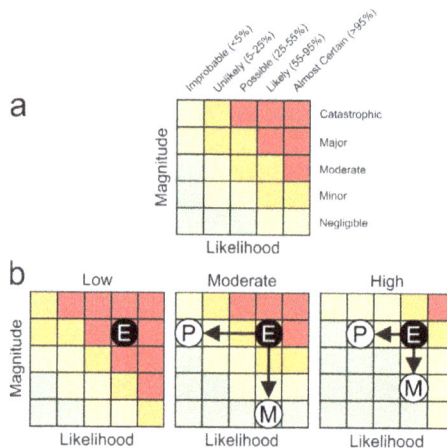

Figure 9. (**A**) Risk criteria and (**B**) risk tolerance matrices to evaluate if a management system should be changed (effects (**E**) are managed through mitigating (**M**) or preventative (**P**) measures). Coloration within the matrices denotes the necessary course of management action (**Green**: No management measures required; **Yellow**: Existing management measures adequate; **Orange**: Existing management measures need enhancement, and **Red**: Additional management measures needed). Modified from [40,77].

Probability impact diagrams can facilitate discussion, highlighting critical areas of uncertainty and win-win or no-regret strategies. However, they are less helpful when there are trade-offs between risks. For example, some strategies to support climate regulation may come at the expense of water availability and biodiversity. Similarly, maximizing fiber production may reduce water availability [97]. In such cases, evaluating the costs and benefits of risks under alternative scenarios may be desirable. Quantitative assessment of risk to AES is complicated by the ecological uncertainties described in previous sections that make it difficult to quantify probabilities. Similarly, the public good nature of AES such as clean water and aquatic biodiversity make a monetary valuation of costs and benefits challenging. The MEA [12] classification of ES as supporting, regulating, provisional, and cultural services is not amenable to valuation because the intermediate nature of supporting and regulating services and feedbacks between services can lead to double counting of benefits [98,99]. Both the EU Forest Action Plan [100] and the Biodiversity Strategy [101] call for the development of a standard framework for valuing forest ES.

Equity is an important component of adaptive capacity. In the case of forest AES, the poorest of the poor may be dependent on forest clearing for subsistence needs and have very little capacity to adapt to changes in water availability outside of further clearing of forest [21,102]. Understanding the distributional impacts of policies can help target resources to ensure that communities have the finances and capacity to adapt in ways that reduce risk and avoid negative cascading consequences.

There are challenging intra- and inter-generational equity issues to address in determining risk tolerances and the need for management action. Equity implies weighting costs and benefits more for the poor and accounting for impacts on future generations in risk management. The burden of forest protection will fall on those who rely on forest products to maintain livelihoods while AES benefits will accrue downstream and to future generations. Indices of relative poverty can be used to weight impacts of wide spread environmental risks (e.g., [103]), and discount rates are used to reduce the relative weight of future to current costs [104]. Since costs and benefits are not borne equally between different communities, weighting schemes have both inter- and intra-generational equity trade-offs (e.g., [105]). One justification for discounting is that growth will ensure that future generations will be wealthier. However, this assumption is false with irreversible loss of natural capital suggesting that discounting may not be suitable for some types of risks that exhibit thresholds and tipping points [106,107]. The choice of weights is probably the most contentious and influential variable in determining the need to act to reduce ecosystem risk as illustrated by the debate on the Stern 2007 Intergovernmental Panel on Climate Change report and the role of discounting [108,109]. Scenarios should be evaluated in terms of the sensitivity of results to different weighting schemes.

Decisions must be made in the face of a lack of knowledge on system behavior and prior probability distributions that describe system dynamics. Strategies for making decisions should involve identifying key sources of uncertainty, and identifying policies that are more forgiving in the event of negative surprise. In other words, costs in terms of system efficiency may have to be traded for reduced vulnerability and risk. This approach is particularly important when there are strong disagreements about assumptions and when decision-making is being done outside of historical context (e.g., [110]).

Effective decision-making strategies are those that perform well over the broadest range of alternative assumptions. A key source of uncertainty is related to interactions between social and ecological systems as humans adapt and respond to new policies that change forest condition. Often these interactions are too complicated to treat analytically and there is a need for multi-scale approaches to understand how the effects of these interactions cascade from individual decisions to communities and regions [111]. One way to deal with this uncertainty is to use agent-based models that are capable of representing individual behaviors and non-linear responses, while incorporating spatial and temporal heterogeneity [112]. Geographic Information Systems can be linked to agent-based models so that it is possible to have a spatial and temporal description of the distribution of risks and vulnerabilities, and reduce unanticipated consequences both locally and globally [113].

Challenges

1.	We must develop standardized methods for valuing ES. There is increasing evidence that AES are linked regionally, nationally and internationally; thus there is a need for consistent and transparent methodologies to compare and aggregate benefits and values of AES at different scales. Both the EU Forest Action Plan [100] and the Biodiversity Strategy [101] call for the development of a standard framework for valuing forest ES.
2.	We must standardize approaches for distinguishing intermediate services and final benefits. The MEA [12] classification of ES as supporting, regulating, provisional and cultural services is not amenable to valuation [98]. Challenges include distinguishing intermediate services from final benefits to ensure there is no double counting, and addressing spatial and temporal dimensions [98,99].
3.	We must choose appropriate discount rates to account for intra- and inter-generational equity. Equity problems are prominent in dealing with AES, because benefits are usually downstream from where management actions take place and costs are incurred. Some benefits have long time lags before they are realized after a management action, whereas most costs are immediate.

2.5. Step 5. Risk Treatment: What Policies and Strategies Can Reduce Risk and Increase the Resilience of Forest Ecosystems and Their Services?

Though forest AES provide large benefits, they are not being adequately protected from the risks of cumulative effects. There is a need to strengthen and develop new policies to protect the valuable regulating and supporting (in addition to the provisioning and cultural) AES, which currently fall outside of markets, on behalf of downstream beneficiaries and future generations. The scale and jurisdiction of forest ownership and management are not typically aligned with management of forests for AES. Forest policy and management decisions are made either at too small a scale (e.g., forest management unit or stand) or too large a scale (national or international), whereas many regulatory and supporting AES require management actions at a watershed scale because that is the scale in which hydrologic processes and other AES typically express themselves.

Protection of AES requires a range of policy approaches from formal protection to incentives for beneficial practices by forest industry and private landowners [114]. Protection policies that emphasize exclusionary zoning are critical for the protection of AES. However, on their own they may be insufficient. Without additional incentives, protective measures may be unsupported and eroded by non-compliance and illegal encroachments, particularly if they reduce livelihood opportunities for those who cannot adapt. Effective forest management will benefit from policies that focus on individual behaviors and responses to price signals and other incentives embedded in tenures and institutions. Protection policies and incentivized approaches are complementary; protected areas act as refugia and perform an insurance role, whereas incentives allow for more adaptive behavior on the ground as conditions change. Unfortunately, these strategies are typically considered separately even though there are feedbacks between the two.

Incentives and payments for ES (PES) are an increasingly common way to internalize the benefits of AES in forest management decisions, particularly in developing countries where they often provide a substantial portion of rural income [115–118]. Getting the prices right is a critical aspect in the design of PES programs. However, the public-good nature of many of the regulating or supporting AES makes it difficult to determine how much the public is willing to pay, leading to budget shortfalls [118]. Water supply utilities, irrigation systems, and power companies are the most frequent buyers of AES (e.g., [118]). However, there is a gap in financing payments for AES that provide purely public benefits such as aquifer recharge. Government PES are particularly important for regulating and supporting AES where traditional private sector options are limited. An example of a successful government PES program is Mexico's Payment for Hydrological Environmental Services Program where the government pays forest landowners for watershed protection and aquifer recharge and collects revenues for the program from water supply charges [119]. However, sustainable financing of PES programs is an ongoing problem.

Multilateral initiatives have provided more than $1 billion in financing for forest carbon investments over the past decade. Commitments to forest conservation were top of the agenda at the Conference of the Parties (COP) 21 climate talks in Paris, particularly for tropical forests where illegal clearing, encroachment, and agricultural pressures continue to be a leading cause of global deforestation. The COP 21 discussions followed on the 2014 New York Declaration on Forests where world leaders committed to reducing natural forest loss by 50% by 2020 and end it altogether by 2030. Britain, Germany and Norway pledged $5 billion for forest conservation in poor countries through 2020 under the New York Declaration. Estimates are that as much as $10 billion a year flow into forest conservation, but this is about half of the funding required to reduce global deforestation by 50% [120].

If these measures are adopted in the COP 21 agreements, then significant investment in forest ecosystems worldwide can be expected, with promising benefits for AES. To date the impetus for forest conservation has been driven by carbon sequestration benefits; however, such a focus could lead to some of the same pitfalls and unanticipated consequences as the previous focus on forests for fiber and fuel. While the New York Declaration mentions the importance of forests for provisioning services including food and water, the ecological functions emphasized in the agreement focus only on biodiversity and carbon. Water regulating functions are not mentioned as a policy priority or objective anywhere in the document. Forests can only take up carbon if they take up water, and part of the price of carbon sequestration is paid in water uptake [32]. To manage forests for water in the 21st century, we need to ensure that carbon and biodiversity policies emphasize the linkages with AES.

Challenges

1. Dealing with complexity means we need to design forest management strategies that reflect feedbacks between forest AES and future landscape conditions, and that signal appropriate scarcities and risks. Regulatory and voluntary (*i.e.*, incentive) strategies must be considered jointly to account for perverse incentives and feedbacks.

2. We must develop incentives that can protect hydrologic regimes that underpin forest AES across multiple boundaries from sub-watersheds to large multi-basin drainage areas. Similarly, we must incorporate signals about future ecological scarcity into current incentives to address lag times in forest restoration.

3. Market mechanisms and PES are important anti-poverty programs. Often PES and anti-poverty programs are linked, but it is important to ensure that these programs are properly targeted and generate beneficial AES outcomes to avoid just becoming income redistribution programs [115,121].

4. The unprecedented level of forest investment under new carbon agreements provides opportunities for new investments in AES. These investments should be undertaken as experiments in order to better understand the relationship between forest management practices and AES at multiple scales. These types of experiments could help us to improve how we manage forests in the face of increasing demands for food, fiber and energy, and to ensure that we avoid some of the unanticipated consequences that have arisen from past carbon-focused policies.

3. Conclusions

Humans are altering the world's remaining natural landscapes at an unprecedented rate. As pressures move ecosystems outside of the natural range of variation, ES from forests are at increasing risk. Governments and companies have committed to reducing deforestation by half by 2020 and ending it altogether by 2030. To accommodate these ambitious targets in the face of growing populations, both forest and non-forest lands will have to be managed more intensively, making a focus on ecological thresholds and protection of AES even more critical.

There is currently a gap in our scientific knowledge about the impacts of various forest management policies on AES. In spite of the enormous progress made in slowing forest loss and fragmentation, international agreements and action plans still tend to operate within "silos" (single-issue oriented policies), even if the silos now include other ES such as carbon. A single-issue focus in policies can create the potential for unintended feedbacks and consequences. An AES approach that considers multiple water-related benefits allows us to explicitly include a broader range of values in forest management decisions, and in particular to recognize the contribution of regulating and supporting AES in maintaining forest and agricultural productivity.

Effective tools will be required to improve the prediction and management of risks to forest AES. We show how the ISO 31000 Risk Management framework can be adapted to forest management risk assessment, and we highlight a suite of challenges that need to be overcome to achieve the five-step implementation of the framework. The forest community should come together to help "customize" tools that will achieve the following:

1. Define a realistic boundary for the forest AES management context that specifies how spatial and temporal scales and lags should be represented in the boundary condition.
2. Develop models and indicators that reveal the pathways (including interactions and feedbacks) among pressures-effects-impacts and that incorporate concepts of complexity, thresholds, tipping points and regime shifts into forest ecosystem monitoring and assessment programs.
3. Develop standardized methods for assessing the cumulative effects on forest AES from multiple stressors and build databases of regulatory/voluntary management measures to assess and monitor management effectiveness and compliance.
4. Develop next generation models and indicators to analyze the adaptability of socio-ecological systems to changing conditions and indicators to track the resilience and robustness of policies operating within these systems.
5. Develop incentives (e.g., payments for ES) that will mitigate impacts of forest management, loss, or degradation of hydrologic function and other AES, and that will overcome some of the complexity highlighted above.

We call for a concerted effort to build these tools as part of the *UN Forest and Water Agenda* announced at the World Forestry Congress in Durban, South Africa. Global leadership and experience are needed to bring together a community of experts, including knowledge developers and users, who can develop effective solutions promptly. Research and advocacy by civil society organizations have improved scientific understanding and helped build public support for forest conservation and restoration. Now we need to focus on not just carbon, but water as the common center of the energy, fiber and food nexus for forest management.

We call for a strengthening of forest governance for water-related values by explicitly identifying the protection of AES in international agreements and policy statements. Furthermore, indicators for crediting the protection of AES should be incorporated in international funds and agreements such as REDD+ (Reducing Emissions from Deforestation and Forest Degradation) transactions. This will enable the development and financing of incentives for AES within existing financial mechanisms such as the Carbon Fund and the Forest Carbon Partnership Facility. It is important to ensure that a substantial share of revenues from these funds goes not just to individual or private tenure holders but also to local communities and governments since the sustainability of AES depends not only on what happens in a single forest stand but cumulatively at watershed levels.

National and international level assessments of risks to AES from forest management, degradation, or loss are required. However, the new "future forests" guide published by the FAO [63] does not assess water. To address risks to whole forest ecosystems and their services, we recommend that AES be specified directly in the objectives of all future international forest agreements and action strategies. If forests are the lungs and sweat glands of the earth, then water is the venous system. The focus on forests for trees without equal consideration of water and AES is akin to providing resuscitation while letting the patient bleed to death. We need to use investments to protect forests under new international commitments as living laboratories in which opportunities for natural and designed experimentation and evaluation of innovative forest management can occur. We further recommend principles from adaptive management to refine hypotheses and assimilate new information to sustain the services provided by forests for future generations.

Acknowledgments: This research was funded by the NSERC Canadian Network for Aquatic Ecosystem Services (http://www.cnaes.ca/) and Alberta Innovates Technology Futures (http://www.albertatechfutures.ca/). We gratefully thank Johnston Miller, David Aldred, Katrina Laurent, and Geraldine Leung Lam Hing for invaluable assistance with figure preparation and proofreading.

Author Contributions: Irena Creed and Marian Weber are the co-lead authors of the paper. Irena Creed conceptualized the paper, analyzed the issues, and led the writing of the paper. Marian Weber contributed to conceptualization of the paper, analysis of the issues, and writing. Francesco Accatino contributed to the research and writing. Dave Kreutzweiser provided a government perspective and edited the paper.

Conflicts of Interest: The authors declare no conflict of interest. The founding sponsors had no role in the design of the study, in the collection, analyses, or interpretation of data, in the writing of the manuscript, and in the decision to publish the results.

References

1. Wilson, E.O. *The Future of Life*; Vintage: New York, NY, USA, 2002; p. 265.
2. United Nations Sustainable Development Goals. In *Transforming Our World: The 2030 Agenda for Sustainable Development*; United Nations: New York, NY, USA, 2015.
3. Sizer, N.; Petersen, R.; Anderson, J.; Hansen, M.; Potapov, P.; Thau, D. Tree Cover Loss Spikes in Russia and Canada, Remains Globally High. World Resources Institute: Available online: http://www.wri.org/blog/2015/04/tree-cover-loss-spikes-russia-and-canada-remains-high-globally (accessed on 18 December 2015).
4. Hansen, M.C.; Potapov, P.V.; Moore, R.; Hancher, M.; Turubanova, S.A.; Tyukavina1, A.; Thau, D.; Stehman, S.V.; Goetz, S.J.; Loveland, T.R.; *et al.* High-resolution global maps of 21st-Century forest cover change. *Science* **2013**, *342*, 850–853. [CrossRef] [PubMed]
5. Henry, J.D. Northern Exposure: Can the planet-encircling boreal forest survive global warming and resource exploitation? *Nat. Hist.* **2005**, *114*, 26–32.
6. Repetto, R. Deforestation in the tropics. *Sci. Am.* **1990**, *262*, 36–42. [CrossRef]
7. Schindler, D.W.; Lee, P.G. Comprehensive conservation planning to protect biodiversity and ecosystem services in Canadian boreal regions under a warming climate and increasing exploitation. *Biol. Conserv.* **2010**, *143*, 1571–1586. [CrossRef]
8. Wells, J.; Roberts, D.; Lee, P.; Cheng, R.; Darveau, M. *A Forest of Blue–Canada's Boreal Forest: The World's Waterkeeper*; International Boreal Conservation Campaign: Seattle, WA, USA, 2012.
9. Biggs, T.W.; Dunne, T.; Roberts, D.A.; Matricardi, E. The rate and extent of deforestation in watershed of the southwestern Amazon basin. *Ecol. Appl.* **2008**, *18*, 31–48. [CrossRef] [PubMed]
10. Brandt, J.P.; Flannigan, M.D.; Maynard, D.G.; Thompson, I.D.; Volney, W.J.A. An introduction to Canada's boreal zone: Ecosystem processes, health, sustainability, and environmental issues. *Environ. Rev.* **2013**, *21*, 207–226. [CrossRef]
11. Lawrence, D.; Vandecar, K. Effects of tropical deforestation on climate and agriculture. *Nat. Clim. Chang.* **2015**, *5*, 27–36. [CrossRef]
12. Millennium Ecosystem Assessment (MEA). *Ecosystems and Human Well-Being: Synthesis*; Island Press: Washington, DC, USA, 2005.
13. Muira, A.; Amacher, M.; Hofer, T.; San-Miguel-Ayanz, J.; Ernawati; Thankway, R. Protective functions and ecosystem services of global forests in the past quarter-century. *For. Ecol. Manag.* **2015**, *35*, 35–45. [CrossRef]
14. Mace, G.M.; Norris, K.; Fitter, A.H. Biodiversity and ecosystem services: A multilayered relationship. *Trends Ecol. Evol.* **2012**, *27*, 19–25. [CrossRef] [PubMed]
15. Naeem, S.; Duffy, L.E.; Zavaleta, E. The functions of biological diversity in an age of extinction. *Science* **2012**, *336*, 1401–1406. [CrossRef] [PubMed]
16. Tilman, D. Biodiversity and ecosystem functioning. In *Nature's Services: Societal Dependence on Natural Ecosystems*; Daily, C.G., Ed.; Island Press: Washington, DC, USA; Covelo, CA, USA, 1997; pp. 93–112.

17. Furniss, M.J.; Staab, B.P.; Hazelhurst, S.; Clifton, C.F.; Roby, K.B.; Ilhadrt, B.L.; Larry, E.B.; Todd, A.H.; Reid, L.M.; Hines, S.J.; *et al. Water, Climate Change, and Forests: Watershed Stewardship for a Changing Climate*; General Technical Report PNW-GTR-812; US Department of Agriculture, Forest Service, Pacific Northwest Research Station: Portland, OR, USA, 2010.

18. Abildtrup, J.; Albers, H.; Stenger-Letheux, A.; Termansen, M. Scale, Location, and Spatial Interactions in the Analysis of Natural Resources: Lessons for Forest Economics. *Ecol. Econ.* **2013**, *92*, 34–36. [CrossRef]

19. Barbier, E.B.; Heal, G.M. Valuing Ecosystem Services. *Econ. Voice* **2006**, *3*, 1–6. [CrossRef]

20. US Forest Service. Watershed Services: The Important Link between Forests and Water. Available online: http://www.fs.fed.us/ecosystemservices/pdf/Watershed_Services.pdf (accessed on 30 November 2015).

21. Corvalan, C.; Hales, S.; McMichael, A.J. *Ecosystems and Human Well-Being: Health Synthesis*; World Health Organization: Geneva, Switzerland, 2005.

22. Mueller, J.M.; Swaffar, W.; Nielsen, E.A.; Springer, A.E.; Lopez, S.M. Estimating the value of watershed services following forest restoration. *Water Resour. Res.* **2013**, *49*, 1–9. [CrossRef]

23. Bargués Tobella, A.; Reese, H.; Almaw, A.; Bayala, J.; Malmer, A.; Laudon, H.; Ilstedt, U. The effect of trees on preferential flow and soil infiltrability in an agroforestry parkland in semiarid Burkina Faso. *Water Resour. Res.* **2014**, *50*, 3342–3354. [CrossRef]

24. Ilstedt, U.; Malmer, A.; Verbeeten, E.; Murdiyarso, D. The effect of afforestation on water infiltration in the tropics: A systematic review and meta-analysis. *For. Ecol. Manag.* **2007**, *251*, 45–51. [CrossRef]

25. Ghimire, C.P.; Bruijnzeel, L.A.; Lubczynski, M.W.; Bonell, M. Negative trade-off between changes in vegetation water use and infiltration recovery after reforesting degraded pasture land in the Nepalese Lesser Himalaya. *Hydrol. Earth Sys. Sci.* **2014**, *18*, 4933–4949. [CrossRef]

26. Committee on Hydrologic Impacts of Forest Management, National Research Council (NRC). *Hydrologic Effects of a Changing Forest Landscape*; The National Academies Press: Washington, DC, USA, 2008.

27. Reese, J.; US Forest Service, Charleston, SC, USA. Personal communication, 2015.

28. Egoh, B.; Drakou, E.G.; Dunbar, M.B.; Maes, J.; Willemen, L. *Indicators for Mapping Ecosystem Services: A Review*; Publications Office of the European Union: Luxembourg, Luxembourg, 2012.

29. Grêt-Regamey, A.; Weibel, B.; Kienast, F.; Rabe, S.E.; Zulian, G. A tiered approach for mapping ecosystem services. *Ecosyst. Serv.* **2014**, *13*, 16–27. [CrossRef]

30. US Environmental Protection Agency. *Valuing the Protection of Ecological Systems and Services: A Report of the EPA Science Advisory Board*; EPA-SAB-09-012; US Environmental Protection Agency: Washington, DC, USA, 2013.

31. Forestry Agency of Japan. Shiga declaration on forests and water. In Proceedings of the International Expert Meeting on Forests and Water, Shiga, Japan, 20–22 November 2002.

32. Food and Agriculture Organization of the United Nations. *Forests and Water: International Momentum and Action*; FAO: Rome, Italy, 2013.

33. Food and Agriculture Organization of the United Nations. Global Forest Resources Assessment 2015. How Are the World's Forests Changing? Available online: www.fao.org/3/a-i4793e.pdf (accessed on 30 November 2015).

34. Daily, G.C.; Polansky, S.; Goldstein, J.; Kareiva, P.M.; Mooney, H.A.; Pejchar, L.; Ricketts, T.H.; Salzman, J.; Shallenberger, R. Ecosystem services in decision making: Time to deliver. *Front. Ecol. Environ.* **2009**, *7*, 21–28. [CrossRef]

35. Norgaard, R.B. Ecosystem services: From eye-opening metaphor to complexity blinder. *Ecol. Econ.* **2010**, *69*, 1219–1227. [CrossRef]

36. Smith, N.; Deal, R.; Kline, J.; Blahna, D.; Patterson, T.; Spies, T.A.; Bennett, K. *Ecosystem Services As a Framework for Forest Stewardship: Deschutes National Forest Overview*; General Technical Report PNW-GTR-852; Department of Agriculture, Forest Service, Pacific Northwest Research Station: Portland, OR, USA, 2011; p. 46.

37. International Organization for Standardization (ISO). ISO 31000:2009. Risk Management—Principles and Guidelines. Available online: http://www.iso.org/iso/catalogue_detail?csnumber=43170 (accessed on 30 November 2015).

38. International Electrotechnical Commission/International Organization for Standardization (IEC/ISO). IEC/ISO 31010:2009. Risk Assessment Techniques. Available online: http://www.iso.org/iso/catalogue_detail?csnumber=51073 (accessed on 10 December 2015).

39. Cormier, R.; Kannen, A.; Elliott, M.; Hall, P.; Davies, I.M. *Marine and Coastal Ecosystem-Based Risk Management Handbook*; International Council for the Exploration of the Seas: Copenhagen, Denmark, 2013.

40. Creed, I.F.; Cormier, R.C.; Laurent, K.L.; Accatino, F.; Igras, J.; Henley, P.; Friedman, K.B.; Johnson, L.B.; Crossman, J.; Dillon, P.J.; *et al.* Formal integration of science and management systems needed to achieve thriving and prosperous Great Lakes. *BioScience* **2016**. in press.

41. Lescourret, F.; Magda, D.; Richard, G.; Adam-Blondon, A.-F.; Bardy, M.; Baudry, J.; Doussan, I.; Dumont, B.; Lefevre, F.; Litrico, I.; *et al.* A social-ecological approach to managing multiple agro-ecosystem services. *Curr. Opin. Environ. Sustain.* **2015**, *14*, 68–75. [CrossRef]

42. Schlüter, M.; Hinkel, J.; Bots, P.W.; Arlinghaus, R. Application of the SES framework of model-based analysis of the dynamics of social-ecological systems. *Ecol. Soc.* **2014**, *19*, 36. [CrossRef]

43. Binder, C.R.; Hinkel, J.; Bots, P.W.G.; Pahl-Wostl, C. Comparison of frameworks for analyzing social-ecological systems. *Ecol. Soc.* **2013**, *18*, 26. [CrossRef]

44. Fremier, A.K.; DeClerck, F.A.J.; Bosque-Pérez, N.A.; Carmona, N.E.; Hill, R.; Joyal, T.; Keesecker, L.; Zion Klos, P.; Martínez-Salinas, A.; Niemeyer, R.; *et al.* Understanding spatiotemporal lags in ecosystem services to improve incentives. *BioScience* **2013**, *63*, 472–482. [CrossRef]

45. Fisher, B.; Turner, R.K.; Morling, P. Defining and classifying ecosystem services for decision making. *Ecol. Econ.* **2009**, *68*, 643–653. [CrossRef]

46. Gayer, T.; Viscusi, W.K. Determining the Proper Scope of Climate Change Benefits. Available online: http://www.brookings.edu/research/papers/2014/06/04-determining-proper-scope-climate-change-benefits-gayer (accessed on 22 February 2016).

47. Costanza, R. Ecosystem services: Multiple classification systems are needed. *Biol. Conserv.* **2008**, *141*, 350–352. [CrossRef]

48. Pattanayak, S.K.; Butry, D.T. Spatial complementarity of forests and farms: Accounting for ecosystem services. *Am. J. Agr. Econ.* **2005**, *87*, 995–1008. [CrossRef]

49. Olander, L.; Johnston, R.J.; Tallis, H.; Kagan, J.; Maguire, L.; Polasky, S.; Urban, D.; Boyd, J.; Wainger, L.; Palmer, M. *Best Practices for Integrating Ecosystem Services into Federal Decision Making*; Duke University National Ecosystem Services Partnership: Durham, NC, USA, 2015.

50. Lewis, D.J.; Wu, J. Land-use patterns and spatially dependent ecosystem services: Some microeconomic foundations. *Int. Rev. Environ. Resour. Econ.* **2015**, *8*, 191–223. [CrossRef]

51. United Nations Department of Economic and Social Affairs, Population Division. *World Population Prospects: The 2015 Revision, Key Findings and Advance Tables*; Working Paper No ESA/P/WP.241; United Nations Department of Economic and Social Affairs: New York, NY, USA, 2015.

52. Waters, C.; Zalasiewicz, J.; Summerhayes, C.; Barnosky, A.D.; Poirier, C.; Gałuszka, A.; Cearreta, A.; Edgeworth, M.; Ellis, E.C.; Ellis, M.; *et al.* The Anthropocene is functionally and stratigraphically distinct from the Holocene. *Science* **2016**, *351*. [CrossRef] [PubMed]

53. Venier, L.; Thompson, I.; Fleming, R.; Malcolm, J.; Aubin, I.; Trofymow, J.; Langor, D.; Sturrock, R.; Patry, C.; Outerbridge, R.; *et al.* Effects of natural resource development on the terrestrial biodiversity of Canadian boreal forests. *Environ. Rev.* **2014**, *22*, 457–490. [CrossRef]

54. Kreutzweiser, D.; Beall, F.; Webster, K.; Thompson, D.; Creed, I. Impacts and prognosis of natural resource development on aquatic biodiversity in Canada's boreal zone. *Environ. Rev.* **2013**, *21*, 227–259. [CrossRef]

55. Webster, K.; Beall, F.D.; Creed, I.F.; Kreutzweiser, D.P. Impacts and prognosis of natural resource development on water and wetlands in Canada's boreal zone. *Env. Rev.* **2015**, *23*, 78–131. [CrossRef]

56. Canadian Environmental Assessment Agency (CEAA). Act and Regulations. Available online: https://www.ceaa-acee.gc.ca/default.asp?lang=en&n=07F0DCD5-1 (accessed on 22 February 2016).

57. Bishop, J.; Kapila, S.; Hicks, F.; Mitchell, P.; Vorhies, F. *Building Biodiversity Business*; Shell International Limited and the International Union for Conservation of Nature (IUCN): London, UK; Gland, Switzerland, 2008; p. 164.

58. Krieger, D.J. *The Economic Value of Forest Ecosystem Services: A Review*; The Wilderness Society: Washington, DC, USA, 2001.

59. Simberloff, D. The role of science in the preservation of forest biodiversity. *Forest Ecol. Manag.* **1999**, *115*, 101–111. [CrossRef]

60. Bergeron, Y.; Cyr, D.; Drever, C.R.; Flannigan, M.; Gauthier, S.; Kneeshaw, D.; Lauzon, È.; Leduc, A.; Le Goff, H.; Lesieur, D.; *et al.* Past, current, and future fire frequencies in Quebec's commercial forests: Implications for the cumulative effects of harvesting and fire on age-class structure and natural disturbance-based management. *Can. J. For. Res.* **2006**, *36*, 2737–2744. [CrossRef]

61. Sibley, P.K.; Kreutzweiser, D.P.; Naylor, B.J.; Richardson, J.S.; Gordon, A.M. Emulation of natural disturbance (END) for riparian forest management: Synthesis and recommendations. *Freshw. Sci.* **2012**, *31*, 258–264. [CrossRef]

62. Thiffault, E.; Paré, D.; Brais, S.; Titus, B.D. Intensive biomass removals and site productivity in Canada: A review of relevant issues. *Forest. Chron.* **2010**, *86*, 36–42. [CrossRef]

63. Food and Agriculture Organization of the United Nations. *Forest Futures Methodology*; Forest Resources Assessment Working Paper 182: Rome, Italy, 2015.

64. Brown, C.J.; Bode, M.; Venter, O.; Barnes, M.D.; McGowan, J.; Runge, C.A.; Watson, J.E.M.; Possingham, H.P. Effective conservation requires clear objectives and prioritizing actions, not places or species. *Proc. Nat. Acad. Sci. USA* **2015**, *112*, E4342–E4342. [CrossRef] [PubMed]

65. International Panel on Climate Change. *Special Report on Emissions*; Nakićenović, N., Swart, R., Eds.; IPCC: Geneva, Switzerland, 2000; p. 27.

66. Carpenter, S.R.; Bennett, E.M.; Peterson, G.D. Editorial: Special feature on scenarios for ecosystem services. *Ecol. Soc.* **2006**, *11*, 32. Available online: http://www.ecologyandsociety.org/vol11/iss2/art32/ (accessed on 22 February 2016). [CrossRef]

67. Calder, I.R. Forests and water—Ensuring forest benefits outweigh water costs. *Forest Ecol. Manag.* **2007**, *25*, 110–120. [CrossRef]

68. Wack, P. Scenarios: Shooting the rapids. *Harvard Bus. Rev.* **1985**, *63*, 139–150.

69. Bishop, P.; Hines, A.; Collins, T. The current state of scenario development: An overview of techniques. *Foresight* **2007**, *9*, 2–25. [CrossRef]

70. Bradfield, R.; Wright, G.; Burt, G.; Cairns, G.; Van Der Heijden, K. The origins and evolution of scenario techniques in long range business planning. *Futures* **2005**, *37*, 795–812. [CrossRef]

71. Huss, W.R.; Honton, E.J. Scenario planning—What style should you use? *Long Range Plan.* **1987**, *20*, 21–29. [CrossRef]

72. Alcamo, J. Introduction: The case for scenarios of the environment. In *Environmental Futures: The Practice of Environmental Scenario Analysis*, 1st ed.; Alcamo, J., Ed.; Elsevier: Amsterdam, The Netherlands, 2008; pp. 1–11.

73. Schwartz, P. *The Art of the Long View*, 2nd ed.; Doubleday: New York, NY, USA, 1996; p. 288.

74. Tapinos, E. Perceived environmental uncertainty in scenario planning. *Futures* **2012**, *44*, 338–345. [CrossRef]

75. Chermack, T.J.; van der Merwe, L.; Lynham, S.A. Exploring the relationship between scenario planning and perceptions of strategic conversation quality. *Technol. Forecast. Soc.* **2007**, *74*, 379–390. [CrossRef]

76. Swart, R.J.; Raskin, P.; Robinson, J. The problem of the future: Sustainability science and scenario analysis. *Global Environ. Chang.* **2004**, *14*, 137–146. [CrossRef]

77. International Council for the Exploration of the Sea. *Report of the Joint Rijkswaterstaat/DFO/ICES Workshop: Risk Assessment for Spatial Management*; ICES CM 2014/SSGHIE:01; ICES: Amsterdam, The Netherlands, 2014.

78. European Union. Directive 2008/56/EC of the European Parliament and of the Council of 17 June 2008. Establishing a Framework for Community Action in the Field of Marine Environmental Policy (Marine Strategy Framework Directive). Available online: http://eur-lex.europa.eu/legal-content/EN/TXT/?uri=CELEX%3A32008L0056 (accessed on 22 February 2016).

79. Gann, G.D.; Lamb, D. Society for Ecological Restoration International, Tucson, Arizona, USA and IUCN, Gland, Switzerland. A call to action by the ecological restoration joint working group of SER International and the IUCN Commission on Ecosystem Management. Available online: http://www.ser.org/resources/resources-detail-view/ecological-restoration-a-means-of-conserving-biodiversity-and-sustaining-livelihoods (accessed on 22 February 2016).

80. Bishop, K.; Baven, K.; Destouni, G.; Abrahamsson, K.; Andersson, L.; Johnson, R.K.; Rodhe, J.; Hjerdt, N. Nature as the "natural" goal for water management: A conversation. *AMBIO* **2009**, *38*, 209–214. [CrossRef] [PubMed]

81. Valinia, S.; Hansen, H.P.; Futter, M.N.; Bishop, K.; Sriskandarajah, N.; Fölster, J. Problems with the reconciliation of good ecological status and public participation in the Water Framework Directive. *Sci. Total Environ.* **2012**, *433*, 482–490. [CrossRef] [PubMed]

82. Ye, H.; Beamish, R.J.; Glaser, S.M.; Grant, S.C.H.; Hsieh, C.; Richards, L.J.; Schnute, J.T.; Sugihara, G. Equation-free mechanistic ecosystem forecasting using empirical dynamic modeling. *Proc. Natl. Acad. Sci. USA* **2015**, *112*, E1569–E1576. [CrossRef] [PubMed]

83. Hodgson, D.; McDonald, J.; Hosken, D. What do you mean "resilient"? *Trends Ecol. Evol.* **2015**, *30*, 503–506. [CrossRef] [PubMed]

84. Kimmins, J.P.H. Future shock in forestry Where have we come from; where are we going; is there a "right way" to manage forests? Lessons from Thoreau, Leopold, Toffler, Botkin and Nature. *Forest. Chron.* **2002**, *78*, 263–271. [CrossRef]

85. Yeung, A.; Richardson, J. Some conceptual operational considerations when measuring resilience: A response to Hodgson *et al. Trends Ecol. Evol.* **2016**, *31*, 2–3. [CrossRef] [PubMed]

86. Newton, A.; Cantarello, E. Restoration or forest resilience: An achievable goal? *New For.* **2015**, *46*, 645–668. [CrossRef]

87. Brock, W.A.; Carpenter, S.R. Variance as a leading indicator of regime shift in ecosystem services. *Ecol. Soc.* **2006**, *11*, 9. Available online: http://www.ecologyandsociety.org/vol11/iss2/art9/ (accessed on 30 November 2015).

88. Guttal, V.; Jayaprakash, C. Spatial variance and spatial skewness: Leading indicators of regime shifts in spatial ecological systems. *Theor. Ecol.* **2009**, *2*, 3–12. [CrossRef]

89. Carpenter, S.R.; Cole, J.J.; Pace, M.L.; Batt, R.; Brock, W.A.; Cline, T.; Coloso, J.; Hodgson, J.R.; Kitchell, J.F.; Seekell, D.A.; *et al.* Early warnings of regime shifts: A whole-ecosystem experiment. *Science* **2011**, *332*, 1079–1082. [CrossRef] [PubMed]

90. Cabezas, H.; Fath, B.D. Towards a theory of sustainable systems. *Fluid Ph. Equilib.* **2002**, *194*, 3–14. [CrossRef]

91. MacDougall, A.S.; McCann, K.S.; Gellner, G.; Turkington, R. Diversity loss with persistent human disturbance increases vulnerability to ecosystem collapse. *Nature* **2013**, *494*, 86–89. [CrossRef] [PubMed]

92. Ulanowicz, R.E.; Goerner, S.J.; Liataer, B.; Gomez, R. Quantifying sustainability: Resilience, efficiency, and the return of information theory. *Ecol. Complex.* **2009**, *6*, 27–36. [CrossRef]

93. Mayer, A.L.; Donovan, R.P.; Pawlowski, C.W. Information and entropy theory for the sustainability of coupled human and natural systems. *Ecol. Soc.* **2014**, *19*, 3. [CrossRef]

94. Dow, K.; Berkhout, F.; Preston, B.L.; Klein, R.J.T.; Midgley, G.; Shaw, M.R. Limits to adaptation. *Nat. Clim. Chang.* **2013**, *3*, 305–307. [CrossRef]

95. Klinke, A.; Renn, O. A new approach to risk evaluation and management: Risk-based, precaution-based, and discourse-based strategies. *Risk Anal.* **2002**, *22*, 1071–1094. [CrossRef] [PubMed]

96. United Nations Framework Convention on Climate Change. *Assessing the Costs and Benefits of Adaptation Options: An Overview of Approaches*; UNFCCC: Bonn, Germany, 2011.

97. Onaindia, M.; de Fernandez Manuel, B.; Madariaga, I.; Rodriguez-Loinaz, G. Co-benefits and trade-offs between biodiversity, carbon storage and water flow regulation. *For. Ecol. Manag.* **2013**, *289*, 1–9. Available online: http://www.sciencedirect.com/science/article/pii/S037811271200607X (accessed on 22 February 2016). [CrossRef]

98. Fisher, B.; Batement, I.; Turner, R.K. *Valuing Ecosystem Services: Benefits, Values, Space and Time*; United Nations Environment Programme: Nairobi, Kenya, 2011.

99. Keeler, B.L.; Polasky, S.; Brauman, K.A.; Johnson, K.A.; Finlay, J.C.; O'Neill, A.; Kovaks, K.; Dalzell, B. Linking water quality and well-being for improved assessment and valuation of ecosystem services. *Proc. Nat. Acad. Sci. USA* **2012**, *109*, 18619–18624. [CrossRef] [PubMed]

100. European Commission. A New EU Forest Strategy: For Forests and the Forest-Based Sector. 2013. Available online: http://eur-lex.europa.eu/legal-content/EN/TXT/?uri=CELEX:52013DC0659 (accessed on 30 November 2015).

101. European Commission. The EU Biodiversity Strategy to 2020. 2012. Available online: http://ec.europa.eu/environment/nature/biodiversity/comm2006/2020.htm (accessed on 30 November 2015).

102. Bele, M.Y.; Sonwa, D.J.; Tiani, A.-M. Adapting the Congo Basin forests management to climate change: Linkages among biodiversity, forest loss, and human well-being. *For. Pol. Econ.* **2015**, *50*, 1–10. [CrossRef]

103. Tol, R.S.J.; Downing, T.W.; Kuik, O.J.; Smith, J.B. Distributional aspects of climate change impacts. *Glob. Env. Chang.* **2004**, *14*, 259–272. [CrossRef]

104. Weisbach, D.A.; Sunstein, C.R. Symposium on Intergenerational Equity and Discounting. *Univ. Chic. Law Rev.* **2007**, *74*, 1–3. Available online: http://www.jstor.org/stable/4495592?seq=1#page_scan_tab_contents (accessed on 22 February 2016).

105. Schneider, M.T.; Traeger, C.P.; Winkler, R. Trading off generations: Equity, discounting and climate change. *Eur. Econ. Rev.* **2012**, *56*, 1621–1644. [CrossRef]

106. Neumayer, E. A Missed Opportunity: The Stern Review on Climate Change Fails to Tackle the Issue of Non-Substitutable Loss of Natural Capital. *Glob. Environ. Chang.* **2007**, *17*, 297–301. [CrossRef]

107. Weitzman, M.L. A review of the Stern review on the economics of climate change. *J. Econ. Lit.* **2007**, *45*, 703–724. [CrossRef]

108. Nordhaus, W.D. A Review of the Stern Review on the Economics of Climate. *J. Econ. Lit.* **2007**, *45*, 686–702. Available online: http://www.jstor.org/stable/27646843?seq=1#page_scan_tab_contents (accessed on 18 December 2015). [CrossRef]

109. Stern, N. *The Economics of Climate Change: The STERN Review*; Cambridge University Press: Cambridge, UK, 2007.

110. Lempert, R.J. Embedding (some) benefit-cost concepts into decision support processes with deep uncertainty. *J. Benefit Cost Anal.* **2014**, *5*, 487–514. [CrossRef]

111. Janssen, M.A.; Bodin, Ö.; Anderies, J.M.; Elmqvist, T.; Ernstson, H.; McAllister, R.R.J.; Olsson, P.; Ryan, P. Toward a network perspective of the study of resilience in social-ecological systems. *Ecol. Soc.* **2006**, *11*, 15. Available online: http://www.ecologyandsociety.org/vol11/iss1/art15/ (accessed on 15 December 2015).

112. Farmer, J.D.; Foley, D. The economy needs agent-based modelling. *Nature* **2009**, *460*, 685–686. [CrossRef] [PubMed]

113. Brown, D.G.; Riolo, R.; Robinson, D.; North, M.; Rand, W. Spatial process and data models: Toward integration of agent-based models and GIS. *J. Geograph. Syst.* **2005**, *7*, 25–47. [CrossRef]

114. Roux, D.J.; Nel, J.L.; Fisher, R.M.; Berendise, J. Top-down conservation targets and bottom-up management action: Creating complementary feedbacks for freshwater conservation. *Aquat. Conserv.* Available online: http://onlinelibrary.wiley.com/doi/10.1002/aqc.2577 (accessed on 30 November 2015). [CrossRef]

115. Barbier, E.B. Poverty, development, and ecological services. *Int. Rev. Environ. Resour. Econ.* **2008**, *2*, 1–27. [CrossRef]

116. Hogarth, N.J.; Belcher, B.; Campbell, B.; Stacey, N. The role of forest-related income in household economies and rural livelihoods in the border-region of Southern China. *World Dev.* **2013**, *43*, 111–123. [CrossRef]

117. Mahanty, S.; Suich, H.; Tacconi, L. Access and benefits in payments for environmental services and implications for REDD+: Lessons from seven PES schemes. *Land Use Policy* **2013**, *31*, 38–47. [CrossRef]

118. Whittington, D.; Pagiola, S. Using contingent valuation in the design of payments for environmental services mechanisms: A review and assessment. *World Bank Res. Obs.* **2012**, *27*, 261–287. [CrossRef]

119. Muñoz-Piña, C.; Guevara, A.; Torres, J.M.; Braña, J. Paying for the hydrological services of Mexico's forests: Analysis, negotiations and results. *Ecol. Econ.* **2008**, *4*, 725–736. [CrossRef]

120. Gillis, J. Delegates at Climate Talks Focus on Saving the World's Forests. *New York Times*, Available online: http://www.nytimes.com/2015/12/11/world/delegates-at-climate-talks-focus-on-saving-the-worlds-forests .html?_r=0 (accessed on 10 December 2015).

121. Barbier, E.B. Poverty, development, and environment. *Environ. Dev. Econ.* **2010**, *15*, 635–660. [CrossRef]

forests

MDPI

Article

Streamflow Regime Variations Following Ecological Management on the Loess Plateau, China

Jianjun Zhang [1,3], Tingting Zhang [2], Yongnan Lei [1,3], Xiaoping Zhang [1,2,*] and Rui Li [1,2]

1   State Key Laboratory of Soil Erosion and Dry land Farming in Loess Plateau, Institute of Soil and Water Conservation, Chinese Academy of Sciences and Ministry of Water Resources, Yang ling 712100, Shaanxi, China; zhangjianjun08@mails.ucas.ac.cn (J.Z.); leiyn604@126.com (Y.L.); lirui@ms.iswc.ac.cn (R.L.)

2   Institute of Soil and Water Conservation, Northwest A & F University, Yangling 712100, China; suztting@126.com

3   University of Chinese Academy of Sciences, Beijing 100049, China

*   Correspondence: zhangxp@ms.iswc.ac.cn; Tel.: +86-29-8701-9327; Fax: +86-29-8701-2210

Academic Editors: Ge Sun and James M. Vose

Received: 6 September 2015; Accepted: 17 December 2015; Published: 25 December 2015

Abstract: The continuous ecological management of the Loess Plateau is known throughout the world for two strategies: the integrated soil conservation project that began in the 1970s, and the "Grain for Green" project that began in the 1990s. Six sub-catchments nested in the Beiluo River basin were selected to investigate streamflow regime variations during the two project periods. The annual streamflow trends and change points were detected using a bootstrap-based Mann-Kendall test and Pettitt test. Annual streamflow (from the 1950s to 2011) exhibited significantly negative trends in five out of six catchments, varying from -0.15 to -0.30 mm/a. During the integrated soil conservation period, the annual streamflow was reduced due to high flow decreases (5% of time exceeded), whereas in the low flows (95%) it increased in all sub-catchments. During the "Grain for Green" period, the annual streamflow decreased due to daily streamflow reductions at four stations. In addition to high flow and low flow decreases at the Wuqi and Liujiahe stations during the "Grain for Green" period, it is significant that the low flows continuously increased. Compared with trends from the forestry area, which includes the Zhangcunyi and Huangling stations, incremental annual streamflow reductions were observed in other sub-catchments, which can be linked to ecological management. This result implies that streamflow can be moderated by appropriate management options, even in semiarid areas. It was concluded that a stable streamflow regime can be achieved in vegetated areas, and streamflow moderation is dependent on ecological management practices.

Keywords: ecological management; climate variability; streamflow regime; Loess Plateau

1. Introduction

Observations in most regions throughout the world show that hydrological cycles are being affected by climate change. Such changes disrupt the hydrology of drainage basins, altering both the balance between rainfall and evaporation and the runoff response of the area [1,2]. Simultaneously, the impact of human activities on streamflow variations is spatially heterogeneous throughout the world [3,4]. Thus, climate change and human activity related to streamflow effects must be investigated to avoid and minimize the economic costs associated with floods and droughts [3,5,6]. Streamflow regime variations must be understood to achieve sustainable water resources management and develop decision-making strategies.

The Loess Plateau (640,000 km^2), located in the middle reaches of the Yellow River basin, generates some of the highest sediment yields observed on earth, with sediment yields exceeding 3×10^4 to 4×10^4 t· km^{-2}· a^{-1} in some tributaries over recent decades [7–9]. Such high soil erosion rates cause serious problems on-site, including soil nutrients and agricultural land losses, degrade the ecologic environment in the middle Yellow River basin and represent the primary cause of sedimentation in the lower Yellow River [10,11]. It has been illustrated that the majority of the sediment yield can be attributed to land use intensification driven by the increasing population [9,12,13]. National ecological management projects have been implemented to control the severe soil erosion. These projects include the integrated soil conservation and "Grain for Green" projects.

The integrated soil conservation project, which focuses on the integrated management of small watersheds, was implemented on the Loess Plateau during the 1970s [11,14,15]. It comprises an extensive series of management actions, including engineering works (building terraces and sediment-trapping dams) and vegetation measures (changing land cover through replanting trees and improving pastures). This project was replaced by the "Grain for Green" project, which mainly consists of vegetation measures. It has been implemented on a massive scale since the 1990s via improving vegetation on slopes [14–17]. The areas that have been treated by management actions in each sub-catchment are listed in Table 1.

Table 1. Cumulative area treated by management actions in the corresponding sub-catchments from 1959 to 2006 [14,18,19].

Corresponding Stations	Year	Management Actions (%)				Total (%)
		Terrace	Afforestation	Pasture	Sediment Trapping Dams	
Wuqi Liujiahe	1959	0.04	0.77	0.02	0.01	0.8
	1969	0.52	2.43	0.19	0.15	3.3
	1979	1.26	4.22	0.53	0.29	6.3
	1989	1.98	8.14	2.47	0.29	12.9
	1999	2.99	12.35	3.95	0.29	19.6
	2006	3.88	22.14	10.06	0.29	36.4
Zhangcunyi Huangling	1959	0.02	0.05	0.00	0.00	0.1
	1969	0.18	0.16	0.01	0.01	0.4
	1979	0.72	0.28	0.02	0.04	1.0
	1989	0.69	0.53	0.08	0.05	1.4
	1999	1.04	0.81	0.13	0.05	2.0
	2006	1.35	0.96	0.17	0.05	2.5
Jiaokou	1959	0.03	0.65	0.01	0.01	0.7
	1969	0.40	2.04	0.11	0.17	2.7
	1979	1.07	3.54	0.31	0.24	5.2
	1989	1.56	6.83	1.43	0.24	10.1
	1999	2.35	10.36	2.28	0.24	15.2
	2006	3.04	18.57	5.79	0.24	27.6
Zhuangtou	1959	0.03	0.44	0.01	0.01	0.5
	1969	0.31	1.40	0.07	0.05	1.8
	1979	0.76	2.43	0.21	0.12	3.5
	1989	1.20	4.69	0.97	0.17	7.0
	1999	4.77	11.80	1.75	0.17	18.5
	2006	6.18	21.16	4.44	0.17	32.0

The processes that reduce streamflow and sediment yields are different. The engineered projects can block or delay the streamflow routing. By depositing the suspended sediment and steadily releasing water [7,20], the engineering projects can effectively slow runoff and attenuate high flow magnitudes and peaks [20–22]. Generally, engineering projects significantly and immediately impact runoff. However, sediment-trapping dams will slowly lose their effectiveness and eventually became abandoned due to sedimentation if proper maintenance is not performed [20,22,23]. Appropriate vegetation measures typically decrease surface runoff and increase *in situ* water infiltration, thereby decreasing the streamflow and sediment yields [24,25]. In addition, vegetation can alter the water balance by increasing rainfall interception and evapotranspiration in a catchment [26–28]. Vegetation measures typically take several years to become effective because vegetative succession is a slow process [28,29]. The effect of appropriate vegetation measures becomes increasingly significant over time [10]. Accordingly, streamflow regime processes and time periods may vary between engineering and vegetation projects.

Numerous studies have analyzed middle Yellow River basin streamflow variations in the context of ecological management. These analyses determined that various management actions have reduced the streamflow in the tributaries, which effectively decreased sediment yields [4,6,28,30,31]. Moreover, these studies also noted that results varied between basins, which may be due to differences in the percentage of an area treated by management actions, vegetation cover, landforms, and other factors. When assessing streamflow variations, it is necessary to consider both climate variability and human activities. Although climate change, such as precipitation variations, have been relatively insignificant on the Loess Plateau [32], climate variability has partly caused streamflow reduction [4,6,30,33,34]. As shown in Table 1, the treated area significantly increased during the 1990s. The transition from the integrated soil conservation project to the "Grain for Green" project represents an intensified process of ecological management process. Previous studies mainly investigated pre- and post-project streamflow changes. However, it is unclear how streamflow regimes concurrently varied during the implementation of these two ecological management projects. The effects of the two projects on streamflow regime changes have been well documented, which in turn indicate if the management actions are appropriate. Accordingly, streamflow regime investigations can help to optimize ecological management.

The aim of this paper is to investigate how the streamflow regime changed during the implementation of the two ecological management strategies. Six sub-catchments from the basin-Beiluo River basin were selected as the study area. We analyzed annual streamflow trends and variations during the two ecological management periods.

2. Study Area and Data

2.1. Study Site

The Beiluo River drains an area of 26,905 km² and is 680 km long. It is a tributary of the Wei River and a secondary tributary of the Yellow River (Figure 1). The wind-deposited loess, which developed during the Quaternary Period, covers the study area with a thickness of 50–200 m. However, a portion of the sub-catchment above Wuqi is semiarid. Otherwise, the basin is mainly semi-humid, with a mean annual PET of 1690.1 mm, precipitation of 534.3 mm and runoff depth of 32.5 mm from 1958 to 2011 (Figure 2 and Table 2). The basin is one of the major coarse sediment source areas of the Yellow River. The mean annual streamflow and sediment yield of the river are 8.65×10^8 m³ and 8.65×10^7 t, respectively. Approximately 76.2% of the annual precipitation occurs during the wet season (between May and September), and 92.6% of the total sediment is transported by the top 5% of the daily sediment load (1958–2011). The mean annual streamflow and sediment yield above the Liujiahe station account for 26.8% and 91.1% of the total basin yield, respectively, with the area accounting for 27.2% of the entire basin [35]. The streamflow below Liujiahe and Zhangcunyi and above Zhuangtou accounts for 61.9% of the entire basin, and accounts for 52.2% of the area [35]. This indicates that the streamflow and sediment source areas are non-uniformly distributed in the basin, which is common in the Yellow River basin. Accordingly, the Beiluo River basin is a representative basin of the Yellow River.

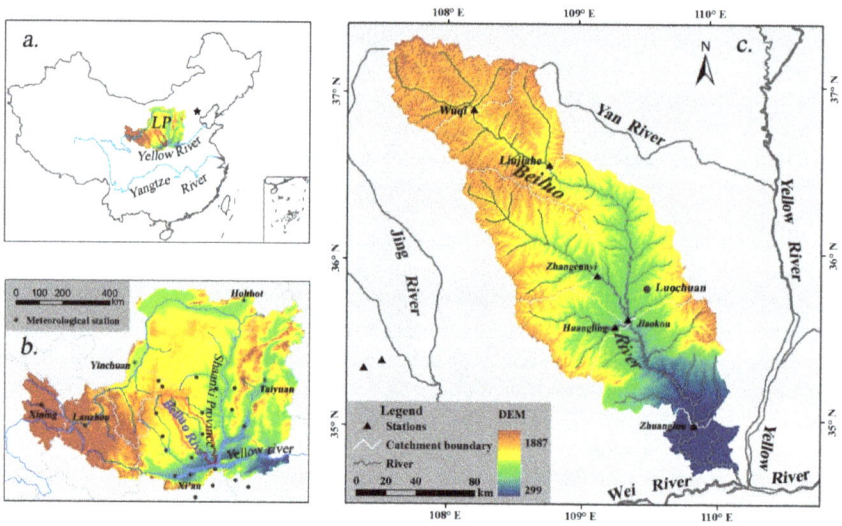

Figure 1. (**a**) The location of the Beiluo River basin and the Loess Plateau in China; (**b**) map of the Loess Plateau in the middle reaches of the Yellow River basin; (**c**) map of the Beiluo River basin.

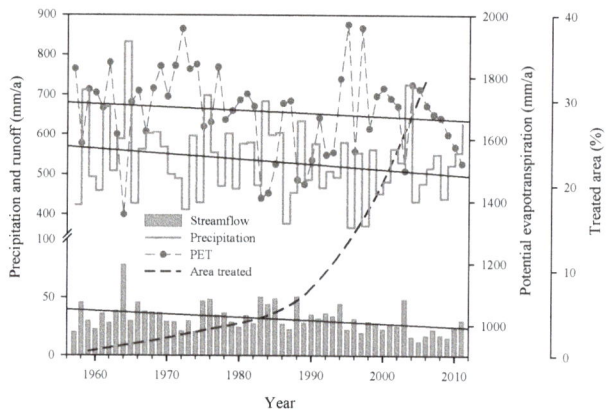

Figure 2. Annual precipitation, runoff, potential evapotranspiration (PET), and the area affected by soil conservation measures in the Beiluo River basin (Upper Zhuangtou station).

Table 2. Characteristics and streamflow records for all sub-catchments.

No.	Stations	Area (km²)	Streamflow Records	Runoff Ranges ($\times 10^{-3}$ mm/d)	Annual Average		
					Runoff (mm/a)	Precipitation (mm/a)	PET (mm/a)	Vegetation Coverage (%)
1	Wuqi	3408	1963–2011	0.15~41831	28.0	415.3	1786.3	34.2
2	Liujiahe	7325	1959–2011	5.66~30195	32.3	446.5	1743.9	32.5
3	Zhangcunyi	4715	1958–2011	0.47~3701	23.0	540.0	1640.4	65.9
4	Huangling	2266	1967–2011	0.31~8922	46.8	563.7	1643.5	68.1
5	Jiaokou	17180	1958–2011	1.51~7041	25.9	502.8	1693.5	47.7
6	Zhuangtou	25654	1958–2011	2.06~6577	32.5	534.3	1690.1	44.7

Extreme precipitation events occasionally occur in the area, but they significantly impact the fragile Loess Plateau ecosystem. For instance, a 1000-year precipitation event was observed in Wuqi on 30 August 1994, when the six-hour precipitation reached 214 mm. A daily sediment concentration of 1060 kg·m^{-3} induced by the event was measured on 31 August 1994 at the Wuqi station. The streamflow/sediment yield was 2.41/25.6 times the mean annual streamflow/sediment load from 2002 to 2011. In addition, and the sediment load was equivalent to 9.6% of the total sediment yields from 1963 to 2011.

Both the integrated soil conservation project and "Grain for Green" project have been implemented on a massive scale in the basin. Generally, management actions such as afforestation on slopes have been implemented based on natural vegetation zones, while the elevations shown in Figure 1 were not seriously considered. Table 1 lists the basin area variations as a result of soil conservation measures, including terracing, afforestation, pasture re-establishment, and the sediment trapping dams. In addition to the soil conservation measures, a large amount of farmland has been abandoned and hillsides have been closed to eliminate grazing. The Zhangcunyi and Huangling basins drain into the only natural secondary forest on the Loess Plateau. They represent sub-catchments with few ecological management actions and minimal human activities.

2.2. Database

Streamflow data for six stations (Table 2) were obtained from the Water Resources Committee of the Yellow River Conservancy Commission. Annual streamflow data ware calculated from the daily data. The daily precipitation and Pan Evaporation (PET) data were observed in meteorological stations and obtained from the State Meteorology Bureau of China (http://cdc.nmic.cn/home.do). The annual precipitation and PET data were calculated based on the daily data. As shown in Figure 1, data from 20 meteorological stations were used to interpolate the annual precipitation and PET data using the kriging data interpolation technique in ArcGIS 9.3 [36]. The annual data from 1994 (Wuqi and Liujiahe stations) were eliminated from the trend analysis to avoid the influence of extreme precipitation events.

3. Methodology

Trends and Change Point Analysis

The Mann–Kendall (MK) rank correlation coefficient [37,38] is commonly used to assess the significance of trends in hydro-meteorological time series and was implemented in this study. The Mann–Kendall test statistic (S) is given by

$$S = \sum_{k=1}^{n=1} \sum_{j=k+1}^{n} \text{sgn}(x_j - x_k), k < j < n \tag{1}$$

where

$$\text{sgn}(x) = \begin{cases} +1, x > 0 \\ 0, x = 0 \\ -1, x < 0 \end{cases}$$

and n is the data set record length; x_j and x_k are the sequential data values. When S is positive, a positive trend is present, and *vice versa*. If no serial correlation is observed in the data, existing formulas can be used to assess the significance of the trend using standard Z score methods. However, the existence of a serial correlation alters the variance of MK statistic estimate [39,40]. Therefore, we have adopted the bootstrap-based procedure proposed by Yue and Pilon [41] to remove the serial correlation effect. The significance of S is assessed based on the bootstrap-based procedure MK test (BS-MK), which can be derived by randomly bootstrapping the sample data X. A bootstrapped sample, denoted by X^*, {$x_1{}^*, x_2{}^*$, ..., $x_n{}^*$}, is obtained by n random samples times with replacements, with an equal probability of $1/n$

from the observed sample $x_1, x_2, ..., x_n$. By bootstrapping X M times, M independent bootstrap samples $X^{*1}, X^{*2}, ..., X^{*M}$ can be obtained, each with sample size n. The S^* for each of the bootstrapped samples is then estimated using Equation (1). By arranging $\{S_1{}^*, S_2{}^*, ..., S_n{}^*\}$ in ascending order, the bootstrap empirical cumulative distribution of the slope can be obtained. The p value of S is estimated as:

$$P = \Pr[S^* \leqslant S] = \frac{m_S}{M} \tag{2}$$

where m_s is the rank corresponding to the largest value when $S^* \leqslant S$.

The nonparametric median-based linear model method proposed by Sen [42] was used to fit trend slopes (β) to the data:

$$\beta = Median \left[\frac{x_j - x_k}{j - k} \right] \text{ for all } k \ < \ j, \tag{3}$$

where $1 < k < j < n$. β is the median of all possible pair combinations in the data set.

The nonparametric method developed by Pettitt [43] was applied to detect the change point using the Mann–Whitney statistic $U_{t,N}$. The $U_{t,N}$ is used to verify if two samples $x_1,..., x_t$ and $x_{t+1},..., x_N$ are from the same population. The test statistic $U_{t,N}$ is given by

$$U_{t-1,N} = U_{t-1,N} + \sum_{j=1}^{N} \text{sgn}(x_t - x_j) \text{ for } t \ = \ 2, \ldots, \ n, \tag{4}$$

where $\text{sgn}(\theta) = 1$ if $\theta > 0$, $\text{sgn}(\theta) = 0$ if $\theta = 0$ and $\text{sgn}(\theta) = -1$ if $\theta < 0$.

The test statistic counts the number of times a member of the first sample exceeds a member of the second sample. The null hypothesis of Pettitt's test is the absence of a changing point. The statistic $K(t)$ and the associated probabilities used in the significance testing are given as

$$K(t) = \max_{1 \leqslant t < N} |U_{t,N}| \tag{5}$$

$$p \cong 2\exp \left\{ -6k_n^2 / \left(N^3 + N^2 \right) \right\} \tag{6}$$

where k_n is numerical value for $K(t)$ (K^+ or K^-) and N is the observed sample.

The trends were determined by applying the BS-MK and Sen tests to the annual and daily series of streamflow series. Incremental percentiles on an annual basis were used to obtain data series [44]. The observed data from each year were sorted in descending order. Then, data from each year within the same exceedance percentile were selected for a daily percentile series. The obtained daily series were sorted by year. The daily series were normalized before applying the BS-MK test and Sen's slope estimation to compare the rates of change of series in various percentiles via:

$$X_i' = (X_i - X_{\min})/(X_{\max} - X_{\min}) \cdot 100 \tag{7}$$

4. Results

4.1. Temporal Trends in Annual Streamflow, Precipitation, and PET

The Mann–Kendall trend test identified negative annual streamflow trends at five out of six stations, with the rate varying from -0.15 to -0.30 mm·a^{-1}. Streamflow changes at the Wuqi, Jiaokou, and Zhuangtou stations exhibited negative trends at a statistically significant level of 0.01 (Table 3). The streamflow decrease at the Zhangcunyi station was significant ($p < 0.05$), whereas the decrease at the Huangling station was insignificant. The rate of streamflow reduction varied among stations. However, the streamflow change rate (Table 3) divided by the mean annual streamflow (Table 2) in the forestry area (Zhangcunyi and Huangling stations) is lower than other stations. The annual precipitation and PET trends were detected to understand the nature of streamflow changes. As shown in Table 3, significantly negetive annual precipitation trends were identified in three sub-catchments (Zhangcunyi, Jiaokou, and Zhuangtou). No significant annual PET trends were identified in any sub-catchment.

4.2. Precipitation, PET, and Streamflow Variation over Time

The water balance in a catchment involves precipitation, evapotranspiration, and streamflow. The streamflow stablity depends on a stable climate system. To fully understand the nature of streamflow changes, it is necessary to determine precipitation regime variations. The means and standard deviations of annual streamflow, precipitation, and PET from each station in three periods were analyzed. Per Table 4, the *t*-tests and *F* tests showed that the mean and the standard deviation of the annual precipitation exhibited insignificant changes in all sub-catchments. The annual PET results suggest that the mean annual PET decreased during PII in four sub-catchments. However, the mean annual PET in PIII was identified to be indifferent from PI.

By contrast, both the mean and the standard deviation of the annual streamflow significantly decreased over the three periods. Moreover, the coefficient of variation (CV) of annual streamflow exhibited a reduction at all stations (Table 4), which was consistent with the expected ecological management effect. A reduced CV indicates that streamflow became less variable, while an increased CV indicates that the proportional reduction in the mean is lower than the reduction in the standard deviation.

Annual streamflow values in all sub-catchments have continuously decreased in recent decades, as shown in Tables 4 and 5. Compared to the streamflow in the forestry area (Huangling and Zhangcunyi stations), incremental annual streamflow reductions were observed at the other four stations. These differences are related to minimal ecological management in the forestry area *versus* intensive ecological management actions in other catchments (Table 1). In addition, the vegetation in the forestry area helps to stabilize the streamflow, making it less sensitive to climate variability and ecological management. In addition, ecological management area increases (Table 1 and Figure 2) and precipitation decreases (Table 3) led to higher streamflow reductions during PIII.

The Pettitt's test at the Wuqi station is shown in Figure 3. No change points for annual precipitation and PET were identified in Wuqi sub-catchment. The annual streamflow curve indicates that the ecological management effects that occurred during the two study periods are well documented in the annual streamflow variation. The change point, e.g., the maximum of the curve, was detected in 2002. Moreover, the integrated soil conservation resulted in a relative maximum in 1979 (Figure 3), which was also determined to be statistically significant. The annual streamflow at Wuqi was divided into three periods, including the baseline period (PI), integrated soil conservation period (PII), and "Grain for Green" period (PIII). The same division process was applied to data from the other stations, such as Zhangcunyi in Figure 3d. In addition, the most likely points-in-time at Huangling station were also selected for comparison.

Table 3. Summary of annual streamflow, precipitation, and PET trends in each sub-catchment from the 1950s to 2011.

Stations	Annual Streamflow				Change Point Year		Annual Precipitation				Annual PET			
	lag 1 Corr.	BS-MK S	BS-MK Sig.	Sen β (mm/a)			*lag 1* Corr.	BS-MK Test S	BS-MK Test Sig.	Sen β (mm/a)	*lag 1* Corr.	BS-MK S	BS-MK Sig.	Sen β (mm/a)
Wuqi	−0.06	−0.339	**	−0.30	1979	2002	−0.14	−0.101	ns	−1.01	0.15	−0.067	ns	0.79
Liujiahe	−0.10	−0.264	*	−0.24	1979	1999	−0.18	−0.129	ns	−1.57	0.24	−0.090	ns	−1.23
Zhangcunyi	0.18	−0.275	*	−0.15	1978	1994	−0.23	−0.172	*	−1.66	0.27	−0.027	ns	−0.36
Huangling	0.14	−0.152	ns	−0.27	1984	1994	−0.20	−0.087	ns	−1.02	0.31	−0.070	ns	−1.14
Jiaokou	0.01	−0.323	**	−0.21	1979	1994	−0.22	−0.166	*	−1.63	0.24	−0.077	ns	−1.26
Zhuangtou	0.15	−0.323	**	−0.26	1978	1994	−0.26	−0.166	*	−1.37	0.24	−0.072	ns	−1.24

Note: ** and * indicate significance levels of 0.01 and 0.05; *ns* indicates that the significance level exceeds 0.05.

Table 4. Summary of the annual streamflow, precipitation, and PET statistics.

Objects	Stations	PI			PII			PIII		
		Mean (mm)	SD (mm)	CV	Mean (mm)	S.D. (mm)	CV	Mean (mm)	SD (mm)	CV
Runoff	Wuqi	32.47 A	12.80 a	0.39	25.49 B	7.99 b	0.31	16.15 C	3.12 c	0.19
	Liujiahe	37.21 A	11.29 a	0.30	31.94 A	8.28 a	0.26	22.65 B	4.86 c	0.21
	Zhangcunyi	26.98 A	11.98 a	0.44	25.42 A	7.07 a	0.28	20.15 B	3.86 b	0.24
	Huangling	50.95 A	33.38 a	0.62	48.64 A	23.33 a	0.51	43.02 B	9.98 b	0.31
	Jiaokou	29.35 A	10.84 a	0.37	27.76 A	7.94 a	0.29	20.66 B	4.47 b	0.22
	Zhuangtou	36.33 A	12.62 a	0.35	35.64 A	9.47 a	0.28	23.78 B	4.92 b	0.25
Precipitation	Wuqi	436.4	108.7	0.25	408.8	84.5	0.21	385.3	74.7	0.19
	Liujiahe	472.6	109.8	0.23	429.9	82.0	0.19	429.4	80.6	0.19
	Zhangcunyi	573.2	112.7	0.20	537.3	87.6	0.16	524.4	94.8	0.19
	Huangling	584.2	101.2	0.17	555.7	87.5	0.16	546.8	109.1	0.20
	Jiaokou	525.7	110.9	0.21	501.4	81.2	0.16	494.3	83.1	0.18
	Zhuangtou	552.1	105.1	0.19	517.3	90.9	0.18	524.3	83.6	0.16
PET	Wuqi	1783.4	145.9	0.08	1789.2	153.5	0.09	1783.6	94.9	0.05
	Liujiahe	1778.9	141.4	0.08	1705.5	163.8	0.10	1754.5	92.3	0.05
	Zhangcunyi	1679.9 A	135.7	0.08	1550.6 B	144.2 a	0.09	1686.6 A	136.7 a	0.08
	Huangling	1661.3 AB	151.7 a	0.09	1546.3 B	134.7 b	0.09	1686.9 A	136.7 b	0.08
	Jiaokou	1733.2 A	125.6 b	0.07	1606.5 B	130.4 a	0.08	1728.0 A	129.8 a	0.08
	Zhuangtou	1730.9 A	121.1 a	0.07	1638.2 B	164.0 a	0.10	1690.8 A	84.1 b	0.05

Note: Different capital letters ("A," "B," and "C") indicate significantly different mean annual streamflow values over three periods at $p < 0.05$, while small letters ("a," "b," and "c") represent standard deviations.

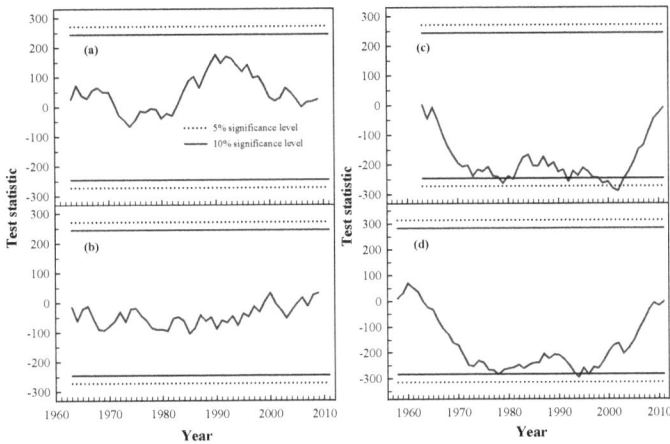

Figure 3. Pettitt's statistical significance, which was used for detecting change points for (**a**) annual PET; (**b**) annual precipitation; and (**c**) annual streamflow at Wuqi station; and (**d**) annual streamflow at Zhangcunyi station.

4.3. Daily Streamflow Regime and Changes

Daily streamflow series were obtained to compare trends in various magnitudes streamflow. These series were normalized using Equation (7) before trend detection. The trends and statistical significance levels were determined using the BS-MK and Sen tests, as shown in Figure 4. For the Wuqi basin (Figure 4a), the high extreme flow series trends (e.g., the annual maximum flow series) are lower than the median flow series. This indicates that high extreme flows, which are induced by extreme precipitation events, are more difficult to effectively moderate. As shown in Figure 4a,b, the daily series trends for the majority of percentiles in Wuqi are higher than those in Zhangcunyi. As noted in Section 2, the forestry area is less influenced by ecological management, implying that larger streamflow variations occurred in response to more intensive ecological management. The gray strip in Figure 4 represents the daily streamflow variation over the past six decades. The dynamic daily streamflow range in Wuqi is an order of magnitude larger than that in Zhangcunyi (Figure 4a,b), which is similar in area and landform, but located in the forestry area. Moreover, the dynamic daily streamflow range in Zhangcunyi is equivalent to that in the entire basin (Zhuangtou) (Figure 4b,c), implying that a much more stable daily streamflow can be achieved in highly vegetated areas.

Flow duration curves help to put the daily streamflow variation magnitudes into perspective, as shown in Figure 5. The relative streamflow change is calculated by $(Q_{after} - Q_{before})/Q_{before}$. Given the mixed nature of both climate variability and human activities, the streamflow variations shown in the flow duration curves likely reflect combined effects. As shown in Figure 5, the relative change curves indicate that daily streamflow sharply decreased at three stations for percentiles <5% (time exceedance) during PII. Relative streamflow changes in the percentile interval from 5% to 70% were generally stable with values between −15% and 15%. However, the relative change curves sharply increased for the >75% percentile. As shown in Table 5 and Figure 5, the streamflow decreased during PIII for all percentiles at four stations. In addition to high and median flow decreases, the low flows continuously increased in Wuqi and Liujiahe stations in PIII. Overall, as shown in Figure 5 and Table 5, high flow (5%) decreased in both PII and PIII; median flow (50%) slightly increased in PII and then slightly decreased in PIII in all sub-catchments. Low flow (95%) highly increased in PII, and then decreased in PIII in four sub-catchments.

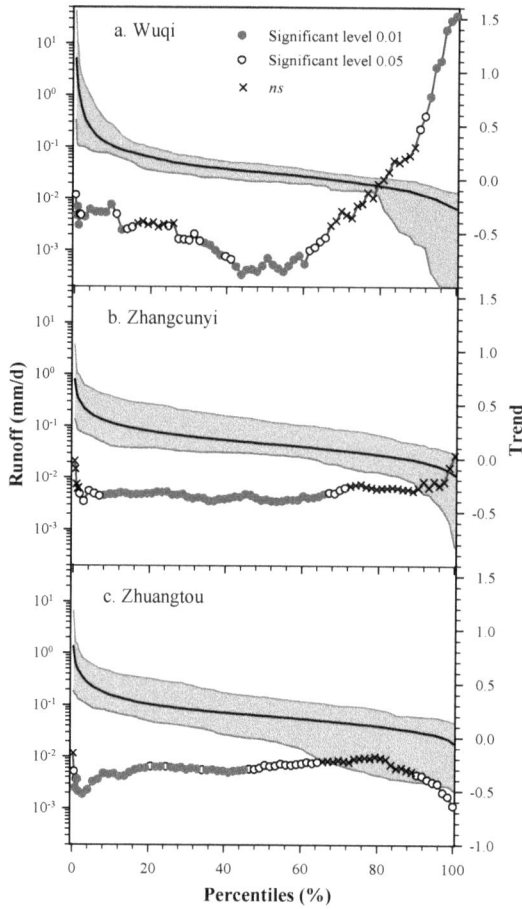

Figure 4. Trends, statistically significant levels, and ranges of daily streamflow series over the past six decades at the (**a**) Wuqi; (**b**) Zhangcunyi; and (**c**) Zhuangtou stations. The solid line represents the means of all daily streamflow series, the upper boundary of the gray strip represents the maximum of all daily series, and the lower boundary represents the minimum of all daily series.

Table 5. Mean annual runoff variation (ΔQ^{tot}) and relative high (Q_5), median (Q_{50}), and low flow (Q_{95}) changes during for the PII and PIII.

Stations	PII				PIII			
	ΔQ^{tot} (mm)	ΔQ_5 (%)	ΔQ_{50} (%)	ΔQ_{95} (%)	ΔQ^{tot} (mm)	ΔQ_5 (%)	ΔQ_{50} (%)	ΔQ_{95} (%)
Wuqi	−7.0	−21.5	−5.8	99.0	−16.3	−23.6	−19.7	5.6
Liujiahe	−5.3	−7.1	10.9	42.5	−14.6	−28.8	−16.6	11.9
Zhangcunyi	−1.6	−11.5	3.2	40.5	−6.8	−34.0	−27.0	−48.1
Huangling	−2.3	−30.9	1.0	61.6	−7.9	−29.8	−13.8	−17.8
Jiaokou	−2.5	−17.5	10.2	30.5	−9.3	−24.7	−23.0	−15.7
Zhuangtou	−3.1	−12.7	11.9	19.5	−13.0	−37.4	−30.7	−80.1

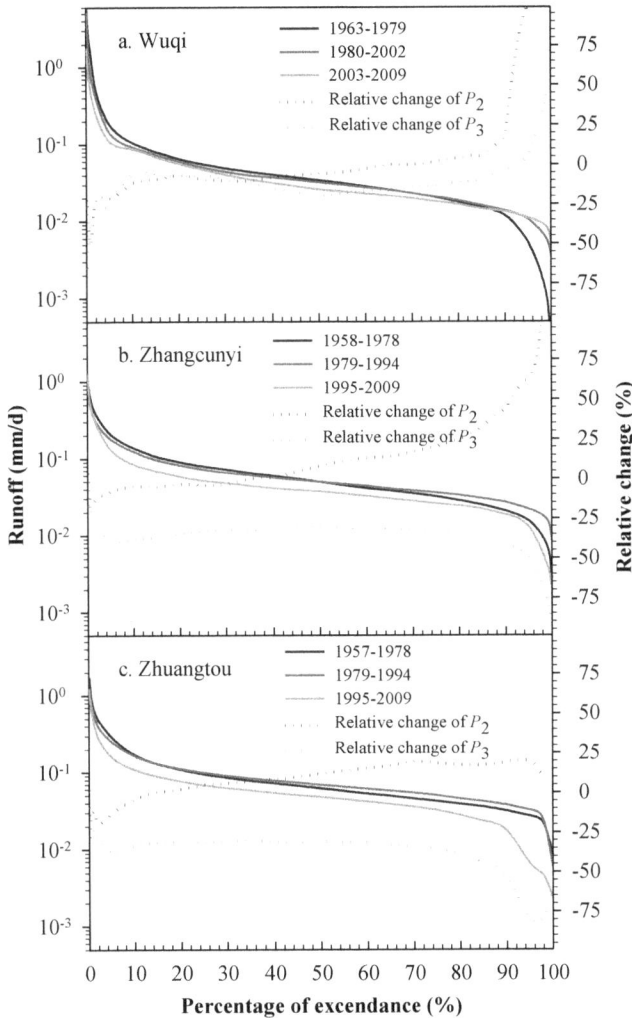

Figure 5. Comparison of daily flow duration curves over three periods at the (**a**) Wuqi; (**b**) Zhangcunyi; and (**c**) Zhuangtou stations.

Note that low flow increased at the Wuqi and Liujiahe stations during the two ecological management periods (Figure 5a and Table 5). This increase is likely due to continuous ecological management. The vegetation in the sub-catchments above the two stations is dominated by grass and shrubs. Wuqi County (3791.5 km^2, Figure 1) converted 1578.6 km^2 of cultivated land to grassland/forestry in 1999, representing the largest cultivated land conversion in China. In addition, Wuqi County exhibits a high revegetation rate [19]. The continuously increasing low flow implies that streamflow regime could be moderated via the appropriate management options, even in semiarid areas.

Moreover, we detected the daily precipitation regime in Wuqi and Luochuan stations using erosive rainfall ($\geqslant$10 mm) data. Generally, daily erosive rainfall is defined as rainfall that can generate surface runoff and produce erosion [45]. The Gumbel and Weibull distribution parameters of erosive rainfall data during PI were estimated using L-moments [46]. A Goodness-of-fit test (Kolmogorov–Smirnov test) showed that the daily precipitation data in three periods provided an excellent fit to the parameters of the two distribution functions ($p > 0.95$). This indicates that the precipitation regime (probability distribution) has not changed, which implies that the water yield capacity of rainfall event has not changed. We have also collected the data for mean daily non-erosive precipitation (<10 mm/day) and the corresponding wet days in each year. The *t*-test showed that the mean non-erosive precipitation was statistically insignificant over three periods, whereas a significant decrease of wet days between PI and PIII was identified. This result indicates that the increase of low flow was not owing to precipitation variation.

5. Discussion

5.1. Processes of Streamflow Reduction between Ecological Management Periods

In this study, the streamflow decreased as the ecological management area increased (Table 1 and Figure 2). This result is supported by Wang and Hejazi [3], who noted that the effect of regional human activities is somewhat heterogeneous owing to different extent. Zhu *et al.* [47] investigated the effect of community functional composition on soil and water conservation in a revegetation area on the Loess Plateau. They indicated that the management strategies led to large areas of mono-specific vegetation, and streamflow had not been substantially decreased by revegetation during the soil conservation period. Sediment trapping dams across eroding gullies and smaller tributaries have been used to control streamflow and sediment yields on the Loess Plateau [7]. These dams impede the flow of water and induce sediment deposition [7,11,14]. During the "Grain for Green" period, the community functional diversity was incorporated into the ecological management design, and streamflow and soil were efficiently conserved [47]. Annual and daily streamflow variations suggest that two corresponding regulation phases exist during the two ecological management periods:

Phase 1: by Impeding Floods

Independent of annual precipitation regime variations, the daily streamflow significantly decreased in multiple percentiles (Figure 4). Revegetation was not dense enough and the revegetated area (Table 1) was not large enough to decrease the streamflow during PII. As noted by Zhu *et al.* [47], the streamflow was not substantially moderated by mono-specific revegetation during this period. However, engineering projects prohibited or delayed the streamflow during PII [7], thus decreasing high flows. Engineering projects also increased the median and low flow (Table 5 and Figure 5) by depositing the suspended sediments and releasing water [20–22]. Therefore, the streamflow was effectively moderated by sediment-trapping dams. As a result, the annual streamflow slightly decreased during PII.

Phase 2: by Reducing Streamflow Effectively

Sediment-trapping dams lose their effectiveness over time if proper maintenance is not performed [20,22,23]. It was reported that more than 100,000 sediment-trapping dams were built on the Loess Plateau in the late 1960s and 1970s [47]. However, a survey in the northern Shaanxi province (shown in Figure 1b) noted that more than 80% of the sediment-trapping dams were destroyed by intensive storms in the early 1980s [14,20]. Thus, the effects of engineering projects were significantly diminished during PIII. However, the implementation of the "Grain for Green" project increased the ecological management area by >30% of the entire basin in 2006 (Table 1). Moreover, the community functional diversity increased over 30 years of vegetation succession and significantly reduced streamflow and sediment yields [47]. Vegetation management effects become significant over time [10]. The surface runoff decreased as *in situ* water infiltration increased [24,25]. Moreover, increasing the rainfall interception and evapotranspiration led to streamflow decreases. As a result, incremental streamflow reductions were observed in PIII compared to PII (Table 5). Thus, the streamflow was efficiently reduced by revegetation during PIII. This result is supported by

Zeng and Ma [48] and Cai [29], who illustrated that artificial vegetation will only reduce streamflow reduction if the accumulated vegetation coverage exceeded a critical value of approximately 20%.

5.2. Can Streamflow Be Successfully Moderated?

Compared with that the Wuqi and Liujiahe stations, the hydrological regime in the secondary forestry area (Zhangcunyi and Huangling stations) exhibits a daily streamflow regime that is more stable (Figure 4) and less in soil erosion (below the soil-loss tolerance). This scenario represents the theoretical basis for ecological management on the Loess Plateau, *i.e.*, to produce an ideal streamflow regime by reducing high flows and increasing low flows, thus reducing the potential for flood hazards and properly allocating water resources [14,17,18]. The incremental annual streamflow reductions in the four non-forest sub-catchments imply that streamflow reduction magnitudes would be lower if no ecological management had been implemented on the vast Loess Plateau in the past decades.

A comparison between Zhangcunyi (forestry area) and Wuqi high flow variations indicates that high flow can be moderated. Streamflow at the Wuqi and Liujiahe stations were moderated by decreasing high flows and increasing low flows, indicating that streamflow can be moderated by appropriate ecological management actions. Streamflow can be moderated into the future via the continuous optimization of ecological management, such as incorporating community functional diversity into ecological management design.

6. Conclusions

The continuous ecological management of the Loess Plateau has involved two strategies: the integrated soil conservation project that began in the 1970s, and the "Grain for Green" project that began in the 1990s. This study investigated the streamflow variations in response to the two ecological management projects by selecting six sub-catchments nested in a representative basin, the Beiluo River basin. Data from the 1950s to 2011 were analyzed, and statistically significant negative annual streamflow trends were identified in five out of six sub-catchments over the past 60 years, with the rates varying from -0.15 to -0.30 mm$\cdot$a^{-1}.

The streamflow regime variations differ between the two ecological management periods. The annual streamflow was reduced by decreasing high flows, whereas low flow increases were observed in all sub-catchments during PII. Conversely, the annual streamflow decreased due to daily streamflow decreases at four stations during PIII. In addition to high and median flow decreases, the low flows continuously increased in Wuqi and Liujiahe stations in PIII. Compared with streamflow changes in the forestry area, incremental annual streamflow reductions were observed in other sub-catchments, which are mainly due to ecological management. These results imply that the streamflow regime can be moderated using appropriate management actions, even in semiarid areas. Moreover, streamflow in the forestry area is more stable, indicating that a stable streamflow regime can be achieved in areas with well-preserved vegetation. In conclusion, ecological management strategies can successfully achieve streamflow moderations.

Acknowledgments: This study was supported by the National Natural Science Foundation of China (Grant No. 41440012, 41230852, and 41101265), and the Knowledge Innovation Program of the Chinese Academy of Sciences (KZZD-EW-04-03-03; KZCX2-XB3-13). The authors thank the two anonymous reviewers for their constructive comments.

Author Contributions: Xiaoping Zhang and Jianjun Zhang conceived and designed the experiments; Jianjun Zhang, Tingting Zhang, and Yongnan Lei performed the data collecting; Jianjun Zhang, Xiaoping Zhang and Rui Li analyzed the data; Xiaoping Zhang and Rui Li contributed reagents/materials/analysis tools; Jianjun Zhang wrote the manuscript.

Conflicts of Interest: The authors declare no conflict of interest.

References

1. Milly, P.C.; Dunne, K.A.; Vecchia, A.V. Global pattern of trends in streamflow and water availability in a changing climate. *Nature* **2005**, *438*, 347–350. [PubMed]
2. Oki, T.; Kanae, S. Global hydrological cycles and world water resources. *Science* **2006**, *313*, 1068–1072. [CrossRef] [PubMed]
3. Wang, D.; Hejazi, M. Quantifying the relative contribution of the climate and direct human impacts on mean annual streamflow in the contiguous United States. *Water Resour. Res.* **2011**, *47*. [CrossRef]
4. Zhang, X.; Zhang, L.; Zhao, J.; Rustomji, P.; Hairsine, P. Responses of streamflow to changes in climate and land use/cover in the Loess Plateau, China. *Water Resour. Res.* **2008**, *44*, W00A07. [CrossRef]
5. Haddad, K.; Rahman, A. Regional flood frequency analysis in eastern Australia: Bayesian GLS regression-based methods within fixed region and ROI framework-Quantile Regression *vs.* Parameter Regression Technique. *J. Hydrol.* **2012**, *430*, 142–161. [CrossRef]
6. Zhao, G.; Tian, P.; Mu, X.; Jiao, J.; Wang, F.; Gao, P. Quantifying the impact of climate variability and human activities on streamflow in the middle reaches of the Yellow River basin, China. *J. Hydrol.* **2014**, *519*, 387–398. [CrossRef]
7. Zhang, X.; Walling, D.E.; Quine, T.A.; Wen, A. Use of reservoir deposits and caesium-137 measurements to investigate the erosional response of a small drainage basin in the rolling loess plateau region of China. *Land Degrad. Dev.* **1997**, *8*, 1–16. [CrossRef]
8. Zhang, X.; Walling, D.E.; Yang, Q.; He, X.; Wen, Z.; Qi, Y.; Feng, M. Cs-137 budget during the period of 1960s in a small drainage basin on the Loess Plateau of China. *J. Environ. Radioactiv.* **2006**, *86*, 78–91. [CrossRef] [PubMed]
9. Shi, H.; Shao, M. Soil and water loss from the Loess Plateau in China. *J. Arid Environ.* **2000**, *45*, 9–20. [CrossRef]
10. Zheng, F.; He, X.; Gao, X.; Zhang, C.E.; Tang, K. Effects of erosion patterns on nutrient loss following deforestation on the Loess Plateau of China. *Agric. Ecosyst. Environ.* **2005**, *108*, 85–97. [CrossRef]
11. Tang, K. The Changes of Erosion, Runoff and Sediment in the Yellow River. Science China Press: Beijing, China, 1993.
12. Xu, J.X. A study of physico-geographical factors for formation of hyperconcentrated flows in the Loess Plateau of China. *Geomorphology* **1998**, *24*, 245–255. [CrossRef]
13. Shi, C.; Dian, Z.; You, L. Changes in sediment yield of the Yellow River basin of China during the Holocene. *Geomorphology* **2002**, *46*, 267–283. [CrossRef]
14. Ran, D.; Liu, L.; Zhao, L.; Bai, Z.; Liu, B.; Wang, H. The Soil Conservation Practices and Streamflow and Sediment Load Changes in the Hekou-Longmen Region of Middle Reaches of Yellow River. Yellow River Water Conservancy Press: Zhengzhou, China, 2000.
15. Yao, W.; Li, Z.B.; Kang, L.L.; Ran, D. *The Effects of Controlling Soil Erosion on Environment on the Loess Plateau*; Science and Technology Press: Beijing, China, 2005.
16. Uchida, E.; Xu, J.; Rozelle, S. Grain for green: Cost-effectiveness and sustainability of China's conservation set-aside program. *Land Econ.* **2005**, *81*, 247–264. [CrossRef]
17. Tang, K. *Soil and Water Conservation in China*; Science China Press: Beijing, China, 2004; In Chinese.
18. Yao, W.; Xu, J.; Ran, D. *Analysis and Evaluation of the Water Sand Changing Regime in Catchments of Yellow River Basin*; Yellow River Water Conservancy Press: Zhengzhou, China, 2011; In Chinese.
19. Zhang, S.; kang, L.; Wei, Y. Research of the Impact of Human Activities on Streamflow and Sediment Load in the Middle Reaches of Yellow River. Yellow River Water Conservancy Press: Zhengzhou, China, 2010; In Chinese.
20. Xu, X.; Zhang, H.; Zhang, O. Development of check-dam systems in gullies on the Loess Plateau, China. *Environ. Sci. Policy* **2004**, *7*, 79–86.
21. Wang, G.; Wu, B.; Wang, Z.Y. Sedimentation problems and management strategies of Sanmenxia Reservoir, Yellow River, China. *Water Resour. Res.* **2005**, *41*. [CrossRef]
22. Wang, Y.; Fu, B.; Chen, L.; Lü, Y.; Gao, Y. Check dam in the Loess Plateau of China: Engineering for environmental services and food security. *Environ. Sci. Technol.* **2011**, *45*, 10298–10299. [CrossRef] [PubMed]
23. Ran, L.; Lu, X.; Xin, Z.; Yang, X. Cumulative sediment trapping by reservoirs in large river basins: A case study of the Yellow River basin. *Glob. Planet. Change* **2013**, *100*, 308–319. [CrossRef]

24. Sahin, V.; Hall, M.J. The effects of afforestation and deforestation on water yields. *J. Hydrol.* **1996**, *178*, 293–309. [CrossRef]

25. Quinton, J.N.; Edwards, G.M.; Morgan, R.P.C. The influence of vegetation species and plant properties on runoff and soil erosion: Results from a rainfall simulation study in south east Spain. *Soil Use Manag.* **1997**, *13*, 143–148. [CrossRef]

26. Zhang, L.; Dawes, W.; Walker, G. Response of mean annual evapotranspiration to vegetation changes at catchment scale. *Water Resour. Res.* **2001**, *37*, 701–708. [CrossRef]

27. Brown, A.E.; Zhang, L.; McMahon, T.A.; Western, A.W.; Vertessy, R.A. A review of paired catchment studies for determining changes in water yield resulting from alterations in vegetation. *J. Hydrol.* **2005**, *310*, 28–61. [CrossRef]

28. Gao, Z.; Fu, Y.; Li, Y.; Liu, J.; Chen, N.; Zhang, X. Trends of streamflow, sediment load and their dynamic relation for the catchments in the middle reaches of the Yellow River over the past five decades. *Hydrol. Earth Syst. Sci.* **2012**, *16*, 3219–3231. [CrossRef]

29. Cai, Q. Soil erosion and management on the Loess Plateau. *J. Geogr. Sci.* **2001**, *11*, 53–70.

30. Zhao, G.; Mu, X.; Tian, P.; Wang, F.; Gao, P. Climate changes and their impacts on water resources in semiarid regions: A case study of the Wei River basin, China. *Hydrol. Process.* **2013**, *27*, 3852–3863. [CrossRef]

31. Mu, X.; Zhang, L.; McVicar, T.R.; Chille, B.; Gau, P. Analysis of the impact of conservation measures on stream flow regime in catchments of the Loess Plateau, China. *Hydrol. Process.* **2007**, *21*, 2124–2134. [CrossRef]

32. Wan, L.; Zhang, X.; Ma, Q.; Zhang, J.; Ma, T.; Sun, Y. Spatiotemporal characteristics of precipitation and extreme events on the Loess Plateau of China between 1957 and 2009. *Hydrol. Process.* **2013**. [CrossRef]

33. Zhao, F.; Zhang, L.; Xu, Z.; Scott, D.F. Evaluation of methods for estimating the effects of vegetation change and climate variability on streamflow. *Water Resour. Res.* **2010**, *46*. [CrossRef]

34. Zhang, X.; Zhang, L.; McVicar, T.R.; Van Niel, T.G.; Li, L.T.; Li, R.; Yang, Q.; Wei, L. Modelling the impact of afforestation on average annual streamflow in the Loess Plateau, China. *Hydrol. Process.* **2008**, *22*, 1996–2004. [CrossRef]

35. Ran, D.; Zuo, Z.; Wu, Y.; Li, X.; Li, Z. Streamflow and Sediment Load Changes Response to Human Activites in the Middle Reaches of the Yellow River. Science China Press: Beijing, China, 2012.

36. Oliver, M.A.; Webster, R. Kriging: A method of interpolation for geographical information systems. *Int. J. Geogr. Inform. Syst.* **1990**, *4*, 313–332. [CrossRef]

37. Mann, H.B. Nonparametric tests against trend. *Econom. J. Econom. Soc.* **1945**, *13*, 245–259. [CrossRef]

38. Kendall, M. *Rank Correlation Methods*; Griffin: London, UK, 1975.

39. Yue, S.; Pilon, P.; Cavadias, G. Power of the Mann-Kendall and Spearman's rho tests for detecting monotonic trends in hydrological series. *J. Hydrol.* **2002**, *259*, 254–271. [CrossRef]

40. Yue, S.; Pilon, P.; Phinney, B.; Cavadias, G. The influence of autocorrelation on the ability to detect trend in hydrological series. *Hydrol. Process.* **2002**, *16*, 1807–1829. [CrossRef]

41. Yue, S.; Pilon, P. A comparison of the power of the t test, Mann-Kendall and bootstrap tests for trend detection/Une comparaison de la puissance des tests t de Student, de Mann-Kendall et du bootstrap pour la détection de tendance. *Hydrol. Sci. J.* **2004**, *49*, 21–37. [CrossRef]

42. Sen, P.K. Estimates of the regression coefficient based on Kendall's tau. *J. Am. Stat. Assoc.* **1968**, *63*, 1379–1389. [CrossRef]

43. Pettitt, A. A non-parametric approach to the change-point problem. *Appl. Stat.* **1979**, *28*, 126–135. [CrossRef]

44. Wilcox, B.P.; Huang, Y.; Walker, J.W. Long-term trends in streamflow from semiarid rangelands: Uncovering drivers of change. *Glob. Change Biol.* **2008**, *14*, 1676–1689. [CrossRef]

45. Xie, Y.; Liu, B.Y.; Zhang, W.B. Study on Standard of Erosive Rainfall. *J. Soil Water Conserv.* **2000**, *14*, 6–11.

46. Haddad, K.; Rahman, A.; Green, J. Design rainfall estimation in Australia: A case study using L moments and generalized least squares regression. *Stoch. Env. Res. Risk A* **2011**, *25*, 815–825. [CrossRef]

47. Zhu, H.; Fu, B.; Wang, S.; Zhu, L.; Zhang, L.; Jiao, L.; Wang, C. Reducing soil erosion by improving community functional diversity in semi-arid grasslands. *J. Appl. Ecol.* **2015**. [CrossRef]

48. Zeng, B.; Ma, W. Study on impact of artificial grass coverage on water-borne silt yield. In *Collected Papers on Sino-Canada Study of Soil Erosion Regularity on Loess Plateau of West Shanxi, China*; Water and Hydropower Publishing House: Beijing, China, 1990.

![forests logo] *forests*

MDPI

Article

Modeling Potential Impacts of Planting Palms or Tree in Small Holder Fruit Plantations on Ecohydrological Processes in the Central Amazon [†]

Norbert Kunert [1,*], Luiza Maria Teóphilo Aparecido [2], Priscila Barros [3] and Niro Higuchi [3]

[1] Department for Biogeochemical Processes, Max-Planck Institute for Biogeochemistry, Jena 07745, Germany
[2] Laboratory of Ecohydrology, College of Agriculture and Life Sciences, Texas A&M University, College Station, TX 505781, USA; luizamaria2000@yahoo.com.br
[3] Laboratory of Forest Management, National Institute for Research in the Amazon, Manaus 69060-001, Brazil; pbarros83@gmail.com (P.B.); niro@inpa.gov.br (N.H.)
*   Author to whom correspondence should be addressed; nkunert@bgc-jena.mpg.de; Tel.: +49-3641-57-6107; Fax: +49-3641-57-7107.
†   A short version of this manuscript has been previously published as conference paper [1] at the 9th International Workshop on Sap Flow in Ghent, Belgium. An extensive analysis and a modeling approach was added to the original paper.

Academic Editors: Ge Sun and James M. Vose
Received: 9 June 2015; Accepted: 22 July 2015; Published: 27 July 2015

Abstract: Native fruiting plants are widely cultivated in the Amazon, but little information on their water use characteristics can be found in the literature. To explore the potential impacts of plantations on local to regional water balance, we studied plant water use characteristics of two native fruit plants commonly occurring in the Amazon region. The study was conducted in a mixed fruit plantation containing a dicot tree species (Cupuaçu, *Theobroma grandiflorum*) and a monocot palm species (Açai, *Euterpe oleracea*) close to the city of Manaus, in the Central Amazon. Scaling from sap flux measurements, palms had a 3.5-fold higher water consumption compared to trees with a similar diameter. Despite the high transpiration rates of the palms, our plantation had only one third of the potential water recycling capacity of natural forests in the area. Converting natural forest into such plantations will thus result in significantly higher runoff rates.

Keywords: sap flux; transpiration; monocot; dicot; terra firme

1. Introduction

Native fruiting plants are widely cultivated in the Amazon, but little information on their water use characteristics can be found in the literature. In the Central Amazon, the native Açai palm (*Euterpe oleracea*), for example, plays a significant role in the local diet, as the fruit pulp is processed into wine, candies, ice creams and jams and the inner core of the stems can be consumed as palm hearts [2,3]. These products have a rich nutritional and energetic value due to high protein, fiber, calcium, iron and vitamin content [4]. Furthermore, there is recently a growing demand for the "superfruit" Açai in North America and Europe, as it is suspected to contain cholesterol-reducing fats and anti-aging antioxidants [5]. Another widely-cultivated native woody plant from the well-drained, species-rich *"terra firme"* forests of the Amazon is the dicot tree *Theobroma grandiflorum* [6]; its fruits are also processed into juice, ice creams, jellies, wine, liqueur and candies [7].

Increased local consumption and the increasing global demand for these fruits mean growing areas devoted to plantations containing these two species in the Brazilian Amazon [8]. Although small-scale land use changes associated with plantations are assumed to have smaller effects on the hydrological cycle than large-scale deforestation [9], to our knowledge, the alterations to the local water regimes after the establishment of this specific sort of small-scale plantation has not yet been studied in the region. However, there is some evidence that trees planted in such plantations are exposed to an environment with higher evaporative demand compared to natural forests, and plantations are characterized by low hydraulic conductivity of the root systems, while showing high transpiration and evapotranspiration rates due to the exposure to high solar energy [10]. Nevertheless, there is an urgent need to increase our knowledge about the water use characteristics of monocot and dicot tropical tree species cultivated in plantations.

Despite the already existing studies on the water use characteristics of trees growing under plantation conditions [11–13], we focused on an almost ignored plant type, as only a few ecophysiological studies exist on neotropical palms [1,14], and additionally increased the species pool of dicot trees studied. Most of the existing literature is focused on "cosmopolitan" palms, such as coconut, date and oil palms [15], whereas publications on the water use characteristics of palm species currently restricted to a small geographic area are almost completely missing. To our knowledge, the only existing study on the water relations of palms in the Amazon attributes only a minor contribution of palm trees to overall stand transpiration in a mixed forest canopy; however, it outlines the relatively high individual water consumption of these plants [1,16].

How palms transport water and how this affects their water use characteristics is especially interesting, as palms do not have any secondary growth, but rather an always growing, very active xylem [17]. The same vascular vessels have to support the very "vulnerable process of water transport throughout the potentially long life of the palm" [18]. Given the structural differences between palms and trees, we hypothesized that there must be significant differences in water use characteristics between the two. The objectives of our study were (1) to compare environmental variables and plant traits controlling plant water use, (2) to identify differences in water use between a woody arborescent monocot and a dicot plant species growing in a fruit plantation and (3) to model possible implications on the overall local water budget in the Central Amazon.

2. Experimental Section

2.1. Study Site, Species Selection and Micrometeorological Measurements

This study was conducted in a fruit plantation near the field station of the forest management site of the National Institute for Research in the Amazon (INPA) approximately 60 km northwest of the Centre of Manaus, Brazil. The annual precipitation at the study site is on average 2547 mm/year [19]. Rainfall is more or less evenly distributed throughout the whole year, but with a lesser amount of rain falling between August and November (<100 mm per month). During El Niño events, longer dry spells can occur. Air temperature is on average 26.7 °C with almost no variation between months. The natural vegetation on plateau areas in the region is species-rich evergreen tropical forest (*terra firme*) growing usually on clay rich Oxisols. For our study, we selected one tree species (Cupuaçu, *Theobroma grandiflorum* (Willd. ex Spreng.) Schum., Malvaceae) and one palm species (Açaí, *Euterpe oleracea*, Mart., Arecaceae). Both species are common fruit-bearing species in the Central Amazon, with fruits that have increased in global demand and popularity in recent decades [5].

The fruit plantation is located adjacent to the field station and was established in the mid-1980s. Palms and trees were randomly planted in a mixed stand approximately 0.8 ha in size with no specific planting scheme, but at least with four meters' distance between tree stems. The plantation was weeded regularly, such that no herbaceous layer was present. Other accompanying species in the plantation are *Astrocaryum aculeatum* (G. May, Arecaceae), *Mangifera indica* (L., Anacardiaceae) and *Syzygium malaccense* ((L.) Merr. & L.M. Perry, Myrtaceae). However, only a few individuals of these other species were planted and broadly scattered on the plantation, so we excluded those from the further analysis. All investigated individuals were in their reproductive state, but flowering or fruiting did not coincide with the study. We chose three individuals with unshaded or only minimally-shaded crowns for each species for the ecophysiological study. Micrometeorological data were gathered in open terrain adjacent to the fruit plantation approximately 30 m away from the plantation edge. Air temperature and relative humidity were measured 2.3 m above the ground with a professional weather station (PCE-FWS 20 weather station, PCE Instruments, Meschede, Germany). A Quantum Sensor (LI-190A, Licor Inc., Lincoln, NV, USA) set up at the same height was used to record photosynthetic photon flux density (PPFD, μ mol s^{-1} m^{-2}).

2.2. Sap Flux Measurements

Sap flux density (J_s, g cm^{-2} h^{-1}) was measured continuously in three individuals of each selected species for six weeks from 1 August 2011 until 6 September 2011 (corresponding to the dry season) and for six weeks between 1 November 2011 and 12 December 2011 (corresponding to the wet season). Each tree and palm individual was equipped with two thermal dissipation probes [20] at breast height (1.30 m, DBH). One sensor was installed on the northern side and the other on the southern side of the stem. Sensors were protected with an aluminum-shielded insulation box and then covered with plastic foil, which was sealed with silicon to the stem above the sensor set up. The voltage output from the thermocouples was measured every 30 s, and 5-min averages were stored on a Delta-T datalogger (DL-2, Delta-T Devices Ltd., Cambridge, U.K.). We decided to use the standard calibration determined by Granier [21] to calculate sap flux density, as Renninger *et al.* [16] did not find considerable variations (within a 95% Confidence Interval) from this equation by calibrating thermal dissipation probes for palms.

2.3. Sap Flux Profile

In the last two weeks of the experiment, J_s was measured at one additional depth below the cambium (20–40 mm) in each palm and tree individual, as well as at an additional depth (40–60 mm) for individuals with an appropriate diameter at breast height (DBH > 11 cm). The additional sensors were placed randomly on the eastern or western side of the stems, at an angle of 90° from each of two reference sensors to reduce possible interference between sensors. The additional measurements were used to construct a sap flux profile and to estimate the conductive area of the xylem.

2.4. Calculation of Water Use and Tree Transpiration

Daily water use rates (Q, kg day^{-1}) were estimated by up-scaling daily modeled sap flux densities to the water flux through the whole conductive xylem area of a given stem [12]. We expressed tree transpiration rates per day (T, mm day^{-1}) by dividing Q through the crown projection area of the respective tree or palm (m^2) (see Table 1). Therefore, the horizontal crown extension of each tree and the horizontal extension of the leaves of each palm were measured in eight cardinal directions. Crown projection area was calculated by summing up the area of the eight pitch circles calculated from the crown/leaf extension in eight cardinal directions [22] (Table 1). We compared tree water use rates among species using the analysis of covariance with DBH as a covariate, as tree water use is often described as a function of tree size and/or DBH [12,23] (analysis of covariance (ANCOVA), followed by a *post hoc* Tukey honest significant difference (HSD) test). Sap flux densities and tree transpiration rates were compared among species by applying the analysis of variance (ANOVA, followed by a *post hoc* Tukey HSD test). The statistical analyses were performed using SPSS 18.0 software (SPSS Inc., Chicago, IL, USA). Daily maximum sap flux rates ($J_{s\ max}$, g cm^{-2} h^{-1}) are maximum values at least lasting for 45 min [12].

Forests **2015**, *6*, 2530–2544

2.5. Sap Flux Density Model

We used a sap flux density model based on changes in radiation and vapor pressure deficit to identify eventually occurring differences in sap flux density among the two investigated species. The sap flux model used is a modified Jarvis-type model originally capturing stomatal controls in relation to environmental parameters [24]. The model was modified in analogy to the work of Diereck and Hölscher [25] and Diereck *et al.* [26]; however, in contrast to the earlier work, we opted for a sap flux density model with PPFD (μ mol s^{-1} m^{-2}) and vapor pressure deficit (VPD) (kPa) as explanatory variables, instead of using global radiation. This resulted in the following model form:

$$J_{s\ model} = a\ \frac{PPFD}{b + PPFD}\ \frac{1}{1 + \exp^{\frac{c - VPD}{d}}} \tag{1}$$

where $J_{s\ model}$: modelled sap flux density (g cm^{-2} h^{-1});

a: maximum modelled sap flux density (g cm^{-2} h^{-1});
b: parameter describing PFFD response;
c,d: parameters describing VPD response.

Table 1. A summary of the plant structural characteristics of the studied trees and palms and a summary of the maximum ($J_{s\ max}$), mean ($J_{s\ mean}$) daily sap flux density, mean daily water use (Q_{mean}) and mean (T_{mean}) transpiration rates (means and standard deviations (SD), $n = 3$). Significant differences between the two species ($p < 0.05$) are indicated by different superscripted letters.

Species	Family	Common Name	DBH (cm)		Height (m)		Crown Projection Area (m²)		Conductive Xylem (cm²)		$J_{s\ max}$ g cm⁻² h⁻¹		$J_{s\ mean}$ g cm⁻² day⁻¹		Q_{mean} kg day⁻¹		T_{mean} mm day⁻¹	
			Mean	SD	Mean	SD	Mean	SD	Mean	SD	Mean	SD	Mean	SD	Mean	SD	Mean	SD
Euterpe oleracea	Arecaceae	Açai	13.7	1.8	7.3	1.8	25.6	2.4	143	14	24.2 [a]	9.8	90.6 [a]	30.3	43.6 [a]	20.2	1.67 [a]	0.66
Theobroma grandiflorum	Malvaceae	Cupuaçu	16.8	1.9	7.9	1.4	51.4	17.5	127	19	17.7 [a]	2.1	114.2 [a]	24.6	14.7 [b]	2.8	0.30 [b]	0.11

DBH, diameter at breast height.

Calculations of model parameters *a*, *b*, *c* and *d* and statistical analyses were performed as described in Diereck *et al.* [26] using R Version 2.6.2 (R Development Core Team, 2008). Model parameters were used to calculate daily sap flux densities of the year 2012 and to upscale sap flux densities to annual values for the period between 1 January 2012 and 31 December 2012. Annual ingoing data (VPD and PFFD) came from the above-mentioned climate station. Daily water use rates (Q, kg day^{-1}) of all of the trees and palms of the plantation were estimated by up-scaling daily modeled sap flux densities to the water flux through the whole conductive xylem area of all trees and palms on the plantation. Therefore, a diameter at breast height to conductive sap wood area relationship was established from the above-mentioned profile measurements. The established equation was used to calculate the conductive sap wood area of all trees and palms on the plantation. Daily values of water use rates were summed up for given time intervals chosen for inclusion in the model (weeks, months or year) and divided by the total area of the plantation to receive the stand transpiration rate (T_s, mm).

3. Results

3.1. Sap Flux Properties and Conductivity of the Xylem

Normalized daily sap flux densities of both species over the whole period corresponded well to the environmental parameter chosen to perform the model (Figure 1). The two investigated species were relatively similar in their mean daily maximum and mean diurnal sap flux densities. However, the midday course seemed to be different between the two species, as shown for one representative individual of each species over five bright sunny days (Figure 1). This variation indicated a midday depression in transpiration in the trees, but not in the palms. However, a clear morning peak was present in the Cupuaçu trees, but not in the palm. Maximum $J_{s\,max}$ measured was 24.2 g cm^{-2} h^{-1} for Açai and 17.7 g cm^{-2} h^{-1} Cupuaçu, and mean daily J_s was 90.6 and 114.2 g cm^{-2} day^{-1} for Açai and Cupuaçu, respectively (Table 1). Neither the observed maximum J_s nor the mean daily J_s differed significantly among the two species (Table 1).

The radial sap flux measurements indicated significant water fluxes even below the reference installation depth of the first 2 cm of the xylem below the cambium (Figure 2). In the Açai palm, the sap flux density in the second depth (2–4 cm below cambium) was revealed to be almost the same as in the peripheral cambium (0–2 cm below cambium) (compare to Figure 2a). Compared to the peripheral xylem, sap flux densities were 4% lower in the second xylem depth (2–4 cm below cambium) and 43% lower in the third depth (4–6 cm below cambium). The sap flux densities in the inner xylem compared to the peripheral xylem declined rapidly in the Cupuaçu trees. In the second depth (2–4 cm below cambium), we found a 65% lower sap flux compared to the peripheral xylem and an 88% lower sap flux in the third depth (4–6 cm below cambium) (compare to Figure 3b). Despite the small dataset, the species-specific conductive xylem area scaled relatively well with the diameter at breast height of a given species.

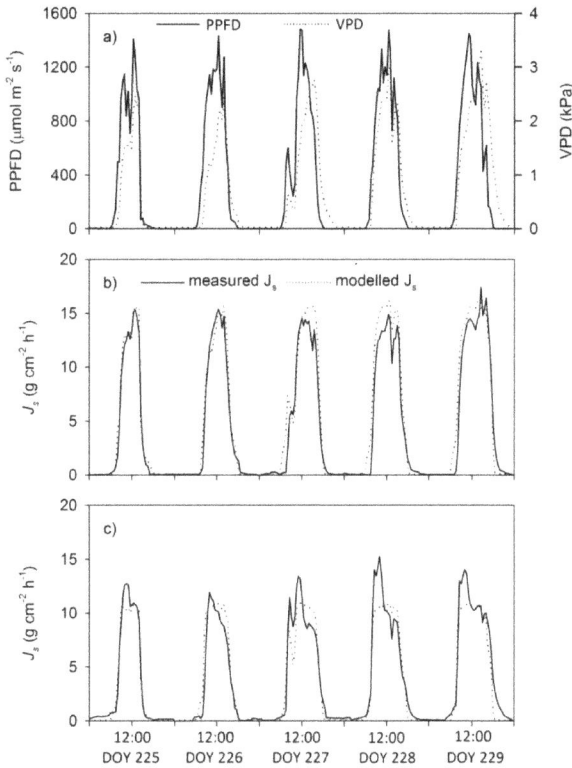

Figure 1. Diurnal courses of (**a**) photosynthetic photon flux density (PPFD), vapor pressure deficit (VPD), measured and modelled sap flux densities in a representative (**b**) Açaí palm and (**c**) Cupuaçu tree over five days in August 2011 (mean of *n* = 3, DOY = day of year, J_s = Sap flux density).

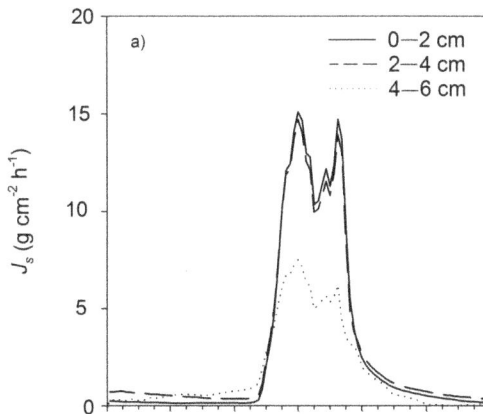

Figure 2. *Cont.*

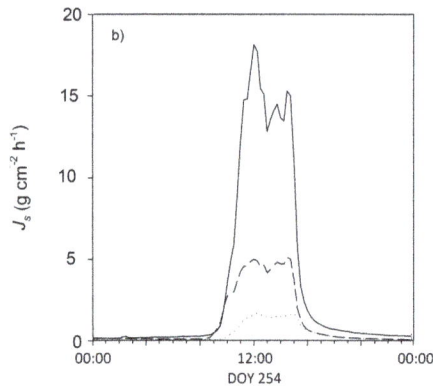

Figure 2. Representative daily courses of sap flux densities at the different xylem depths (0–2 cm, 2–4 cm and 4–6 cm below cambium) for (**a**) one Açaí palm and (**b**) one Cupuaçu tree over 24 h on 5 September 2011, J_s = Sap flux density.

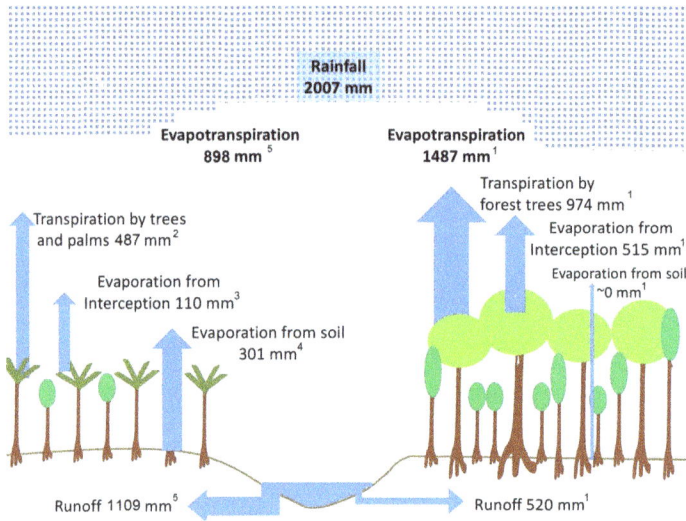

Figure 3. Changes in the water budget after forest conversion into fruit plantation. The origin and reference of the different values are given by the subscripted numbers. [1] Compiled after values given for Manaus by Salati and Vose [27] and Leopolodo *et al.* [28], we took the actual precipitation input of the year 2012, which differs only minimally from the original studies by Salati and Vose [27] and Leopolodo *et al.* [28]. [2] Estimates derived from measurements conducted by this study. [3] The intercept was assumed to scale with leaf area [29] (average leaf area in the planation 1.8 m^2 m^{-2} and in the rainforest 8 m^2 m^{-2}), and the leaves in the plantation had intermediate interception properties. [4] Soil evaporation was assumed to be in accordance to average values found in tropical tree plantations [30]. [5] We used the commonly-recognized function to calculate evapotranspiration as the sum of evapotranspiration from intercepted rainwater, tree transpiration and evaporation by the soil. The runoff was calculated as the subtraction of evapotranspiration from annual rainfall.

3.2. Response of Sap Flux to Environmental Parameters

The applied sap flux model captured the relation between observed sap flux densities and the describing environmental variables well. Adjusted coefficient of determination (R^2_{adj}) ranged between 0.62 and 0.93 for all plant individuals and was on average 0.87 over all study plants. The root mean square error (RMSE) of the modeled sap flux densities was 2.56 g cm^{-2} h^{-1} for the Açai palms and 1.65 g cm^{-2} h^{-1} for the Cupuaçu trees (Table 2). All estimated model parameters and standard deviations are presented in Table 2. Means of the parameter *a* (modeled $J_{s\ max}$) and parameter *b* (species-specific PPFD response) were significantly different (*post hoc* Tukey test), whereas no differences between species were indicated for parameter *c* (VPD response). Modeled mean daily sap flux densities differed from the actual measured mean daily sap flux densities by 3.9% and 4.9% for the Açai palms and the Cupuaçu trees, respectively (compare Tables 1 and 2).

Table 2. Estimated daily mean sap flux density ($J_{s\ mean}$), estimated model parameters (*a*, *b*, *c* and *d*) and measures of model performance (adjusted coefficient of determination (R^2_{adj}); root mean square error (RMSE)) for the two studied species (means and standard deviations (SD), *n* = 3 plant individuals). Significant differences (*p* < 0.05) between species for the estimated sap flux density and individual model parameters are indicated by different superscripted letters.

Species	$J_{s\ max}$ (g cm^{-2} day^{-1})		*a* (g cm^{-2} h^{-1})		*b* µ mol s^{-1} m^{-2}		*c* (kPa)		*d* (kPa)		R^2_{adj} (-)	RMSE (g cm^{-2} h^{-1})	
	Mean	SD	Mean	SD	Mea	SD	Mean	SD	Mean	SD		Mean	SD
Euterpe oleracea	87.1 [a]	50.8	12.5 [a]	5.3	311.7 [a]	290.4	0.38 [a]	0.29	0.46	0.16	0.67	2.56	0.57
Theobroma grandiflorum	108.6 [a]	21.0	13.3 [b]	1.8	79.1 [b]	51.0	0.30 [a]	0.09	0.24	0.08	0.92	1.65	0.27

a: maximum modelled sap flux density (g cm^{-2} h^{-1}); b: parameter describing photosynthetic photon flux density (PFFD) response; c,d: parameters describing vapor pressure deficit (VPD) response.

3.3. Water Use and Transpiration Rates

Species' means of daily mean and maximum water use rates (*Q* and Q_{max} in kg day^{-1}) were significantly different among the two investigated species. We estimated the mean daily water use rate of Açai to be 43 kg day^{-1} with maximum rates up to 90 kg day^{-1}. The Cupuaçu trees for the mean used 14.7 kg day^{-1} with maximum water use rates of 23.9 kg day^{-1} (compare to Table 1). The difference in maximum water use rates between the two species was largely defined by the strong dependency of the water use rates on the conductivity of the xylem, and the conductive xylem area explained 85% of the observed variability in the maximum water use rates. An often described interspecific relationship between water use rates and diameter at breast height (which leaves out possible differences in area, which explained the conductive tissues) was not indicated. Species differed significantly in their water use rates expressed per unit crown projection area (Table 1). Mean transpiration rates averaged 1.67 mm day^{-1} for the Açai palm and 0.30 mm day^{-1} for the Cupuaçu trees over the whole study period. Maximum transpiration rates observed in the six plant individuals varied from 0.34–5.52 mm day^{-1}. We estimated that the plantation transpired 24.3% of the annual rainfall summing up to 487 mm/year (Figure 3). Palms contributed the greatest fraction of the overall stand transpiration rate.

4. Discussion

4.1. Sap Flux Characteristics and Model Performance

Our observed maximum sap flux densities for Cupuaçu (*Theobroma grandiflorum*) and Açai (*Euterpe oleracea*) are in accordance to reported values for tropical tree species growing in plantations in the Neotropics, which mostly fall between 7 and 46 g cm^{-2} h^{-1} [13,31]. Overall, we achieved a very satisfying fit of the model describing the sap flux density of both species, and the models estimating sap flux using the parameter we used are recommended for tropical regions. The good model fit was illustrated by high to very high R^2_{adj} values and by very low root mean square errors for all of our studied palm and tree individuals (Table 2) [25,26]. All three estimated parameter were within the range of values estimated for 17 species from three different secondary forests [26]; hence, sap flux sensors can be applied in palms without any disadvantage with respect to their differing stem structure compared to trees.

A detailed comparison of the day time variation in sap flux between species indicates a pronounced midday depression in the sap flux of the Cupuaçu tree that was not indicated by the model. Unfortunately, no soil moisture was measured, but we speculate that this midday depression might have been caused by soil water limitation, as sap flux densities were reduced after noon with continuing high evaporative demand (Figure 1). Kunert *et al.* [12] found similar behavior in water-limited trees, which showed reduced sap flux densities compared to times under ample water conditions and similar availability of radiation. Another explanation could be that the climate station was too close to the stand and not installed at a representative height [25] for the canopy of the Cupuaçu trees, as they were much higher than the Açai palms. Nevertheless, the two environmental parameters we used to explain variations in sap flux define a great portion of the diurnal changes in sap flux densities of the Açai palm and the Cupuaçu tree. The model might not have captured the morning peak in the Cupuaçu trees, but had a high fit when comparing the estimated and measured daily sap flux densities. These values are the important estimates to up-scale from the sap flux densities to whole tree water use and transpiration rates. However, under different circumstances (e.g., most probably under severe water limitation during the dry season), a similar good model fit might not be achieved, and as already mentioned, soil moisture content could be an additional explanatory parameter [26]. That we only found a midday depression of transpiration in the Cupuaçu trees and not in the palms could be explained by the exceptionally high water storage capacity in the palm stems [18]. Evidence for this can be found from the profile measurements; higher nighttime refilling activity took place in the deeper xylem of the palms (2–4 cm) (Figure 2).

4.2. Xylem Conductivity and Water Use Rates

Water use in the palm trees was up to 3.5-times higher than in the Cupuaçu trees for a given diameter at breast height (Table 1). This difference in water use results from a much greater conductive xylem area in the palm trees, as sap flux densities in the outer 2 cm were not significantly different, but sap flux densities in deeper sap wood profiles were much higher in palms than in trees. In general, total plant water use is assumed to "universally scale" with the size of the conductive xylem area [32]. In our diffuse porous Cupuaçu trees, the conductivity of the xylem was already significantly reduced within the second depth of the profile measurements (20–40 mm, a reduction of 65% compared to 0–20 mm), and only a small fraction of the out sap flux density was measured at the third depth (40–60 mm, a reduction of 88% compared to 0–20 mm). In contrast, sap flux densities were almost the same in the deeper xylem of the Açai palm as in the outer xylem (Figure 2). Palms are commonly known to have vascular bundles throughout the whole stem cross-section and are able to transport water also within the center of the stem [14]. Nevertheless, the slightly reduced sap flux densities measured at the deepest depth of the palm xylem (40–60 mm) indicate that there is a lower concentration of vascular bundles towards the center. Similar results are reported by anatomical studies on the structure of palm stems from the genus *Euterpe* in the Central Amazon and in Costa Rica, where a higher concentration of vascular bundles was found at the stem periphery [14,18].

We estimated the mean daily water use rate of Açai as 43 kg day^{-1} with maximum rates up to 90 kg day^{-1} during days with high evaporative demand. High water use rates have already been estimated for other palm species, e.g., coconut palm trees, in various studies. Adult coconut trees use between 30 and 120 kg day^{-1} [33], but high water consumption only occurs during periods with high evaporative demand [34]. The extreme high water use rate of the Açai palm might also explain why this species, or in general arborescent palms, is more common in the flood plains where the water table is higher than in plateau areas of the *terra firme* forest in the Amazon. Observed water use rates of the Cupuaçu trees had a mean of 14.7 kg day^{-1} and were in line with other studies on tropical trees.

Mean daily water use rates of 10 kg day^{-1} are reported for *Theobroma cacao* (mean DBH 10 cm) in Indonesia [11] and water use rates between 10 and 20 kg day^{-1} (mean DBH 15 cm) for a variety of tree species, even sized and growing under plantation conditions in mono-specific and mixed stands in Panama [31,35].

4.3. Plant Transpiration Rates

Maximum transpiration rates observed in the six plant individuals varied from 0.34–5.52 mm day^{-1}. This wide range of individual tree transpiration is confirmed by various studies in the tropics. Daily transpiration rates, for example, in individual trees growing in a Panamanian plantation, had a mean between 0.36 and 1.16 mm day^{-1} per unit crown projection area during the wet season [31], whereas values up to 4.9 mm day^{-1}, with one exceptional tree transpiring 7.5 mm day^{-1} per unit crown projection area, were also recorded in a study comparing data from three different secondary tropical forests, one located in Indonesia, one in the Philippines and one in Panama [26]. In our case, the palm trees had significantly higher transpiration rates. High transpiration rates of native palm trees occurring in the Amazon were already outlined by Renninger *et al.* [16]. In the mentioned study, the palm species *Iriartea deltoidea* contributed significantly more to the stand transpiration per unit leaf area "than the average leaf found in the rain forest".

4.4. Stand Transpiration Rate and Impact on the Local Water Budget

Land use change is significantly affecting the local budget and drastically reduces the recycling rate of precipitation [9,27]. Deforestation has thus a significant effect on the rainfall pattern of the whole Amazon Basin and with teleconnections on rainfall in the Southern parts of South America [36]. Conversion of natural forests to anthropogenic forest systems, such as tree plantations, is supposed to have lower effects on the overall water budget [37]. However, we found in this study that the evapotranspiration was drastically reduced above the plantation compared to estimates from the natural undisturbed forest. Estimates for the Central Amazon for years with similar rainfall rates as during our study period assume that approximately 74.1% of the annual rainfall is evapotranspired [27], which would be 1487 mm for our study year. Assuming a significant increase of soil evaporation from 0% in the forest [27,28] to up to 15% of the annual rainfall in the plantation [30] and a reduced evaporation of rainfall interception due to reduced leaf area in the plantation, we estimated an annual evapotranspiration rate of 898 mm above the plantation (Figure 3). This means locally an up to 40% reduction of evapotranspiration through land use conversion to such small-holder plantations and that the runoff rate would be significantly increased.

5. Conclusions

The observed individual water uses and transpiration rates might give only limited information on how the stand transpiration rates will change if natural forests are altered into plantations, as we considered only unshaded or minimally-shaded palm and tree individuals. However, we assumed that these palms and trees contribute a major part to the overall stand transpiration, although differences in individual tree development within a stand and contrasting stand structure due to species mixtures might reduce the observed species-specific transpiration rates [26]. Nevertheless, we suggest that the distinct difference in water use and transpiration rates between monocot and dicot species will have a major effect on changes in the water table of newly established fruit plantations and on variations within the water table compared to former land uses in the affected area.

Acknowledgments: We thank Alida Mercado Cárdenas for critical proof reading and Susan Trumbore for valuable comments on an earlier version of the manuscript. We would like to thank two anonymous reviewers for their comments on and suggestion for how to improve the clarity of this manuscript.

Author Contributions: Norbert Kunert and Priscila Barros conducted the field work. Norbert Kunert, Luiza Maria Teóphilo Aparecido and Niro Higuchi analyzed the data. Norbert Kunert took the lead in writing the manuscript. All authors contributed to the revision of the final manuscript.

Conflicts of Interest: The authors declare no conflict of interest.

References

1. Kunert, N.; Barros, P.; Higuchi, N. Do palm water use characteristics explain the spatial distribution of palms in the Central Amazon? *Acta Hortic.* **2013**, *991*, 197–204.
2. Henderson, A. *The Palms of the Amazon*; University Press: Oxford, UK, 1995.
3. Nogueira, O.; Carvalho, C.; Muller, C.; Galvao, E.; Silva, H.; Rodrigues, J.; Ooliveira, M.; Carvalho Neto, J.; Nascimento, W.; Calvazarra, B. *A Cultura do Açaí.*; Embrapa/Centro de Pesquisa Agroflorestal da Amazônia Oriental: Beasilia, Brazil, 1995.
4. Santos, G.M.; Maia, G.; Sousa, P.; Costa, J.; Figueiredo, R.; Prado, G. Correlação entre atividade antioxidante e compostos bioativos de polpas comerciais de açaí (*Euterpe oleracea* Mart). *Archivos Latinoam. Nutr.* **2008**, *58*, 187–192. (In Portuguese)
5. Colapinto, J. Strange fruit: The rise and fall of Acai. *New Yorker* **2011**, *87*, 37–41.
6. Lorenzi, H. *Árvores brasileiras: Manual de Identificação e Cultivo de Plantas Arbóreas Nativas*; Nova Odessa: Brasilia, Brazil, 1998.
7. Venturieri, G. *Cupuaçu: A Espécie, sua Cultura, usos e Processamento*; Clube do Cupu: Belém, Brazil, 1993.
8. Bastos, M.; Gurgel, T.; De Sousa Filho, M. Efeito da aplicação de enzimas pectinolíticas no rendimento da extração de polpa de cupuaçu. *Rev. Bras. Frutic.* **2002**, *24*, 240–242, (In Portuguese). [CrossRef]
9. D'Almeida, C.; Vörösmarty, C.J.; Hurtt, G.C.; Marengo, J.A.; Dingman, S.L.; Keim, B.D. The effects of deforestation on the hydrological cycle in Amazonia: A review on scale and resolution. *Int. J. Climatol.* **2007**, *27*, 633–647. [CrossRef]
10. Flore, J.A.; Lakso, A.N. Environmental and physiological regulation of photosynthesis in fruit crops. In *Horticultural Reviews*; John Wiley & Sons, Inc.: Hoboken, NJ, USA, 1989; pp. 111–157.
11. Köhler, M.; Schwendenmann, L.; Hölscher, D. Throughfall reduction in a cacao agroforest: Tree water use and soil water budgeting. *Agric. For. Meteorol.* **2010**, *150*, 1079–1089. [CrossRef]
12. Kunert, N.; Schwendenmann, L.; Hölscher, D. Seasonal dynamics of tree sap flux and water use in nine species in Panamanian forest plantations. *Agric. For. Meteorol.* **2010**, *150*, 411–419. [CrossRef]
13. Dünisch, O.; Morais, R. Regulation of xylem sap flow in an evergreen, a semi-deciduous, and a deciduous meliaceae species from the amazon. *Trees* **2002**, *16*, 404–416.
14. Aparecido, L.M.T.; dos Santos, J.; Higuchi, N.; Kunert, N. Ecological applications of differences in the hydraulic efficiency of palms and broad-leaved trees. *Trees* **2015**, 1–15. [CrossRef]
15. Niu, F.; Röll, A.; Hardanto, A.; Meijide, A.; Köhler, M.; Hendrayanto; Hölscher, D. Oil palm water use: Calibration of a sap flux method and a field measurement scheme. *Tree Physiol.* **2015**, *35*, 563–573. [CrossRef] [PubMed]
16. Renninger, H.J.; Phillips, N.; Salvucci, G.D. Wet- *vs.* dry-season transpiration in an Amazonian rain forest palm *Iriartea deltoidea*. *Biotropica* **2010**, *42*, 470–478. [CrossRef]
17. Basset, Y. Communities of insect herbivores foraging on saplings *versus* mature trees of *Pourouma bicolor* (Cecropiaceae) in Panama. *Oecologia* **2001**, *129*, 253–260. [CrossRef]
18. Rich, P.M. Developmental anatomy of the stem of *Welfia georgii, Iriartea gigantea*, and other arborescent palms: Implications for mechanical support. *Am. J. Bot.* **1987**, *74*, 792–802. [CrossRef]
19. Da Silva, F.; Suwa, R.; Kajimoto, T.; Ishizuka, M.; Higuchi, N.; Kunert, N. Allometric equations for estimating biomass of *Euterpe precatoria*, the most abundant palm species in the Amazon. *Forests* **2015**, *6*, 450–463. [CrossRef]
20. Granier, A. Une nouvelle méthode pour la mesure du flux de sève brute dans le tronc des arbres. *Ann. For. Sci.* **1985**, *42*, 193–200. (In French) [CrossRef]
21. Granier, A. Evaluation of transpiration in a Douglas-fir stand by means of sap flow measurements. *Tree Physiol.* **1987**, *3*, 309–320. [CrossRef] [PubMed]
22. Röhle, H. Vergleichende Untersuchungen zur Ermittlung der Genauigkeit bei der Ablotung von Kronenradien mit dem Dachlot und durch senkrechtes anvisieren des Kronenrandes. *Forstarchiv* **1986**, *57*, 67–71. (In German)
23. Andrade, J.; Meinzer, F.; Goldstein, G.; Schnitzer, S. Water uptake and transport in lianas and co-occurring trees of a seasonally dry tropical forest. *Trees* **2005**, *19*, 282–289. [CrossRef]

24. Jarvis, P.G. The interpretation of the variations in leaf water potential and stomatal conductance found in canopies in the field. *Philos. Trans. R. Soc. Lond. B Biol. Sci.* **1976**, *273*, 593–610. [CrossRef]

25. Dierick, D.; Hölscher, D. Species-specific tree water use characteristics in reforestation stands in the Philippines. *Agric. For. Meteorol.* **2009**, *149*, 1317–1326. [CrossRef]

26. Dierick, D.; Kunert, N.; Köhler, M.; Schwendenmann, L.; Hölscher, D. Comparison of tree water use characteristics in reforestation and agroforestry stands across the tropics. In *Tropical Rainforests and Agroforests under Global Change*; Tscharntke, T., Leuschner, C., Eds.; Spinger: Berlin, Germany, 2010; pp. 293–308.

27. Salati, E.; Vose, P.B. Amazon basin: A system in equilibrium. *Science* **1984**, *225*, 129–138. [CrossRef] [PubMed]

28. Leopoldo, P.R.; Franken, W.K.; Salati, E. Balanço hídrico de pequena bacia hidrográfica em floresta amazônica de *terra firme*. *Acta Amazon.* **1982**, *12*, 33–337. (In Portuguese)

29. Schneebeli, M.; Wolf, S.; Kunert, N.; Eugster, W.; Mätzler, C. Relating the X-band opacity of a tropical tree canopy to sapflow, rain interception and dew formation. *Remote Sens. Environ.* **2011**, *115*, 2116–2125. [CrossRef]

30. Lane, P.N.J.; Morris, J.; Ningnan, Z.; Guangyi, Z.; Guoyi, Z.; Daping, X. Water balance of tropical eucalypt plantations in south-eastern China. *Agric. For. Meteorol.* **2004**, *124*, 253–267. [CrossRef]

31. Kunert, N. *Tree Transpiration in Forest Plantations: Effects of Species, Seasonality and Diversity (Panama)*; Georg-August-Universität Göttingen: Goettingen, Germany, 2010.

32. Meinzer, F.; Andrade, J.; Goldstein, G.; Holbrook, N.; Cavelier, J.; Wright, S. Partitioning of soil water among canopy trees in a seasonally dry tropical forest. *Oecologia* **1999**, *21*, 293–301. [CrossRef]

33. Jayasekara, K.; Jayasekara, C. Efficiency of water use in coconut under different soil/plant management systems. In *Advances in Coconut Research and Development*; Nair, M., Khan, H., Eds.; Oxford & IBH Publishing: New Delhi, India, 1993.

34. Yusuf, M.; Varadan, K. Water management studies on coconut in india. In *Advances in Coconut Research and Development*; Nair, M., Khan, H., Eds.; Oxford & IBH Publishing: New Delhi, India, 1993; pp. 337–346.

35. Kunert, N.; Schwendenmann, L.; Potvin, C.; Hölscher, D. Tree diversity enhances tree transpiration in a Panamanian forest plantation. *J. Appl. Ecol.* **2012**, *49*, 135–144. [CrossRef]

36. Spracklen, D.V.; Arnold, S.R.; Taylor, C.M. Observations of increased tropical rainfall preceded by air passage over forests. *Nature* **2012**, *489*, 282–285. [CrossRef] [PubMed]

37. Kunert, N.; Cardenas, A.M. Are diverse tropical tree plantations more resistant to drought than monocultures? *Forests* **2015**, *6*, 2029–2046. [CrossRef]

forests

MDPI

Article

Effects of Land Use on Flow Rate Change Indices

Ali Assani *, Francis Delisle †, Raphaëlle Landry † and Mushombe Muma

Department of Environmental Sciences, University of Quebec at Trois-Rivières, 3351 Boulevard des Forges, Trois-Rivières QC G9A 5H7, Canada; francis.delisle1@uqtr.ca (F.D.); raphaelle.landry@uqtr.ca (R.L.); mushome.muma@uqtr.ca (M.M.)

* Author to whom correspondence should be addressed; ali.assani@uqtr.ca;
  Tel.: +1-819-376-5011 (ext. 3669); Fax: +1-819-376-5179.
† These authors contributed equally to this work.

Academic Editors: James M. Vose and Ge Sun
Received: 10 September 2015; Accepted: 18 November 2015; Published: 24 November 2015

Abstract: The goal of this study was to analyze the impact of agriculture on the spatial and temporal variability of flow rate change indices from 1930 to 2008. The two indices used are the coefficient of immoderation (CI) and the coefficient of variation (CV). Values of these two indices are higher for the L'Assomption River agricultural watershed than for the Matawin River forested watershed due to higher runoff in the former than in the latter. The difference in these values between the two watersheds is greater for winter, but it is lower for summer, when the difference in runoff between the two watersheds is strongly attenuated by the presence of crops. Regarding the temporal variability, a difference between the two watersheds is observed in the fall. For the agricultural watershed, mean values of neither index show a break in slope, while a break is observed for the forested watershed. In both watersheds, both indices are positively correlated with maximum temperature and total rainfall in winter, but only to this latter climate variable in the fall. In springtime, the two indices are negatively correlated with minimum temperature in the forested watershed, but only CV is correlated, positively, with this same climate variable in the agricultural watershed.

Keywords: flow rate change; coefficient of variation; coefficient of immoderation; temperature; precipitation; agriculture

1. Introduction

According to the ecological natural flow regime concept, the flow regime of a river comprises five fundamental components [1,2]: magnitude, duration, timing, frequency and flow rate change. Many fluvial ecology studies have demonstrated the influence of flow rate change on the dynamics and evolution of aquatic and semi-aquatic organisms [3–11] both in natural and in regulated rivers. Indeed, flow rate change affects the composition, structure and abundance of macrophytes and riparian vegetation. It also affects habitat volumes and the availability of food for aquatic and semi-aquatic animals, as well as transfers between the low-flow channel and adjacent alluvial plain. From a morphological standpoint, flow rate change affects the evolution of banks and their sensitivity to erosion through humectation-desiccation and freeze-thaw processes, as well as the evolution of meanders and other landforms [12]. It also determines whether streamflow is permanent or intermittent [13,14].

Unlike the other four components, however, flow rate change remains little studied in hydrology despite its role in fluvial ecosystem function and evolution [15–17]. As a result, the watershed climate and physiographic factors that affect the spatial and temporal variability of this component of the flow regime remain unknown, as do human factors. In Quebec, although several studies have analyzed the hydrologic impacts of deforestation and agriculture on various components of flow [18–22], none has looked at the impacts of these two human activities on flow rate change. The goal of the present study is to fill this gap. To do so, the following two major points are addressed:

- An analysis of the impacts of agriculture on the spatial and temporal variability of flow rate change indices. This objective is based on the following hypothesis: flow rate change in an agricultural watershed is much greater than in a forested watershed due to high runoff;
- An analysis of the impacts of agriculture on the relationship between climate variables (temperature and precipitation) and flow rate change indices, the underlying assumption being that agriculture changes the relationship between climate variables and flow rate change indices.

This study is carried out as part of a vast research program aimed at constraining the influence of agriculture on the spatial and temporal variability of the five components of the flow regime and its implications for the morphological and ecological evolution of fluvial ecosystems in Quebec. The ultimate goal of this research program is to develop flow management practices for restoring and conserving the ecological integrity of these ecosystems.

2. Methods

2.1. Description of Watershed

The choice of watersheds to study was based on the following criteria:

- The existence of continuous flow and climate data measured over at least 50 years;
- Similar geological, physiographic and climate characteristics in the selected watersheds in order to constrain better the impacts of land use on flow rate change indices;
- Two selected watersheds with differing land uses.

Two watersheds met these three criteria, namely the adjacent L'Assomption River and Matawin River watersheds. These watersheds have already been described in detail in some of our previous work [18,22]. The Matawin River watershed is fully contained within the Canadian Shield. It is covered entirely by forest and no farming takes place within it. This forested area, which also extends to the L'Assomption River watershed, comprises essentially sugar maple-yellow birch stands. For the Matawin River, the watershed upstream from the Saint-Michel-des-Saints station covers 1390 km^2 (Figure 1). Flows have been measured continuously at the Saint-Michel-Des-Saints station since 1931. This station was not affected by the dam built further downstream in 1930 because it is located far from the impounded lake that makes up the Taureau reservoir. With regard to the L'Assomption River watershed, two thirds (approximately 66%) of it is located within the Canadian Shield and one third (approximately 33%) in the St. Lawrence Lowlands, where intensive agriculture (mostly grains and fodder crops) is practiced. At the Joliette station, the geographic area of the L'Assomption River watershed is 1340 km^2. Flows have been measured there on an ongoing basis since 1925. For both watersheds, flow data as well as temperature and precipitation data were taken from the Environment Canada websites [23]. However, unlike for flow data, temperatures and precipitation were measured fairly regularly until 2008 for both watersheds, and then only intermittently afterwards.

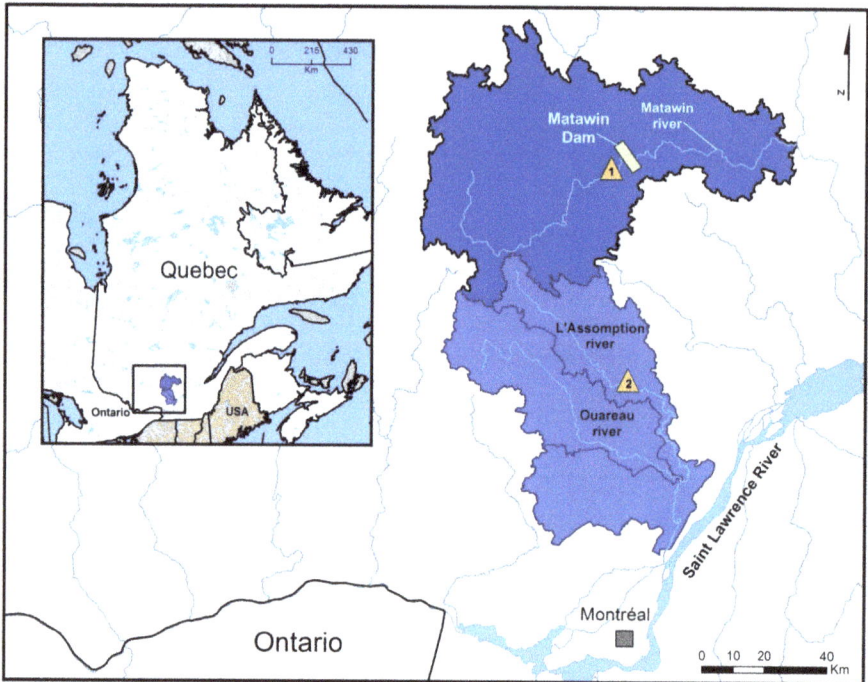

Figure 1. Location of stations. 1, Saint-Michel-des-Saints station on Matawin river. 2, Joliette station on L'Assomption River.

2.2. Definition of Flow Rate Change Indices and Statistical Analysis

The index that is commonly used to characterize flow rate change in the literature is the number of phases of increasing and decreasing flow [1]. Although this approach is precise, it is cumbersome and long because it requires detailed analysis of flow hydrographs. To streamline these processing steps, we propose the use of two indices to characterize flow rate change. The first index is the coefficient of variation (CV) of flows, which is in fact the ratio of the standard deviation and the mean value calculated for a series of daily flows. It is expressed as a percentage. This index measures between-day flow variations at the annual and seasonal scales. Higher values of CV indicate stronger flow variations from one day to the next. The second index is the coefficient of immoderation (CI), which is the ratio of the highest daily flow (maximum daily flow) and the lowest daily flow (minimum daily flow) measured during a given year or season [24]. It is also expressed as a percentage. CI is a measure of the maximum amplitude of flow fluctuations at the annual or seasonal scale. Higher CI values indicate a greater difference between the maximum and minimum daily flows. We calculated the two indices using daily flows for each of the following four seasons: winter (January–March), spring (April–June), summer (July–September) and fall (October–December).

For the statistical analysis, the mean values of these two indices were compared using the paired *t* test to analyze the impacts of differing land uses in the two watersheds on the spatial variability of the two indices. The use of the paired *t* test is warranted by the normal distribution and the lack of autocorrelation in the CI and CV series for both watersheds. For its part, the temporal variability of the two indices was compared using the Lombard test [25,26]. The choice of this method is warranted by its general nature, it being the only method that can detect both sharp and gradual breaks in mean values of a statistical series, unlike other statistical tests commonly used in hydrology (e.g. test de Pettitt). The mathematical development of the Lombard test was presented by [25] and [26] and will not be addressed further. It should be noted, however, that a break in mean values of a statistical series is statistically significant at the 95% confidence level when the Sn value (score) calculated for the series of observations is greater than 0.0403, which is the Lombard test theoretical value.

Finally, to test the second hypothesis, we correlated the two flow rate change indices (CI and CV) with climate variables using the linear correlation method. The climate variables that were correlated with the two indices include:

- The series of mean daily maximum temperatures (TMAX);
- The series of mean daily minimum temperatures (Tmin);
- The series of daily mean temperatures (Tme);
- The series of total snowfall (TSF);
- The series of total rainfall (TRN);
- The series of total precipitation (rain and snow) (TP).

These series were assembled for each of the four seasons (except for snowfall in summer) over the period from 1930 to 2008.

3. Results and Discussion

3.1. Comparison of the Mean Values of Flow Rate Change Indices between the Two Watersheds

Mean values of CI and CV, the flow rate change indices, are shown in Table 1, from which it can be seen that the mean values of both indices are higher for the L'Assomption River agricultural watershed than for the Matawin River forested watershed. For CI, the difference between the two watersheds is much greater for winter than for other seasons and much lower for summer. For CV, the difference between the two watersheds is greater for winter and spring, and is low for summer.

Table 1. Comparison of mean values of coefficient of immoderation (CI) and the coefficient of variation (CV) using the paired *t* test (1930–2008).

Seasons	CI			CV		
	L'Assomption Watershed	Matawin Watershed	*p*-Values	L'Assomption Watershed	Matawin Watershed	*p*-Values
Winter	55.3	3.5	0.000	57.4	32.6	0.000
Spring	19.7	10.7	0.000	81.5	61.9	0.000
Summer	9.3	7.0	0.000	57.0	52.2	0.000
Fall	9.6	5.0	0.000	53.7	39.9	0.000

These results show that streamflow varies considerably in the agricultural watershed compared to the forested watershed due to higher runoff in the former than in the latter [18]. However, in summer, when the fields are covered by crops, the difference between the two watersheds is lower due to reduced runoff in the agricultural watershed, accounting for the small difference in values of the two indices between the watersheds in summer. During the other seasons, soil cover is generally limited in the agricultural watershed, a situation which favors higher runoff than in the forested watershed, resulting in greater flow variations in the agricultural watershed than in the forested watershed. It follows that differences in morphological and physiographic characteristics between the two watersheds cannot account for the seasonal differences in CI and CV values observed between the two watersheds, because, unlike plant cover, these morphological and physiographic characteristics do not vary according to the season. In addition, it should be recalled that, in the agricultural area, ground slopes are nearly zero (ancient seafloor), which should have produced lower streamflow variability in the agricultural watershed than in the forested watershed.

3.2. Comparison of the Temporal Variability of Flow Rate Change Indices between the Two Watersheds

Results of the Lombard analysis are shown in Table 2. For CI, breaks in mean values are observed for winter and summer in both watersheds. For summer, the timing of this break is the same for the two watersheds (1993–1994), while for winter, the break in mean values took place roughly 30 years later in the agricultural watershed than in the forested watershed. In this latter watershed, aside from breaks for winter and summer, another break in mean values is observed for fall in 1983–1985. All breaks in means values are sharp for both watersheds. CI values are significantly larger in both watersheds after these breaks (Figure 2).

Table 2. Analysis of the temporal variability of two flow indices in the two watersheds using the Lombard test (1930–2008).

| Seasons | CI | | | | CV | | | |
| | L'Assomption Watershed | | Matawin Watershed | | L'Assomption Watershed | | Matawin Watershed | |
	Sn	T1/T2	Sn	T1/T2	Sn	T1/T2	Sn	T1/T2
Winter	**0.0601**	1970/71	**0.0613**	1945/46	**0.0499**	1972/73	0.0248	-
Spring	0.0386	-	0.0211	-	0.0065	-	0.0400	-
Summer	**0.0633**	1993/94	**0.0620**	1993/94	**0.1019**	1993/94	**0.0620**	1993/94
Fall	0.0116	-	**0.0833**	1983/85	0.0044	-	**0.0419**	1984/85

Sn, Lombard test statistic. Statistically significant *Sn* values at the 5% levels are shown in bold. T1 and T2, dates of start and end, respectively, of shift in mean.

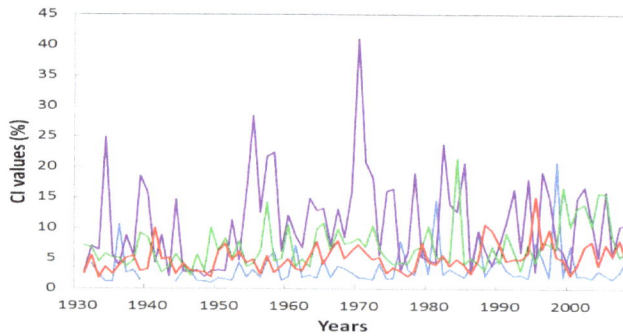

(a)

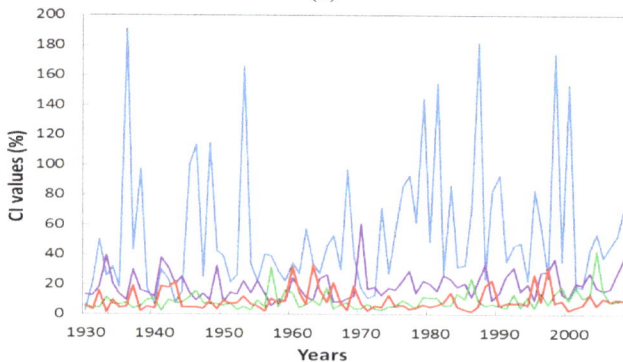

(b)

Figure 2. Temporal variability of the CI index in the Matawin River forested watershed (**a**) and the L'Assomption River agricultural watershed; (**b**) for the four seasons. Winter: blue curve; Spring: pink curve; Summer: green curve; fall: red curve.

The same trend as for CI is observed for CV values, with breaks in mean values of CV observed for the same seasons as for CI in both watersheds, except for winter in the forested watershed. Moreover, the timing of these breaks is nearly the same as that for breaks in CI values. These breaks are sharp and CV values increase significantly after the breaks (Figure 3).

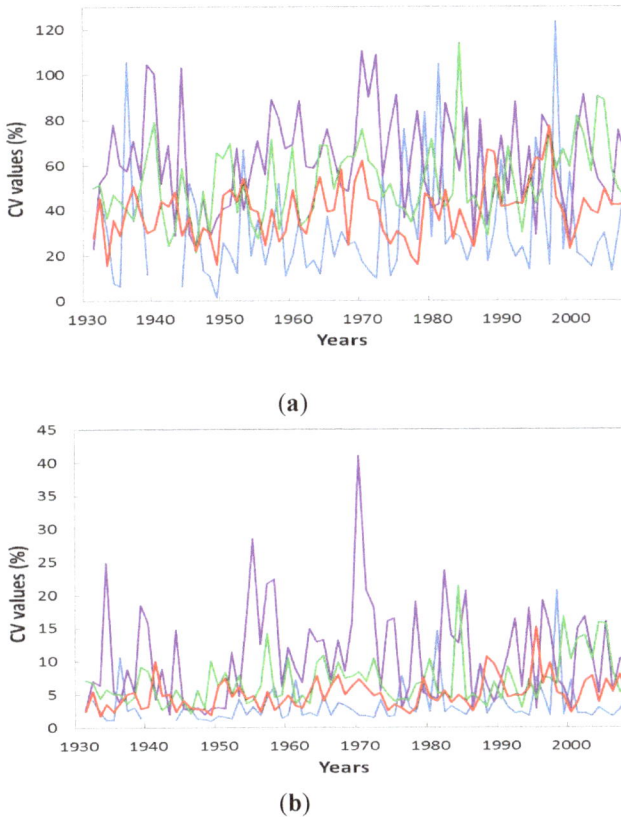

(a)

(b)

Figure 3. Temporal variability of the CV index in the Matawin River forested watershed (**a**) and the L'Assomption River agricultural watershed; (**b**) for the four seasons. Winter: blue curve; Spring: pink curve; Summer: green curve; fall: red curve.

These results generally support the previous conclusions regarding the spatial variability of the two indices. Thus, for summer, the two watersheds behave similarly, reflecting the synchronous nature of the breaks in mean values. Differences between the two watersheds are observed for fall and winter, two seasons that show a large difference in runoff between the two watersheds as a result of soil being exposed in the agricultural watershed. In any case, CV and CI values increase significantly after the breaks in both watersheds. In other words, variations in streamflow increase significantly over time in both watersheds. In the agricultural watershed, this increase may be related to increasing rainfall [18,22], while in the forested watershed, only summer rainfall has increased significantly. In addition, minimum temperatures have also increased significantly in the four seasons [18].

3.3. Relationship between Climate Variables and Flow Rate Change Indices

Coefficient of correlation values are shown in Table 3. In winter, the indices for both watersheds are positively correlated to maximum temperature and total rainfall, two factors that influence runoff during that season. In the Matawin River forested watershed, CV is also correlated with minimum temperature. For springtime, the CI index for the agricultural watershed is not correlated with any climate variable, whereas CV is positively correlated with maximum and minimum temperatures. In the forested watershed, the two indices are negatively correlated with minimum temperature. For summer, neither index is correlated with any climate variable in either watershed. For fall, the two indices are positively correlated with total rainfall in both watersheds, and are also positively correlated with total precipitation, but only in the forested watershed. It is quite likely that snow cover in the agricultural watershed does not stay on the ground very long in the fall as a result of higher temperatures than in the forested watershed. In addition, [18] have shown that fall temperatures are much more strongly affected by site-specific conditions.

This analysis indicates that the difference between the two watersheds is observed in the spring, when the watersheds show opposite correlations. No climate variable can account for these opposite correlations because, in both watersheds, daily minimum temperatures increase significantly over time. The difference in land use between the two watersheds seems to be the factor that accounts for these opposite correlations. In the forested watershed, an increase in spring minimum temperature is related to a decrease in flow variations (lower values of the two flow rate change indices), due to sustained snowmelt promoting sustained runoff. This results in a decrease in flow variations between days. This processes is thought to be dampened in the agricultural watershed, likely as a result of the rapid and transient nature of snowmelt-generated runoff.

4. Conclusions

Flow rate change is a major component of the flow regime due to its effect on fluvial ecosystem function and evolution. Few studies have looked at the natural and human factors that affect its spatial and temporal variability, however. In this study, we compared the values of two indices (the coefficient of variation and the coefficient of immoderation) in an agricultural and a forested watershed. The influence of agriculture produces higher values of the two indices in the agricultural watershed than in the forested watershed due to higher runoff in the former than in the latter. The difference in index values between the two watersheds is greater for winter and lower for summer. As far as the temporal variability of these two indices is concerned, the Lombard analysis revealed breaks in mean values for winter and summer in both watersheds. The timing of these breaks is nearly similar for summer only. Breaks in mean values are also observed for fall in the forested watershed. Values of both indices increase significantly after these breaks. It follows that flow variations increase over time in both watersheds, likely as a result of higher rainfall and temperature. Finally, in both watersheds, the two flow rate change indices are correlated with the same climate variables. However, for springtime, the sign of this correlation is opposite for the two watersheds. This study shows that agriculture increases flow variations in all four seasons, but its impact is dampened in summer as a result of the presence of crops, which slow runoff.

Table 3. Coefficients of correlation calculated between climate variables and seasonal daily flow variability indices.

Variables	Winter				Springs				Summer				Fall			
	L'Assomption		Matawin		L'Assomption		Matawin		L'Assomption		Matawin		L'Assomption		Matawin	
	CI	CV	CI	CV	CI	CV	CI	CV	CI	CV	CI	CV	CI	CV	CI	CV
Tmax	**0.304**	**0.270**	**0.367**	**0.364**	0.194	**0.276**	−0.099	−0.130	0.052	0.105	0.125	0.070	0.030	−0.064	−0.025	0.031
Tmin	0.72	0.160	0.205	**0.272**	0.205	**0.292**	**−0.287**	**−0.338**	0.129	0.204	0.0023	0.018	−0.051	−0.046	0.008	0.007
Tme	0.222	0.200	**0.313**	**0.294**	0.255	**0.345**	−0.099	−0.130	0.124	0.169	0.084	0.048	−0.044	−0.060	−0.038	−0.040
TSF	−0.158	−0.158	−0.171	−0.191	0.152	0.072	0.024	0.200	-	-	-	-	−0.080	−0.183	0.034	−0.082
TRN	**0.533**	**0.533**	**0.413**	**0.546**	−0.218	−0.199	−0.038	−0.161	0.160	0.160	0.134	0.063	**0.243**	**0.319**	**0.416**	**0.295**
TP	0.219	0.219	0.101	15.4	0.183	0.175	−0.032	−0.107	0.160	0.160	0.134	0.063	0.155	0.160	**0.353**	**0.232**

Statistically significant coefficient of correlation values at the 5% level are shown in bold.

Acknowledgments: The authors would like to acknowledge financial support from the Natural Sciences and Engineering Research Council of Canada and from the RIVE research center at Université du Québec à Trois-Rivières.

Author Contributions: Ali Assani, Francis Delisle and Raphaëlle Landry conducted data analyses, participated in writing all sections of the manuscript and to the elaboration of figures. Muma Mushombe contributed to writing of the results and discussion sections.

Conflicts of Interest: The authors declare no conflict of interest.

References

1. Ritcher, B.D.; Baumgartner, J.V.; Braun, D.P.; Powell, J. A spatial assessment of hydrologic alteration within a river network. *Regul. Rivers Res. Manag.* **1996**, *14*, 329–340.
2. Poff, N.L.; Allan, J.D.; Bain, M.B.; Karr, J.R.; Prestegaard, K.L.; Richter, B.D.; Sparks, R.E.; Stromberg, J.C. The natural flow regime. *Bioscience* **1997**, *47*, 769–784. [CrossRef]
3. Beche, L.A.; McElravy, E.P.; Resh, V.H. Long-term seasonal variation in the biological traits of benthic-macroinvertebrates in two Mediterranean-climate streams in California, USA. *Freshw. Biol.* **2006**, *51*, 56–75. [CrossRef]
4. Cushman, R.M. Review of ecological effects of rapidly varying flows downstream from hydroelectric facilities. *N. Am. J. Fish. Manag.* **1985**, *5*, 330–339. [CrossRef]
5. Enders, E.C.; Scruton, D.A.; Clarke, K.D. The "Natural flow paradigm" and Atlantic salmon-moving from concept to practice. *Rivers Res. Appl.* **2009**, *25*, 2–15. [CrossRef]
6. Hudon, C. Impact of water level fluctuations on St. Lawrence River aquatic vegetation. *Can. J. Fish. Aquat. Sci.* **1997**, *54*, 2853–2865. [CrossRef]
7. Merritt, D.M.; Scott, M.L.; Poff, N.L.; Auble, G.T.; Lytle, D.A. Theory, methods and tools for determining environmental flows for riparian vegetation : Riparian vegetation-flow response guilds. *Freshw. Biol.* **2010**, *55*, 206–225. [CrossRef]
8. Nilsson, C.; Svedmark, M. Basic principles and ecological consequences of changing water regimes: Riparian plant communities. *Environ. Manag.* **2002**, *30*, 468–480. [CrossRef]
9. Petts, G.E. *Impounded Rivers: Perspective for Ecological Management*; John Wiley & Sons: New York, NY, USA, 1984.
10. Poff, N.L.; Zimmerman, K.H. Ecological responses to altered flow regimes: A literature review to inform the science and management of environmental flows. *Freshw. Biol.* **2010**, *55*, 194–205. [CrossRef]
11. Riis, T.; Hawes, I. Relationships between water level fluctuations and vegetation diversity in shallow water of New Zealand lakes. *Aquat. Bot.* **2002**, *74*, 133–148. [CrossRef]
12. Richter, B.D.; Richter, H.E. Prescribing flood regimes to sustain riparian ecosystems along meandering rivers. *Conserv. Biol.* **2000**, *14*, 1467–1478. [CrossRef]
13. Assani, A.A.; Simard, É.; Gravel, É.; Ibrahim, G.; Campeau, S. The impact of "Man-Made Hydrological drought" on plant species abundance in the low-flow channel downstream from the Matawin dam, Quebec. *Water* **2013**, *5*, 875–892. [CrossRef]
14. Larned, S.T.; Datry, T.; Arscott, D.B.; Tockner, K. Emerging concepts in temporary-river ecology. *Freshw. Biol.* **2010**, *55*, 717–738. [CrossRef]
15. Assani, A.A.; Quéssy, J.-F.; Mesfioui, M.; Matteau, M. An example of application: The ecological "natural flow regime" paradigm in hydroclimatology. *Adv. Water Resour.* **2010**, *33*, 537–545. [CrossRef]
16. Mazouz, R.; Assani, A.A.; Quessy, J.-F.; Légaré, G. Comparison of the interannual variability of spring heavy floods characteristics of tributaries of the St. Lawrence River in Quebec (Canada). *Adv. Water Resour.* **2012**, *35*, 110–120. [CrossRef]
17. Mazouz, R.; Assani, A.A.; Rodríguez, M.A. Application of redundancy analysis to hydroclimatology: A case study of spring heavy floods in southern Québec (Canada). *J. Hydrol.* **2013**, *496*, 187–194. [CrossRef]
18. Assani, A.A.; Landry, R.; Kinnard, C.; Azouaoui, O.; Demers, C.; Lacasse, K. Comparison of the Spatiotemporal Variability of Temperature, Precipitation, and Maximum Daily Spring Flows in Two Watersheds in Quebec Characterized by Different Land Use. Available online: http://www.hindawi.com/journals/amete/aa/238029/ (accessed on 20 November 2015).

19. Lavigne, M.-P.; Rousseau, A.N.; Turcotte, R.; Laroche, A.-M.; Fortin, J.-P.; Villeneuve, J.-P. Validation and use of a semidistributed hydrological modelling system to predict short-term effects of clear-cutting on a watershed hydrological regime. *Earth Interact.* **2004**, *8*, 1–19. [CrossRef]
20. Muma, M.; Assani, A.A.; Landry, R.; Quessy, J.-F.; Mesfoui, M. Effects of the change from forest to agriculture land use on the spatial variability of summer extreme daily flow characteristics in Southern Quebec (Canada). *J. Hydrol.* **2011**, *407*, 153–163. [CrossRef]
21. Quilbé, R.; Rousseau, A.N.; Moquet, J.-S.; Savary, S.; Ricard, S.; Garbouj, M.S. Hydrological response of watershed to historical land use evolution and future land use scenarios under climate change. *Hydrol. Earth Syst. Sciences* **2008**, *12*, 101–110. [CrossRef]
22. Sylvain, J.-M.; Assani, A.; Landry, R.; Quessy, J.-F.; Kinnard, C. Comparison of the spatio-temporal variability of annual minimum daily extreme flow characteristics as a function of land use and dam management mode in Quebec, Canada. *Water* **2015**, *7*, 1232–1245. [CrossRef]
23. Environnement Canada. Water Survey of Canada. Available online: https://www.ec.gc.ca/rhc-wsc/default.asp? (accessed on 5 May 2013).
24. Assani, A.A.; Landry, R.; Labrèche, M.; Frenette, J.-J.; Gratton, D. Temporal variability of monthly daily extreme water levels in the St. Lawrence river at the Sorel station from 1912 to 2010. *Water* **2014**, *6*, 196–212. [CrossRef]
25. Lombard, F. Rank tests for changepoint problems. *Biometrika* **1987**, *74*, 615–624. [CrossRef]
26. Quessy, J.-F.; Favre, A.-C.; Saïd, M.; Champagne, M. Statistical inference in Lombard's smooth-change model. *Environmetrics* **2011**, *22*, 882–893. [CrossRef]

![forests logo] *forests*

MDPI

Article

Modeling Ecohydrological Processes and Spatial Patterns in the Upper Heihe Basin in China

Bing Gao [1], Yue Qin [2], Yuhan Wang [2], Dawen Yang [2,*] and Yuanrun Zheng [3]

[1]   School of Water Resources and Environment, China University of Geosciences, Beijing 100083, China; gb03@cugb.edu.cn

[2]   State Key Laboratory of Hydroscience and Engineering, Department of Hydraulic Engineering, Tsinghua University, Beijing 100084, China; qiny13@mails.tsinghua.edu.cn (Y.Q.); wangyuha14@mails.tsinghua.edu.cn (Y.W.)

[3]   State Key Laboratory of Vegetation and Environmental Change, Institute of Botany, Chinese Academy of Sciences, Beijing 100093, China; zhengyr@ibcas.ac.cn

*   Correspondence: yangdw@tsinghua.edu.cn; Tel.: +86-10-6279-6976; Fax: +86-10-6279-6971

Academic Editors: Ge Sun and James M. Vose

Received: 29 September 2015; Accepted: 21 December 2015; Published: 25 December 2015

Abstract: The Heihe River is the second largest inland basin in China; runoff in the upper reach greatly affects the socio-economic development in the downstream area. The relationship between spatial vegetation patterns and catchment hydrological processes in the upper Heihe basin has remained unclear to date. In this study, a distributed ecohydrological model is developed to simulate the hydrological processes with vegetation dynamics in the upper Heihe basin. The model is validated by hydrological observations at three locations and soil moisture observations at a watershed scale. Based on the simulated results, the basin water balance characteristics and their relationship with the vegetation patterns are analyzed. The mean annual precipitation and runoff increase with the elevation in a similar pattern. Spatial patterns of the actual evapotranspiration is mainly controlled by the precipitation and air temperature. At the same time, vegetation distribution enhances the spatial variability of the actual evapotranspiration. The highest actual evapotranspiration is around elevations of 3000–3600 m, where shrub and alpine meadow are the two dominant vegetation types. The results show the mutual interaction between vegetation dynamics and hydrological processes. Alpine sparse vegetation and alpine meadow dominate the high-altitude regions, which contribute most to the river runoff, and forests and shrub contribute relatively small amounts of water yield.

Keywords: distributed ecohydrological model; vegetation dynamics; hydrological processes; water balance characteristics

1. Introduction

Vegetation, topography and climate variables interactively influence multi-scale ecohydrological processes in a large catchment. Vegetation patterns are a key factor affecting the water balance and catchment water yield. Previous studies have demonstrated the impact of forest change on river discharge in China [1,2]. However, few studies have addressed the relationship between hydrological processes and vegetation patterns. In particular, the relationship between forest and water in the headwater catchments of arid inland basins remains unclear [3]. In arid inland basins, the river discharge generated from the mountain regions greatly affects the socio-economic development and ecosystem sustainability of the downstream regions. Therefore, understanding the complex relationship between spatial vegetation patterns and hydrological processes is important for integrated river basin management. Hydrological observations and small-scale experiments provide limited information for understanding the spatial patterns of ecohydrological processes in a large river basin [4].

Instead, a physically based distributed model that links ecohydrological processes across scales is needed to analyze the spatial variability of hydrology with vegetation pattern.

In the past few decades, with global climate change and population growth, the water shortage and ecosystem degradation in many river basins have gained increasing concern worldwide. Meanwhile, changes in natural river runoff in the headwater catchments worldwide have been reported in previous studies [5–11]. Because of the less direct influence of human activities in headwater areas, runoff changes are mainly caused by the mutual interactions among climate, vegetation and hydrology. Yang *et al.* [12] reported that climate contributions to river runoff showed a large spatial variation over China, and several studies attempted to attribute runoff change to the impacts of climate and vegetation changes [13–15]. However, vegetation is absent or simply parameterized in traditional hydrological models [16]. It is relatively difficult to evaluate the influence of vegetation change on runoff due to data availability and methodological limitations [17,18]. Therefore, it is important to develop the ecohydrological models for understanding and predicting changes in the regional water availability under the changing environment.

Modeling hydrological processes at the catchment scale requires a flexible distributed scheme to represent the catchment topography, river network and vegetation patterns [19]. Previous studies of distributed hydrological models focused on the representation of the heterogeneity of catchment landscape and physically based descriptions of hydrological processes, such as the Systeme Hydrologique Europeen (SHE) and the Variable Infiltration Capacity (VIC) model [20,21]. Yang *et al.* [22,23] proposed the geomorphology-based hydrological model (GBHM) considering sub-grid parameterization, which has been employed in macroscale studies [24,25] and mesoscale studies [13,14,26,27]. To better simulate the hydrological changes in a catchment, it is necessary to couple the vegetation pattern and vegetation dynamics in hydrological models [19]. Land surface models, such as the second version of the Simple Biosphere model (SiB2) [28], have mainly focused on the role of vegetation in the water-heat-carbon cycle. However, the catchment hydrology was poorly represented in SiB2. Further research embedded the SiB2 into the GBHM and developed a distributed biosphere hydrological model called the Water and Energy Budget-Based Distributed Hydrological Model (WEB-DHM) [29]. A comparative analysis of the WEB-DHM and GBHM has been carried out and indicated that the WEB-DHM could be used to predict streamflow and conduct the water and energy flux estimations [30]. Several land surface models can simulate the cryosphere processes, such as the Community Land Model (CLM) [31]. However, they typically simplify the catchment hydrological processes and cannot accurately simulate streamflow. Several studies attempt to develop physically based models to couple hydrological processes with ecological processes. Tague and Band [32] developed the Regional Hydro-Ecologic Simulation System (RHESSys) to simulate both hydrological processes and vegetation dynamics. However, in RHESSys, the frozen soil process is not considered and the soil temperature is estimated based on the average daily temperature. Maneta and Silverman [33] and Ivanov *et al.* [34] developed spatial distributed models to simulate the water, energy balance and vegetation dynamics. However, the frozen soil is not adequately considered, as there are only two soil thermal layers in this model. Therefore, it is important to develop a distributed model that couples hydrological processes, cryosphere processes and vegetation dynamics.

There are several previous studies focusing on the hydrological modeling in the Heihe River basin. Jia *et al.* [35] applied the water and energy transfer process (WEP) model to simulate and predict the annual runoff changes due to climate and land use changes. Wang *et al.* [36] and Zhang *et al.* [37] applied heat and water coupling models to a small experimental catchment in the upper Heihe basin to test the model applicability in the high, cold mountainous area. Zhou *et al.* [38] chose several modules for the hydrological processes in cold regions and linked them to a catchment hydrological model to improve the hydrological modeling capability in the cold mountainous area. Zang and Liu [39] applied the Soil and Water Assessment Tool (SWAT) in the Heihe basin to analyze the flow trends of green and blue water. Yang *et al.* [19] developed a distributed scheme for ecohydrological modeling in the upper Heihe River. However, this scheme needs further coupling of vegetation dynamics into the hydrological simulation and improvement of the cryosphere hydrological processes. Because of the complexity of ecohydrological processes in the upper Heihe basin, further research to develop a sophisticated ecohydrological model is still ongoing. A major research plan entitled "Integrated research on the ecohydrological processes of the Heihe basin" has been launched by the National Natural Science Foundation of China since 2010 [40]. One of the integrated research projects in this research plan aims to develop a distributed ecohydrological model for the cold mountainous regions of inland basins. With the help of the Heihe Watershed Allied Telemetry Experimental Research (HiWATER), which is a comprehensive ecohydrological experiment in this research plan [4], there are new opportunities for ecohydrological model development in the Heihe basin.

The major objectives of this study are to (1) develop a distributed ecohydrological model by coupling hydrological processes with vegetation dynamics and (2) analyze the relationship between the water balance and vegetation patterns in the upper Heihe basin.

In the following sections, the features of the study area are presented, followed by the data descriptions. The distributed ecohydrological model is then introduced. In the results and discussion section, the model validation is presented, followed by the analysis of water balance characteristics and the spatiotemporal variability of runoff. Finally, the catchment ecohydrological pattern is analyzed from the water balance and its relation to the vegetation distribution.

2. Study Area and Data Used

2.1. The Upper Heihe Basin

Heihe basin is the second largest inland basin in Northwest China. The upper reach of the Heihe River, which is gauged at the Yingluoxia hydrological station (see Figure 1), has a drainage area of 10,005 km^2. The upper Heihe basin generates nearly 70% of the total river runoff, which supplies agricultural irrigation and benefits the social economy development in the middle and lower basin [19,41]. There are two tributaries in the upper Heihe basin, namely, the West Tributary and East Tributary, both of which originate in the Qilian Mountains. The annual precipitation is between 200 mm and 700 mm with highly seasonal variability, and nearly 60% of the total annual rainfall is concentrated in summer from June to September. The upper Heihe basin has an elevation of 1700–5200 m, low temperature and relatively abundant vegetation types [41–44]. The major vegetation types include coniferous forest (*Picea crassifolia* Kom.), shrub (*Potentilla fruticosa* Linn.), steppe (*Stipa purpurea* Griseb), alpine meadow (*Kobresia pygmaea* Clarke), alpine sparse vegetation (*Saussurea medusa* Maxim.), and desert (*Sympegma regelii* Bunge) (see Figure 2).

2.2. Data Used in the Study

Two types of data are used in this study: the first type is the data used to build and run the ecohydrological model, which include the geographic information and climatic forcing data, and the second type is the data used for model validation.

Meteorological observations are available at several stations within the study basin and its surrounding areas, as shown in Figure 1. The data are acquired from the National Meteorological Information Center affiliated with the China Meteorological Administration [45]. The observed meteorological data include daily precipitation, temperature, sunshine hour, wind speed and relative humidity. In this study, daily gridded precipitation is interpolated from the gauge data using the method developed by Shen and Xiong [46]. Other forcing data are interpolated using the inverse distance method. The hourly temperature is estimated from the daily maximum and minimum temperature using a sine curve. Hourly precipitation is estimated from the daily data according to the duration. Duration of precipitation within a day is determined by the precipitation amount estimated from the regional historical records. The starting time of the precipitation in a day is decided randomly and the hourly precipitation is specified using a normal distribution. The wind speed and relative humidity are assumed uniform in a day. The location of glaciers and their areas and volumes are obtained from the first and second glacier inventory datasets of China [47–49], which is downloaded from the Cold and Arid Regions Science Data Center at Lanzhou [50]. Digital elevation data with a resolution of 90 m resolution are downloaded from the Shuttle Radar Topography Mission (SRTM) database [51]. The vegetation map (see Figure 2) is obtained from the Institute of Botany, Chinese Academy of Sciences [52,53]. The leaf area index (LAI) is estimated from the remote sensing data by Fan [54]. The soil map of Heihe basin is produced by the second national soil survey [55]. We use the van Genuchten model to represent the retention curve of soil water. The soil water parameters used in this study, including the saturated hydraulic conductivity, residual soil moisture, saturated soil moisture, and parameters α and n in the van Genuchten model, are provided by the China soil dataset developed by Dai *et al.* [56]. The spatial resolution of this dataset is 1 km.

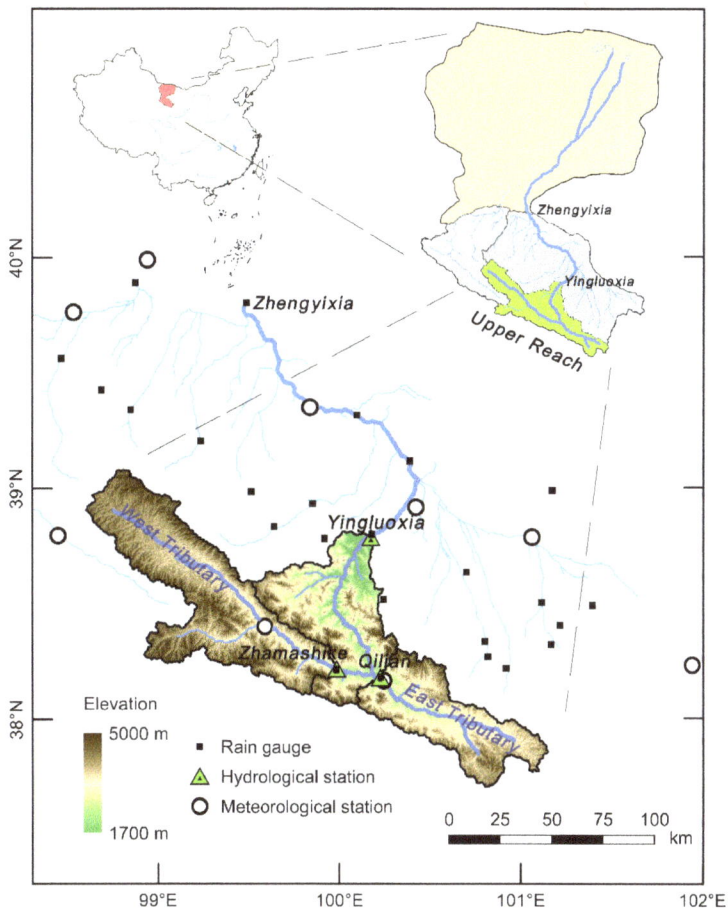

Figure 1. Location and topography of the upper Heihe basin.

To validate the runoff simulation, the stream discharge data are obtained from the Hydrology and Water Resources Bureau of Gansu Province. Soil moisture measured by the wireless sensor network (WSN) in the East Tributary is obtained from the HiWATER [57,58]. The actual evapotranspiration dataset estimated by remote sensing is available in the study basin at a 1 km spatial resolution and monthly temporal scale [59,60], which is used for comparison with the simulated result.

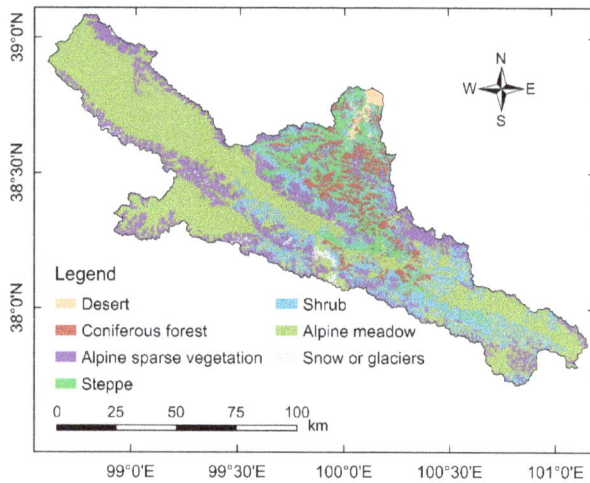

Figure 2. Vegetation map of the upper Heihe basin.

3. Distributed Ecohydrological Model

3.1. Representation of the Landscape

The distributed scheme used to develop the ecohydrological model is originally from the geomorphology-based hydrological model (GBHM) [61–64] and was improved by Yang *et al.* [19] for ecohydrological modeling. The distributed ecohydrological model developed in this study is called the geomorphology-based ecohydrological model (hereafter referred to as the GBEHM). The major development in the GBEHM includes replacing the evapotranspiration estimation from the Penman-Monteith equation to a simple biosphere model used in SiB2 [65] and adding an energy balance based module for simulating the cryosphere hydrological processes.

A grid system with a resolution of 1 km × 1 km is used to discretize the study catchment, and the river network is extracted from the 1-km digital elevation model (DEM), by which the study catchment is divided into 461 sub-catchments. The main rivers of 461 sub-catchments are used to represent the streamflow pathway of the study catchment, and the Horton-Strahler ordering system is used to define the flow routing sequence. The mean terrain properties (slope length and gradient) and a particular soil type are assigned to each 1-km grid and the area ratios of vegetation types are determined for each grid.

Furthermore, each 1-km grid cell is represented by a number of topographically similar "hillslope-valley" systems. Length, gradient and aspect of the hillslope are estimated from the 90-m DEM and averaged on the 1-km grid [19]. The hillslopes within a 1-km grid are grouped according to vegetation type. The vertical structure of a hillslope is then subdivided into vegetation canopy, soil and bedrock.

3.2. Simulation of Ecohydrological Processes

Hillslope is the basic unit of ecohydrological simulation in the GBEHM, in which vegetation dynamics are coupled with the hillslope hydrological processes. The descriptions of hydrological processes, which mainly include the transfer of energy, water and carbon dioxide in the soil-plant-atmosphere continuum, are especially designed for better simulation in the cryosphere.

During the growing season, the photosynthesis process of vegetation is simulated together with canopy energy transfer and canopy evapotranspiration. The radiation transfer in the vegetation canopy layer includes interception, reflection, transmission and absorption and is described by the same scheme in SiB2 [28,66]. The energy balance equation in the canopy layer is expressed as [28]

$$C\frac{\partial T_c}{\partial t} = R_n - H - \lambda E - \xi \tag{1}$$

where C is the effective heat capacity of the canopy ($J \cdot m^{-2} \cdot K^{-1}$), T_c is the canopy temperature (K), t is the time (s), R_n is the absorbed net radiation ($W \cdot m^{-2}$), H is the sensible heat flux ($W \cdot m^{-2}$), λ is the latent heat of vaporization ($J \cdot kg^{-1}$), E is the evapotranspiration rate ($kg \cdot m^{-2} \cdot s^{-1}$), and ξ is the energy transfer due to water phase change ($W \cdot m^{-2}$), which is caused by the melting/freezing of the snow intercepted by the canopy. Thus, the energy budget is linked with water balance by the evapotranspiration component. The absorbed net radiation is calculated using the radiation transfer model described by Sellers *et al.* [65]. The sensible heat flux of the canopy H is calculated as

$$H = \rho c_p \frac{T_c - T_a}{r_b} \tag{2}$$

where ρ is the air density ($kg \cdot m^{-3}$), c_p is the specific heat of air ($J \cdot K^{-1} \cdot kg^{-1}$), T_c is the canopy temperature (K), T_a is the air temperature (K), and r_b is the bulk canopy boundary layer resistance ($s \cdot m^{-1}$).

The actual evapotranspiration rate of the vegetation layer is influenced by the leaf stomatal conductance, which is related to environmental properties, such as the canopy temperature, carbon dioxide concentration and water vapor in the air. In this study, canopy conductance is estimated as [28]

$$g_c = m\frac{A_c}{C_s}h_s p + bL_T \tag{3}$$

where g_c is the canopy conductance ($m \cdot s^{-1}$), m and b are the empirical coefficients of vegetation types, C_s is the carbon dioxide partial pressure at the leaf surface (Pa), h_s is the relative humidity, p is the atmospheric pressure (Pa), L_T is the total leaf area index ($m^2 \cdot m^{-2}$), and A_c is the canopy photosynthesis rate ($mol \cdot m^{-2} \cdot s^{-1}$) and is calculated as [67]

$$A_c = A_{n0}\Pi \tag{4}$$

$$\Pi = FPAR/k \tag{5}$$

where A_{n0} is the net assimilation rate for the leaves at the top of the canopy ($mol \cdot m^{-2} \cdot s^{-1}$), FPAR is the fractional interception of photosynthetically active radiation, and k is the time-mean extinction coefficient for photosynthetically active radiation. The net assimilation rate of the leaf is calculated as

$$A_n = A - R_d \tag{6}$$

where A_n is the leaf net assimilation rate ($mol \cdot m^{-2} \cdot s^{-1}$), A is the leaf photosynthetic rate ($mol \cdot m^{-2} \cdot s^{-1}$), and R_d is the leaf respiration rate ($mol \cdot m^{-2} \cdot s^{-1}$). A and R_d are estimated by the functions of the maximum catalytic capacity of the photosynthetic enzyme (V_{max}), canopy temperature and other environmental factors [28,68,69]. Details about the calculation of g_c, A and R_d were given by Sellers *et al.* [28]. Based on the canopy conductance g_c, the canopy transpiration rate is expressed as [28]

$$\lambda E_c = \left[\frac{e^*(T_c) - e_a}{1/g_c + 2r_b}\right]\frac{\rho c_p}{\gamma}(1 - W_c) \tag{7}$$

where E_c is the canopy transpiration rate ($kg \cdot m^{-2} \cdot s^{-1}$), e^* is the saturation vapor pressure (Pa), e_a is the vapor pressure in the canopy (Pa), r_b is the canopy boundary layer resistance ($s \cdot m^{-1}$), ρ is the density of air ($kg \cdot m^{-3}$), c_p is the specific heat of air ($J \cdot kg^{-1} \cdot K^{-1}$), and γ is the psychrometric constant

(Pa·K^{-1}), W_c is the canopy wetness-snow cover fraction, and the other parameters are the same as in Equations (1) and (3). The soil evaporation rate E_g of the surface soil layer and the evaporation rate of the canopy interception E_i are calculated using the same methods in SiB2 [28]. E_g and E_i are added to E_c as the total actual evapotranspiration over the hillslope unit.

In the non-growing season, ecohydrological simulation focuses on the cryosphere hydrological processes, which mainly include the snow melting process, soil freezing and thawing process, and glacier melting process. We use a similar scheme as in the Community Land Model version 4.0 (*i.e.*, CLM4.0) [31] to represent the heat transfer in snow and frozen soil:

$$c\frac{\partial T_s}{\partial t} = \frac{\partial}{\partial z}\left[K_T\frac{\partial T_s}{\partial z}\right] \tag{8}$$

where c is the volumetric snow/soil heat capacity (J·m^{-3}·K^{-1}), T_s is the temperature (K) of the snow/soil layers, z is the vertical depth of snow/soil (m), and K_T is the thermal conductivity (W·m^{-1}·K^{-1}). Equation (8) solves the snow/soil temperature with the boundary condition as the heat flux into the top surface layer of the snow/soil and zero heat flux at the bottom of the soil column. The surface layer heat flux from the atmosphere is expressed as

$$h = S_g - L_g - H_g - \lambda E_g \tag{9}$$

where h is the upper boundary heat flux into the snow/soil layer (W·m^{-2}), S_g is the solar radiation absorbed by the top layer (W·m^{-2}), L_g is the long-wave radiation absorbed by the ground (W·m^{-2}), H_g is the sensible heat flux from the ground (W·m^{-2}), and λE_g is the latent heat flux from the ground (W·m^{-2}).

After solving Equation (8), the soil or snow layer temperature is evaluated to determine whether the phase change will take place [31]. For the soil or snow layers, melting takes place under the condition of

$$T_i > T_f \text{ and } W_{ice} > 0. \tag{10}$$

For the snow layers, freezing takes place under the condition of

$$T_i < T_f \text{ and } W_{liq} > 0 \tag{11}$$

and for the soil layers, freezing takes place under the condition of

$$T_i < T_f \text{ and } W_{liq} > W_{liq,max.} \tag{12}$$

In Equations (10)–(12), T_i is the temperature of the soil or snow layers (K), T_f is the freezing temperature of water (K), W_{ice} is the mass of ice in the soil or snow layers (kg·m^{-2}), W_{liq} is the mass of liquid water in soil or snow layers (kg·m^{-2}), and $W_{liq,max}$ is the maximum mass of supercooled soil water, which is the liquid water that coexists with the ice (kg·m^{-2}). The phase change rate is determined by the energy excess (or deficit) needed to change the temperature of soil or snow layers (T_i) to the freezing temperature (T_f). If the melting criteria in Equation (10) is met and energy excess is greater than zero, then the ice mass is calculated by [31]

$$W_{ice}^{n+1} = W_{ice}^n - \frac{U_i\Delta t}{L_f} \tag{13}$$

where W_{ice}^{n+1} is the ice mass after the phase change (kg·m^{-2}), W_{ice}^n is the ice mass before the phase change (kg·m^{-2}), $n + 1$ and n refer to the time steps, U_i is the energy excess (W·m^{-2}), Δt is the length of time step (s), and L_f is the latent heat of ice fusion (J·kg^{-1}). If the freezing criteria in

Equations (11) or (12) is met and energy excess is less than zero, then the ice mass in the snow layers is adjusted by

$$W_{ice}^{n+1} = \min\left(W_{ice}^{n} + W_{liq}^{n}, W_{ice}^{n} - \frac{U_i \Delta t}{L_f}\right).$$ (14)

The ice mass in the soil layers is adjusted by

$$W_{ice}^{n+1} = \begin{cases} \min(W_{ice}^{n} + W_{liq}^{n} - W_{liq,max}, W_{ice}^{n} - \frac{U_i \Delta t}{L_f}) & W_{ice}^{n} + W_{liq}^{n} \geqslant W_{liq,max} \\ 0 & W_{ice}^{n} + W_{liq}^{n} < W_{liq,max} \end{cases}$$ (15)

and the mass of liquid water is adjusted by

$$W_{liq}^{n+1} = W_{liq}^{n} + W_{ice}^{n} - W_{ice}^{n+1}$$ (16)

where W_{liq}^{n+1} and W_{liq}^{n} are the mass of liquid water after and before the phase change (kg·m^{-2}), respectively, in Equations (14)–(16), and the other parameters are the same as in Equation (13). Moreover, glacier melting is simulated using the degree-day model [70,71].

The surface runoff is from the infiltration excess and saturation excess calculated by solving Richards' equation using an implicit finite difference method. The surface runoff flows through the hillslope into the stream via kinematic wave. The groundwater aquifer is treated as an individual storage corresponding to each grid. The exchange between the groundwater and river water is considered as steady flow and calculated using Darcy's law [64]. The runoff generated from the grid is the lateral inflow into the river of the sub-catchment. The flow routing in the river network of the whole study catchment is solved using the kinematic wave approach:

$$\begin{cases} \frac{\partial A}{\partial t} + \frac{\partial Q}{\partial x} = q \\ Q = \frac{S_0^{1/2}}{n_r \cdot p^{2/3}} A^{5/3} \end{cases}$$ (17)

where Q is the discharge (m^3·s^{-1}), t is the time (s), x is distance along the river (m), A is the area of the cross-section (m^2), q is the lateral inflow to the river from the hillslope (m^3·s^{-1}), S_0 is the slope of the river bed, n_r is the roughness of the river bed, and p is the wetting perimeter of cross-section (m). Equation (17) is solved using a nonlinear explicit finite difference method and Newton's iteration scheme. The time step of the GBEHM model is one hour.

3.3. Model Calibration and Performance Evaluation Metrics

Most model parameters are estimated from field observations or remote sensing data, and some vegetation parameters are specified from previous studies [19]. The major parameters related to vegetation type are listed in Table 1. Considering the equilibration time for the hydrological state variables (e.g., soil moisture, soil temperature, groundwater table), a warm-up run of the model in the period of 1999–2000 is used to update the model state variables. We perform our analysis in the period from 2001 to 2012. The Nash-Sutcliffe efficiency (NSE) coefficient and relative error (RE) are used to evaluate the model performance.

Table 1. Major parameters related to vegetation and soil types in the geomorphology-based ecohydrological model (GBEHM).

	Coniferous Forest	Shrub	Steppe	Alpine Meadow	Alpine Sparse Vegetation	Desert
Dominant species	*Picea crassifolia* Kom.	*Potentilla fruticosa* Linn.	*Stipa purpurea* Griseb	*Kobresia pygmaea* Clarke	*Saussurea medusa* Maxim.	*Sympegma regelii* Bunge
Root depth (m)	2.0	1.0	0.4	0.4	0.1	0.0
Surface storage (mm)	30.0	25.0	10.0	15.0	15.0	5.0
Leaf reflectance to visible light	0.105	0.105	0.105	0.105	0.105	—
Leaf reflectance to near-infrared radiation	0.35	0.58	0.58	0.58	0.58	—
Leaf transmittance to visible light	0.05	0.07	0.07	0.07	0.07	—
Leaf transmittance to near-infrared radiation	0.10	0.25	0.25	0.25	0.25	—
Maximum Rubsico capacity of top leaf (10^{-5} mol·m^{-2}·s^{-1})	6.0	6.0	3.3	3.3	3.0	—
Intrinsic quantum efficiency (mol·mol^{-1})	0.08	0.08	0.05	0.05	0.05	—
Mean (standard deviation) of saturated hydraulic conductivity (mm·hour^{-1})	18.71 (7.86)	20.32 (6.64)	18.59 (8.89)	24.64 (9.83)	25.23 (6.48)	11.18 (5.87)
Mean (standard deviation) of the saturated soil moisture content (cm^3·cm^{-3})	0.470 (0.010)	0.465 (0.009)	0.468 (0.011)	0.465 (0.014)	0.458 (0.011)	0.475 (0.033)
Mean (standard deviation) of the residual soil moisture content (cm^3·cm^{-3})	0.100 (0.002)	0.100 (0.001)	0.100 (0.001)	0.096 (0.019)	0.099 (0.005)	0.100 (0.000)
Mean (standard deviation) of n in van Genuchten Model	1.195 (0.011)	1.205 (0.019)	1.197 (0.012)	1.205 (0.023)	1.215 (0.022)	1.187 (0.005)
Mean (standard deviation) of α in van Genuchten Model	0.020 (0.003)	0.021 (0.003)	0.021 (0.003)	0.022 (0.004)	0.022 (0.004)	0.017 (0.003)

4. Results and Discussion

4.1. Model Validation

The model has been validated using the soil moisture measured in the East Tributary of Heihe River, streamflow discharge observed at three hydrological stations (Figure 1) and actual evapotranspiration estimated from the remote sensing observations.

At the catchment scale, the model is validated using the streamflow and spatial distribution of observed soil moisture. Figure 3 illustrates the monthly river discharge of the Yingluoxia, Zhamashike and Qilian hydrological stations, which are located at the outlet of upper Heihe River, the West Tributary and the East Tributary, respectively. The simulated streamflow generally shows a good agreement with the observed one. The NSE values for the three observation stations are 0.77, 0.80 and 0.67, respectively, and the absolute values of RE are smaller than 10%. The distributed soil moisture simulation of the top 5-cm layer is compared with the WSN observation at 4 cm from the surface of the HiWATER in the East Tributary of the upper Heihe basin. A comparison of the simulations and observations for the monthly averaged soil moisture over the East Tributary is shown in Figure 4. The areal average values of the simulated and observed soil moistures are highly similar at 0.41 and 0.40 in August, 0.40 and 0.39 in September, and 0.31 and 0.29 in October, respectively. The simulated soil moisture generally captures the spatial pattern of the observed soil moisture. However, the details need to be checked carefully in future research.

In addition, the simulated actual evapotranspiration (ET) is compared with the remote sensing-based estimation. Figure 5 illustrates the comparison of annual average ET between the model simulation and remote sensing-based estimation in the study catchment in the 2001–2012 period [59,60]. Both of the estimations have close long-term basin average ETs and similar spatial patterns over the study catchment. The areal average ET is 310.8 mm for the model simulation and 306.7 mm for the remote sensing-based estimation. However, the remote sensing-based estimation shows a higher spatial variability than the GBEHM simulation. The remote sensing-based estimation mainly considers the energy balance, and the land surface roughness plays an important role. In addition, the ecohydrological model considers both energy and water balances when estimating the actual evapotranspiration, in which vegetation plays an important role. Vegetation may re-distribute the precipitation and moderate the spatial variability of soil moisture and evapotranspiration.

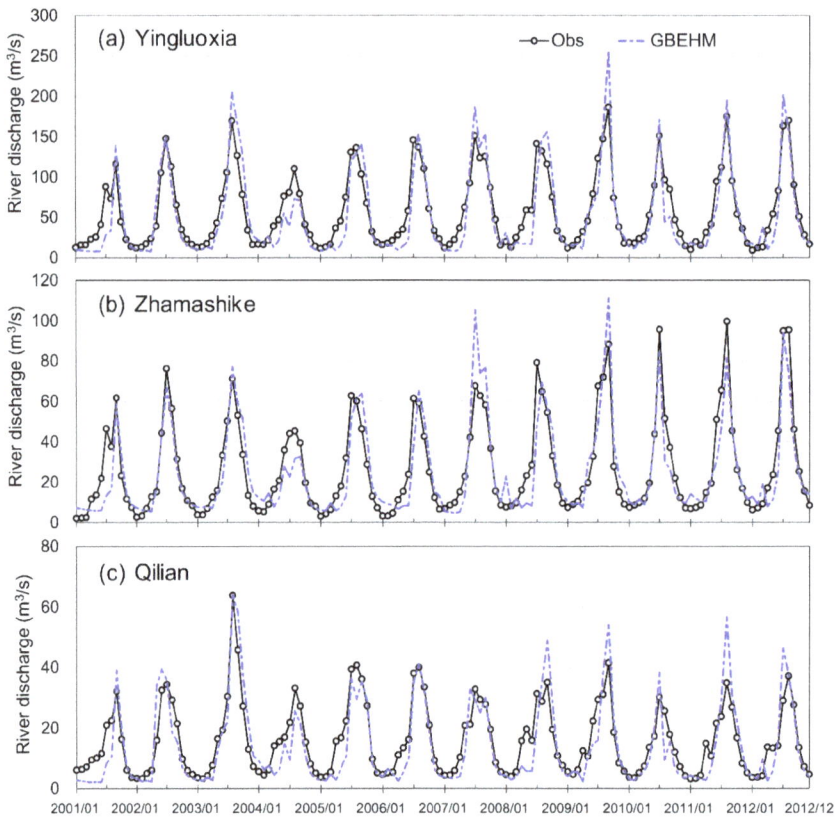

Figure 3. Comparison of the monthly observed and simulated river discharge at the three hydrological stations: (**a**) Yingluoxia; (**b**) Zhamashike; and (**c**) Qilian, in the 2001–2012 period.

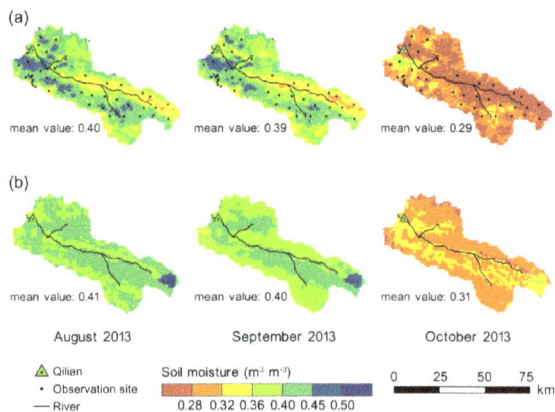

Figure 4. Spatial distributions of monthly average soil moisture ($m^3 \cdot m^{-3}$) in the East Tributary: (**a**) observed soil moisture at 4 cm from the surface and (**b**) simulated soil moisture of the top 5-cm layer.

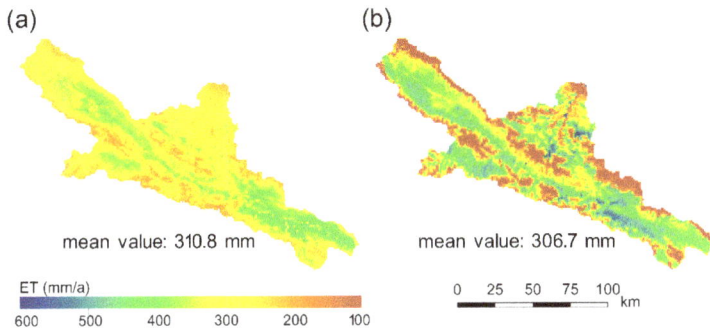

Figure 5. Comparison of the annual average evapotranspiration between the (**a**) GBEHM simulation and (**b**) remote sensing-based estimation during the 2001–2012 period [59].

4.2. Water Balance Characteristics and Spatio-Temporal Variability of Runoff

Based on the simulation, the annual average water balance during 2001–2012 is calculated for the East and West Tributaries and the entire catchment, and the results are given in Table 2. For the upper Heihe basin, the annual average precipitation, actual evapotranspiration (ET) and runoff are 479.9 mm, 310.8 mm and 169.0 mm, respectively. Comparing the water balance in the East and West Tributaries, the East Tributary has higher actual ET and runoff due to its higher precipitation. However, the West Tributary has a larger runoff ratio compared to the East Tributary due to the higher altitudes and relatively larger areas of glaciers.

Table 2. Water balance for the East and West Tributaries and the entire catchment during the 2001–2012 period.

Catchment	Drainage Area (km²)	Precipitation (mm/a)	Actual ET (mm/a)	Runoff (mm/a)	Runoff Ratio
East Tributary	2457	529.8	344.9	186.9	0.35
West Tributary	4586	485.3	304.8	178.3	0.37
Entire catchment	10,005	479.9	310.8	169.0	0.35

The seasonal characteristics of water balance for the East and West Tributaries and the entire catchment are also estimated and are shown in Table 3. In general, the East and West Tributaries and the entire catchment show similar seasonal patterns. For the entire catchment, the precipitation in winter (from December to February) is only 11.5 mm, and the actual evapotranspiration (ET) and runoff is also rather small (6.2 mm and 8.9 mm, respectively). The precipitation in spring (from March to May) is 81.4 mm, which is lower than the sum of the actual ET (66.0 mm) and runoff (19.3 mm). This implies that the runoff in spring is generated from not only precipitation but also snow and glacier melting. This characteristic is more obvious for the West Tributary due to the relatively larger area of glaciers (see Figure 2). As the glacier area is relatively small (less than 1% of the basin area), the contribution of glacier melting to river discharge in summer and autumn is quite low. In summer (from June to August), the precipitation is 281.6 mm, which is larger than the total of the actual ET (180.1 mm) and runoff (78.3 mm). This result implies that precipitation recharges the soil water and groundwater in summer. In autumn (from September to November), the precipitation is 105.4 mm for the entire basin, and it is lower than the total of the actual ET (58.5 mm) and runoff (62.5 mm). This result implies that the runoff is generated from the precipitation and also from the soil water and groundwater storage.

Table 3. Seasonal water balance for the East and West Tributaries and the entire catchment during the 2001–2012 period.

Season	Water Balance Components	East Tributary	West Tributary	Whole Catchment
Spring (Mar.–May)	Precipitation (mm/a)	98.2	76.8	81.4
	Actual ET (mm/a)	71.1	64.2	66.0
	Runoff (mm/a)	19.0	18.2	19.3
Summer (Jun.–Aug.)	Precipitation (mm/a)	297.6	294.3	281.6
	Actual ET (mm/a)	201.8	176.5	180.1
	Runoff (mm/a)	83.8	80.2	78.3
Autumn (Sep.–Nov.)	Precipitation (mm/a)	124.8	100.3	105.4
	Actual ET (mm/a)	65.6	56.3	58.5
	Runoff (mm/a)	70.8	63.7	62.5
Winter (Dec.–Feb.)	Precipitation (mm/a)	9.2	13.9	11.5
	Actual ET (mm/a)	6.2	6.3	6.2
	Runoff (mm/a)	13.2	16.6	8.9

4.3. Spatial Pattern of Water Balance and Relation to Vegetation

To better understand the ecohydrological pattern in the upper Heihe basin, the spatial distributions of the water balance components are further analyzed, including the precipitation, evapotranspiration (ET), runoff and soil moisture in the top one meter during the vegetation growing season from May to October, based on a 30-year model simulation during 1981–2010. Figure 6 shows that annual precipitation and runoff have a similar spatial pattern, annual actual evapotranspiration has a similar pattern with the soil moisture of the top layer in the growing season. The mean soil moisture values are relatively high (0.22–0.41) because of the selected wet season and possible uncertainties of soil water parameters. As shown in Figure 6a, annual precipitation over the study catchment ranges from 220 mm to 630 mm, and the East Tributary has the highest annual precipitation. Comparing Figure 6b with Figure 2, the areas with relatively high ET correspond to the two major vegetation types, namely, steppe and alpine meadow. Figure 6b illustrates that ET has a similar pattern in the East and West Tributaries corresponding with the distribution of alpine meadow vegetation. However, the steep and narrow valley area along the main stream (*i.e.*, downstream of the junction of East and West Tributaries) has relatively low ET and low soil moisture due to the lower precipitation, and this is also related to the steep hillslope and sparse vegetation. In general, the spatial distribution of runoff is mainly controlled by the precipitation and also affected by the topography and vegetation.

The area percentage of each vegetation type is calculated at a 200-m elevation interval in the basin. Accordingly, the water balance components (*i.e.*, annual precipitation, ET and runoff) are also calculated in the same elevation intervals. Figure 7 shows the distributions of vegetation types, annual precipitation, ET and runoff along with the elevation. The vegetation areas of the four major vegetation types (namely, steppe, shrub, coniferous forest and alpine meadow) increase with altitude in the elevation range of 1700–3000 m. Vegetation coverage increases with elevation in the order of steppe, shrub, coniferous forest and alpine meadow. Desert dominates the lowest elevation area, and alpine sparse vegetation dominates the highest elevation area. This spatial vegetation pattern is closely related to the changes in precipitation and temperature along the elevation.

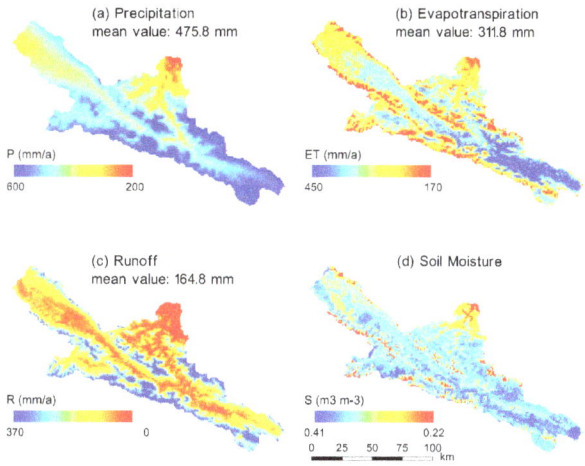

Figure 6. Spatial distributions of the mean values of (**a**) annual precipitation; (**b**) annual evapotranspiration; (**c**) annual runoff and (**d**) growing season soil moisture of the top 1 m during 1981–2010.

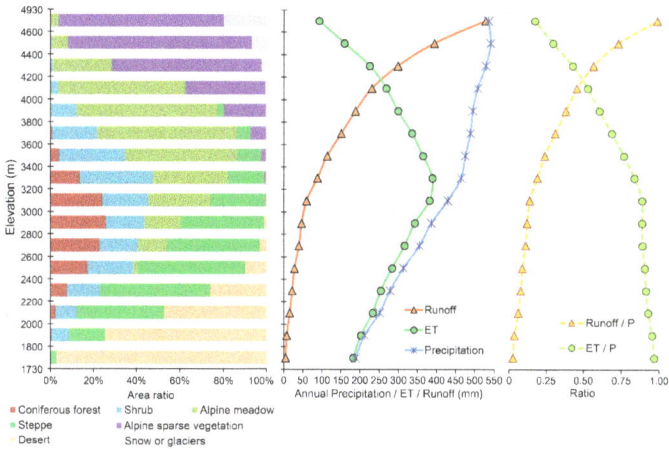

Figure 7. Changes in vegetation, annual average precipitation, evapotranspiration (ET), runoff, runoff/P, and ET/P ratios along with elevation during 1981–2010.

Precipitation and runoff have a similar pattern, both increasing with elevation. The actual evapotranspiration shares a similar pattern with the four major vegetation types (*i.e.*, steppe, shrub, coniferous forest and alpine meadow) along the elevation. Actual evapotranspiration increases with elevation when the elevation is lower than 3000 m. The highest actual evapotranspiration is at the elevations of 3000–3600 m, where shrub and alpine meadow are the dominant vegetation types. Previous research has found that during the growing season, vegetation cover is the densest in the elevation range of 3200–3400 m in the Qilian Mountains [44]. This implies that vegetation dynamics are most intensive in the elevation range of 3200–3400 m. When elevation is higher than 3400 m, actual evapotranspiration gradually decreases and vegetation dynamics gradually weaken due to the decreasing temperature. The region with elevation above 4200 m has the highest runoff depth due to high precipitation and lower evapotranspiration. Glacier melting is also a reason for the high runoff depth. Regarding the annual water balance characteristics, the regions with elevations lower than 3200 m are water limited. In these regions, actual evapotranspiration and vegetation growth are controlled by water availability (precipitation). The regions with elevation higher than 3400 m are temperature/energy limited. In these regions, actual evapotranspiration and vegetation growth are mainly controlled by temperature, and the actual evapotranspiration decreases with increasing elevation. Vegetation grows best and the actual evapotranspiration has the highest value in the region with elevations ranging from 3200 to 3400 m. The above spatial patterns of vegetation and water balance components confirm that climate variability has a significant effect on ecohydrological patterns in the high mountainous region.

The water balance of the three different elevation intervals of the East Tributary and West Tributary are calculated and shown in Table 4. The water balance (actual ET and runoff) differs among vegetation types in each elevation interval where the precipitation is close. Both of the runoff depth and runoff ratio for the coniferous forest is less than other vegetation types within the same elevation interval. This implies that vegetation type enhanced the differences in water balance in addition to the climate variability.

Table 4. Water balance in different elevation intervals of the East Tributary and West Tributary during the 2001–2012 period.

East Tributary						
Elevation Interval and the Area	Major Vegetation Types	Area Ratio	Precipitation (mm/a)	Actual ET (mm/a)	Runoff Depth (mm/a)	Runoff Ratio
2800–2999 m (89 km^2)	Shrub	16%	413.2	371.1	39.1	0.09
	Steppe	22%	410.9	358.0	50.9	0.12
	Coniferous forest	12%	402.0	376.7	25.3	0.06
	Alpine meadow	51%	395.0	359.5	37.8	0.10
3400–3599 m (458 km^2)	Shrub	42%	498.0	428.4	75.9	0.15
	Steppe	2%	460.1	413.8	50.3	0.11
	Coniferous forest	1%	468.9	406.6	61.9	0.13
	Alpine meadow	52%	513.4	439.6	78.1	0.15
4200–4399 m (78 km^2)	Alpine meadow	8%	564.4	400.9	170.0	0.30
	Alpine sparse vegetation	87%	606.0	299.6	307.8	0.51
West Tributary						
Elevation interval and the area	Major vegetation types	Area ratio	Precipitation (mm/a)	Actual ET (mm/a)	Runoff depth (mm/a)	Runoff ratio
3000–3199 m (123 km^2)	Shrub	24%	436.5	381.1	53.2	0.12
	Steppe	12%	439.6	398.6	37.7	0.09
	Coniferous forest	13%	450.8	421.9	34.1	0.08
	Alpine meadow	51%	418.5	383.8	36.0	0.09
3400–3599 m (590 km^2)	Shrub	18%	447.5	384.4	68.8	0.15
	Steppe	2%	466.6	401.5	68.3	0.15
	Coniferous forest	1%	458.1	402.5	56.4	0.12
	Alpine meadow	78%	437.8	384.4	65.6	0.15
4200–4399 m (634 km^2)	Alpine meadow	35%	458.4	337.3	129.7	0.28
	Alpine sparse vegetation	60%	526.8	264.8	259.0	0.49

The water balance of the entire catchment for each vegetation type is also calculated and shown in Table 5, which is the result of the combined effects of climate and vegetation. Because the annual precipitation increases with elevation and different vegetation types grow at different elevations, the annual precipitation of alpine meadow, alpine sparse vegetation and shrub are 488.5 mm, 547.3 mm and 495.9 mm, respectively, which are higher than those of coniferous forest (402.1 mm) and steppe (396.7 mm). The annual average actual evapotranspiration (ET) of coniferous forest, shrub, steppe and alpine meadow ranges from 331.5 mm to 355.0 mm, whereas the actual ET of alpine sparse vegetation is relatively lower (237.2 mm). Table 5 shows that the annual runoff depth varies for different vegetation types. Alpine meadow and alpine sparse vegetation have higher annual runoff (147.8 mm and 310.1 mm, respectively) than forest and steppe (70.5 mm and 65.2 mm, respectively). The runoff ratios of the four major vegetation types, namely, steppe, shrub, coniferous forest and alpine meadow, range from 0.16 to 0.30, whereas alpine sparse vegetation has higher runoff ratio of close to 0.5 due to the high altitude. The water yield per unit area from different vegetation type is in order of alpine sparse vegetation, alpine meadow, shrub, coniferous forest and steppe. The top three largest vegetation areas are covered by alpine meadow (with an area of 4549 km^2), alpine sparse vegetation (with an area of 2009 km^2) and shrub (with an area of 1652 km^2), which are also located in relatively high-elevation regions. The total runoff amount produced by the top three largest vegetation areas are 6.72 × 10^8 m^3/a (alpine meadow), 6.23 × 10^8 m^3/a (alpine sparse vegetation) and 2.33 × 10^8 m^3/a (shrub) (see Table 5). The runoff amount produced by forests (with area of 561 km^2) is 0.40 × 10^8 m^3/a. The coniferous forest has a small area (561 km^2) and produces a small amount of runoff (0.40 × 10^8 m^3/a).

Figure 8 shows the decadal changes in water balance components. Annual precipitation, actual ET and runoff show similar patterns along the elevation. However, decadal variability of the water balance is also observed. Compared with the 1980s, precipitation decreased and ET increased in the 1990s, which caused a reduction in runoff. However, in the 2000s, precipitation increased in the high-altitude region with elevations above 3600 m, which led to a significant increase in runoff compared to the 1990s.

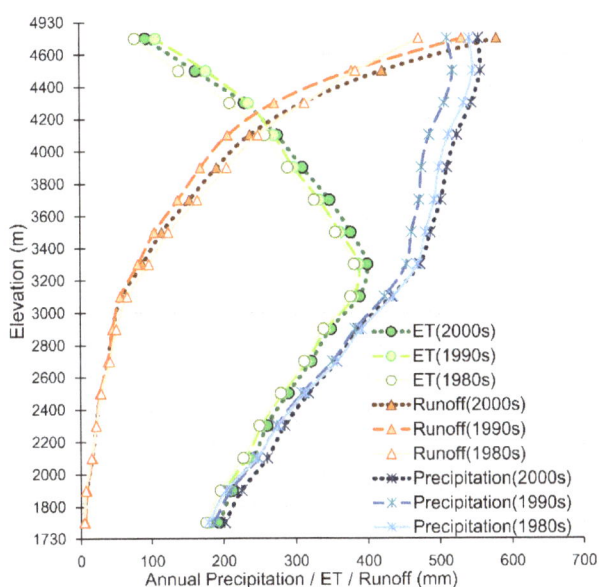

Figure 8. Changes in annual average precipitation, evapotranspiration and runoff along with elevation during the 1980s, 1990s and 2000s.

Table 5. Water balance of the entire catchment for each vegetation type during the 2001–2012 period.

Vegetation Type and Area Covered by Each Type (km^2)		Precipitation (mm/a)	Actual ET (mm/a)	Runoff Depth (mm/a)	Runoff Ratio	Runoff Amount (10^8 m^3/a)
Desert	91	253.1	238.0	15.1	0.06	0.01
Shrub	1652	495.9	355.0	140.9	0.28	2.33
Steppe	1063	396.7	331.5	65.2	0.16	0.69
Coniferous forest	561	402.1	331.6	70.5	0.18	0.40
Alpine meadow	4549	488.5	348.7	147.8	0.30	6.72
Alpine sparse vegetation	2009	547.3	237.2	310.1	0.57	6.23
Snow or glaciers	80	586.7	82.7	846.2	1.44	0.68

4.4. Comparison with Previous Studies in the Same and Similar Regions

In this study, the model simulation shows that the precipitation recharges soil water and groundwater in the summer. This result is consistent with a previous study by Yang *et al.* [72] on the Heihe River. Using the hydrochemistry approach, it is found that the precipitation contributes only slightly to the total surface runoff, instead mainly recharging the sub-surface soil and groundwater.

The interflow and groundwater flow dominate the total runoff. Additionally, Wang *et al.* [73] inferred that as the air temperature has risen in the Heihe basin during the last 50 years, the active layer of frozen soil has increased in thickness. This may lead to the increase of both soil water storage and interflow and thus change the contribution of each runoff component in the future.

Our study shows that forests contribute only a small amount of the water yield. In a previous study, He *et al.* [3] analyzed the water balance of a small experimental catchment (2.91 km²) in the upper Heihe basin and found that the forests contribute only 3.5% to the total runoff, which is similar to this study. This result is also supported by model simulations. For example, using the Topography Driven Flux Exchange (FLEX-Topo) model, Gao *et al.* [74] report that forest hillslope generates only a small amount of runoff in the upper Heihe basin. Qin *et al.* [75] analyze the water balance components of different landscapes in the upper Heihe basin using the VIC model and find that glaciers contribute 3.57% of the total runoff and that the contribution of forests is also quite small (0.49%). This result also implies that the barren regions contribute most of the total runoff (52.46%) and steppe contributes 34.15% to the total runoff. This is in accordance with our results, as Qin *et al.* [75] consider the steppe and alpine meadow as the same vegetation type and consider regions in high elevation as barren.

Our study shows that the runoff ratio of coniferous forest has the lowest value (0.18) comparing with other vegetation types except the desert in the upper Heihe River basin. This is similar to the findings by Yaseef *et al.* [76], which shows that when precipitation larger than 300 mm ET accounts 85% of precipitation for Aleppo pine forest in Southern Israel. Wang *et al.* [77] analyzed the annual water balance of shrub at a station in the Inner Mongolian Highland Region with elevation of 1300 m and found that ET/P ratio is about 94%, which is higher than the results of the present study because of the differences of elevation and air temperature in the two study areas. Wang *et al.* [78] analyzed the water balance of different vegetation in a small watershed in the Liupan Mountains, Northwest China, based on field measurements. They found that the evaporation rate (ratio of ET to precipitation) was about 60% for grassland, 93% for shrubs, and >95% for forest. This also shows that the forest has the least water yield compared with other vegetation types in the Liupan Mountains.

5. Conclusions

A geomorphology-based ecohydrological model (GBEHM) is developed in the upper Heihe basin, and this model is validated using available observations, including soil moisture, streamflow discharge, and actual evapotranspiration estimated from remote sensing. The catchment water balance characteristics and their spatial-temporal variability are analyzed based on the ecohydrological simulation. The following conclusions can be drawn from the results of this study:

(1)   At the basin scale, the model provides a good simulation of streamflow discharge in the two tributaries and the entire catchment of the study area. It also captures the spatial pattern of soil moisture appropriately. In addition, the simulated actual evapotranspiration and remote sensing-based estimation have close long-term average values and similar spatial patterns over the entire study catchment. The GBEHM may be useful for ecohydrological simulation and prediction in cold high-altitude regions.

(2)   Analysis of the water balance characteristics shows that water balance characteristics are closely related to the altitude and vegetation patterns in the study catchment. Regarding the annual water balance characteristics, the low-altitude regions with elevations below 3200 m are water limited. The actual annual evapotranspiration and vegetation distribution and growth are controlled by water availability (precipitation). Seasonal analysis indicates that river runoffs are mainly in summer and autumn, and runoff in spring is generated from precipitation and snow melt.

(3)   In the upper Heihe basin, the precipitation and runoff share a similar pattern, increasing with elevation. Actual evapotranspiration has a similar pattern with the four major vegetation types (*i.e.*, steppe, shrub, coniferous forest and alpine meadow) along the elevation. The highest actual evapotranspiration is at the elevations of 3000–3600 m, where shrub and alpine meadow are the two dominant vegetation types. Precipitation controls the spatial pattern of annual runoff and

determines the spatial pattern of vegetation together with the air temperature. Climate variability in the high mountainous region has a significant effect on ecohydrological patterns.

(4)   At the same time, vegetation type enhanced the differences in annual runoff and actual evapotranspiration. In the same elevation interval with similar precipitation, differences in the runoff depth (and the actual evapotranspiration) were caused mainly by the vegetation types. For the whole study area, the water yield per unit area from different vegetation types is in order of alpine sparse vegetation, alpine meadow, shrub, coniferous forest and steppe. The three major vegetation types, namely, alpine meadow (with an area of 4549 km^2), alpine sparse vegetation (with an area of 2009 km^2) and shrub (with an area of 1652 km^2), located in relatively higher elevation contribute most of the river runoff.

Several limitations remain in the current study. The GBEHM simulates the vegetation dynamics with the known leaf area index and other vegetation parameters. Further improvement of the model should include carbon partitioning to simulate the vegetation growth. The uncertainty of the model parameters should be assessed to apply this model to other catchments.

Acknowledgments: This research was supported by the major plan of "Integrated Research on the Ecohydrological Processes of the Heihe Basin" (Project Nos. 91225302, 91425303) funded by the National Natural Science Foundation of China (NSFC).

Author Contributions: Dawen Yang conceived and designed the research. Yuanrun Zheng performed the classification of vegetation types. Bing Gao performed the model programming and simulation. Yue Qin and Yuhan Wang analyzed the simulated data. Yue Qin and Bing Gao took the lead in writing the manuscript. All authors contributed to the revision of the final manuscript.

Conflicts of Interest: The authors declare no conflict of interest.

References

1.   Zhou, G.; Wei, X.; Luo, Y.; Zhang, M.; Li, Y.; Qiao, Y.; Liu, H.; Wang, C. Forest recovery and river discharge at the regional scale of Guangdong Province, China. *Water Resour. Res.* **2010**, *46*, 5109–5115. [CrossRef]
2.   Liu, W.; Wei, X.; Liu, S.; Liu, Y.; Fan, H.; Zhang, M.; Yin, J.; Zhan, M. How do climate and forest changes affect long-term streamflow dynamics? A case study in the upper reach of Poyang River basin. *Ecohydrology* **2015**, *8*, 46–57. [CrossRef]
3.   He, Z.B.; Zhao, W.Z.; Liu, H.; Tang, Z.X. Effect of forest on annual water yield in the mountains of an arid inland river basin: A case study in the Pailugou catchment on northwestern China's Qilian Mountains. *Hydrol. Process.* **2012**, *26*, 613–621. [CrossRef]
4.   Li, X.; Cheng, G.D.; Liu, S.M.; Xiao, Q.; Ma, M.G.; Jin, R.; Che, T.; Liu, Q.H.; Wang, W.Z.; Qi, Y.; *et al.* Heihe Watershed Allied Telemetry Experimental Research (HiWATER): Scientific Objectives and Experimental Design. *Bull. Am. Meteorol. Soc.* **2013**, *94*, 1145–1160. [CrossRef]
5.   Chang, H.J.; Jung, I.W. Spatial and temporal changes in runoff caused by climate change in a complex large river basin in Oregon. *J. Hydrol.* **2010**, *388*, 186–207. [CrossRef]
6.   Belmont, P.; Gran, K.B.; Schottler, S.P.; Wilcock, P.R.; Day, S.S.; Jennings, C.; Lauer, J.W.; Viparelli, E.; Willenbring, J.K.; Engstrom, D.R.; *et al.* Large Shift in Source of Fine Sediment in the Upper Mississippi River. *Environ. Sci. Technol.* **2011**, *45*, 8804–8810. [CrossRef] [PubMed]
7.   Taye, M.T.; Ntegeka, V.; Ogiramoi, N.P.; Willems, P. Assessment of climate change impact on hydrological extremes in two source regions of the Nile River Basin. *Hydrol. Earth Syst. Sci.* **2011**, *15*, 209–222. [CrossRef]
8.   Zhou, D.G.; Huang, R.H. Response of water budget to recent climatic changes in the source region of the Yellow River. *Chin. Sci. Bull.* **2012**, *57*, 2155–2162. [CrossRef]
9.   Wu, L.; Long, T.Y.; Liu, X.; Guo, J.S. Impacts of climate and land-use changes on the migration of non-point source nitrogen and phosphorus during rainfall-runoff in the Jialing River Watershed, China. *J. Hydrol.* **2012**, *475*, 26–41. [CrossRef]
10.   Ficklin, D.L.; Stewart, I.T.; Maurer, E.P. Climate Change Impacts on Streamflow and Subbasin-Scale Hydrology in the Upper Colorado River Basin. *PLoS ONE* **2013**, *8*, e71297. [CrossRef] [PubMed]
11.   Cuo, L.; Zhang, Y.X.; Gao, Y.H.; Hao, Z.C.; Cairang, L.S. The impacts of climate change and land cover/use transition on the hydrology in the upper Yellow River Basin, China. *J. Hydrol.* **2013**, *502*, 37–52. [CrossRef]

12. Yang, H.B.; Qi, J.; Xu, X.Y.; Yang, D.W.; Lv, H.F. The regional variation in climate elasticity and climate contribution to runoff across China. *J. Hydrol.* **2014**, *517*, 607–616. [CrossRef]
13. Ma, H.; Yang, D.W.; Tan, S.K.; Gao, B.; Hu, Q.F. Impact of climate variability and human activity on streamflow decrease in the Miyun Reservoir catchment. *J. Hydrol.* **2010**, *389*, 317–324. [CrossRef]
14. Xu, X.Y.; Yang, H.B.; Yang, D.W.; Ma, H. Assessing the impacts of climate variability and human activities on annual runoff in the Luan River basin, China. *Hydrol. Res.* **2013**, *44*, 940–952. [CrossRef]
15. Tang, Y.; Tang, Q.; Tian, F.; Zhang, Z.; Liu, G. Responses of natural runoff to recent climatic variations in the Yellow River basin, China. *Hydrol. Earth Syst. Sci.* **2013**, *17*, 4471–4480. [CrossRef]
16. Peel, M. Hydrology: Catchment vegetation and runoff. *Prog. Phys. Geogr.* **2009**, *33*, 837–844. [CrossRef]
17. Samaniego, L.; Bardossy, A. Simulation of the impacts of land use/cover and climatic changes on the runoff characteristics at the mesoscale. *Ecol. Model.* **2006**, *196*, 45–61. [CrossRef]
18. Marshall, E.; Randhir, T.O. Spatial modeling of land cover change and watershed response using Markovian cellular automata and simulation. *Water Resour. Res.* **2008**, *44*, W044234. [CrossRef]
19. Yang, D.W.; Gao, B.; Jiao, Y.; Lei, H.M.; Zhang, Y.L.; Yang, H.B.; Cong, Z.T. A distributed scheme developed for eco-hydrological modeling in the upper Heihe River. *Sci. China Earth Sci.* **2015**, *58*, 36–45. [CrossRef]
20. Abbott, M.B.; Bathurst, J.C.; Cunge, J.A.; O'connell, P.E.; Rasmussen, J. An introduction to the European Hydrological System—Systeme Hydrologique Europeen, "SHE", 2: Structure of a physically-based, distributed modelling system. *J. Hydrol.* **1986**, *87*, 61–77. [CrossRef]
21. Liang, X.; Lettenmaier, D.P.; Wood, E.F. One-dimensional statistical dynamic representation of subgrid spatial variability of precipitation in the two-layer variable infiltration capacity model. *J. Geophys. Res.* **1996**, *101*, 21403–21422. [CrossRef]
22. Yang, D.W.; Koike, T.; Tanizawa, H. Application of a distributed hydrological model and weather radar observations for flood management in the upper Tone River of Japan. *Hydrol. Process.* **2004**, *18*, 3119–3132. [CrossRef]
23. Yang, D.W.; Li, C.; Ni, G.H.; Hu, H.P. Application of a distributed hydrological model to the Yellow River basin. *Acta Geogr. Sin.* **2004**, *59*, 143–154. (In Chinese)
24. Xu, J.J.; Yang, D.W.; Yi, Y.H.; Lei, Z.D.; Chen, J.; Yang, W.J. Spatial and temporal variation of runoff in the Yangtze River basin during the past 40 years. *Quat. Int.* **2008**, *186*, 32–42. [CrossRef]
25. Cong, Z.T.; Yang, D.W.; Gao, B.; Yang, H.B.; Hu, H.P. Hydrological trend analysis in the Yellow River basin using a distributed hydrological model. *Water Resour. Res.* **2009**, *45*, W00A13. [CrossRef]
26. Valeriano, O.; Koike, T.; Yang, K.; Yang, D.W. Optimal Dam Operation during Flood Season Using a Distributed Hydrological Model and a Heuristic Algorithm. *J. Hydrol. Eng.* **2010**, *15*, 580–586. [CrossRef]
27. Alam, Z.R.; Rahman, M.M.; Islam, A.S. Assessment of Climate Change Impact on the Meghna River Basin using geomorphology based hydrological model (GBHM). In Proceedings of the ICWFM 2011—The 3rd International Conference on Water and Flood Management, Dhaka, Bangladesh, 8–10 January 2011.
28. Sellers, P.J.; Randall, D.A.; Collatz, G.J.; Berry, J.A.; Field, C.B.; Dazlich, D.A.; Zhang, C.; Collelo, G.D.; Bounoua, L. A Revised Land Surface Parameterization (SiB2) for Atmospheric GCMS. Part I: Model Formulation. *J. Clim.* **1996**, *9*, 676–705. [CrossRef]
29. Wang, L.; Koike, T.; Yang, K.; Jackson, T.J.; Bindlish, R.; Yang, D.W. Development of a distributed biosphere hydrological model and its evaluation with the Southern Great Plains Experiments (SGP97 and SGP99). *J. Geophys. Res.* **2009**, *114*. [CrossRef]
30. Wang, L.; Koike, T. Comparison of a distributed biosphere hydrological model with GBHM. *Annu. J. Hydraul. Eng.* **2009**, *53*, 103–108.
31. Oleson, K.W.; Lawrence, D.M.; Bonan, G.B.; Flanner, M.G.; Kluzek, E.; Lawrence, P.J.; Levis, S.; Swenson, S.C.; Thornton, P.E.; Dai, A.G.; et al. *Technical Description of Version 4.0 of the Community Land Model (CLM), NCAR Technical Note*; National Center for Atmospheric Research: Boulder, CO, USA, 2010; p. 257.
32. Tague, C.; Band, L. RHESSys: Regional Hydro-ecologic simulation system: An object-oriented approach to spatially distributed modeling of carbon, water and nutrient cycling. *Earth Interact.* **2004**, *19*, 1–42. [CrossRef]
33. Maneta, M.; Silverman, N. A spatially-distributed model to simulate water, energy and vegetation dynamics using information from regional climate models. *Earth Interact.* **2013**, *17*, 1–44. [CrossRef]
34. Ivanov, V.Y.; Bras, R.L.; Vivoni, E.R. Vegetation-Hydrology Dynamics in Complex Terrain of Semiarid Areas: I. A mechanistic Approach to Modeling Dynamic Feedbacks. *Water Resour. Res.* **2008**, *44*. [CrossRef]

35. Jia, Y.W.; Wang, H.; Yan, D.H. Distributed model of hydrological cycle system in Heihe River basin I Model development and Verification. *J. Hydraul. Eng.* **2006**, *37*, 534–542. (In Chinese).

36. Wang, L.; Koike, T.; Yang, K.; Jin, R.; Li, H. Frozen soil parameterization in a distributed biosphere hydrological model. *Hydrol. Earth Syst. Sci.* **2010**, *14*, 557–571. [CrossRef]

37. Zhang, Y.L.; Cheng, G.D.; Li, X.; Han, X.J.; Wang, L.; Li, H.Y.; Chang, X.L.; Flerchinger, G.N. Coupling of a simultaneous heat and water model with a distributed hydrological model and evaluation of the combined model in a cold region watershed. *Hydrol. Process.* **2013**, *27*, 3762–3776. [CrossRef]

38. Zhou, J.; Pomeroy, J.W.; Zhang, W.; Cheng, G.D.; Wang, G.X.; Chen, C. Simulating cold regions hydrological processes using a modular model in the west of China. *J. Hydrol.* **2014**, *509*, 13–24. [CrossRef]

39. Zang, C.F.; Liu, J.G. Trend analysis for the flows of green and blue water in the Heihe River basin, northwestern China. *J. Hydrol.* **2013**, *502*, 27–36. [CrossRef]

40. Cheng, G.; Li, X.; Zhao, W.; Xu, Z.; Feng, Q.; Xiao, S.; Xiao, H. Integrated study of the water-ecosystem-economy in the Heihe River Basin. *Natl. Sci. Rev.* **2014**, *1*, 413–428. [CrossRef]

41. Chen, Y.; Zhang, D.; Sun, Y.; Liu, X.; Wang, N.; Savenije, H. Water demand management: A case study of the Heihe River Basin in China. *Phys. Chem. Earth* **2005**, *30*, 408–419. [CrossRef]

42. Herzschuh, U.; Kurschner, H.; Mischke, S. Temperature variability and vertical vegetation belt shifts during the last similar to ~50,000 yr in the Qilian Mountains (NE margin of the Tibetan Plateau, China). *Quat. Res.* **2006**, *66*, 133–146. [CrossRef]

43. Wang, P.; Li, Z.Q.; Gao, W.Y. Rapid Shrinking of Glaciers in the Middle Qilian Mountain Region of Northwest China during the Last similar to 50 Years. *J. Earth Sci.* **2011**, *22*, 539–548. [CrossRef]

44. Deng, S.F.; Yang, T.B.; Zeng, B.; Zhu, X.F.; Xu, H.J. Vegetation cover variation in the Qilian Mountains and its response to climate change in 2000–2011. *J. Mt. Sci.* **2013**, *10*, 1050–1062. [CrossRef]

45. National Meteorological Information Center, the China Meteorological Administration. Available online: http://cdc.nmic.cn (accessed on 24 December 2015).

46. Shen, Y.; Xiong, A. Validation and comparison of a new gauge-based precipitation analysis over mainland China. *Int. J. Climatol.* **2015**. [CrossRef]

47. Wu, L.; Li, X. *Dataset of the First Glacier Inventory in China*; Cold and Arid Regions Science Data Center: Lanzhou, China, 2004.

48. Guo, W.; Liu, S.; Yao, X.; Xu, J.; Shangguan, D.; Wu, L.; Zhao, J.; Liu, Q.; Jiang, Z.; Wei, J.; *et al.* *The Second Glacier Inventory Dataset of China (Version 1.0)*; Cold and Arid Regions Science Data Center: Lanzhou, China, 2014.

49. Wei, J.F.; Liu, S.Y.; Guo, W.Q.; Yao, X.J.; Xu, J.L.; Bao, W.J.; Jiang, Z.L. Surface-area changes of glaciers in the Tibetan Plateau interior area since the 1970s using recent Landsat images and historical maps. *Ann. Glaciol.* **2014**, *55*, 213–222. [CrossRef]

50. Cold and Arid Regions Science Data Center at Lanzhou. Available online: http://westdc.westgis.ac.cn (accessed on 24 December 2015).

51. Jarvis, A.; Reuter, H.I.; Nelson, A.; Guevara, E. Hole-filled seamless SRTM data (Version 4). International Centre for Tropical Agriculture. 2008. Available online: http://srtm.csi.cgiar.org (accessed on 31 July 2015).

52. Hou, X. *China Vegetation Map (1:1,000,000)*; Science Press: Beijing, China, 2001. (In Chinese)

53. Zhou, J.H.; Zheng, Y.R. *Vegetation Map of the Upper Heihe Basin V2.0*; Heihe Plan Science Data Center: Lanzhou, China, 2014.

54. Fan, W. *Heihe 1 km LAI Production*; Heihe Plan Science Data Center: Lanzhou, China, 2014.

55. Shi, X.; Yu, D.; Pan, X. A framework for the 1:1,000,000 soil database of China. In Proceedings of the 17th World Congress of Soil Science, Bangkok, Thailand, 14–21 August 2002; pp. 1–5.

56. Dai, Y.J.; Shangguan, W.; Duan, Q.Y.; Liu, B.Y.; Fu, S.H.; Niu, G. Development of a China Dataset of Soil Hydraulic Parameters Using Pedotransfer Functions for Land Surface Modeling. *J. Hydrometeorol.* **2013**, *14*, 869–887. [CrossRef]

57. Jin, R.; Li, X.; Yan, B.P.; Li, X.H.; Luo, W.M.; Ma, M.G.; Guo, J.W.; Kang, J.; Zhu, Z.L.; Zhao, S.J. A Nested Ecohydrological Wireless Sensor Network for Capturing the Surface Heterogeneity in the Midstream Areas of the Heihe River Basin, China. *IEEE Geosci. Remote Sens. Lett.* **2014**, *11*, 2015–2019. [CrossRef]

58. Kang, J.; Jin, R.; Li, X.; Ma, M. *HiWATER: WATERNET Observation Dataset in the Upper Reaches of the Heihe River Basin in 2013*; Cold and Arid Regions Science Data Center: Lanzhou, China, 2014.

59. Wu, B.F. *Monthly Evapotranspiration Datasets (2000–2012) with 1 km Spatial Resolution over the Heihe River Basin;* Heihe Plan Science Data Center: Lanzhou, China, 2013.

60. Wu, B.F.; Yan, N.N.; Xiong, J.; Bastiaanssen, W.; Zhu, W.W.; Stein, A. Validation of ETWatch using field measurements at diverse landscapes: A case study in Hai Basin of China. *J. Hydrol.* **2012**, *436*, 67–80. [CrossRef]

61. Yang, D.W.; Herath, S.; Musiake, K. Development of a geomorphology-based hydrological model for large catchments. *Annu. J. Hydraul. Eng.* **1998**, *42*, 169–174. [CrossRef]

62. Yang, D.W.; Herath, S.; Musiake, K. Comparison of different distributed hydrological models for characterization of catchment spatial variability. *Hydrol. Process.* **2000**, *14*, 403–416. [CrossRef]

63. Yang, D.W.; Herath, S.; Musiake, K. Spatial resolution sensitivity of catchment geomorphologic properties and the effect on hydrological simulation. *Hydrol. Process.* **2001**, *15*, 2085–2099. [CrossRef]

64. Yang, D.W.; Herath, S.; Musiake, K. A hillslope-based hydrological model using catchment area and width functions. *Hydrol. Sci. J.* **2002**, *47*, 49–65. [CrossRef]

65. Sellers, P.J. Canopy reflectance, photosynthesis, and transpiration. *Int. J. Remote Sens.* **1985**, *8*, 1335–1372. [CrossRef]

66. Sellers, P.J.; Mintz, Y.; Sub, Y.C.; Dalcher, A. A Simple Biosphere Model (SiB) for Use within General Circulation Models. *J. Atmos. Sci.* **1986**, *43*, 505–531. [CrossRef]

67. Sellers, P.J.; Berry, J.A.; Collatz, G.J.; Field, C.B.; Hall, F.G. Canopy reflectance, photosynthesis, and transpiration Part III: Are analysis using improved leaf models and a new canopy integration scheme. *Remote Sens. Environ.* **1992**, *42*, 187–216. [CrossRef]

68. Collatz, G.J.; Ball, J.T.; Grivet, C.; Berry, J.A. Physiological and environmental regulation of stomatal conductance, photosynthesis and transpiration: A model that includes a laminar boundary layer. *Agric. For. Meteorol.* **1991**, *54*, 107–136. [CrossRef]

69. Collatz, G.J.; Ribas-Carbo, M.; Berry, J.A. Coupled Photosynthesis-Stomatal Conductance Model for leaves of C4 plants. *Aust. J. Plant Physiol.* **1992**, *19*, 519–538. [CrossRef]

70. Zhang, Y.; Liu, S.Y.; Ding, Y.J. Spatial Variation of Degree-day Factors on the Observed Glaciers in Western China. *Acta Geogr. Sin.* **2006**, *61*, 89–98. (In Chinese) [CrossRef]

71. Gao, X.; Ye, B.S.; Zhang, S.Q.; Qiao, C.J.; Zhang, X.W. Glacier runoff variation and its influence on river runoff during 1961–2006 in the Tarim River Basin, China. *Sci. China Earth Sci.* **2010**, *53*, 880–891. (In Chinese) [CrossRef]

72. Yang, Y.; Xiao, H.; Wei, Y.; Zhao, L.; Zou, S.; Qiu, Y.; Yin, Z. Hydrological processes in the different landscape zones of alpine cold regions in the wet season, combining isotopic and hydrochemical tracers. *Hydrol. Process.* **2012**, *26*, 1457–1466. [CrossRef]

73. Wang, Y.; Yang, D.; Lei, H.; Yang, H. Impact of cryosphere hydrological processes on the river runoff in the upper reaches of Heihe River. *J. Hydraul. Eng.* **2015**, *46*, 1064–1071. (In Chinese)

74. Gao, H.; Hrachowitz, M.; Fenicia, F.; Gharari, S.; Savenije, H. Testing the realism of a topography-driven model (FLEX-Topo) in the nested catchments of the Upper Heihe, China. *Hydrol. Earth Syst. Sci.* **2014**, *18*, 1895–1915. [CrossRef]

75. Qin, J.; Ding, Y.; Wu, J.; Gao, M.; Yi, S.; Zhao, C.; Ye, B.; Li, M.; Wang, S. Understanding the impact of mountain landscapes on water balance in the upper Heihe River watershed in northwestern China. *J. Arid Land* **2013**, *5*, 366–384. [CrossRef]

76. Yaseef, N.R.; Yakir, D.; Rotenberg, E.; Schiller, G.; Cohen, S. Ecohydrology of a semi-arid forest: Partitioning among water balance components and its implications for predicted precipitation changes. *Ecohydrology* **2009**. [CrossRef]

77. Wang, X.; Ronny, B.; Li, X.; Kang, E. Water balance change for a re-vegetated xerophyte shrub area. *Hydrol. Sci. J.* **2004**, *49*, 283–295. [CrossRef]

78. Wang, Y.; Yu, P.; Xiong, W.; Shen, Z.; Guo, M.; Shi, Z.; Du, A.; Wang, L. Water-yield reduction after afforestation and related processes in the semiarid Liupan Mountains, Northwest China. *J. Am. Water Resour. Assoc.* **2008**, *44*, 1086–1097. [CrossRef]

![forests logo] *forests*

MDPI

Article

Influences of Land Use Change on Baseflow in Mountainous Watersheds

Xu-Dong Huang [1], Zhi-Hua Shi [1,2,*], Nu-Fang Fang [2] and Xuan Li [1]

[1]   College of Resources and Environment, Huazhong Agricultural University, Wuhan 430070, China;
      huangxudong269@163.com (X.-D.H.); gstslixuan@163.com (X.L.)
[2]   State Key Laboratory of Soil Erosion and Dryland Farming on the Loess Plateau, Institute of Soil and Water
      Conservation, Chinese Academy of Sciences, Yangling, Shaanxi 712100, China; fnf@ms.iswc.ac.cn
*   Correspondence: shizhihua70@gmail.com; Tel.: +86-27-8728-8249; Fax: +86-27-8767-1035

Academic Editors: Ge Sun and James M. Vose
Received: 18 September 2015; Accepted: 24 December 2015; Published: 6 January 2016

Abstract: It is crucial for effective water resource management in a watershed that the relationship between land use changes and baseflow. This study quantifies the influence of land use changes on the baseflow dynamics using a hydrological model and partial least-squares (PLS) regression in the Upper Du Watershed (8961 km^2), China. Our study suggests that forest can be a major factor with a negative impact on the baseflow. Additionally, farmland and urban land have second-order negative effects on the baseflow dynamics. Baseflow increases when forest is replaced by farmland because the evapotranspiration (ET), associated with baseflow recession, is weaker and shorter in duration in the farmland than in the forest. The conversion of forest to urban land increases baseflow owing to the presence of non-contributing impervious surfaces in urban areas, which prevents the urban land from intercepting the baseflow discharge. These results indicate that the baseflow dynamics are closely associated with varying land use types within a watershed. Thus, this study is intended to provide a deeper understanding of the baseflow processes and useful quantitative information on land use factors in watersheds, enabling more informed decision-making in forest and watershed management.

Keywords: baseflow; land use; forest; farmland; urban land; hydrological model; watershed management

---

1. Introduction

Baseflow is the sustained flow of water that exists between precipitation events; it feeds the water to stream channels in a delayed manner through subsurface pathways [1]. Understanding baseflow is essential for water-supply planning and design, reservoir storage design, managing the maintenance of water for irrigation (both quantity and quality), wildlife conservation and recreation [2]. The magnitude of the baseflow in streams is controlled by many factors, e.g., fluvial geomorphology, soils, land use, and climate [3,4]. Among these factors, topography and soil properties are relatively constant in short periods, whereas land use changes are variable, especially in forestlands [5,6]. The effects of forest and other land use changes are associated with changes in evapotranspiration (ET), infiltration, and the recharge of watershed subsurface storage, all of which may influence baseflow [3,7]. Watershed management and planning require practical knowledge of the relationships between forest and other land use changes and baseflow processes. Most previous studies, however, have not quantified the relative importance of land use types' variation to baseflow. The impact of changes on hydrologic components in forest areas and other land use classes may be understated or exaggerated, or even misinterpreted without accurate quantification. Use of multiple regression analysis and the Soil and Water Assessment Tool (SWAT) model can offer a simple method to quantify the effect of land use changes on hydrological components [8].

Multivariate regression approaches have great potential for analyzing diverse land use to derive the causes of baseflow fluctuation [9,10]. However, the types of land use are highly co-linear or co-dependent and are not independent predictors [11,12]. There are inherent defects in the traditional regression algorithms regarding multicollinearity and noisy data [13,14]. Therefore, an extensive multivariate data analysis technique must be applied [13,14]. Partial least-squares (PLS) regression is an advanced method that combines features of a principal component analysis and the multiple linear regression [15]. PLS regression has been widely used to overcome the issue of multicollinearity and noisy data in many fields for quantitative analyses [16]. Thus, in our hypothesis, PLS regression can be used for the evaluation of forest and other land use influences on baseflow.

China has a highly variable distribution of water resources. The northern regions account for less than 20% of the nation's total runoff [17,18]. To mitigate the ongoing water crisis, China implemented the South-to-North Water Transfer (SNWT) Scheme. The Danjiangkou Reservoir Area (DRA), located at the water source of the SNWT [19], is a crucial setting for assessing land use changes and how they influence baseflow dynamics. The project has greatly changed land use patterns in the DRA as a result of many national water-soil conservation programs [17]. In our study, we validated the SWAT model that is used to estimate the baseflow of the un-gauged areas. We also addressed the importance of land use changes on baseflow on a watershed scale. Finally, we quantified the individual land use type contributions to changes in baseflow at the sub-watershed scale using PLS regression.

2. Study Area and Methods

2.1. Study Area

The Upper Du Watershed is located in the DRA and lies between $31°25'$ N and $32°48'$ N and between $109°10'$ E and $110°45'$ E and covers an area of 8973 km^2 (Figure 1). Average annual temperature was 12.4 °C to 18.4 °C, and the average annual precipitation was 728 mm to 1480 mm over the past 50 years. The topography of the watershed is undulating and characterized by mountain ranges, steep slopes, and deep valleys. The elevation ranges from 220 m at the outlet of the Upper Du Watershed to 2833 m at the highest point in the watershed. The main soil types are yellow-brown soil (71.5%) and brown soil (18.5%), which correspond to Alfisols and Entisols, respectively, based on the USA Soil Taxonomy [20]. The main land use types are forest, shrubland, farmland, urban land and grassland. Most areas are covered by subtropical evergreen broad-leaved forest and mixed coniferous broad leaved forest. The main agricultural crops are corn and wheat.

2.2. Methods

2.2.1. Data Collection

In this study, we used daily streamflow data, daily meteorological data, digital elevation data, soil type information and four sets of land use data. Daily streamflow data (1965–2010) from two hydrological stations (Zhushan and Xinzhou) were obtained from the Hubei Provincial Water Resources Bureau. Daily meteorological data, which included daily precipitation; solar radiation; wind speed and direction; humidity; and maximum, minimum, and mean air temperature data from 1965 to 2010 were obtained from nine weather stations that were within or close to the watershed (Figure 1). Digital elevation data were obtained from the National Geomatics Center of China and are presented at a 25 m × 25 m spatial resolution. The soil type information was extracted from a soil type map (1:100,000) that was issued by the Soil Hubei Provincial Survey Office. Four sets of land use data (1978, 1987, 1999 and 2000) were obtained from the Changjiang River Water Resources Commission. Seven land use categories were identified: forest, farmland, urban land, grassland, shrub land, barren land, and water (Figure 2).

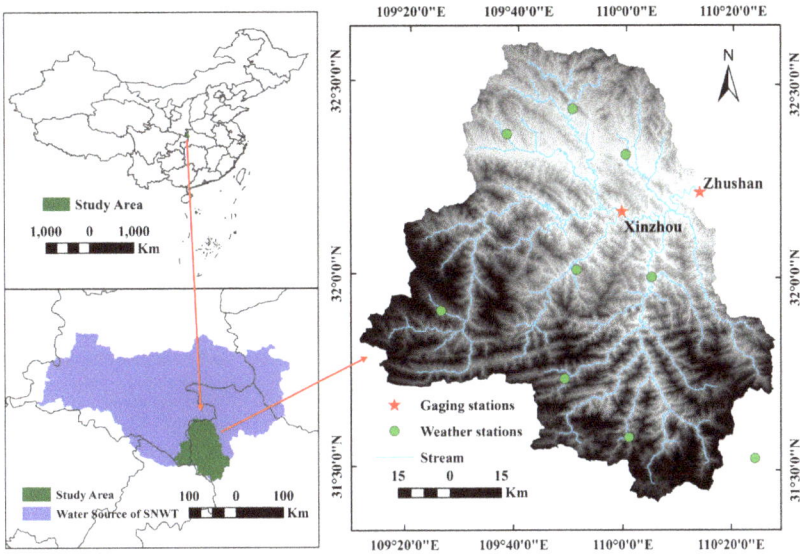

Figure 1. Location map and observation sites in the Upper Du Watershed. SNWT: South-to-North Water Transfer.

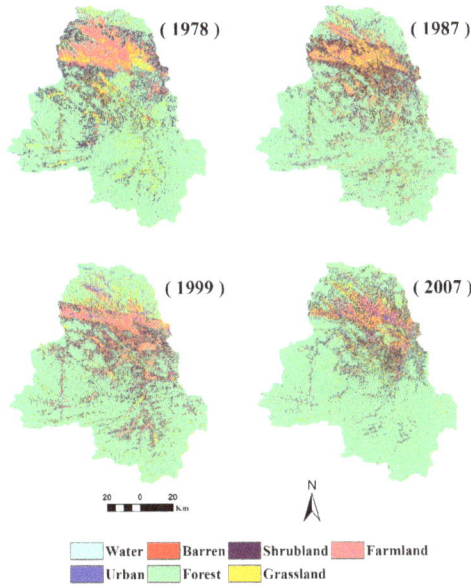

Figure 2. Land use maps of the Upper Du Watershed.

2.2.2. Baseflow Separation

The program "Bflow.exe" is a recursive digital filter used for baseflow separation that was first suggested by Lyne and Hollick [21]. It works on the premise that direct runoff and baseflow are the components of streamflow [22]. Streamflow data could be similarly partitioned by analyzing high- and low-frequency signals using a recursive filter technique [21]. Low-frequency signals are related to baseflow and high-frequency signals are related to direct runoff [23]. This technique is physically unrealistic but is objective, reproducible, and easily automated [18]. The equation of the filter is:

$$BF_t = \beta BF_{t-1} + \frac{1-\beta}{2}(Q_t + Q_{t-1})$$

(1)

where BF is the baseflow, Q is the total streamflow, β is the filter parameter (0.925), and t is the time step [23]. Equation (1) is restricted with the condition that $BF_t \leq Q_t$ [1]. The BLOW program computes baseflow by filtering the streamflow data three times; *i.e.*, 1-Pass, 2-Pass and 3-Pass after opening a DOS prompt window and switching to the directory that contains the streamflow and program data files. With every pass, there is a reduction in the baseflow as a percentage of the streamflow. The 1-Pass baseflow, which is consistent with manually estimated baseflow [22,23], was used in this study. The BFI (baseflow/streamflow) values generated with these parameters were similar to those reported by many studies in the nearby watersheds [12,24].

2.2.3. SWAT Model Setup

The SWAT model is able to assess the influence of land management methods on hydrological components in complicated watersheds that have various land cover areas, varying soils and different climate scenarios, by employing parameters with time step at daily scale [19]. Hydrology in small and large watersheds have been studied with numerous SWAT applications in many regions of the world [8,25]. The dynamics of the initiation of baseflow were studied with SWAT in detail. In addition, SWAT was used to simulate baseflow with deterministic equations and the spatial variability of baseflow processes were considered as well as the consequent changes in baseflow. This allowed the model to be used to support land use management [26]. Overall, the SWAT program is a suitable model for simulating baseflow considering various land use and management scenarios [27].

The SWAT model embedded within GIS requires the input of various spatial environmental data. First, based on the data, came from topography (from the DEM), soil, and land use maps, watershed areas were divided into 107 sub-watersheds and these were then further sub-divided into 674 hydrological response units. Second, watershed management information, the daily precipitation, insolation, wind speed and direction, humidity, and temperature data were input to improve the modeling accuracy. Third, the model calculated the baseflow data for each sub-watershed automatically based on all of the input data. The algorithmic equations for baseflow are:

$$Q_{b,i} = Q_{b,i-1} \cdot \exp(-\alpha \cdot t) + W_i \cdot [1 - \exp(-\alpha \cdot t)]$$

(2)

where $Q_{b,i}$ is the baseflow from the aquifer of watershed on day i (mm/day), α is the baseflow recession coefficient, and t is the time step. W_i indicates the recharge to the aquifer on the given day i (mm/day), which is calculated as follows:

$$W_i = [1 - \exp(-\frac{1}{\delta})] \cdot W_{seep} + \exp(-\frac{1}{\delta})W_{i-1}$$

(3)

where δ is the delay time of the overlying geologic formations, and W_{seep} is the total amount of water exiting the bottom of the soil profile (mm/day) [28].

2.2.4. SWAT Calibration for Un-Gauged Sub-Watershed Baseflow

Digital filter-based programs have been widely used for model calibration because of the difficulties with measuring baseflow [29]. The daily data were aggregated to the monthly time scale for the model evaluation. In calibration of the model, the 1978 land use map and other spatial environmental data were input in the SWAT model. We calibrated the model parameters (Table 1) to make the watershed simulated (model-based) baseflow data from January 1971 to December 1980 correspond to the digital-based baseflow data in gauging stations with multiple runs. Based on the 1987 land use map, data from the Zhushan gauging station from January 1981 to December 1990 were used for validation. Based on the 1999 land use map, data for the subperiod from January 1991 to December 1990 from the Xinzhou gauging station were also used for the validation. The performance of the model was evaluated with E_{NS}, which ranged from $-\infty$ to 1. Higher values indicated higher acceptable levels of performance. The range of R^2 from 0 to 1 indicated the degree of collinearity between the observed and simulated data. The average tendency of the simulated data to differ from the observed counterparts was measured with the percent bias ($PBLAS$) [30]. Low-magnitude values indicating accurate model simulation [30]. According to Moriasi [31], a model simulation is judged to be very good if $E_{NS} > 0.75$, $R^2 > 0.75$, and $PBIAS = \pm 10$. A similar approach was used by Nie [8].

Table 1. Parameters of the SWAT model used to calibrate baseflow in the Upper Du Watershed.

Parameter Database	Parameter	Definition	Optimal Value
.bsn	ESCO	Soil evaporation compensation factor	1
	EPCO	Plant water uptake compensation factor	1
	SURLAG	Surface runoff lag time	2
.GW	GW_DELAY	Delay days	10
	GW_REVAP	Re-evaporation coefficient	0.05
	ALPHA_BF	Baseflow alpha factor	0.5
.soil	SOL_AWC	Available soil water capacity	0.2
.sub	CH_N1	Manning's "n" of tributary channels	0.1
.rte	CH_N2	Manning's "n" of the main channel	0.02
.mgt	CN2	SCS curve number	39 (Forest)
			48 (Shrubland)
			68 (Grassland)
			81 (Farmland)
			89 (Urban)
			92 (Barren)
.GW	GWQMN	Threshold of return flow occurring in aquifer	0
	RCHRGDP	Deep aquifer percolation factor	0.05
.hru	SLSUBBSN	Slope length of the sub-basin	1.1
	HRU_SLP	Slope of Hydrological Response Unit (HRU)	0.1

SWAT: the Soil and Water Assessment Tool.

2.2.5. Model Application

Land use maps from 1978 and 2007 were used in model calibration. The DEM and soil data was kept constant from January 1970 to December 2010. Only the land use maps are "changing", while the other input data are "fixed". Then, we obtained the data for the baseflow changes from the land use scenarios for 1978 to 2007 in the 107 sub-watersheds. We then extracted the data (area) on the changes in the individual land use types from the land use maps from 1978 to 2007 in the 107 sub-watersheds. The results were used to illustrate the baseflow change under the effects of land use changes in the watershed scale and to quantify the influences of land use changes on seasonal baseflow at the sub-watershed scale.

2.2.6. Statistical Analyses

To estimate the variables' variability, the robust coefficient of variation (CV) was calculated as follows:

$$\text{Rubost CV} = 100\% \times \text{normalized interquartile range (NIR)/median} \qquad (4)$$

where NIR is interquartile range multiplied by 0.7413 [32]. The PLS regression was used to determine the main watershed land use type that controls baseflow. For the analysis of the contribution of changes in influencing factors to baseflow at the sub-watershed scale, the following independent variables corresponded to changes in the seven land use types, barren, forest, shrubland, water, farmland, grassland, and urban, and the dependent variables corresponded to baseflow changes. In the PLS method, X is a matrix with n rows and p columns and Y is a matrix with n rows and q columns. Multivariate response variables are processed with the PLS method when Y is an $n \times q$ vector with $q > 1$. However, in this work, it was supposed that Y is a single variable, *i.e.*, Y is $n \times 1$ and X is $n \times p$. To build a PLS model, X needs to be regressed onto the x-scores (T), which are used to predict the y-scores (U), which in turn are used to predict the responses Y. To avoid overfitting, the analyses searched for a set of components with the minimum value difference (cross-validated root mean squared error, RMSECV) between the explained variation in response (R^2) and the predictive ability of the model (maximum cross-validated goodness of prediction, Q^2). The regression coefficient indicates the direction of the relationship between each independent and dependent variable. Modeling of the PLS, which has several components, and calculating the Variable Influence on Projection (VIP) can indicate the importance of a predictor for variations. The information over all predictors and PLS dimensions was pooled with the VIP. The strength of influence for each predictor is indicated by the VIP values. The direction of the relationship between baseflow and the changes in land use types were described by the regression coefficients of the PLS models.

3. Results and Discussion

3.1. Un-Gauged Sub-Watersheds Baseflow

Figure 3 shows the monthly model-based and digital filter-based baseflow of the Upper Du Watershed during calibration and validation. The statistical performance was satisfactory according to the monthly E_{NS}, R^2, and *PBIAS* (Table 2). The statistical results showed good agreement by comparing the digital-based baseflow with the simulation, and the parameters calibrated for baseflow of the model could be used to simulate every sub-watershed. However, as shown in Figure 3, there was a difference between the filtered-based value and the simulated value. The filter-based value accounted for 34.3% of the annual flow volume and the model-based baseflow volume accounted for 35.0% of the annual flow volume. Most summers, the simulated value was overestimated, whereas it tended to be too low in winter. The depletion of a portion of the shallow aquifer storage of the watershed during the simulation accounted for the slight difference. The simulation revealed that there was seasonal storage fluctuation and equilibrium was maintained for the deep aquifer. Rapid percolation of rainfall occurs during the summer, and the shallow aquifer, which is the important resource for baseflow, quickly receives recharge from the unsaturated soil profile percolation; in winter, the underground storage is released more slowly [29].

Table 2. Examination of the performance of SWAT in the Upper Du Watershed.

Stations	Period	E_{NS} [a]	*PBIAS* [b]	R^2	Rating
Zhushan	Calibration (1971–1980)	0.83	3.9	0.85	Very good [c]
	Validation (1981–1990)	0.80	4.5	0.81	Very good
	Overall (1971–1990)	0.82	4.2	0.83	Very good
Xinzhou	Validation (1991–2000)	0.77	1.5	0.87	Very good
	Overall (1991–2010)	0.77	1.5	0.87	Very good

[a] Sampling E_{NS} = Nash-Sutcliffe efficiency; [b] Sampling *PBIAS* = Percent Bias; [c] The performance of the SWAT model is very good when $E_{NS} > 0.75$ and *PBIAS* values are in the range of $\pm 10\%$.

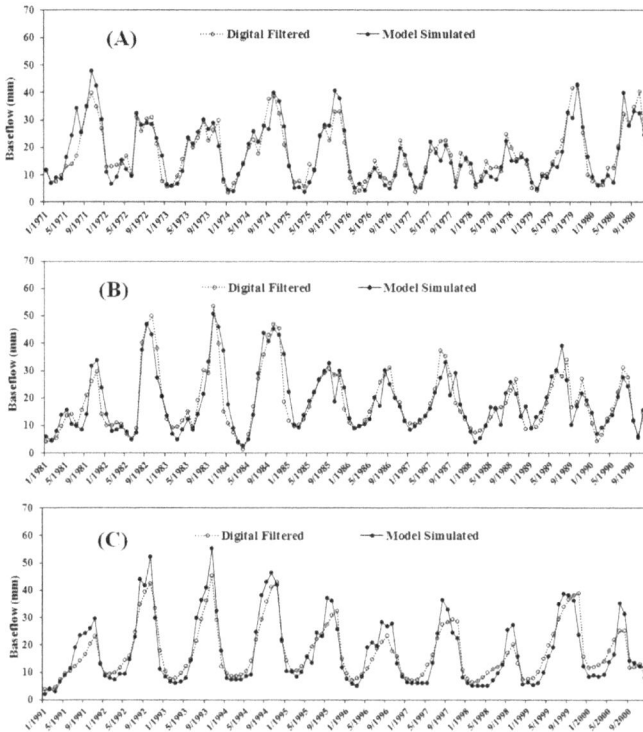

Figure 3. Monthly digital filtered-based and model-based baseflow in the Upper Du Watershed for the calibration (from 1 January 1971 to 31 December 1980) at Zhushan station (**A**); validation (from 1 January 1981 to 31 December 1990) at Zhushan station (**B**); and validation (from 1 January 1991 to 31 December 2000) in Xinzhou station (**C**).

3.2. Temporal and Spatial Distribution of Baseflow

Figure 4 shows the changes in the timing of digital-based baseflow. The average annual baseflow over the entire watershed for four study periods (1970s, 1980s, 1990s, and 2000s) was 205.0, 220.1, 201.3, and 198.2 mm, respectively. The mean monthly baseflow showed a prominent increased in spring, which might have been affected by the rainfall increase (3 mm) from the 1970s to the 2000s in this season. The prominent late-autumn peaks were likely to diminish and a larger proportion of discharge shifted to early winter. The processes causing the temporal changes in baseflow also resulted in spatial changes. Figure 5 shows the model-based baseflow changes between 1978 and 2007 at the sub-watershed scale and Table 3 shows that the seasonal baseflow in the 107 sub-watersheds varied substantially according to CV. The spatial distribution of the baseflow changes of this watershed can be broadly divided into two parts: the area near the major stream channels mainly covered by farmland and urban areas, and the more distant area that is mainly covered by forest. The baseflow change during February, March, and April (spring) of 2007 was not substantially different from the conditions during 1978 for much of the Upper Du Watershed (Figure 5A), as the increase was inconspicuous (less than 2 mm). The decrease in baseflow was less than 3.9 mm in the area along the major stream channels. Simulations indicated that the baseflow during May, June, and July (summer) of 2007 declined (0.1–1.9 mm) throughout the area, which was mainly covered by forest, relative to 1978. Larger decreases in baseflow, ranging from 2.0 to 18.9 mm, were simulated in the area mainly covered by farmland and urban land use near the main stream channel in the middle and northern parts of the watershed. The baseflow decreased during August, September, and October (autumn) in the middle and northern parts of the watershed in 2007. The baseflows in the northern, southwestern, and southeastern portions distant from the major stream network of the watershed showed a slight increase, whereas they showed a slight decrease in the summer months and were not markedly different volumetrically from the historic period. Patterns of baseflow changes in November, October, and January (winter) were similar to those in the autumn months; however, the baseflow recession expanded to areas distant from the major stream network.

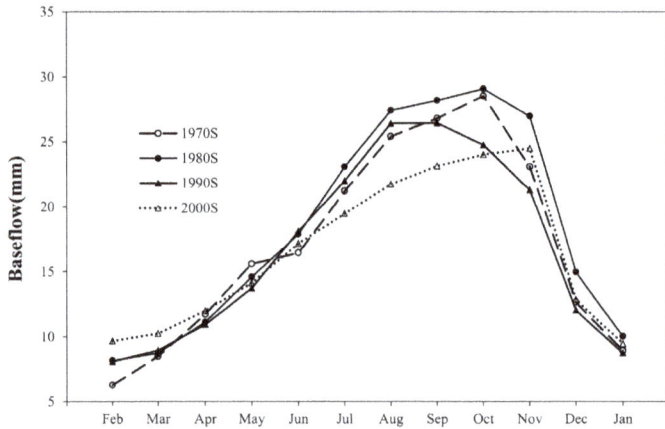

Figure 4. Watershed-scale average monthly baseflow for the 1970s, 1980s, 1990s, and 2000s.

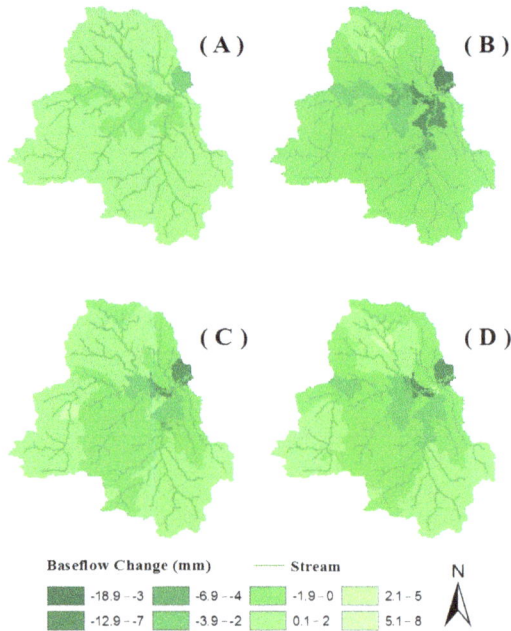

Figure 5. Changes in baseflow from 1970s to 2000s calculated for spring (**A**); summer (**B**); autumn (**C**); and winter (**D**) seasons.

Table 3. Robust coefficient of variation (CV) for the average monthly baseflow of each sub-watershed in this study.

Seasonal Baseflow	Land Use Scenarios	Robust Coefficient of Variation
Spring baseflow	1978	216.8%
	2007	239.2%
Summer baseflow	1978	241.5%
	2007	260.4%
Autumn baseflow	1978	232.8%
	2007	234.5%
Winter baseflow	1978	219.3%
	2007	226.3%

3.3. Influences of Forest and Other Land Use Changes on Baseflow

The land use changes during the four periods are given in Table 4. Comparing the land cover maps for 1978 and 1999, the area corresponding to forest decreased from 6365.5 km^2 to 6232.1 km^2 with an annual reduction of 6.1 km^2, whereas the area corresponding to farmland increased by 15.2 km^2 per year. However, after 1999, rapid forest expansion and urban development occurred in this region. The most remarkable land use variations are the increase in forest of 76.1 km^2 per year and the decline in farmland by 86.9 km^2 per year. These dynamics were associated with government policy. In 1978, "Household Responsibility System" was initiated by the central government, and most areas of China entered into the period of cultivation [33]. In 1999, Grain for Green (GFG) was implemented and directly engaged millions of farmers in protecting certain areas, thus, China entered into the period of ecological restoration [34].

Table 4. Percent of land use areas and changes in the Upper Du Watershed (1978–2007).

Land Use (%)	1978	1987	1999	2007	1978–1987	1987–1999	1999–2007	1978–2007
Forest	70.9	70.4	69.3	76.2	−0.5	−1.1	+6.9	+5.3
Farmland	9.8	10.2	13.6	5.8	+0.4	+3.4	−7.8	−4.0
Urban	0.8	0.9	1.1	1.4	+0.1	+0.2	+0.4	+0.6
Grassland	7.6	7.3	5.9	6.1	−0.3	−1.4	+0.2	−1.5
Shrubland	10.2	10.4	9.4	9.5	−0.2	+1.0	−0.1	−0.7
Barren	0.3	0.4	0.4	0.7	+0.1	0	+0.3	+0.4
Water	0.4	0.4	0.3	0.3	0	−0.1	0	−0.1

Table 5 shows statistics of individual land use changes at the sub-watershed scale. The CV values indicated that the land use types varied substantially in the 107 sub-watersheds, except the water. This phenomenon was caused by the non-uniform distribution of forests and changes in farmland. First, before 1999, diminishing forests are linked with the efficiency of deforestation, which was affected by the physical accessibility of the forest stand, as exemplified through such metrics as the linear distances to highways, roads, and navigable rivers [35]. Second, expanded farmland associated with cultivation mainly occurred in land near stream channels over the entire watershed. Finally, after 1999, the land use distribution at the sub-watersheds scale became more irregular because only specific farmland (normally with slopes >25°) was transformed into forests [36].

Land use transformation maps were produced based on the intersecting of the 1978 and 2007 land use maps (Figure 6). Since the land use maps have six land use types, the land use transformations can have a maximum of 36 classes. However, many transformations were not evident in the maps. In this study, only forest/farmland/urban transformations were considered. The farmland and urban expansion mainly development in the lower stretches and middle of the northern area of the watershed, largely matching the decreases in baseflow. Baseflow change during the spring of 2007 was only slightly different from the conditions during 1978 throughout most of the watershed with a change of less than

2 mm over most of the watershed away from the main stream network, which is mainly covered by forest. This is because spring is the initial growing season for trees and ET is much lower than in other growing seasons [37]. In summer, the majority of the farmland converted to forest and there was high seasonal evapotranspiration in the sub-watersheds and this spatially corresponded with the decrease in baseflow in the northern, southwestern and southeastern portions of the watershed.

Table 5. Robust Coefficient of Variation for the land use types of each sub-watershed in Upper Du Watershed.

Land Use Maps	Land Use Types	Robust Coefficient of Variation
1978	Forest	159.6%
	Farmland	350.0%
	Urban	304.0%
	Grassland	159.8%
	Shrubland	223.1%
	Barren	197.9%
	Water	279.8%
2007	Forest	193.7%
	Farmland	394.8%
	Urban	352.9%
	Grassland	396.7%
	Shrubland	203.5%
	Barren	514.1%
	Water	213.3%

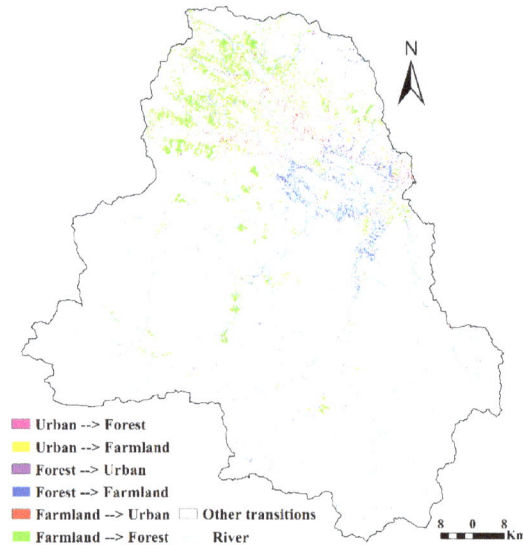

Figure 6. Land use transformation maps of the Upper Du Watershed from 1978 to 2007.

In autumn and winter, simulations indicated a general increase in the baseflow of 0.1–2.0 mm in 2007 compared to 1978 over much of northern, southwestern and southeastern portions of the watershed. This change in baseflow was due to the large effects of forests in this area far from the stream network as well as the low ET during later growing and non-growing seasons. A larger proportion of baseflow recharge occurred in these seasons. Evapotranspiration diminished the baseflow recharge pulse from May to January, and the comparison of variations of baseflow and changes in land use types suggests a strong negative relationship between baseflow and the forest and farmland in these three seasons (average R^2 is 0.83 and 0.79, respectively).

3.4. Contribution of Land Use Changes to Baseflow

Table 6 provided the summaries of the PLS model constructed for the four seasons. For the spring, autumn, and winter models, the first component explains 74.7%, 74.4%, and 69.1% of the variation in baseflow, respectively. The addition of the second component explained, respectively, 79.1%, 78.8%, and 71.3% of the variation and generated a minimum RMSECV. The addition of components to the PLS led to higher RMSECV values (Table 6). For these models, two predictor variables, namely, forest and urban land, had VIP scores greater than 1, followed by farmland, shrubland, grassland, and barren land with VIP scores less than 1 (ranges from 0.991 to 0.433). Forest also had larger negative regression coefficients (-0.708, -0.854, and -1.108) (Figure 7).

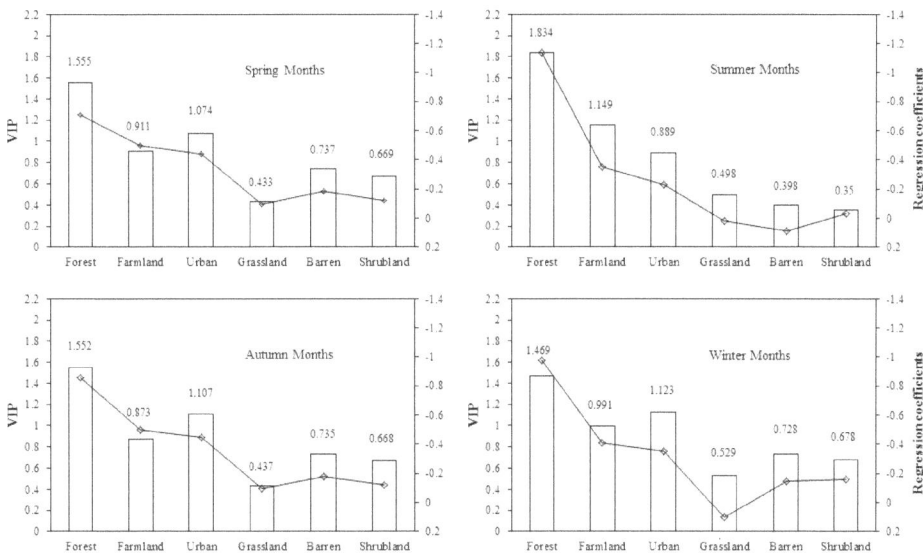

Figure 7. Regression coefficients (lines) and the Variable Influence on Projection (VIP) (bars) of each land use type.

Table 6. Summary of partial least-squares (PLS) regression models of baseflow for all sub-watersheds.

Response Y	R^2 [a]	Q^2 [b]	Component	% of Explained Variability in Y	Cumulative Explained in Y (%)	RMSECV [c]	Q^2_{cum} [d]
Spring baseflow	0.79	0.67	1	74.7	74.7	0.88	0.634
			2	4.4	79.1	0.80	0.666
			3	0.4	79.5	0.81	0.656
Summer baseflow	0.82	0.72	1	71.8	71.8	6.09	0.658
			2	9.8	81.6	5.12	0.718
			3	1.2	82.8	5.70	0.709
Autumn baseflow	0.79	0.68	1	74.4	74.4	0.88	0.644
			2	4.4	78.8	0.80	0.682
			3	0.4	79.2	0.81	0.667
Winter baseflow	0.71	0.55	1	69.1	69.1	1.29	0.597
			2	2.2	71.3	1.26	0.547
			3	0.1	71.4	1.27	0.494

[a] Sampling R^2 = goodness of fit; [b] Q^2 = maximum cross-validated goodness of prediction; [c] RMSECV = cross-validated root mean squared error; and [d] Q^2_{cum} = cumulative cross-validated goodness of prediction.

In the summer model, the first component was dominated by forest and farmland and explained 71.8% of the variance in the dataset regarding changes in baseflow (Table 6). The second component was dominated by farmland and urban areas and addition of this component explained 81.6% of the total variance. Adding more components to the PLS models failed to substantially improve the explained variance (Table 6). The lower importance of some variance predictors in a particular component was indicated by the distance of the PLS weights from the original variables. Also, a more convenient and comprehensive expression of the relative importance of predictors can be derived from exploring their VIP values [38]. As shown in Figure 7, two predictor variables, namely forest and farmland, had VIP scores greater than 1 (1.834 and 1.149, respectively) and regression coefficients of -1.135 and -0.350, respectively, followed by the percentage of urban (VIP = 0.889; coefficient = -0.231), grassland (VIP = 0.498; coefficient = 0.020), and barren land (VIP = 0.398; coefficient = 0.091). Hence, these variables are used in the prediction model to obtain projected predictands. The negative regression coefficient of forestland was due to the greater interception of the canopy and ET rates (trees transfer subsurface water to leaves and then to the atmosphere) [39]. According to Price [3], the baseflow response to farmland may be positivity or negativity associated with the crop irrigation practices, natural losses via ET, and variable infiltration. Our results suggest that the negative relationships between farmland and baseflow in the Upper Du Watershed may be correlated with crops, which are irrigated from surface water storage associated with the stream network, and the great ET loss of crops, which is agreed with the conclusions of many researchers [9,40]. Following urbanization, throughfall decreases in building zones where rainfall interception occurs; additionally, infiltration is reduced by soil compaction and impervious surface additions, and water flushes more quickly through the watershed as a result of decreases in the hydraulic resistance of land surfaces and channels [3,41,42].

The effects of forested areas are greater than that of agricultural areas. This phenomenon can be explained as follows. First, baseflow regression associated with ET in a watershed with perennial vegetation (e.g., trees) is generally higher than crops (*i.e.*, farmland) [37,39]. Second, the transpiration of perennial forest vegetation influences the baseflow regression throughout the whole growing season, whereas the transpiration of seasonal crops influences the baseflow regression only during the mid-growing and late-growing seasons [9]. Overall, the strong baseflow regression of forests is sustained for a longer time. Thus, we can suggest that the baseflow will increase with the replacement of forest by farmland. These results are consistent with Sun [43] pertaining to a study on the water yield response to forest management. The effects of forested areas are greater than that of urban land due to the increase of non-contributing impervious surfaces in urban areas, which mitigate the negative influences of urbanization on baseflow [44]. The impacts of urbanization are characterized by the total area of impervious surfaces in a watershed [45]. The total impervious area can be divided into the effective impervious area and the non-contributing impervious area (such as pervious areas and leaky water infrastructure) [45,46]. However, considering only the effective impervious area of a watershed is not sufficient [44]. Non-contributing impervious areas, which are formally addressed through effective impervious areas [47], increase with increases in urban land. Thus, baseflow maybe increase when forestland changes to urban. Similar conclusions were reported by Boggs and Sun [48].

4. Conclusions

Our study quantifies the relative importance of the land use types on baseflow at the sub-watershed scale. The results indicate that the dynamics of baseflow are closely associated with changes of land use. The major negative factors that affect baseflow were found to be changes to forest, followed by farmland and urban land. Grassland, barren land, and shrubland did not result in a significant impact on baseflow in our study watershed.

This study could be applied to many types of watersheds if the time series data and special land use information are available, and thereby provides useful quantitative information on internal dynamics of baseflow and major drivers in watersheds for forest and watershed management. From a forest landscape ecology perspective, a watershed's land cover patterns might be important for determining hydrological processes. Therefore, future research should focus on the influence of forestland cover patterns on baseflow changes.

Acknowledgments: Financial support provided by the National Natural Science Foundation of China (41525003).

Author Contributions: Xu-Dong Huang and Zhi-Hua Shi conceived and designed the experiments; Xu-Dong Huang and Nu-Fang Fang performed the experiments; Xu-Dong Huang and Xuan Li analyzed the data; and Xu-Dong Huang wrote the paper.

Conflicts of Interest: The authors declare no conflict of interest.

References

1. Eckhardt, K. A comparison of baseflow indices, which were calculated with seven different baseflow separation methods. *J. Hydrol.* **2008**, *352*, 168–173. [CrossRef]
2. Smakhtin, V.U. Low flow hydrology: A review. *J. Hydrol.* **2001**, *240*, 147–186. [CrossRef]
3. Price, K. Effects of watershed topography, soils, land use, and climate on baseflow hydrology in humid regions: A review. *Prog. Phys. Geogr.* **2011**, *35*, 465–492. [CrossRef]
4. Knox, J.C. Floodplain sedimentation in the Upper Mississippi Valley: Natural *versus* human accelerated. *Geomorphology* **2006**, *79*, 286–310. [CrossRef]
5. Varis, O.; Vakkilainen, P. China's 8 challenges to water resources management in the first quarter of the 21st Century. *Geomorphology* **2001**, *41*, 93–104. [CrossRef]
6. Zhuang, D.F.; Deng, X.Z.; Zhan, J.Y.; Zhao, T. A study on the spatial distribution of land use change in Beijing. *Geogr. Res.* **2002**, *21*, 667–674. (In Chinese)
7. Dou, X.; Chen, B.; Black, T.A.; Jassal, R.S.; Che, M. Impact of nitrogen fertilization on forest carbon sequestration and water loss in a chronosequence of three Douglas-fir stands in the pacific northwest. *Forests* **2015**, *6*, 1897–1921. [CrossRef]
8. Nie, W.M.; Yuan, Y.P.; Kepner, W.; Nash, M.S.; Jackson, M.; Erickson, C. Assessing impacts of land use changes on hydrology for the upper San Pedro watershed. *J. Hydrol.* **2011**, *407*, 105–114. [CrossRef]
9. Zhang, Y.K.; Schilling, K.E. Increasing streamflow and baseflow in Mississippi River since the 1940s: Effect of land use change. *J. Hydrol.* **2006**, *324*, 412–422. [CrossRef]
10. Ma, X.; Xu, J.C.; Luo, Y.; Aggarwal, S.P.; Li, J.T. Response of hydrological processes to land-cover and climate changes in Kejie watershed, south-west China. *Hydrol. Process.* **2009**, *23*, 1179–1191. [CrossRef]
11. Artita, K.S.; Kaini, P.; Nicklow, J.W. Examining the possibilities: Generating alternative watershed-scale BMP designs with evolutionary algorithms. *Water Resour. Manag.* **2013**, *27*, 3849–3863. [CrossRef]
12. Zhou, F.; Xu, Y.; Chen, Y.; Xu, C.Y.; Gao, Y.; Du, J. Hydrological response to urbanization at different spatio-temporal scales simulated by coupling of CLUE-S and the SWAT model in the Yangtze River Delta region. *J. Hydrol.* **2013**, *485*, 113–125. [CrossRef]
13. Luedeling, E.; Gassner, A. Partial least squares regression for analyzing walnut phenology in California. *Agric. For. Meteorol.* **2012**, *158*, 43–52. [CrossRef]
14. Shi, Z.H.; Ai, L.; Li, X.; Huang, X.D.; Wu, G.L.; Liao, W. Partial least-squares regression for linking land-cover patterns to soil erosion and sediment yield in watersheds. *J. Hydrol.* **2013**, *498*, 165–176. [CrossRef]
15. Abdi, H.; Williams, L.J. Principal component analysis. *Wiley Interdiscip. Rev. Comput. Stat.* **2010**, *2*, 433–459. [CrossRef]
16. Geladi, P.; Sethson, B.; Nyström, J.; Lillhonga, T.; Lestander, T.; Burger, J. Chemometrics in spectroscopy. *Spectrochim. Acta B At. Spectrosc.* **2004**, *59*, 1347–1357. [CrossRef]
17. Li, L.; Shi, Z.; Yin, W.; Zhu, D.; Ng, S.L.; Cai, C.; Lei, A. A fuzzy analytic hierarchy process (FAHP) approach to eco-environmental vulnerability assessment for the Danjiangkou Reservoir Area, China. *Ecol. Model.* **2009**, *220*, 3439–3447. [CrossRef]
18. Wang, J.; Huang, B.; Fu, D.; Atkinson, P.M. Spatiotemporal variation in surface urban heat island intensity and associated determinants across major Chinese cities. *Remote Sens.* **2015**, *7*, 3670–3689. [CrossRef]
19. Yan, B.; Fang, N.F.; Zhang, P.C.; Shi, Z.H. Impacts of land use change on watershed streamflow and sediment yield: An assessment using hydrologic modelling and partial least squares regression. *J. Hydrol.* **2013**, *484*, 26–37. [CrossRef]

20. Soil Survey Staff. *Soil Taxonomy, A Basic System of Soil Classification for Making and Interpreting Soil Surveys*, 2nd ed.; Agriculture Handbook No. 436; USDA Natural Resources Conservation Service, U.S. Government Printing 23 Office: Washington, DC, USA, 1999; pp. 160–162, 494–495.
21. Lyne, V.; Hollick, M. Stochastic time-variable rainfall-runoff modelling. *Canberra* **1979**, *79*, 89–93.
22. Arnold, J.G.; Allen, P.M. Automated methods for estimating baseflow and ground water recharge from streamflow records. *J. Am. Water Resour. Assoc.* **1999**, *35*, 411–424. [CrossRef]
23. Ahiablame, L.; Chaubey, I.; Engel, B.; Cherkauer, K.; Merwade, V. Estimation of annual baseflow at ungauged sites in Indiana USA. *J. Hydrol.* **2013**, *476*, 13–27. [CrossRef]
24. Fang, N.F.; Shi, Z.H.; Li, L.; Guo, Z.L.; Liu, Q.J.; Ai, L. The effects of rainfall regimes and land use changes on runoff and soil loss in a small moutainous watershed. *Catena* **2012**, *99*, 1–8. [CrossRef]
25. Shi, Z.H.; Huang, X.D.; Ai, L.; Fang, N.F.; Wu, G.L. Quantitative analysis of factors controlling sediment yield in mountainous watersheds. *Geomorphology* **2014**, *226*, 193–201. [CrossRef]
26. Salerno, F.; Tartari, G. A coupled approach of surface hydrological modelling and Wavelet Analysis for understanding the baseflow components of river discharge in karst environments. *J. Hydrol.* **2009**, *376*, 295–306. [CrossRef]
27. Kushwaha, A.; Jain, M.K. Hydrological simulation in a forest dominated watershed in Himalayan region using SWAT model. *Water Resour. Manag.* **2013**, *27*, 3005–3023. [CrossRef]
28. Neitsch, S.L.; Arnold, J.G.; Kiniry, J.R.; Williams, J.R.; King, K.W. Soil Water Assessment Tool Theoretical Document, Version 2000, Grassland, Soil and Water Research Laboratory. Available online: http://www.brc.tamus.edu/swat/doc.html (accessed on 7 May 2012).
29. Luo, Y.; Arnold, J.; Allen, P.; Chen, X. Baseflow simulation using SWAT model in an inland river basin in Tianshan Mountains, Northwest China. *Hydrol. Earth Syst. Sci.* **2012**, *16*, 1259–1267. [CrossRef]
30. Gupta, H.V.; Sorooshian, S.; Yapo, P.O. Status of automatic calibration for hydrologic models: Comparison with multilevel expert calibration. *J. Hydrol. Eng.* **1999**, *4*, 135–143. [CrossRef]
31. Moriasi, D.N.; Arnold, J.G.; van Liew, M.W.; Bingner, R.L.; Harmel, R.D.; Veith, T.L. Model evaluation guidelines for systematic quantification of accuracy in watershed simulations. *Trans. ASABE* **2007**, *50*, 885–900. [CrossRef]
32. Temnerud, J.; Düker, A.; Karlsson, S.; Allard, B.; Köhler, S.; Bishop, K. Landscape scale patterns in the character of natural organic matter in a Swedish boreal stream network. *Hydrol. Earth Syst. Sci.* **2009**, *13*, 1567–1582. [CrossRef]
33. Li, X.B. Change of cultivated land area in china during the past 20 years and its policy implications. *J. Nat. Resour.* **1999**, *14*, 329–333. (In Chinese)
34. Lü, Y.H.; Fu, B.J.; Feng, X.M.; Zeng, Y.; Liu, Y.; Chang, R.Y.; Sun, G.; Wu, B.F. A policy-driven large scale ecological restoration: Quantifying ecosystem services changes in the Loess Plateau of China. *PLoS ONE* **2012**, *7*, e31782. [CrossRef] [PubMed]
35. Laurance, W.F.; Albernaz, A.K.M.; Schroth, G.; Fearnside, P.M.; Bergen, S.; Venticinque, E.M.; da Costa, C. Predictors of deforestation in the Brazilian Amazon. *J. Biogeogr.* **2002**, *29*, 737–748. [CrossRef]
36. Gao, Z.L.; Fu, Y.L.; Li, Y.H.; Liu, J.X.; Chen, N.; Zhang, X.P. Trends of streamflow, sediment load and their dynamic relation for the catchments in the middle reaches of the Yellow River over the past five decades. *Hydrol. Earth Syst. Sci.* **2012**, *16*, 3219–3231. [CrossRef]
37. FAO (Food and Agriculture Organization of the United Nations). *Crop Evapotranspiration, Guidelines for Computing Crop Water Requirements*; FAO Irrigation and Drainage Paper 56; Food and Agriculture Organization of the United Nations: Rome, Italy, 1998.
38. Onderka, M.; Wrede, S.; Rodný, M.; Pfister, L.; Hoffmann, L.; Krein, A. Hydrogeologic and landscape controls of dissolved inorganic nitrogen (DIN) and dissolved silica (DSi) fluxes in heterogeneous catchments. *J. Hydrol.* **2012**, *450*, 36–47. [CrossRef]
39. Wittenberg, H. Effects of season and man-made changes on baseflow and flow recession: Case studies. *Hydrol. Process.* **2003**, *17*, 2113–2123. [CrossRef]
40. Juckem, P.F.; Hunt, R.J.; Anderson, M.P.; Robertson, D.M. Effects of climate and land management change on streamflow in the driftless area of Wisconsin. *J. Hydrol.* **2008**, *355*, 123–130. [CrossRef]
41. Burns, D.; Vitvar, T.; McDonnell, J.; Hassett, J.; Duncan, J.; Kendall, C. Effects of suburban development on runoff generation in the Croton River Basin, New York, USA. *J. Hydrol.* **2005**, *311*, 266–281. [CrossRef]
42. Woltemade, C.J. Impact of residential soil disturbance on infiltration rate and stormwater runoff. *J. Am. Water Resour. Assoc.* **2010**, *46*, 700–711. [CrossRef]

43. Sun, G.; Zhou, G.; Zhang, Z.; Wei, X.; McNulty, S.G.; Vose, J.M. Potential water yield reduction due to forestation across China. *J. Hydrol.* **2006**, *328*, 548–558. [CrossRef]
44. Hamel, P.; Daly, E.; Fletcher, T.D. Source-control stormwater management for mitigating the impacts of urbanisation on baseflow: A review. *J. Hydrol.* **2013**, *485*, 201–211. [CrossRef]
45. Jacobson, C.R. Identification and quantification of the hydrological impacts of imperviousness in urban catchments: A review. *J. Environ. Manag.* **2011**, *92*, 1438–1448. [CrossRef] [PubMed]
46. Shuster, W.D.; Bonta, J.; Thurston, H.; Warnemuende, E.; Smith, D.R. Impacts of impervious surface on watershed hydrology: A review. *Urban Water J.* **2005**, *2*, 263–275. [CrossRef]
47. Booth, D.B.; Jackson, C.R. Urbanization of aquatic systems: Degradation thresholds, stormwater detection, and the limits of mitigation. *J. Am. Water Resour. Assoc.* **1997**, *33*, 1077–1090. [CrossRef]
48. Boggs, J.L.; Sun, G. Urbanization alters watershed hydrology in the Piedmont of North Carolina. *Ecohydrology* **2011**, *4*, 256–264. [CrossRef]

forests

MDPI

Article

Attribution Analyses of Impacts of Environmental Changes on Streamflow and Sediment Load in a Mountainous Basin, Vietnam

Jie Wang [1,*], Ishidaira Hiroshi [2], Shaowei Ning [3], Timur Khujanazarov [4], Guiping Yin [5] and Lijuan Guo [5]

[1] College of Hydrometeorology, Nanjing University of Information Science & Technology, Nanjing 210044, China
[2] International Research Center for River Basin Environment, University of Yamanashi, Kofu, Yamanashi 4008511, Japan; ishi@yamanashi.ac.jp
[3] School of Civil Engineering, Hefei University of Technology, Hefei 230009, China; yantaigold@sina.com
[4] Water Resources Research Center, Disaster Prevention Research Institute, Kyoto University, Uji, Kyoto 6110011, Japan; exider@gmail.com
[5] Nanjing Water Planning and Designing Institute Co., Ltd, Nanjing 210006, China; yingp008@126.com (G.Y.); 365843295@163.com (L.G.)
* Correspondence: wangjie0775@163.com; Tel.: +86-25-5869-5622

Academic Editors: James M. Vose and Ge Sun
Received: 29 November 2015; Accepted: 21 January 2016; Published: 29 January 2016

Abstract: Located in the southeastern China and northern Vietnam, the Red River is an important international trans-boundary river that has experienced rapid deforestation and environmental changes over the past decades. We conducted attribution analysis of impacts of various environmental changes on streamflow and sediment load. The contribution of reclassified environmental changes to total change of the streamflow and sediment load was separated. Land cover change based on climate-induced and human-induced indicators were defined. We found that human-induced land cover change was the main factor affecting changes of the streamflow and sediment load. Changes of the land cover were more pronounced in the dry season than in the wet season whereas sediment load changed more in the wet season than in the dry season. In addition, changes in sediment load were mainly caused by human-induced land cover change and the changes of land cover were more influential on sediment load than on streamflow in the Red River basin.

Keywords: human activities; climate change; land cover change; separation; streamflow; sediment load

1. Introduction

Understanding hydrological responses to catchment environmental changes is important in watershed management worldwide [1,2]. The hydrological cycles of river basins depend on climatic regime, land cover, geology, topography and other human activities. However, climate change has been the main concern recently. Climate change has resulted in rise of the atmospheric temperature and modified precipitation patterns, which has directly led to alteration in runoff [3] and thus sediment load in the river flow [4]. Another important factor altering hydrological cycles is land cover change, such as deforestation, farming activities, climate-induced and human-induced land cover change. Such land cover changes are directly linked to changes to the ecosystem structure (e.g., leaf area index) altering the evapotranspiration rates and flow velocity [5] and physical structure such as surface roughness that can also modify soil erodibility and consequently impact the sediment load in river basins [6]. River discharge and sediment load are affected by various environmental changes within a drainage basin in an integrated way [7,8].In addition, human activities such as dam construction and agricultural irrigation, had seriously changed hydrological cycle in most river basins.

Streamflow or sediment load characteristics of a watershed are closely related to the geology, topography, climate, land cover and human activities within the basin. While geologic and topographic variables are fixed in the short term, long-term changes occur in climatic conditions. On the other hand, human activities or land cover changes would produce abrupt alterations in streamflow, erosion process and sediment load [7]. All environmental changes play an important role in altering surface flow and sediment yield. Sun *et al.* [2] argued that climate change was more crucial to the hydrological cycle changes in four Poyang Lake basins than vegetation. Wang and Ishidaira [4] suggested that the total changes of runoff or sediment load in Red River basin was caused by climate variation and human activities, mainly on land cover change. Nguyen Ngoc and Lung [9] concluded that if the forest cover of the catchment is reduced from 70%–80% to 40%–50%, soil erosion will increase by 27.1% and surface flows will increase by 33.8%. Land cover change was demonstrated as a crucial factor of changes in water yield, sediment load and nonpoint water pollution [6–8].

Quantitative contribution of all these impacts on changes in the streamflow and sediment load has been thoroughly investigated [4,8,10]. However, little quantitative knowledge is available on individual impacts of the various environmental changes on streamflow and sediment load. There are two main ways to study separating effects of the climate and the land cover change. One traditional way is a paired catchments experiment [10]. Although this approach is the "good standard" in quantifying the impacts of land cover changes, it is quite costly and time-consuming. Another approach is a simulation method. Model simulation methods account for streamflow or sediment load change response to climate variability and land cover change or human activities [4,8], with the assumption that the total changes of runoff or sediment load is caused by climate variation and human activities or land cover change. For instance, Zhao *et al.* [11] calculated different contributions of human activities and climate change on streamflow change in the upper catchment of the Yellow River Basin using the Geomorphology Based Hydrological Model (GBHM) and sensitivity-based method. Tang *et al.* [8] evaluated separated effects of variations in land cover and climate on runoff and water quality in the upper catchment of the Miyun Reservoir in northern China using the GBHM hydrological model. Wang and Ishidaira [4] applied the Soil and Water Assessment Tool (SWAT) model to separate impacts of climate change and human activities on the streamflow and sediment flow in the Red River basin and concluded that land cover change is the main human activity to alter the streamflow and sediment flow in this basin. Most of these studies assumed that land cover changes were caused by human activities without separating the climate-induced land cover change from human-induced land cover change and other human activities, and climate change only included meteorological changes (such as precipitation, temperature changes). Climate-induced land cover change has been rarely considered as part of climate change in assessing impacts of the climate change on water resources.

To distinguish climate/human-induced land cover change and evaluate the effects of land cover change on the streamflow and sediment load, dynamics of land cover change should be investigated first. While long-term time series of land cover change is not readily available, the Normalized Difference Vegetation Index (NDVI) and Leaf Area Index (LAI) are two of the most widely used vegetation indices to reflect dynamics of land cover degradation caused by human activities and climate changes [12,13]. However, NDVI or LAI obtained from remote sensing data can only explain the current vegetation cover with dual influence of climate change and human activities. To investigate potential vegetation cover (e.g., potential LAI) under climate change scenarios excluding human activities, ecosystem simulation models are required. Ecosystem models have additional advantage to considering effects of not only climatic conditions but also other factors such as carbon dioxide concentrations.

The objective of this study is to design framework to quantitatively assess the impacts of various environment changes on the streamflow and sediment load in the Da River Basin. We used a hydrological model and new sediment rating curve to conduct multiple scenario analysis to separate the individual effects of environment changes on streamflow and sediment load. Specifically, our main focuses are: (1) to determine the period with the most drastic artificial disturbance; (2) to determine LAI time series from Glaobal Inventory Modelling and Mapping Studies (GIMMS) to analyze changing trends of the actual land/vegetation cover in the past years, and to model potential LAI by an ecosystem model to describe the potential land/vegetation cover condition without human activities; (3) to evaluate hydrological models and new sediment rating curves; (4) and to separate environment change effects on streamflow and sediment load.

2. Study Area and Data Description

2.1. Study Area

The Da River, originated from Yunnan Province, China, is one of the largest tributaries of the Red River representing a trans-boundary river shared between Vietnam and China (Figure 1). The catchment area of the Da River is approximately 55,000 km^2. Mountainous landscapes dominate in the Da River Basin (DRB), with narrow and steep slopes. Mean elevation is at 1836 m, but maximal elevation reaches 3318 m and the minimal one is of 5 m (Figure 1). The geologic substratum of the upper basin is dominated by consolidated paleozoic sedimentary rocks of complex lithology, with variable contributions of mesozoic silicic or carbonate rocks [3]. Soils in the upper basin are typically Ultisols and alluvial soils with little variation spatially [14]. Mountain areas in the upstream are tectonically active and unstable, and this, combined with intense rainfall, causes high erosion [15].

Climate is dominated by tropical monsoon with annual mean rainfall about 1320 mm, in two seasons with the wet season (May to October) receiving 85% of total precipitation [3,8]. The annual mean runoff is about 1168 m^3/s from 1988 to 2004 at the Lai Chau Station and a total annual sediment load about is 40.1 × 10^6 ton. The annual mean runoff is about 1660 m^3/s at Hoa Binh station, which accounts for about half of the maximum discharge in the Red River basin.

The overall sediment load of the Red River ranks ninth in the world. Sediment yield of the river is important to investigate as the Vietnamese government has decided to build a cascade of five dams and hydropower facilities in the DRB (Figure 1), for flood control, irrigation and hydropower generation. Up to now, two dams, Son La and Hoa Binh have been completely finished. The Son La reservoir in the DRB with effective storage of 16.2 km^3 [3,4] has just been completed in October 2012, becoming the largest dam in Vietnam (Figure 1). The Hoa Binh dam (V = 9.5 km^3) located downstream of the Son La dam, was completely finished in 1993 [3].

Deforestation has been a growing concern in the region and upstream of DRB in particular. The region was originally dominated by forest: 70% of the total DRB was covered by evergreen broadleaf forests with remaining area as croplands and shrublands. The forest coverage of the Chinese part of the river has declined by half [16] from 1950 to 1990 and most rapidly in 1993 [17]. Vietnamese forest cover decline has been even more rapid over the same time period replacing or felling more than 70% of previously forest area especially in upstream mountainous regions [18]. Since 1995, several forest rehabilitation programs have been established and overall forest area of Vietnam has continuously increased; however, the Da River Basin still has limited forest plantations due to poor accessibility [19]. Compared with original natural forests, young man-made forests have lower canopy density, shallower rooting depth and had limited soil erosion function. Over the last 500 years, deforestation had raised the soil erosion rate by 15-fold resulting in increased sediment load in the DRB [3]. In addition, according to the observed meteorological data, both rainfall and air temperature show an ascending trend with the average slope of 0.863 mm/year and 0.014 °C/year in the past 50 years. Thus, deforestation and climate change have been main factors in intensified soil erosion in the basin.

The Da River has received increasing attention [20] for many eco-hydrological issues, such as flooding, sediment changes and biodiversity losses. Land cover change has caused a great impact on the streamflow and sediment yield process in the Red River basin [4]. For the streamflow of this river, Tuan [21] concluded that the peak discharge and the total runoff volume increased as the forest cover area decreased because of the Hoa Binh Reservoir constructions. Ye *et al.* applied Mann–Kendall and cluster technique methods to analyze the variability of the 45-year runoff series at the Manhao station in the Red River and showed an inverse trend between annual runoff and NDVI [17]. As for the sediment load, Ren *et al.* [22] analyzed annual sediment load of different periods in Yuan Jiang in the Red River Basin, and showed that annual sediment load in the 1980s was less than in the 1990s, and forest cover had a reverse relationship with sediment load. Dang *et al.* [23] detected a significant decrease of sediment load after 1990 in the downstream of reservoir, which indicated that the Hoa Binh dam reduced its annual sediment by half. Wang *et al.* [4] concluded that human activities such as dams or land use changes are the main causes affecting the changes of sediment flow in Red River Basin. However, it is not clear how much each environment change factor affected streamflow and sediment load in the Red River basin.

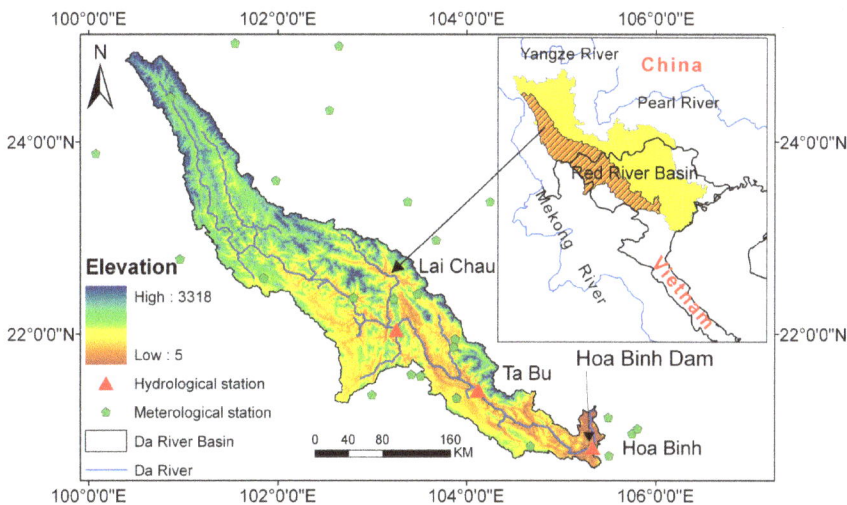

Figure 1. Location of the DRB and the meteorological stations.

2.2. Dataset

The hydrological and meteorological datasets covering 1960–2008 were provided by the Vietnam Academy of Science and Technology and the China Meteorological Data Sharing Service Center and are used as inputs for hydrological simulation and sediment load calculations. Daily streamflow data collected from the Lai Chau (LC) and the Ta Bu (TB) stations in the DRB (Figure 1) were used in calibrating and validating the hydrological model. Monthly suspended sediment concentration (SSC) data are also available at the Lai Chau station. Daily meteorological data including precipitation, wind speed, relative humidity, hours of sunshine as well as maximum, minimum, and mean air temperatures were well distributed in the study area, reflecting the climatic characteristics of DRB.

We also used 0.25 degree gridded daily precipitation and average temperature data from APHRODITE's Water Resources Project [24]. In addition, 0.5 degree gridded monthly average daily maximum and minimum temperature data from Climatic Research Unit [25] was introduced to calculate the diurnal temperature range (DTR), which was applied to transform daily average temperature from APHRODITE into daily maximum and minimum temperature. As for other geographical information, elevation data with 1 km resolution was provided by Global 30 Arc-Second Elevation (GTOPO30) from the U.S. Geological Survey [26,27]. Global Digitized Soil Map and effective Soil Depth of FAO-UNESCO with a spatial resolution of 1 km were used to obtain the soil properties [28]. Global 1 km Land Cover data obtained from the USGS National Center for Earth Resources Observation Science was employed (http://edcdaac.usgs.gov/glcc/ea_int.html), and the land cover was reclassified into the following seven types: evergreen needle-leaf forest, evergreen broadleaf forest, deciduous broadleaf forest, deciduous needle-leaf forest, evergreen shrubs, C3 and C4 (photosynthesis type) grassland in the study. In addition, annual mean global Carbon Dioxide (CO_2) data from Ed Dlugokencky and Pieter Tans, Earth System Research Laboratory, National Oceanic & Atmospheric Administration (NOAA/ESRL) (www.esrl.noaa.gov/gmd/ccgg/trends/) was also used in the ecological model. Global Data Sets of Vegetation Leaf Area Index (LAI 3 g) including a 30 year period from 1982 to 2011 [29] was used to analyze the land cover and develop the new sediment rating curve in our study area. All the geographic data were re-gridded into the same spatial resolution of 0.25 degree to feed with the Biome-Bio Geochemical Cycle (Biome-BGC) ecological model.

3. Methodology

3.1. Determination of Period with Human Distubances

In order to evaluate environment change effects on streamflow and sediment load, the period of most drastic artificial disturbance should be first determined. The Pettitt mutation approach, widely-used to detect the time of the change in time series [30], was employed to detect the time with an abrupt change in annual streamflow in this study. When this break point was determined, the research period could be divided into two parts: the pre-change period before this year represented as the baseline period without strong human activities and post-change period after the abrupt year was recognized as the most serious period of human activities effect compared with the pre-change period (Figure 2). In addition, time series of NDVI and precipitation was also analyzed to confirm this period. In this study, we only focus on the post-change period associating with significant human activities.

3.2. Analysis Method

The total change of streamflow or sediment load should be caused by climate change and human activities in one period. Climate changes include climate-induced land cover change and meteorological change, and human activities include human-induced land cover change and others.

$$\Delta Q^{tot} = \Delta Q^{cli} + \Delta Q^{hum}, \tag{1}$$

$$\Delta Q^{hum} = \Delta Q^{hum-lcc} + \Delta Q^{\circ\ thers}, \tag{2}$$

$$\Delta Q^{cli} = \Delta Q^{cli-lcc} + \Delta Q^{met}, \tag{3}$$

where ΔQ^{tot}, ΔQ^{cli}, ΔQ^{hum}, $\Delta Q^{hum-lcc}$, $\Delta Q^{cli-lcc}$, ΔQ^{met} and $\Delta Q^{\circ\ thres}$ represent the change of streamflow caused by all environment changes, climate variability, human activities, human-induced land cover change, climate-induced land cover change, meteorological change and other artificial disturbances, respectively. Calculation of sediment load changes follows the same rule with streamflow. According to Figure 2, effects of different environmental changes on the streamflow and sediment load were estimated as the following:

$$\Delta Q^{tot} = \overline{Q}_2^{obs} - \overline{Q}_1^{obs}, \tag{4}$$

$$\Delta Q^{hum} = \overline{Q}_2^{obs} - \overline{Q}_2^{sim_{cli}}, \tag{5}$$

$$\Delta SL^{tot} = \overline{SL}_2^{obs} - \overline{SL}_1^{obs}, \tag{6}$$

$$\Delta SL^{hum} = \overline{SL}_2^{obs} - \overline{SL}_2^{sim_{cli}}, \tag{7}$$

in which ΔQ^{hum} and ΔSL^{hum} are the change of streamflow and sediment load due to human activities; $\overline{Q}_1^{obs}$, $\overline{Q}_2^{obs}$, $\overline{SL}_1^{obs}$, and $\overline{SL}_2^{obs}$ is the observed streamflow or sediment load in the first or second period, respectively; and $\overline{Q}_2^{sim_{cli}}$ and $\overline{SL}_2^{sim_{cli}}$ are the simulated potential streamflow and sediment load only considering climate change effect in the second period.

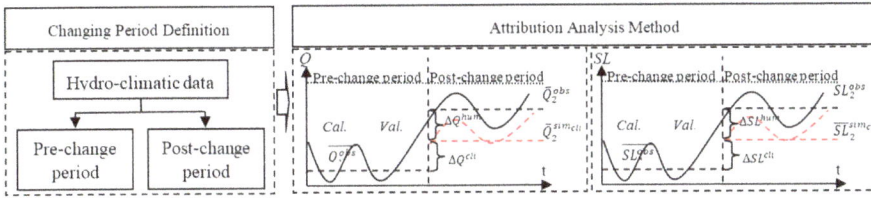

Figure 2. Different period separation and schematic diagram of ΔQ, ΔSL.

Three models are used to evaluate environment changes and their impacts on streamflow and sediment load in DRB: the Biome-BGC Model, the Block wise use of Topography hydrological model with Muskingum–Cunge routing model (BTOPMC) and the New Sediment Rating Curve (NSRC). The models are coupled in a "one-way" manner (Figure 3) and datasets used in these models are summarized in Table 1. A feedback loop is not included, as spatial changes in land cover and temporal dynamic change in LAI are reflected in the basin scale streamflow and sediment load simulation. Biome-BGC is first used to simulate the potential LAI under climate change effect, and BTOPMC and NSRC are validated in the pre-change period in DRB. After this, the potential LAI and actual meteorological data in the post-change period are then inputted into the validated BTOPMC to calculate $\overline{Q}_2^{sim_{cli}}$. Then, potential LAI and $\overline{Q}_2^{sim_{cli}}$ are used to drive validated NSRC to get $\overline{SL}_2^{sim_{cli}}$. Finally, the effect of human activities on streamflow and sediment load can be calculated by the differences between simulated and observed value in the post-change period and the effect of climate variability is the remaining part of the total change.

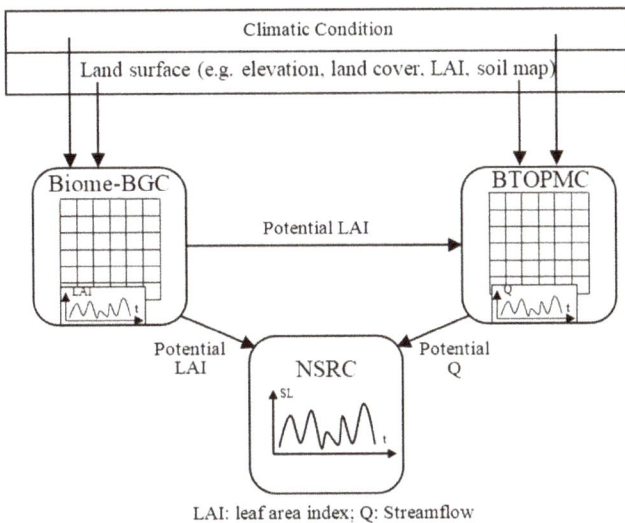

LAI: leaf area index; Q: Streamflow

Figure 3. Model integration and data flow within models.

Table 1. A summary of input datasets for parameterizing different models.

Data	Temporal Scale	Time Span	Spatial Scale	Data Source
Sreamflow	Monthly	1988–2004	Point	Lai Chau station
Sediment flow	Monthly	1988–2004	Point	Lai Chau station
CO_2	Annual	1959–2014	Point	NOAA/ESRL
LAI/NDVI	Monthly	1982–2006	Grid (8 km)	AVHRR-GIMMS(LAI3g)
Precipitation	Daily	1951–2007	Grid (0.25°)	APHRODITE's Water Resources Project
Average Temp	Daily	1951–2007	Grid (0.25°)	Same as above
Max & Min Temp	Monthly	1901–2009	Grid (0.5°)	Climatic Research Unit
DEM			Grid (1 km)	GTOPO30 (USGS)
Soil		2000	Grid (1 km)	FAO-UNESCO
Land Cover		1992	Grid (1 km)	USGS

3.2.1. Hydrological Model

The BTOPMC is a blockwise grid-based distributed hydrological model developed by the University of Yamanashi, Japan [30,31]. The model extends TOPMODEL concept [32] by adopting the Muskingum–Cunge method for flow routing component on a grid basis and sub-catchments served as blocks [30,31]. This concept helps to address TOPMODEL's limitation in flow timing and heterogeneity for modeling large river basins in the warm humid regions [31,33]. For each grid, four vertical zones are considered for hydrological calculation: vegetation zone, root zone, unsaturated zone and saturated zone [30,31]. The model has been validated on several river basins with various resolutions using remote sensing data and global datasets on ungauged catchments with good performance [30–33]. A more detailed description of the BTOPMC model and its underlying conceptualizations and parameters is found in one reference [30].

In this paper, BTOPMC is applied to simulate streamflow controlled by environment changes such as climate change scenario and LAI change. The maximum soil water capacity of the root zone, the LAI for calculation of actual evapotranspiration, and canopy interception were key parameters to evaluate land cover change effects on the streamflow. Three statistics are applied to assess the performance of BTOPMC model [34]:

(i) Nash–Sutcliffe efficiency (*NSE*): *NSE* ranges between $-\infty$ and 1.0 (1 inclusive), with *NSE* = 1 being the optimal value. Values between 0.0 and 1.0 are generally viewed as acceptable levels of performance;

$$NSE = 1 - \frac{\sum_{i=1}^{n}(Qobs_i - Qsim_i)^2}{\sum_{i=1}^{n}\left(Qobs_i - \overline{Qobs}\right)^2} \tag{8}$$

(ii) The ratio of root mean squared error to observations standard deviation (*RSR*): *RSR* varies from the optimal value of 0, which indicates perfect performance in simulation, to a large positive value. The lower the RSR, the better the model simulation performance:

$$RSR = \frac{RMSE}{STDEV_{obs}} = \frac{\sqrt{\sum_{i=1}^{n}(Qobs_i - Qsim_i)^2}}{\sqrt{\sum_{i=1}^{n}\left(Qobs_i - \overline{Qobs}\right)^2}} \tag{9}$$

(iii) Percent bias (*PBIAS*): *PBIAS* value should be close to zero. Positive values indicate the model underestimation bias and *vice versa*;

$$PBIAS = \frac{MAE}{Qobs} = \frac{\left|Qsim - \overline{Qobs}\right|}{\overline{Qobs}} * 100\%, \tag{10}$$

where *Qsim* is simulated value, *Qobs* is observed value, $\overline{Qsim}$ is average simulated value, $\overline{Qobs}$ is average observed value, and MAE is mean absolute error.

When the RSR is less than 0.7 and the NSE is greater than 0.5, the model performance for both streamflow and sediment load calculation is considered as being good [34]. However, values of PBIAS for streamflow and sediment load vary significantly [34]. Moriasi [34] defines PBIAS being less than 25% of a satisfactory indication for the streamflow simulation and PBIAS results less than 55% are considered acceptable for the sediment load.

3.2.2. Ecological Model

Biome-BGC is a biogeochemical point-scale simulation model [35] to estimate the storage and fluxes of carbon, nitrogen and water within terrestrial ecosystems. The model simulates the potential LAI under present climate conditions without human activities, considering changes of both climatic conditions and carbon dioxide concentrations. The model requirement includes daily climate data, CO_2, information of the general environment (*i.e.*, soil, vegetation type and site conditions) and parameters describing the eco-physiological characteristics of vegetation. The missing daily meteorological data, which is not available from APHRODITE or Climate Research Unit (CRU) dataset, are estimated by the Mountain Microclimate Simulation Model (MTCLIM) [36]. The Biome-BGC needs "spin-up" simulations to achieve equilibrium conditions when the initial soil and plant compartment pools match the mass balance equations [35]. Biome-BGC emphasizes leaf area index (LAI) as a key structural output, which is calculated by multiplying carbon allocated to leaves times the specific leaf area. Ichii *et al.* [37] applied this model to simulate the carbon fluxes and gross primary productivity in Amazonian, African and Asian areas. As a result, we also used the model to simulate potential LAI since our study basin is one part of the Asian area. In order to obtain LAI values for all grids, instead of previous point simulation vision for DRB, we developed the grid-based Biome-BGC model with the spatial resolution of 0.25 degree.

3.2.3. New Sediment Rating Curve

The calculation of sediment load requires both streamflow and sediment concentration data in river basins. Sediment concentration data are rare since data collection requires manual individual sampling taken at fixed temporal intervals. This type of data is still absent at most hydrological stations especially in developing countries. Physically-based models or sediment rating curves have been used to estimate suspended sediment concentration (SSC). However, physically-based models universally used to simulate SSC tend to suffer from problems associated with the difficulty of huge dataset and the identifiability of parameter values. Conversely, traditional sediment rating curve [38] generally represents a simple power functional relationship relating SSC to streamflow that unfortunately, does not consider temporal dynamic changes of vegetation cover. Vegetation cover, as was discussed above, should have important effects on soil erosion and sediment transport capacity by slowing flow through friction losses [39]. Hence, low intensity vegetation cover condition should provide more sediment flux for the same streamflow. The New Sediment Rating Curve (NSRC) considers vegetation cover (NDVI or LAI) and gives better agreement in sediment simulation result in several Asian basins [40]. The sediment load (SL) is calculated by:

$$SSC = a(1-M_{LAI}{}^c)Q^b \tag{11}$$

$$M_{LAI} = (LAI - LAI_{min})/(LAI_{max} - LAI_{min}) \tag{12}$$

in which a, b and c are model parameters for a particular stream; Q (m^3/s) is streamflow; SSC (g/m^3) is suspended sediment concentration; M_{LAI} is standardized LAI; and $LAI_{min/max}$ is the minimum and maximum LAI value.

Then, the sediment load (*SL*) can be calculated by:

$$SL = Q \times SSC. \tag{13}$$

Considering data shortage in DRB, NSRC is developed based on time series of M_{LAI} and streamflow to estimate sediment load changes from the changing streamflow and land cover in this study. To provide comprehensive assessment of this sediment model performance and indicate the accuracy of calculated curve, the same statistics and evaluation rules as in the BTOPMC model are used.

4. Results and Discussion

4.1. Determination of Time Period with Human Distubances

As mentioned before, we first determined the period affected the most strongly by human activities. According to the previous study [4], the Pettitt mutation test results indicated a change point in annual streamflow occurring in 1993 for both Lai Chau and Ta Bu hydrologic stations, which showed a significant upward trend in DRB. The period after 1993 was recognized as the period with the most serious human activities impact compared with the period before 1993. In addition, we also analyzed the change of NDVI from 1982 to 2006 and detected one obvious downward shift. Additionally, the average NDVI before and after 1993 also indicated that vegetation cover change affected by human activities was more serious after 1993 (Figure 4). Therefore, the period was divided into two parts: a pre-change period (1988–1993), representing streamflow under natural conditions, and a post-change period (1994–2004), representing streamflow under drastic human activities control. As a result, the period from 1994 to 2004 was selected as the target period to separate impacts of different environment changes on the streamflow and sediment load in this research.

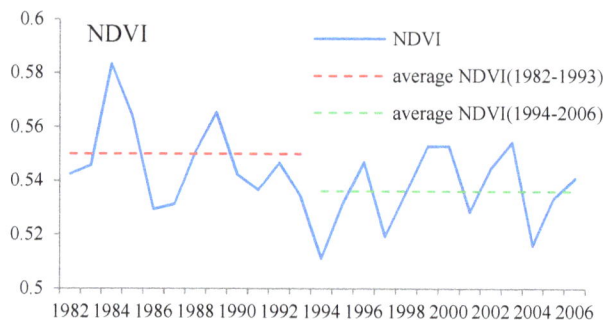

Figure 4. Change of annual maximum NDVI in the upstream of Laichau station (1982–2006).

4.2. Hydrological Model and NSRC Model Simulation

In this study, daily streamflow data for 1988–1993 are used for model calibration and validation of the BTOPMC hydrological model.The statistics for evaluation of the BTOPMC model give consistent results and good accuracy according to established criteria (Table 2).Direct comparison of the daily simulated to observed data of the streamflow in the pre-change period shows a reasonable match with observed data at the Lai Chau and the Ta Bu stations (Figure 5). Thus, the BTOPMC hydrological model could simulate streamflow in DRB well.

Table 2. Evaluation of model simulation during the pre-change period for the catchments controlled by Laichau and Tabu stations in the Da River Basin (DRB).

	Laichau		Tabu	
	Calibration	Validation	Calibration	Validation
R^2	0.92	0.88	0.94	0.89
NSE	0.93	0.89	0.90	0.87
MAE(mm)	3.76	4.49	2.96	3.71
PBIAS (%)	0.37	0.41	0.26	0.27

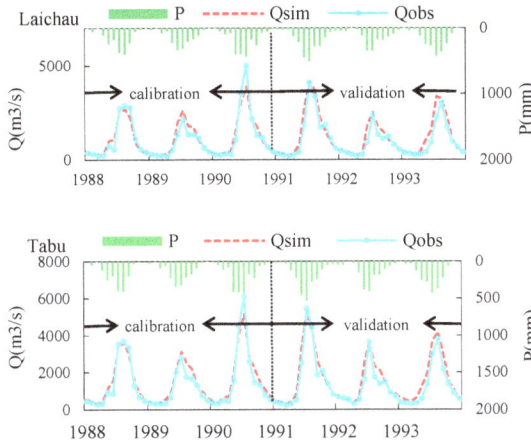

Figure 5. Comparison of observed and simulated monthly streamflow in the DRB.

NSRC model is used to calculate SSC for the period from 1988 to 1993, as the following equation:

$$SSC = 0.41(1-M_{LAI}{}^{6.5})Q^{1.5}. \qquad (14)$$

Results show well noted correlation between simulated and observed monthly SSC (Figure 6). The same three statistical criteria to evaluate new sediment rating curves indicate good agreement with established validation techniques. High NSE (0.86), low RSR and PBIAS (Table 3) suggest that NSRC can evaluate SSC accurately at the Lai Chau station and can be applied to well simulate SSC or sediment load in the DRB.

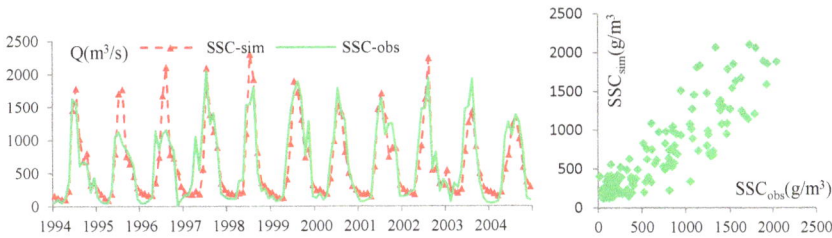

Figure 6. Comparison of observed and simulated monthly SSC at the Laichau station.

Table 3. Performance of new sediment rating curve for the Laichau station.

Catchment	NSE	MAE (g/m³)	PBIAS (%)
Laichau	0.86	3.21	0.634

4.3. Modeled Actual and Potential LAI Analysis

As mentioned above, the point-scale Biome-BGC model was used for simulating gridded basin to evaluate land cover change under climate change. Comparing simulated and observed monthly basin average LAI from 1982 to 1993, the simulated LAI showed a good match with the satellite observed values (Figure 7). In addition, the high R^2 value (0.772) also suggests that this ecological model is capable of simulating LAI reasonably well. Moreover, we compared simulated and satellite annual maximum LAI from 1982 to 2006 shown on Figure 8. It is obvious that the annual simulated LAI matches the observed values before 1994 well, and there is some partial difference in the post-change period. Then, grid maximum monthly and annual potential LAI from 1994 to 2004 were generated from the model to analyze the potential land cover conditions.

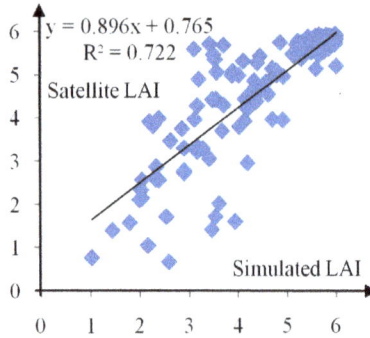

Figure 7. Scatterplot of satellite and simulated monthly basin average LAI.

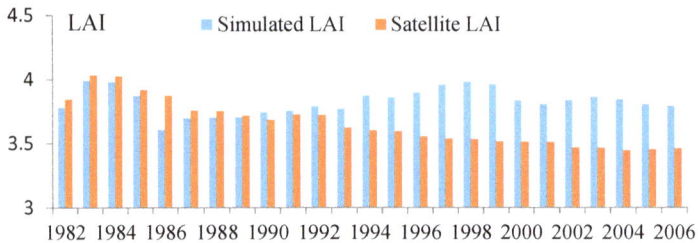

Figure 8. Comparison between simulated and satellite annual maximum LAI.

In order to quantify land cover change in detail, satellite observed LAI was used to reflect actual land cover change caused by combination of climate change and human activities, and simulated potential LAI by an ecological model representing climate-induced land cover change. The difference between the two was considered the true impacts from human-induced land cover change. Thus, the linear trend of annual LAI from GIMMS and potential LAI from the Biome-BGC model forced by real climate data alone were further calculated to identify these complex land cover changes (Figure 9), which expressed some inverse trend between actual LAI and potential LAI from 1982 to 2006. Almost all of the area in the basin showed a decreasing trend for the actual LAI whereas most grids had an increasing trend for potential LAI. On the other hand, the maximum decreasing trend of actual LAI is 0.12, much higher than the increasing slope of 0.01, and the maximum increasing trend of potential LAI is 0.13, much higher than the decreasing slope of 0.05. This unsymmetrical result also showed that human actives aversely changed the trend of land cover. To quantify this type of land cover change, LAI were then standardized according to the Equation (12). Results showed that the average standardized potential LAI (M_{LAIp}) was larger than the standardized actual LAI (M_{LAIc}) for almost all the months including the wet and dry season (Figure 10). As shown in Table 4, two statistics were used to evaluate changes of the land cover without the effect of human activities. The changes between M_{LAIp} and M_{LAIc} for the wet season, dry season, and annual average were different, which indicated that land cover changed severely and human activities affected it stronger in the dry season in the DRB.

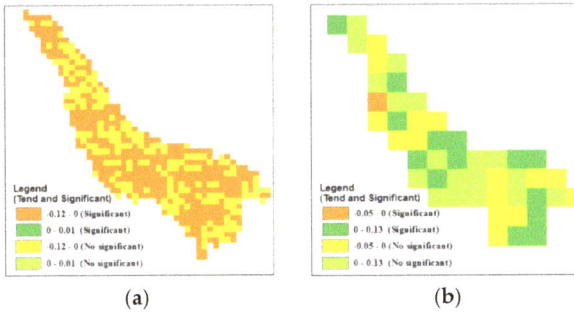

Figure 9. (a) Linear slope of annual maximum LAI from GIMMS; (b) Linear slope of annual maximum LAI from the Biome-BGC model (1982–2006) (Significant: passed significance level of 0.05).

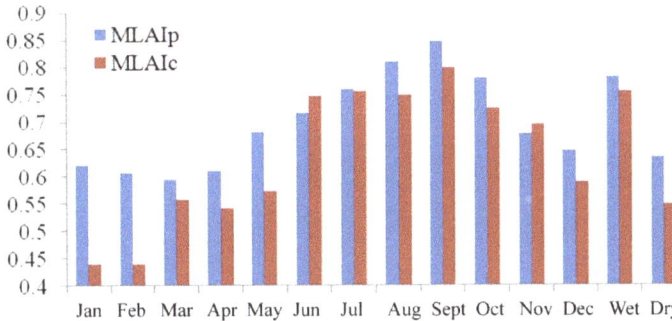

Figure 10. Comparison of average standardized potential LAI (M_{LAIp}) and actual LAI (M_{LAIc}) from 1994 to 2004.

Table 4. Statistic results of comparison between M_{LAIp} and M_{LAIc} from 1994 to 2004.

	Wet Season	Dry Season	Annual Average
M_{LAIp}	0.783	0.635	0.696
M_{LAIc}	0.756	0.548	0.636
MAE	0.027	0.087	0.06
PBIAS(%)	3.57	15.88	9.43

4.4. Effects of New Reclassified Environmental Changes on Streamflow and Sediment Load

In this research, we reclassified all environmental changes related to river streamflow and sediment load as the following: climate change including meteorological changes (such as precipitation, temperature changes) and climate-induced land cover change; human activities including human-induced land cover change and other human activities. According to attribution analysis method, the total change of the streamflow (ΔQ^{tot}) was separated as ΔQ^{cli} and ΔQ^{hum} in different seasons, which was listed in Table 5. Seasonal and annual changes show expected increase for both the Lai Chau and Ta Bu with different magnitudes. Results show that human activities account for 65%, 56.0% in the wet season and the dry season for the Lai Chau catchment, and 62.5% of the total streamflow change for the whole year, and 69.0%, 59.0% and 66.4% for the Ta Bu catchment respectively. Climate change contribution accounts for 35.0% of the wet season, 44% of the dry season, and 37.5% of the whole year at the Lai Chau and 31.0% of the wet season, 41.0% of the dry season, and 33.6% of the whole year at the Ta Bu catchments. Generally, an increase of annual and seasonal streamflow caused by artificial disturbances is larger than the increment caused by climate change in the DRB. The contribution ratio of human activities effect to streamflow changes is a little higher in the wet season at the Lai Chau and Ta Bu station.

Table 5. Effects of human activities and climate change on the annual streamflow (mm) across catchments controlled by hydrological stations in the DRB (subscript 1: 1988–1993; subscript 2: 1994–2004).

Station	Time Scale	$\overline{Q}_1^{obs}$	$\overline{Q}_2^{obs}$	$\overline{Q}_2^{sim_{cli}}$	ΔQ^{tot}	ΔQ^{cli}	ΔQ^{hum}	Clim	Hum
								%	%
	wet season	1726.8	1982.9	1816.4	256.1	89.6	166.5	35.0	65.0
LC	dry season	381.5	479.5	424.6	98.0	43.1	54.9	44.0	56.0
	annual	1054.2	1231.1	1120.5	176.9	66.3	110.6	37.5	62.5
	wet season	2235.2	2784.9	2405.6	549.7	170.4	379.3	31.0	69.0
TB	dry season	493.8	690.6	574.5	196.8	80.7	116.1	41.0	59.0
	annual	1364.6	1738.0	1490.1	373.4	125.5	247.9	33.6	66.4

(Wet season: May to October; dry season: November to April).

Table 6. Effects of human activities and climate change on the annual sediment load (10^6 ton/year) of Lai Chau station (subscript 1: 1988–1993; subscript 2: 1994–2004).

Station	Time Scale	$\overline{SL}_1^{obs}$	$\overline{SL}_2^{obs}$	$\overline{SLQ}_2^{sim_{cli}}$	ΔSL^{tot}	ΔSL^{cli}	ΔSL^{hum}	Clim	Hum
								%	%
	Wet season	65.3	79.8	69.2	14.5	3.9	10.6	26.9	73.1
LC	Dry season	4.8	5.9	5.3	1.1	0.4	0.7	40.0	60.0
	Annual	35.1	42.9	37.4	7.8	2.3	5.5	29.5	70.5

The contribution of climate change and artificial disturbance in sediment load changes is calculated in Table 6. Similar with streamflow, sediment load also shows an obvious increase in the post-change period for the whole year, wet season and dry season. The results show that the proportions of artificial disturbance effect to the total change of sediment load accounts for 70.5%, 73.1% and 60.0% in the whole year, in the wet season and the dry season, and 29.5%, 26.9% and 40.0% for climate change at the Lai Chau station.

4.5. Discussion

4.5.1. Changes of Land Cover Changes and Their Impacts

Generally, human activities and climate variability are the main factors affecting streamflow or sediment load. Land cover changes' effects are more challenging to diagnose and quantify since we reclassified it in two parts in this study: climate-induced and human-induced land cover change. Previous research confirmed climate-induced land cover change as human activities. On the contrary, we considered its effects as a part of climate change impacts. As a result, human-induced land cover changes were the main human activities in our research period since no other drastic human activities were found in the DRB [4,16,17]. Although the spatial distribution of land cover is dominantly controlled by climate on a global scale [41–43], recent studies concluded that regional land cover change has been mainly changed by humans [44–46]. Our results support that human actions are the main factor altering the land cover changes in the DRB through analyzing differences between satellite LAI and simulated LAI from Biome-BGC model. Deforestation was confirmed as the main land cover change in the DRB [16,17,19]. On the other hand, potential LAI without impacts of human activities indicated that forests would have flourished more due to the increased rainfall [42,43]. From the view of different seasons, changes of the human-induced land cover in the dry season are strongest because it is the best season of logging in the DRB. Climate-induced land cover changes are hardly to be controlled in a short time period, however, it is easy to carry out countermeasures for slowing down streamflow and sediment load changes by reversing human-induced land cover changes.

Deforestation was demonstrated to increase river streamflow and sediment load as the main human-induced land cover change [8,15,17,22]. Similar with this study, Wang *et al.* [4] concluded that human activities (land cover changes) are the main reason to affect changes in streamflow in the DRB. Nevertheless, a higher contribution of human activity impacts on streamflow and sediment load (Table 7) was calculated in our study because climate-induced land cover change played a negative role (Table 8) on the increase of streamflow and sediment load. This higher rate contribution indicated climate-induced land cover change could weaken the increase of streamflow and sediment load in the DRB. Although human-induced land cover changed more in the dry season than in the wet season, the absolute change of streamflow and sediment load affected by human-induced land cover changes was higher in the wet season (Tables 4–6). This is due to its rainy weather, which implied that a precondition of land cover change impacts on streamflow and sediment load was the occurrence of enough precipitation. Comparing results of streamflow and sediment load changes separation, we can find that human-induced land cover change effect on sediment load is stronger than the streamflow in the DRB, which argued that changes of land cover may be more sensitive to sediment load [8]. Sediment load of the Lai Chau station draining 2/3 of the area of the DRB was considered as the main sediment flow into the Hoa Binh reservoir downstream. Therefore, due to the increased sediment flow into the reservoir and the reservoir siltation itself, the useful lifetime of the Hoa Binh reservoir would be shortened quickly, which would cause the risk of flood risk to increase and hydropower generation reduction in the Red River area. Thus, countermeasures to protect land cover should be carried out to extend useful lifetime of the reservoir.

Table 7. Comparison with previous research.

Station	Results Source	Clim %	Hum %
LC(Streamflow)	A	37.5	62.5
	B	46.0	54.0
TB(Streamflow)	A	33.6	66.4
	B	40.0	60.0
LC(Sediment load)	A	29.5	70.5
	B	36.0	64.0

Note: A: Our results; B: Results from Reference [4].

Table 8. Environmental changes and their impacts.

Type	Behaviour	Increase of Streamflow and Sediment Load
Climate change	Increasing rainfall	Positive
Climate-Induced land cover change	More frequent forest	Negative
Human-induced land cover change	Forest degradation	Positive

4.5.2. Uncertainties Analysis

Despite the fact that well validated models gave us much information for ungauged watersheds, uncertainties still existed in our study due to many factors: potential errors in input datasets, model parameters and simplification of ecological or hydrological process [47–49]. For example, Li *et al.* found that high uncertainty existed in various model parameters and different scale model simulations [47]. Additionally, although atmospheric CO_2 concentration was considered to simulate potential LAI in ecological models, it was not included in our hydrological and sediment simulation models [30,31,40].

Other human disturbances such as agricultural irrigation water use, urban water consumption and especially dam construction have also likely affected streamflow and sediment load [23,50].

All factors mentioned above may have led to unrealistic simulation results in our study. To effectively reduce uncertainty in model simulations, more field observations should be done [47,48]. It was also demonstrated that ensemble techniques are helpful for uncertainty analysis. Therefore, more field observations should be carried out and an integrated approach considering other influencing factors should be developed in the future.

5. Conclusions

The interaction and feedback among streamflow, sediment load and land cover is complex. Degradation of forests in DRB is caused by humans. As the main human-induced land cover changes, especially in the dry season, deforestation could result in a bigger increase of water yield and sediment load than climate change. Climate change would have the potential to increase vegetation greenness, which could weaken the increase of streamflow and sediment load in the Da River Basin. Deforestation impacts on water yield and sediment load are more pronounced in the wet season, with a stronger influence on the sediment load due to its being doubly affected by changes of streamflow and land cover.

Overall, the research provided a framework for attribution analyses of multiple environmental changes on streamflow and sediment load in a mountainous basin. Since climate-induced land cover changes may not stop in a short time period in this study region, impact analysis on the individual contributions of human-induced land cover changes could be valuable for the local government in decision-making. This study also could provide guidance for future similar studies in other basins that are rarely gauged. Such information could be critically important in directing efforts in managing land use, improving agricultural practices, flood control and soil conservation in the rapidly changed environments in Vietnam.

Acknowledgments: This research was supported by the National Natural Science Foundation of China (Grant No. 41501029, No. 91425301 and No. 41202174), the Natural Science Foundation of Jiangsu Province (Grant No. BK20150922, BK20151525), and the Startup Foundation for Introducing Talent of Nanjing University of Information Science & Technology (NUIST). The authors are also thankful to the Vietnam Academy of Science and Technology and China Meteorological Data Sharing Service Center for providing the hydro-meteorological data.

Author Contributions: This manuscript was primarily designed and written by Jie Wang; Shaowei Ning contributed to its model simulation and calculation. Guiping Yin and Lijuan Guo supported the dataset and data analysis; Hiroshi Ishidaira supervised the research and critically reviewed the draft; Timur Khujanazarov polished the English writing of this draft.

Conflicts of Interest: The authors declare no conflict of interest.

References

1. Schulze, R.E. Modelling hydrological responses to land use and climate change: A southern African perspective. *Ambio* **2000**, *29*, 12–22. [CrossRef]
2. Sun, S.L.; Chen, H.S.; Ju, W.M.; Hua, W.J.; Yu, M.; Yin, Y.X. On the attribution of changing hydrological cycle in Poyang Lake Basin, China. *J. Hydrol.* **2014**, *514*, 214–225. [CrossRef]
3. Le, T.P.Q.; Garnier, J.; Gilles, B.; Sylvain, T.; van Minh, C. The changing flow regime and sediment load of the Red River, Viet Nam. *J. Hydrol.* **2007**, *334*, 199–214. [CrossRef]
4. Wang, J.; Ishidaira, H. Effects of climate change and human activities on streamflow and sediment flow into the Hoa Binh reservoir. *J. Jpn. Soc. Civil Eng. Ser.B1 (Hydraul. Eng.)* **2012**, *68*, I91–I96. [CrossRef]
5. Wardrop, D.H.; Brooks, R.P. The Occurrence and impact of sedimentation in central Pennsylvania wetlands. *Environ. Monit. Assess.* **1998**, *51*, 119–130. [CrossRef]
6. Garcia-Ruiz, J.M.; Lana-Renault, N. Hydrological and erosive consequences of farmland abandonment in Europe, with special reference to the Mediterranean region—A review. *Agric. Ecosyst. Environ.* **2011**, *140*, 317–338. [CrossRef]

7.   José Marques, M.; Bienes, R.; Jiménez, L.; Pérez-Rodríguez, R. Effect of vegetation cover on runoff and soil erosion under light intensity events. Rainfall simulation over USLE. *Sci. Total Environ.* **2007**, *378*, 161–165. [CrossRef] [PubMed]

8.   Tang, L.H.; Yang, D.W.; Hu, H.P.; Gao, B. Detecting the effect of land-use change on streamflow, sediment and nutrient losses by distributed hydrological simulation. *J. Hydrol.* **2011**, *409*, 172–182. [CrossRef]

9.   Nguyen, N.L.; Vo, D.H. *Initiate Results of Research on Impacts of Several Main Vegetative Types on Water Sources and the Principles to Establish Forests for Water Protection*; Agricultural Publishing House: Hochiminh, Vietnam, 1997; p. 156.

10.   Brown, A.E.; Zhang, L.; McMahon, T.A.; Western, A.W.; Vertessy, R.A. A review of paired catchment studies for determining changes in water yield resulting from alterations in vegetation. *J. Hydrol.* **2005**, *310*, 28–61. [CrossRef]

11.   Zhao, F.F.; Xu, Z.X.; Zhang, L.; Zuo, D.P. Streamflow response to climate variability and human activities in the upper catchment of the Yellow River Basin. *Sci. China Ser. E: Technol. Sci.* **2009**, *52*, 3249–3256. [CrossRef]

12.   Stephen, J.W.; Thomas, W.C.; William, F.W.; Kelley, A.C.M. A multiscale analysis of LULC and NDVI variation in Nang Rong district, northeast Thailand. *Agric. Ecosyst. Environ.* **2001**, *85*, 47–64.

13.   Tucker, C.J.; Pinzon, J.E.; Brown, M.E.; Slavback, D.; Park, E.W.; Mahoney, R.; Vermote, E.; Saleous, N.E. An extended AVHRR 8-km NDVI dataset compatible with MODIS and SPOT vegetation NDVI data. *Int. J. Remote Sens.* **2005**, *26*, 4485–4498. [CrossRef]

14.   MOSTE. *Vietnamese General Statistics Officer, Ministry of Science, Technology and Environment of Vietnam, General Statistics Editor*; MOSTE: Hanoi, Vietnam, 1997.

15.   Fullen, M.A.; Mitchell, D.J.; Barton, A.P.; Hocking, T.J.; Liu, L.G.; Wu, B.Z.; Zheng, Y.; Xia, Z.Y. Soil erosion and Conservation in the Headwaters of the Yangtze River, Yunnan Province, China. In *Headwaters: Water Resources and Soil Conservation*, Proceedings of the Headwater '98, the Fourth International Conference on Headwater Control, Merano, Italy, 1998; Haigh, M.J., Krecek, J., Rajwar, S., Kilmartin, M.P., Eds.; pp. 299–306.

16.   United Nations Environment Programme (UNEP). *China Conservation Strategy*; UNEP & China Environmental Science Press: Beijing, China, 1990.

17.   Ye, C.Q.; Gan, S.; Wang, W.L.; Deng, Q.Y.; Chen, W.H.; Li, Y.G. Analysis on the runoff distribution and the variability in the downstream of Honghe River. *Resour. Environ.* **2008**, *17*, 886–891.

18.   World Bank. *Vietnam Water Resources Sector Review. Selected Working Papers of the World Bank, ADB, FAO/UNP and NGO Water Resources Sectoral Group*; World Bank: Hanoi, Vietnam, 1996; p. 340.

19.   Forest Science Institute of Vietnam (FSIV). *Vietnam Forestry Outlook Study, Asia-Pacific Forestry Sector Outlook Study II. Working Paper Series*; Forest Science Institute of Vietnam (FSIV): Hoanoi, Vietnam, 2009.

20.   He, D.M.; Wu, S.H.; Peng, H.; Yang, Z.F.; Ou, X.K.; Cui, B.S. A study of ecosystem changes in Longitudinal Range-Gorge Region and transboundary eco-security in southwest China. *Adv. Earth Sci.* **2005**, *20*, 338–344.

21.   Tuan, V.V. Evaluation of the impact of deforestation to inflow regime of the Hoa Binh Reservoir in Vietnam. In Proceedings of the Yokohama Symposium, Hydrology of Warm Humid Regions, Yokohama, Japan, 13–15 July 1993; pp. 135–138.

22.   Ren, J.; Hen, D.M.; Fu, K.D.; Li, Y.G. Sediment change under climate changes and human activities in the Yuanjiang-Red River Basin. *Chin. Sci. Bull.* **2007**, *52*, 164–171.

23.   Dang, T.H.; Coynel, A.; Orange, D.; Blanc, G.; Etcheber, H.; Le, L.A. Long-term monitoring (1960–2008) of the river-sediment transport in the Red River Watershed (Vietnam): Temporal variability and dam-reservoir impact. *Sci. Total Environ.* **2010**, *408*, 4654–4664. [CrossRef] [PubMed]

24.   Yatagai, A.; Kamiguchi, K.; Arakawa, O.; Hamada, A.; Yasutomi, N.; Kitoh, A. APHRODITE: Constructing a Long-term Daily Gridded Precipitation Dataset for Asia based on a Dense Network of Rain Gauges. *Bull. Am. Meteorol. Soc.* **2012**, *93*, 1401–1415. [CrossRef]

25.   Harris, I.; Jones, P.D.; Osborn, T.J.; Lister, D.H. Updated high-resolution grids of monthly climatic observations—The CRU TS3.10 Dataset. *Int. J. Climatol.* **2013**, *34*, 623–642. [CrossRef]

26.   Bliss, N.B.; Olsen, L.M. Development of a 30-arc-second digital elevation model of South America. In Proceedings of the Pecora Thirteen, Human Interactions with the Environment—Perspectives from Space, Sioux Falls, SD, USA, 20–22 August 1996.

27.   Global 30 Arc-Second Elevation (GTOPO30). Available online: https://lta.cr.usgs.gov/GTOPO30 (accessed on 27 Jananury 2016).

28. DIGITAL SOIL MAP OF THE WORLD. Available online: http://www.fao.org/geonetwork/srv/en/metadata. show?id=14116 (accessed on 27 Janunary 2016).

29. Zhu, Z.C.; Bi, J.; Pan, Y.Z.; Ganguly, S.; Anav, A.; Xu, L.; Samanta, A.; Piao, S.L.; Nemani, R.R.; Myneni, R.B. Global Data Sets of Vegetation Leaf Area Index (LAI) 3 g and Fraction of Photosynthetically Active Radiation (FPAR) 3 g Derived from Global Inventory Modeling and Mapping Studies (GIMMS) Normalized Difference Vegetation Index (NDVI3g) for the Period 1981 to 2011. *Remote Sens.* **2013**, *5*, 927–948.

30. Pettitt, A. A nonparametric approach to the change-point problem. *Appl. Stat.* **1979**, *28*, 126–135. [CrossRef]

31. Takeuchi, K.; Ao, T.Q.; Ishidaira, H. Introduction of blockwise use of TOPMODEL and Muskingum–Cunge method for the hydro-environmental simulation of a large ungauged catchment. *Hydrolog. Sci. J.* **1999**, *44*, 633–646. [CrossRef]

32. Ishidaira, H.; Takeuchi, K.; Ao, T. Hydrological simulation of large river basins in Southeast Asia. In Proceedings of the Fresh Perspectives on Hydrology and Water Resources in Southeast Asia and the Pacific, ChristChurch, New Zealand, 21–24 November 2000; pp. 53–54.

33. Beven, K. Linking parameters across scales-sub grid parameterizations and scale-dependent hydrological models. *Hydrol. Process.* **1995**, *9*, 507–525. [CrossRef]

34. Shrestha, S.; Bastola, S.; Babel, M.S.; Dulal, K.N.; Magome, J.; Hapuarachchi, H.A.P.; Kazama, F.; Ishidaira, H.; Takeuchi, K. The assessment of spatial and temporal transferability of a physically based distributed hydrological model parameters in different physiographic regions of Nepal. *J. Hydrol.* **2007**, *347*, 153–172. [CrossRef]

35. Moriasi, D.N.; Arnold, J.G.; van Liew, M.W.; Bingner, R.L.; Harmel, R.D.; Veith, T.L. Model evaluation guidelines for systematic quantification of accuracy in watershed simulations. *Trans. ASABE* **2007**, *50*, 885–900. [CrossRef]

36. Running, S.W.; Gower, S.T. FOREST-BGC, A general model of forest ecosystem processes for regional applications. *Tree Physiol.* **1991**, *9*, 147–160. [CrossRef] [PubMed]

37. Thornton, P.E.; Hasenauer, H.; White, M.A. Simultaneous estimation of daily solar radiation and humidity from observed temperature and precipitation: An application over complex terrain in Austria. *Agric. For. Meteorol.* **2000**, *104*, 255–271. [CrossRef]

38. Ichii, K.; Hashimoto, H.; Nemani, R.; White, M. Modeling the interannual variability and trends in gross and net primary productivity of tropical forests from 1982 to 1999. *Glob. Planet. Chang.* **2005**, *48*, 274–286. [CrossRef]

39. Asselman, N.E.M. Fitting and interpretation of sediment rating curves. *J. Hydrol.* **2000**, *234*, 228–248. [CrossRef]

40. Howe, A.; Rodriguez, J.; MacFarlane, G. Vegetation Sediment Flow Interactions in Estuarine Wetlands. In Proceedings of the MODSIM 2005 International Congress on Modelling and Simulation Zerger, Modelling and Simulation Society of Australia and New Zealand, Melbourne, Australia, 12–15 December 2005; pp. 332–338.

41. Wang, J.; Ishidaira, H.; Sun, W.C.; Ning, S.W. Development and Interpretation of New Sediment Rating Curve Considering the Effect of Vegetation Cover for Asian Basins. *Sci. World J.* **2013**, *2013*, 154375. [CrossRef] [PubMed]

42. Gallimore, R.; Jacob, R.; Kutzbach, J. Coupled atmosphere-ocean-vegetation simulations for modern and mid Holocene climates: Role of extratropical vegetation cover feedbacks. *Clim. Dyn.* **2005**, *25*, 755–776. [CrossRef]

43. Liu, Z.; Notaro, M.; Kutzbach, J.; Liu, N. Assessing global vegetation-climate feedbacks from observations. *J. Clim.* **2006**, *19*, 787–814. [CrossRef]

44. Smith, V.B.; David, C.H.; Cardenas, M.B.; Yang, Z.L. Climate, river network, and vegetation cover relationships across a climate gradient and their potential for predicting effects of decadal-scale climate change. *J. Hydrol.* **2013**, *488*, 101–109. [CrossRef]

45. Tilman, D.; Lehman, C. Human-caused environmental change: Impacts on plant diversity and evolution. *Proc. Natl. Acad. Sci. USA* **2001**, *98*, 5433–5440. [CrossRef] [PubMed]

46. Chaudhry, G.P.; Saroha, B.S.; Yadav, M. Human Induced Land Use/Land Cover Changes in Northern Part of Gurgaon District, Haryana, India: Natural Resources Census Concept. *J. Hum. Ecol.* **2008**, *23*, 243–252.

47. Taub, D. Effects of Rising Atmospheric Concentrations of Carbon Dioxide on Plants. *Nat. Educ. Knowl.* **2010**, *3*, 21.

48. Li, N.; McLaughlin, D.; Kinzelbach, W.; Li, W.; Dong, G. Using an ensemble smoother to evaluate parameter uncertainty of an integrated hydrological model of Yanqi basin. *J. Hydrol.* **2015**, *529*, 146–158. Available online: http://dx.doi.org/10.1016/j.jhydrol.2015.07.024. [CrossRef]

49. Arnold, S.; Attinger, S.; Frank, K.; Hildebrandt, A. Uncertainty in parameterisation and model structure affect simulation results in coupled ecohydrological models. *Hydrol. Earth Syst. Sci.* **2009**, *13*, 1789–1807.

50. Christiaens, K.; Feyen, J. Use of sensitivity and uncertainty measures in distributed hydrological modeling with an application to the MIKE SHE model. *Water Resour. Res.* **2002**, *38*. [CrossRef]

51. Zhao, G.; Tian, P.; Mu, X.; Jiao, J.; Wang, F.; Gao, P. Quantifying the impact of climate variability and human activities on streamflow in the middle reaches of the Yellow River basin, China. *J. Hydrol.* **2014**, *519*, 387–398. [CrossRef]

Article

Impacts of Forest to Urban Land Conversion and ENSO Phase on Water Quality of a Public Water Supply Reservoir

Emile Elias [1,*,†], **Hugo Rodriguez** [2,†], **Puneet Srivastava** [3,†], **Mark Dougherty** [3,†], **Darren James** [1,†] **and Ryann Smith** [4,†]

1   U.S. Department of Agriculture—Agricultural Research Service, Wooton Hall, New Mexico State University, Las Cruces, NM, 88003, USA; eliaseh@nmsu.edu (E.E.); darren.k.james@gmail.com (D.J.)
2   TetraTech, Inc., 2110 Powers Ferry Rd., Atlanta, GA 30326, USA; hugo.rodriguez@tetratech.com
3   Auburn University, 206 Tom Corley Bldg., Auburn, AL 36832, USA; srivapu@auburn.edu (P.S.); doughmp@auburn.edu (M.D.)
4   New Mexico State University, Las Cruces, NM, 88003 USA; rxsmith3@nmsu.edu
*   Correspondence: eliaseh@nmsu.edu or emile.elias@ars.usda.gov; Tel.: +1-575-646-5190; Fax: +1-575-646-5889
†   These authors contributed equally to this work.

Academic Editors: James M. Vose and Ge Sun
Received: 15 November 2015; Accepted: 18 January 2016; Published: 27 January 2016

Abstract: We used coupled watershed and reservoir models to evaluate the impacts of deforestation and l Niño Southern Oscillation (ENSO) phase on drinking water quality. Source water total organic carbon (TOC) is especially important due to the potential for production of carcinogenic disinfection byproducts (DBPs). The Environmental Fluid Dynamics Code (EFDC) reservoir model is used to evaluate the difference between daily pre- and post- urbanization nutrients and TOC concentration. Post-disturbance (future) reservoir total nitrogen (TN), total phosphorus (TP), TOC and chlorophyll-a concentrations were found to be higher than pre-urbanization (base) concentrations ($p < 0.05$). Predicted future median TOC concentration was 1.1 mg· L^{-1} (41% higher than base TOC concentration) at the source water intake. Simulations show that prior to urbanization, additional water treatment was necessary on 47% of the days between May and October. However, following simulated urbanization, additional drinking water treatment might be continuously necessary between May and October. One of six ENSO indices is weakly negatively correlated with the measured reservoir TOC indicating there may be higher TOC concentrations in times of lower streamflow (La Niña). There is a positive significant correlation between simulated TN and TP concentrations with ENSO suggesting higher concentrations during El Niño.

Keywords: reservoir model; urbanization; deforestation; drinking water treatment; total organic carbon; disinfection byproducts; ENSO

---

1. Introduction

Forested watersheds provide essential ecosystem services such as the provision of high quality water. As watershed land becomes increasingly urbanized, valuable filtration services once provided by the forested catchments are lost. Drinking water treatment authorities in locations such as Boston, MA, Portland, OR, and New York, NY recognize the water quality benefits from forested catchments and actively purchase natural land in supplying watersheds. For example, an improvement in turbidity of 30% saved $90,000 to $553,000 per year for drinking water treatment in the Neuse Basin of North Carolina [1]. An analysis of 27 US water suppliers concluded that a reduction from 60% to 10% forest land increased drinking water treatment costs by 211% [2]. The progressive loss of forest ecosystem services risks harm to human health through lowered drinking water quality, as well as increased drinking water treatment cost [2].

One water quality variable of particular interest to water providers is total organic carbon (TOC) because of disinfection byproduct (DBP) formation. Source water TOC is a good indicator of the amount of DBP that may form as a result of chemical disinfection [3]. TOC reacts with chlorine during the disinfection phase of water treatment to form DBPs. Several DBPs have been identified by the US Environmental Protection Agency (US EPA) as probable human carcinogens. Evidence is insufficient to support a causal relationship between chlorinated drinking water and cancer. However, the US EPA concluded that epidemiology studies support a potential association between exposure to chlorinated drinking water and bladder cancer leading to the introduction of the Stage 2 DBP rule. The American Cancer Society (ACS) estimates that there will be about 74,000 new cases of bladder cancer diagnosed in the United States each year [4]. Approximately 2260 drinking water treatment plants nationwide are estimated to make treatment technology changes to comply with the Stage 2 DBP rule [5]. An alternate method to mitigate DBP formation is the management of watershed land to reduce source water TOC [6,7].

While water providers are struggling to maintain low source water TOC concentrations and minimize DBP formation potential, many source water catchments are undergoing rapid forest to urban land use change [8]. The impact of forest to urban land conversion on lotic TOC concentrations varies, however literature reports elevated TN and TP concentrations in urban streams [9]. Elevated nutrient concentrations can support increased algae growth thereby increasing overall TOC in reservoirs regardless of the allochthonous contribution.

Here we assess the impact of forest to urban land conversion on reservoir TOC concentrations at Converse Reservoir, which supplies the drinking water for the City of Mobile, Alabama through the Mobile Area Water and Sewer Systems (MAWSS). MAWSS is one of the >2000 water treatment facilities nationally making changes to comply with the Stage 2 DBP rule because of existing elevated TOC concentrations. Rapid urbanization is occurring in the contributing watershed and urbanization projections concur that the watershed will undergo significant urbanization in the coming decades [8,10,11]. Like other urbanizing watersheds, the concern is that Mobile source water TOC concentrations may increase as watershed urbanization continues.

Along with watershed forest to urban land conversion, changes in reservoir concentrations may be related to variations in ocean-atmosphere oscillation, known as El Niño Southern Oscillation (ENSO). In southern Alabama, interannual variations in precipitation and streamflow are related to ENSO. El Niño events, which occur every 2 to 10 years, are caused by positive sea surface temperature anomalies. Conversely, La Niña events are caused by negative sea surface temperature anomalies (SST). Strong relationships have been established between ENSO and precipitation in certain regions including southern Alabama, ENSO and water temperature and ENSO and streamflow in the Converse watershed [12]. El Niño seasonal precipitation has been shown to be higher than normal and La Niña precipitation in the three southern climate divisions in Alabama [13]. Precipitation during JFM in the La Niña phase is lower than normal for the southern climate divisions [14]. TOC loads from watershed sources have also been linked with ENSO phase and reflect a seasonal component wherein El Niño TOC loads are higher than neutral or La Niña phase loads during Jan-Mar, but lower than La Niña during Aug-Oct [15]. During El Niño events in January to March, the higher precipitation and streamflow could lead to higher nutrient loads delivered to Converse or similar reservoirs.

Changes in precipitation and temperature can have a significant effect on surface water quality [16]. There is a relationship between ENSO phase, precipitation and streamflow in Alabama [13]. Seasonal streamflow is related to both ENSO phase and surface water nutrient loadings [17]. ENSO phase has been found to have strong nitrate concentration, streamflow and precipitation predictive effects in a southeastern U.S. watershed [18]. ENSO phase has been linked to flow, stream temperature, dissolved oxygen and water quality parameters in southeast Alabama and related to ENSO phase for predicting periods restrictive to point-source discharge to limit water quality impairment [19].

Changes in land use can significantly alter the quality of adjacent surface waters [16]. Increased nutrient concentrations are associated with urban streams [9]. However, the relationship between land use and water quality can vary regionally and even on a stream-by-stream basis due to many factors including land use intensity, geology, precipitation patterns. In the greater Converse Watershed urban subwatersheds had higher TP and TN loads and concentrations than undisturbed forested watershed [20,21]. Watershed simulations also support elevated post-urbanization nutrient concentrations [22]. Converse Reservoir response to changing land use was evaluated previously using a BATHTUB reservoir model [23]. Modelers found increased TP and TN loads, changes in trophic state and increased algal blooms.

This study improves upon previous research by evaluating the impacts of two major stressors to water resources of Converse Reservoir simultaneously. Here we concurrently evaluate the impacts of watershed urbanization and ENSO phase on reservoir water quality. The modeling utilized in this study expands previous efforts by utilizing coupled watershed and reservoir models rather than the BATHTUB model [23], simulating the entire year, rather than April to September only, and using a realistic estimate of watershed urbanization, rather than the expectation of 100% land development. This study builds upon previous efforts [15,19] by relating ENSO phase to reservoir, rather than stream, water quality. Reservoir modeling studies most often evaluate nitrogen and phosphorous fractions, but here we simulate TOC, the variable of most interest to drinking water managers. The rigor of modeling efforts used here, the relation to multiple watershed stressors and the incorporation of reservoir water quality serve to enhance our understanding of the relationship between urbanization, ENSO phase and water quality. To evaluate the impact of forest to urban land conversion and ENSO phase on reservoir water quality, linked watershed [24] and reservoir [25] models were used. Daily nutrient concentrations and streamflow from watershed simulations provide input data to estimate the effects on nutrient and TOC concentrations within the reservoir under base and future land use conditions. Total (1992 to 2005) and monthly median TOC concentrations at a source water intake from base and future scenarios were compared. Additionally, six ENSO indices were correlated with (1) measured TOC; (2) simulated pre-urbanization monthly nutrient and reservoir TOC concentrations; and (3) simulated post- urbanization monthly nutrient and TOC concentrations.

The objectives of this study were to (1) utilize linked watershed and reservoir models to test the hypothesis that watershed nutrient loads during future scenarios will lead to increased TOC concentrations and algae growth at the source water intake when compared with base scenarios; (2) evaluate the influence of anticipated forest to urban land use change in terms of the daily and monthly changes in source water nutrient and TOC concentrations; and (3) evaluate the influence of ENSO phase on measured TOC and simulated pre- and post- urbanization TN, TP, chlorophyll-a and TOC concentrations.

Study Area

Converse Reservoir supplies the majority of drinking water for the City of Mobile, Alabama through the Mobile Area Water and Sewer Service (MAWSS). Past concerns about the quality of Converse Reservoir as a supply source for drinking water prompted various scientific investigations [20,21,23,26–28]. Tributary and reservoir water quality data were collected by the United States Geological Survey (USGS), Auburn University (AU) and MAWSS under various sampling programs beginning in 1990.

Converse Reservoir was formed in 1952 by impoundment of Big Creek in Mobile County, Alabama with a 37 m high earthen dam. The physical characteristics of the reservoir include: volume 64,100,000 m^3, surface area 14.6 km^2, mean depth 4.4 m, and maximum depth 15.2 m. Converse Reservoir has two main branches, Big Creek, which is the reservoir mainstem, and Hamilton Creek, which contains the drinking water intake 4.8 km from the reservoir mainstem (Figure 1).

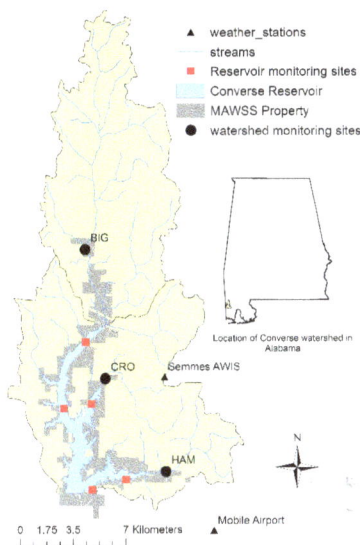

Figure 1. Monitoring locations, weather stations, and Mobile Area Water and Sewer System (MAWSS) property in the Converse watershed and reservoir located in southwestern Alabama.

Precipitation near the study area is some of the highest in the US, with a 48-year (1957–2005) median monthly precipitation of 12.40 cm (1953–2005). A firm-yield analysis of Converse Reservoir estimated ~5% of the total reservoir volume is from groundwater [29]. Streamflow from the 3 major tributaries has been monitored by USGS gauging stations since 1990.

A 267 km^2 watershed drains to the reservoir. Within the watershed there are wetlands, forests, dairy farms, plant nurseries, pecan groves and residential areas using septic tanks for sewage disposal. Watershed soils are generally acidic, low in organic matter content and composed of fine sand or loamy find sand [30]. The eastern watershed boundary extends to within 500 m of Mobile, Alabama city limits. Local, regional and national urbanization studies concur that the study area will likely experience significant urbanization in the coming decades [8,10,11,31].

2. Methods

Long-term simulations using measured hydrologic data were conducted for 1991 to 2005. Environmental Fluid Dynamics Code (EFDC) model simulations were first conducted using uncorrected inflows from the Loading Simulation Program C++ (LSPC) watershed model and water surface elevation. Next, 4 s time-step simulations were conducted using constant outflows. Corrected water surface elevation is recorded daily. After hydrodynamic routines were executed water quality simulations were conducted.

2.1. Software: EFDC Hydrodynamic Model

The EFDC hydrodynamic model was developed at the Virginia Institute of Marine Science beginning in 1988 [25]. EFDC has been applied in various locations, including Chesapeake Bay estuarine system [32], the Neuse Estuary in North Carolina [33] and the Florida Everglades [34]. It has been used in a wide range of environmental studies including simulations of pollutant and pathogenic organism transport, simulation of power plant cooling water discharges, simulation of oyster and crab larvae transport, and evaluation of dredging and dredge spoil disposal alternatives [35]. EFDC has evolved over the past several decades to become one of the most technically defensible and widely used reservoir models available [24]. The EFDC hydrodynamic model provides the hydrologic basis for a number of other water quality models such as Water Quality Analysis Simulation program (WASP5) [36] and the multi-dimensional surface water model (CE-QUAL-ICM) [37]. Details regarding model set-up and theoretical basis are provided in the EFDC User's Manual [35] and the EFDC Theory and Computation Manual [38].

EFDC is an open-access FORTRAN 77 based hydrodynamic model particularly adept at simulating estuarine and reservoir systems. EFDC is an orthogonal, grid-based model, so model execution requires computation of an orthogonal grid with specified number of vertical layers, which is easiest to create using a specialized program (visual orthogonal grid generator). The model solves three-dimensional, vertically hydrostatic equations of motion with many aspects computationally equivalent to the Blumberg-Mellor model [39]. Multiple text files supply various functions in model computation including control files (efdc.inp, show.inp), grid specification files (cell.inp, depth.inp, gcellmap.inp, dxdy.inp, lxly.inp), and time series files (aser.inp (atmospheric information), pser.inp (surface water elevation), qser.inp (volumetric source-sink). EFDC produces various output file classes, all controlled by the master input file (efdc.inp). Modelers can specify diagnostic output files, restart files, two-dimensional graphic and visualization files and three-dimensional graphic and visualization files.

2.2. Scenarios

The 1992 multi-resolution land cover (MRLC) land cover served as the base (pre-urbanization) scenario for comparison with the future (2020; post-urbanization) scenario (Table 1). The 2020 scenario is based on the population-based housing density forecasts of the Forests On The Edge Project [40]. During base and future simulations only daily LSPC-derived streamflow and TN, TP and TOC loads to Converse Reservoir change [22,41].

Table 1. Comparison of 1992 multi-resolution land cover percentages within the Converse Watershed, AL.

Land Use	1992		Post-Urbanization
	Watershed Area (km^2)	Watershed (%)	Watershed Area (km^2)
Urban	7.7	2.9%	59.7
Barren	0.0	0.0%	0.0
Forest	165.6	61.6%	113.6
Pasture	45.3	16.9%	45.3
Cropland	32.8	12.2%	32.8
wetlands	4.8	1.8%	4.8
Water	12.5	4.6%	12.5
Total	268.7	100%	268.7

2.3. Model Configuration

2.3.1. Orthogonal Reservoir Model Grid Generation

Reservoir bathymetry data were unavailable so topographic maps, which reflect the watershed prior to reservoir impoundment in 1952, were used to delineate reservoir bathymetry. We imported photographs of the maps into ArcMap Version 9.1 and georeferenced them to 7.5-min topographic maps. VOGG: A Visual Orthogonal Grid Generation Tool for Hydrodynamic and Water Quality Modeling generates the grid required for reservoir modeling [42]. The grid serves as the reference system for EFDC modeling. A total of 575 grid cells in a curvilinear grid array represented the Converse Reservoir (Figure 2). The mean cell width is 178 m (range: 139–208 m) and mean cell height is 186 m (range: 97–390 m).

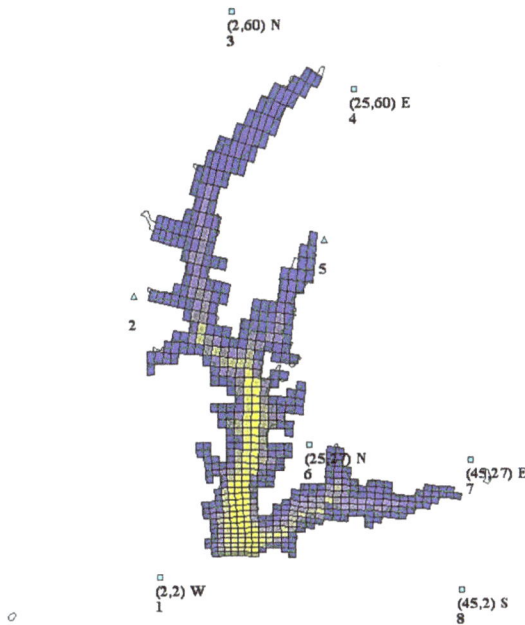

Figure 2. Grid showing the Converse Reservoir with eight control points and 575 cells used in Environmental Fluid Dynamics Code (EFDC) modeling. Cell colors correspond with bottom elevation in meters above mean sea level. Numbers represent the horizon.

2.3.2. Atmospheric Data

We used hourly local climatological data from the National Climatic Data Center (NCDC) for the Mobile Regional Airport weather station for the monitoring period. Atmospheric input files include hourly barometric pressure, air temperature, dewpoint temperature, rainfall, solar radiation, and cloud cover, wind speed and wind direction.

2.3.3. Reservoir Inflows and Outflows

The input file of streamflow and outflow data (qser.inp) was created using modeled LSPC streamflow. Simulated inflows from all subwatersheds draining to Converse Reservoir were apportioned to one of five inflows (Hamilton Creek, Crooked Creek, Big Creek, Long Branch, and Boggy Branch). The two simulated outflows are dam spillage and pumpage for drinking water treatment, taken from MAWSS records. Water level was the measured water surface elevation during the first day of simulation and fluctuated with each time step during the simulation. Dam and lake seepage and groundwater interaction are not simulated by EFDC and estimated to be negligible. Losses to lake evaporation are approximately equal to precipitation in this humid, subtropical region.

2.3.4. Tributary Water Quality Inputs

Daily TN, TP and TOC concentrations from the watershed model [22] were partitioned into nutrient fractions for the EFDC model based upon measured data for each stream (Table 2).

Table 2. Environmental Fluid Dynamics Code (EFDC) water quality simulation variables and measured data used to partition simulated total nitrogen (TN), total phosphorus (TP) and total organic carbon (TOC) into nutrient fractions.

EFDC Simulation Variable	Measured Data Used to Partition Simulated TN, TP and TOC into Fractions
Green Algae	= Daily inflow $\times$ 0.002 mg·L^{-1} $\times$ 2.447 = kg·d^{-1}
Refractory Particulate Organic C	= TOC (680 [†]) − DOC (681 [†]).
Dissolved Organic C	= 681 [†]
Refractory Particulate Organic P	= TP (665 [†]) − dissolved orthophosphate (671 [†]) and dissolved organic P (below).
Dissolved Organic P	= [dissolved P (666 [†]) − dissolved orthophosphorus (671 [†])].
Total Phosphate	= TP (665[†]) − organic P (above)
Refractory Particulate Organic N	= 20% of the total organic N. TON = ammonium (625 [†]) − organic N (610 [†]).
Dissolved Organic N	= 80% of the total organic N.
Ammonium N	= 610 [†]
Nitrate N	= 630 [†]
Dissolved O$_2$	Mean monthly measured dissolved O$_2$ concentrations are used to estimate daily tributary dissolved O$_2$.

[†] indicates USGS parameter code.

Measured data provided the basis for partitioning watershed model TN concentrations into TON, nitrate and ammonium values based upon the following relationship; TN is the sum of inorganic N [nitrate and ammonium] and organic N. Organic N was simulated in either the dissolved or particulate form. TON was assumed to be ~20% particulate and 80% dissolved based upon the measured proportions in samples at Big, Crooked and Hamilton creeks (TON n = 61; DON n = 52). Dissolved and particulate organic P are partitioned based upon the following relationship; TP = particulate organic P + dissolved organic P + orthophosphate. Measured TP, dissolved P and orthophosphorus were used to calculate the percentage of incoming simulated TP as dissolved organic, particulate organic and inorganic (orthophosphate) at all 5 tributaries flowing into Converse Reservoir. Organic C was simulated in particulate and dissolved forms. Measured TOC and DOC data are used to partition the simulated TOC from the watershed model into dissolved and particulate fractions. Daily values of 2 μg·L^{-1} for green algae chlorophyll-a were input. Measured data provided an estimate of mean monthly dissolved oxygen at each stream.

2.4. Calibration and Validation

Reservoir calibration (2001 to 2003) and validation (1996 to 1999) time periods were selected based upon monitoring data availability. The calibration period included one year of below average precipitation (2001) and two years of above average precipitation (2002 and 2003). The validation period also had one year of below average precipitation (1999) and three years of above average precipitation (1996 to 1998).

Measured data were used to assess model calibration and validation. Temperature data are collected using an YSI thermistor and DO was collected using the membrane electrode method [43]. Chlorophyll-a samples are analyzed using standard method 10200H, a high-performance liquid chromatography method [43]. TOC was analyzed using method 5310-B [43]. Colorimetric methods were used to analyze TP and TN (mg·L^{-1}). Chlorophyll-a, TN, TP and TOC model parameters were adjusted to achieve similar simulated and measured water quality near the drinking water intake.

2.5. Data Analyses

2.5.1. Model Calibration and Validation Statistics

EFDC produced daily results for each cell (n = 575) at 5 depths. We calculate the mean of the values for each depth at the MAWSS source water intake (cell 34,18). To assess model performance we calculate absolute mean error (AME), fractional AME and percent bias (PBIAS) performance ratings (Table 3). Fractional AME (or relative error) is a normalized statistic and allows for comparison with other model applications. PBIAS performance ratings [44] are published for monthly mean values, but here were applied to daily grab samples because multiple monthly samples for water quality were unavailable. Moriasi *et al.* (2007) recommend the use of graphs to evaluate calibration and validation quality where a continuous dataset is unavailable. Time-series plots of simulated and measured water quality were developed for visual comparison. Profile plots of measured and simulated temperature and DO in the channel near the drinking water intake (cell 27,18) were also used to assess performance. Model calibration and validation were deemed acceptable based upon time-series plots, as well as comparison of AME and PBIAS performance ratings.

Table 3. Environmental Fluid Dynamics Code (EFDC) calibration (1 August 2001 to 31 December 2003) and validation (1 July 1996 to 31 December 1999) statistics at Converse Reservoir drinking water intake for temperature (TEMP), dissolved oxygen (DO), total nitrogen (TN), total phosphorus (TP), total organic carbon (TOC), and chlorophyll-a (CHL a). Unavailable performance ratings are based on temperature (for dissolved oxygen) and nutrient (for TOC and chlorophyll-a) ratings.

Variable	Units	N	Mean		SD		Fractional AME	AME	PBIAS
			Obs	Sim	Obs	Sim			
Calibration									
TEMP	°C	17	26.2	27.0	3.2	3.4	0.04	1.0	−3.1% VG
DO	mg·L^{-1}	17	6.3	6.1	1.35	0.9	0.14	0.86	3.6% VG
TN	mg·L^{-1}	18	0.39	0.42	0.13	0.04	0.26	0.10	−9.0% VG
TP	mg·L^{-1}	18	0.007	0.006	0.008	0.002	0.66	0.004	9.0% VG
TOC	mg·L^{-1}	38	3.90	3.50	1.12	0.64	0.21	0.81	10.2% VG
CHL a	µg·L^{-1}	17	4.82	7.5	4.48	1.84	0.94	4.5	−54% S
Validation									
TEMP	°C	38	21.5	21.3	6.58	6.50	0.05	1.0	1.7% VG
DO	mg·L^{-1}	38	7.95	6.91	1.78	1.30	0.16	1.3	13.0% F
TN	mg·L^{-1}	24	0.38	0.47	0.07	0.09	0.29	0.11	−25% G
TP	mg·L^{-1}	23	0.015	0.010	0.010	0.005	0.56	0.009	40% G
TOC	mg·L^{-1}	143	3.54	3.48	1.16	0.34	0.28	0.97	2% VG
CHL a	µg·L^{-1}	21	4.19	5.0	5.77	3.16	0.82	3.4	19% VG

Profiles of temperature and dissolved oxygen collected over 17 days during calibration and 13 days during validation. Individual temperature and dissolved oxygen samples collected on 25 days during validation. N = sample size; SD = standard deviation; Fractional AME = fractional absolute mean error; AME = absolute mean error; PBIAS = percent bias.

2.5.2. Base and Future Scenario Statistics

We analyze daily concentrations at the MAWSS source water intake for the simulated water quality variables and urbanization scenarios for normality using histograms and quantile-quantile normal plots of residuals. When data were not normally distributed, differences between scenarios were conducted using nonparametric comparison methods such as the Wilcoxon Sign-Ranked (WSR) test to compare daily and monthly median base and future concentrations [45].

We report the change in overall median (1992 to 2005) and median monthly TN, TP and TOC concentration and percent difference between base and future scenarios. Reservoir concentration change following deforestation is reported in terms of land use change. The percent change per area change (%Δ/areaΔ) metric is the percent difference between base and future concentrations divided by the simulated change in forest to urban land (km^2). Time-series plots display differences between daily base and future TN, TP, TOC and chlorophyll-a concentrations.

2.5.3. El Niño Southern Oscillation Index

Various indices are used to estimate ENSO phase. The oldest indicator if ENSO is based on air pressure differences at sea level at two locations (Tahiti and Darwin) in the southern Pacific Southern Oscillation Index (SOI). Sea surface temperature data in different regions of the Pacific Ocean were later added to ENSO indices. An area of the Pacific was identified as being the most representative of ENSO phase [46] and this area is reflected in the Oceanic Niño Index and the Niño 3.4 Index.

We use three common indices to represent ENSO phase, the National Oceanic and Atmospheric Administration's (NOAA) official ENSO indicator, the Oceanic Niño Index (ONI) [47], Niño 3.4 Index [48] and the Multivariate ENSO Index (MEI) [49]. The Niño 3.4 Index values, which represent a 3 month running mean of sea surface temperature anomalies in the Niño 3.4 region (5° N–5° S, 120°–170° W) was obtained from the NOAA Climate Prediction Center [50]. The Multivariate ENSO Index (MEI) is based upon the six main observed variables over the tropical Pacific Ocean. MEI is computed for bi-monthly seasons and here the Dec/Jan value is attributed to January for analysis purposes. Since the impact of precipitation on reservoir water quality may be delayed, we also shifted the ONI, Niño 3.4 and MEI forward one month, facilitating comparison of, for example, March concentrations with February ENSO index to determine if there is a lagged response between ENSO and reservoir water quality.

2.5.4. Correlation Analysis

MAWSS collected TOC data in Converse Reservoir and at both drinking water treatment plants between 1995 and 2007 (n = 334 samples at each location). Pearson correlation coefficients between measured TOC concentrations with six representative indices (ONI, ONI + 1, Niño 3.4, Niño 3.4 + 1, MEI, MEI + 1) were calculated using SAS Version 9.4 (SAS Institute Inc., North Carolina, USA) to study the relationship between ENSO and TOC. Correlation analysis between simulated monthly mean TN, TP, TOC and chlorophyll-a concentrations (n = 141 months) at the drinking water intake with the six ENSO indices for both pre- and post- urbanization were also evaluated. The null hypothesis of no correlation was tested at the 95% level for all correlations.

3. Results and Discussion

3.1. Calibration and Validation Results

Measured and simulated water level correspond well. Mean simulated water surface elevation (WSE) during calibration was 0.03 m higher than mean measured WSE (33.42 and 33.39 m, respectively). Mean simulated WSE during validation was 0.21 m higher than mean measured WSE (33.32 and 33.53, respectively). Results of simulated and observed mean, standard deviation, absolute mean error (AME), fractional AME and percent bias (PBIAS) for calibration and validation are provided in Table 3.

During calibration, mean values for temperature profiles collected on 17 days for observed and simulated data were 26.2 °C and 27.0 °C, respectively (Table 3). An AME of 1.0 indicates that, on average, the predicted temperature values were within 1.0 °C of the observed values. The PBIAS of −3.1% for temperature calibration indicates "very good" performance [51]. Temperature fractional AME was 4%. Temperature and DO profiles of observed and simulated data during calibration and validation indicate good model performance. DO fractional AME was 0.14, similar to EFDC modeling applications at Cape Fear River, NC (0.12–0.15), Charleston Harbor, SC (0.08–0.21), and Charles River, MA (0.07–0.21) [38]. During calibration and validation, the Converse EFDC model predicted DO levels well and within ranges reported by other EFDC applications.

Nutrient and TOC Calibration and Validation

During calibration, TN, TP and TOC concentration performance ratings were "very good" based upon PBIAS. On average, predicted TN values were within 0.1 mg·L^{-1} of observed values. Mean of daily observed and predicted TP concentrations were 0.007 and 0.006 mg·L^{-1}, respectively. Mean daily observed and predicted TOC are 3.9 and 3.5 mg·L^{-1}, respectively. On average, predicted TOC values were within 0.8 mg·L^{-1} of observed TOC values. TN fractional AME is 0.26, within the range reported for a calibrated model of St. Johns River [52] and other calibrated EFDC models [38]. TP fractional AME was 0.66, within the ranges reported for other calibrated reservoir models [38]. TOC fractional AME was 0.21, less than values reported for Florida Bay [53] and similar to St. Johns River [52].

During validaiton, TN, TP and TOC concentration performance ratings were "good" to "very good" based upon PBIAS. The mean observed and simulated TN concentrations during validation were 0.38 and 0.47 mg· L^{-1}, respectively. Simulated TN was higher than observed TN, with an AME indicating that predicted TN was within 0.11 mg· L^{-1} of observed TN. Fractional AME for TN (0.29) was within the range of reported values from other EFDC applications. TN validation performance rating based upon a PBIAS of 25% was "good" [44]. While the Converse Reservoir EFDC model slightly overpredicted in-reservoir TN concentrations, it slightly underpredicted TP concentrations. Mean observed and simulated TP concentrations during validation were 0.015 and 0.010 mg· L^{-1}, respectively. The fractional AME of 0.56 for TP validation was within reported values for other EFDC applications [38]. PBIAS for TP during validation was 40% indicating "good" model performance. Observed (3.54 mg· L^{-1}) and simulated (3.48 mg· L^{-1}) mean daily TOC concentrations (n = 143) during validation correspond well. The TOC PBIAS of 2% was considered 'very good' based upon the nutrient performance ratings of Moriasi *et al.* (2007).

Mean measured chlorophyll-a during the calibration period was 4.8 µg· L^{-1}, while simulated mean chlorophyll was 7.5 µg· L^{-1}. Seven of the 17 measured chlorophyll-a samples were below the detection limit of 0.1 µg· L^{-1}. Time-series plots of simulated and measured chlorophyll-a revealed that simulated values did not decrease to the detection limit. On average, predicted calibration chlorophyll-a was 4.5 µg· L^{-1} higher than measured chlorophyll-a. PBIAS performance critera specific to chlorophyll-a were not provided by Moriasi *et al.* (2007) or Donigian (2002), but applying TN and TP performance ratings of Moriasi to chlorophyll-a, the validation PBIAS of 19% indicated "very good" reservoir model performance. During validation, mean observed and simulated chlorophyll-a (n = 21) were 4.19 and 5.0 µg· L^{-1}, respectively. The fractional AME for chlorophyll-a during validation was 0.82 and within the range of values reported for a calibrated model of Charles River, MA (0.76–1.37) and St. Johns River, FL (0.37–1.10) [38,52]. The relative error for Converse Reservoir chlorophyll-a simulation during both calibration and validation (0.94 and 0.82, respectively) were within the range of errors reported for other EFDC simulations. Chlorophyll-a concentrations are inherently difficult to measure accurately due to chlorophyll-a overestimation from the presence of phaeophytin [54], decomposition during the process of measurement and variations in collection methodology [55]. Consequently, the differences between simulated and observed chlorophyll-a during calibration and validation, which are commonly attributed to model errors, may in fact be a consequence of errors in determining measured chlorophyll-a.

3.2. Measured Concentrations Used to Partition Total Loads

We partitioned watershed model TN concentrations into TON, nitrate and ammonium values using measured data. The mean N percentages ranged from 32% to 65% for TON, 30% to 65% for nitrate and 3% to 5% for ammonium. These percentages were applied to the daily TN values for each stream to calculate input TON, nitrate and ammonium values. Measured TP data were used to estimate the percentage of incoming simulated TP as dissolved organic, particulate organic and inorganic (orthophosphate) at all 5 tributaries to Converse Reservoir. The TP percentages ranged from 33% to 38% for dissolved organic P, 18% to 23% for particulate organic P and 44% to 49% for orthophosphate. Measured TOC and DOC data was used to partition the simulated TOC from the watershed model into dissolved and particulate fractions. Most of the organic C was in the dissolved form, with average percentages at the five tributaries ranging from 89% to 93%. Particulate organic carbon was between 7% and 11% of the TOC.

3.3. Comparison of Simulated Nutrient, TOC and Chlorophyll-a Concentrations

3.3.1. Daily Simulated Reservoir Concentrations at the Intake

We used nonparametric tests in data comparisons because histograms, quantile-quantile normal plots of residuals and skewness coefficients using simulated daily TN, TP and TOC concentrations indicate data follow a non-normal distribution. The WSR test using daily TN, TP, TOC, and chlorophyll-a concentrations at MAWSS drinking water intake indicated that pre- and post-urbanization reservoir concentrations were significantly different for all variables ($p < 0.05$). In each case, future daily concentrations from the urbanized watershed were higher than pre-urbanization concentrations.

Median future TN, TP, TOC, and chlorophyll-a concentrations were higher than median base concentrations for each scenario and nutrient (Table 4). Future (urban) TN concentrations at MAWSS drinking water intake were 55% (0.21 mg·L^{-1}) higher than base scenario (forested) TN concentrations. Median TN concentration increased by 0.004 mg·L^{-1} km^{-2}. Median future TP concentrations increased by 0.004 mg·L^{-1} (67%) above median base TP concentrations. Median TP concentrations increased by 0.0002 mg·L^{-1} km^{-2} urbanized. Median future TOC concentrations increased by 1.1 mg·L^{-1} (41%) over median base TOC concentrations due to simulated urbanization. Median TOC concentration increased by 0.02 mg·L^{-1} for each km^2 urbanized. The percent TOC change per area urbanized (%Δ/areaΔ) was 0.8% per km^2 urbanized indicating that for each km^2 of forest land converted to urban land reservoir, TOC concentrations at the source water intake increase by 0.8%.

Table 4. Median total nitrogen (TN), total phosphorus (TP) and total organic carbon (TOC) concentrations using daily simulated data at the drinking water intake on Converse Reservoir, AL, 1992 to 2005 (n = 4292 days).

Scenario	Units	TN	TP	TOC
Base	mg·L^{-1}	0.38	0.006	2.59
Future	mg·L^{-1}	0.59	0.010	3.65
Difference	mg·L^{-1}	0.21	0.004	1.1
Percent change	%	55%	67%	41%
Difference/km^2	mg·L^{-1}·km^{-2}	0.004	0.0001	0.02

3.3.2. Simulated Reservoir Concentrations by Month at the Drinking Water Intake

Simulated urbanization significantly increased TN, TP, TOC and chlorophyll-a levels during each monthly comparison. A comparison of median concentration by month (*i.e.*, Jan base concentrations compared with Jan future concentrations, Feb base concentrations compared with Feb future concentrations, *etc.*) indicated base and future TN, TP, TOC, and chlorophyll-a by month were significantly different ($p < 0.05$) (Table 5).

Monthly median TP concentrations were highest from January to March, when simulated median TOC concentrations were least. Analysis of monthly median TP and chlorophyll-a showed an increase in median chlorophyll-a in April that coincided with decreased median TP concentrations indicating simulated P limitation. Monthly analysis indicated that TN and TP concentrations declined as TOC concentrations increased, likely due to the influence of algae growth, which utilized TN and TP and incorporated C into biomass, thereby increasing simulated TOC. Simulated monthly median chlorophyll-a was highest in May and June and TOC was highest in June. However, the strong seasonal influence evident in monthly median chlorophyll-a concentrations was not as evident in TOC concentrations indicating both algae growth and other factors influence TOC concentration at the drinking water intake.

Table 5. Monthly median base, future and measured (n = 382) total organic carbon (TOC) concentration ($mg \cdot L^{-1}$) and monthly TOC percent increase in concentration and percent of days with TOC concentration >2.7 $mg \cdot L^{-1}$ before and following urbanization at the drinking water intake on Converse Reservoir, AL, 1992 to 2005.

	Jan.	Feb.	Mar.	Apr.	May.	Jun.	Jul.	Aug.	Sep.	Oct.	Nov.	Dec.
Base	2.4	2.6	2.5	2.7	2.9	2.9	2.8	2.5	2.4	2.5	2.6	2.5
Future	3.3	3.0	3.0	3.3	3.8	4.0	3.9	3.7	3.6	3.8	3.7	3.7
Simulated percent increase in TOC concentration following urbanization												
	37	19	21	22	33	40	41	49	49	49	43	46
Measured median TOC concentration at source water intake (n = 382; 1995 to 2005)												
	3.3	3.0	3.2	3.3	3.6	3.5	4.4	4.2	4.2	4.6	3.9	2.9
Simulated percent of days with TOC concentration > 2.7 $mg \cdot L^{-1}$ before and after urbanization												
Base	41	34	29	52	72	62	54	37	24	37	41	38
Future	100	85	72	87	97	100	100	100	100	100	100	100
Wilcoxon sign ranked test of simulated monthly median base and future concentrations												
TN	*	*	*	*	*	*	*	*	*	*	*	*
TP	*	*	*	*	*	*	*	*	*	*	*	*
TOC	*	*	*	*	*	*	*	*	*	*	*	*
Chlorophyll-a	*	*	*	*	*	*	*	*	*	*	*	*

* indicates significant difference between base and future monthly median values from 1992 to 2005, excluding drought year of 2000 (n = 141 months).

3.3.3. Comparison of Simulated and Measured Monthly Reservoir TOC

Between May and October, simulated TOC concentrations at the source water intake increased by 33% to 49% (Table 5). The largest increase occurred from August to October. Since additional drinking water treatment is related to elevated water temperatures between May and October, the elevated reservoir TOC concentrations between May and October here can increase DBP formation potential. Changes to existing drinking water treatment to minimize the increased May to October TOC concentrations will be necessary to achieve future compliance with the Stage 2 DBP legislation.

3.3.4. TOC Concentration and Potable Water Treatment

Between May and October, simulated base scenario reservoir TOC was less than the drinking water treatment threshold (2.7 $mg \cdot L^{-1}$) on 1118 of 2117 d (53%). Thus, prior to urbanization, additional drinking water treatment would be required 47% of the days between May to October. Future scenario simulated reservoir TOC concentrations were <2.7 $mg \cdot L^{-1}$ on 11 of 2117 d (0.5%) between May and October. The monthly simulated percent of days with TOC concentrations >2.7 $mg \cdot L^{-1}$ using the base simulation indicated that 24% to 72% of days required additional drinking water treatment prior to urbanization. Following urbanization, 97% to 100% of days between May and October required additional drinking water treatment. To comply with the DBP treatment level of 2.7 $mg \cdot L^{-1}$, additional future drinking water treatment would be continuously necessary and significantly increase treatment costs [56,57]. Mean increase in daily treatment cost ranged from $91–$95 per km^2 converted for forest to urban land use per day [57].

3.3.5. Effects of ENSO on Reservoir Nutrient Concentrations

Other researchers report higher January to March precipitation in Southern Alabama during El Niño events than normal or La Niña phases [12]. We anticipate the reported increases in precipitation and streamflow may lead to measurable changes in reservoir TOC, nutrients and chlorophyll-a.

We compared measured TOC data at three locations with six ENSO indices. Results indicate no significant correlation between MEI, MEI + 1, Niño3.4, Niño3.4 + 1 and ONI + 1 with measured TOC concentrations. While there is a significant correlation between ONI and drinking water treatment plant

TOC at both plants ($p = 0.04$), the correlation coefficient (-0.11) is low in both cases, suggesting that while ENSO may be related to TOC concentration at the drinking water treatment plants, other factors, such as seasonal in-reservoir algae growth, likely have a greater impact on concentrations. A strong positive relationship between ENSO and TOC would indicate watershed TOC sources associated with elevated precipitation and streamflow of El Niño likely driving TOC concentrations. A strong negative relationship between ENSO and TOC may suggest internal factors such as in-reservoir algae growth since La Niña is associated with lower streamflow during most of the year [12]. Given the small negative correlation, there may be slightly higher TOC concentrations at the drinking water plants associated with La Niña events, which are associated with lower streamflow all months except September and October. The small significant correlation between ONI and TOC should be interpreted conservatively because (1) it is evident in only one of six ENSO indices and (2) it explains relatively little of the variance in TOC concentrations. However, further evaluation of the relationship between ONI and reservoir TOC data is warranted. Recent research using long-term instrumented data found a relationship between ENSO phase, streamflow and reservoir dissolved oxygen content [58]. This supports the possible relationship between ENSO and reservoir water quality and indicates dissolved oxygen analysis at Converse Reservoir may be warranted.

There was no significant relationship between simulated monthly chlorophyll-a concentration with ENSO indices or simulated monthly TOC with ENSO indices for either pre- or post- urbanization. There was, however, an observed positive correlation between both TN and TP with ENSO indices (Table 6). The correlation between simulated monthly TN concentrations and ENSO phase was significant for all indices for both forested and urban scenarios. ENSO phase explained between 27% and 37% of the variance in TN concentrations before urbanization and slightly less following urbanization. The correlations between ENSO phase and TP were not as strong as those with TN, however urbanization appears to strengthen the relationship between ENSO and TP concentration. The correlations were positive, indicating higher concentrations associated with El Niño events, which corroborates a recent finding that TN and TP loads to Converse Reservoir were higher during El Nino [59]. Our research indicates that the relationship evident in streamflow modeling is also reflected in reservoir nutrient concentrations, thereby reverberating through the reservoir ecosystem. The positive correlation in simulated reservoir TN and TP concentrations associated with ENSO phase were not apparent in simulated TOC and chlorophyll-a. It is possible that the nutrient additions associated with urbanization and El Niño have a delayed effect on reservoir algae growth and TOC concentrations or that other factors, such as temperature and light, are more important in controlling chlorophyll-a and TOC in Converse Reservoir. The lower flows of La Niña events may serve to promote TOC increase in Converse Reservoir because of lower flushing rates.

Table 6. Correlation between ENSO indices and Converse Reservoir simulated monthly TN and TP concentrations at the Mobile Area Water and Sewer Systems drinking water intake.

Index	TN				TP			
	Baser	*p*-value	Futurer	*p*-value	Baser	*p*-value	Futurer	*p*-value
MEI	0.32	0.0001	0.31	0.0002	0.12	0.1429	0.18	0.0377
MEI + 1	0.27	0.0012	0.24	0.0040	0.13	0.1272	0.17	0.0488
Niño 3.4	0.37	0.0000	0.35	0.0000	0.17	0.0398	0.26	0.0021
Niño 3.4 + 1	0.36	0.0000	0.34	0.0000	0.22	0.0104	0.27	0.0010
ONI	0.37	0.0000	0.33	0.0001	0.17	0.0390	0.26	0.0021
ONI + 1	0.37	0.0000	0.33	0.0001	0.22	0.0088	0.28	0.0007

4. Conclusions

Simulated forest to urban land conversion of 52 km^2 in the 267 km^2 Converse Reservoir watershed increased monthly median TN, TP, TOC and chlorophyll-a concentrations ($p < 0.05$) at a source water intake located 4.8 km upstream of the mainstem of Converse Reservoir. Expected increases in future

TOC concentrations are important due to the potential for increased carcinogenic DBP formation. Simulated forest to urban land conversion to 2020 in the Converse Watershed increased median overall TOC concentrations, calculated from daily concentrations, from 1992 to 2005, by 1.1 mg· L^{-1} (41%). Total median TOC concentrations (1992 to 2005) increased by 0.02 mg· L^{-1} km^{-2} following urbanization. The percent TOC change per area urbanized (%Δ/areaΔ) was 0.8% per km^2 urbanized over the 15-year simulation period, indicating that for each km^2 of forest land converted to urban land, reservoir TOC concentrations at the source water intake increased 0.8%. Monthly median TOC concentrations between May and October increased between 33% and 49% following urbanization during the same simulation period. Chlorophyll-a, indicating algae growth, accounted for most of the variance ($R^2 > 0.37$; $p < 0.05$) in simulated TOC concentration between May and November. In early spring (March and April), prior to high algae growth, allochthonous TOC load predicted 47% to 58% of the variance in intake TOC concentration. Simulated urbanization was associated with a significant relationship between chlorophyll-a and intake TOC concentrations earlier in the spring season of most years. It was found that under simulated 1992 land cover conditions, additional drinking water treatment is necessary in 47% of the simulated days between May and October. Reservoir modeling with future land use indicated the need for continuous additional treatment in Converse Reservoir between May and October based on daily TOC concentrations at the drinking water intake. Simulated urbanization indicated the need for continuous additional drinking water treatment between May and October to comply with the Safe Drinking Water Act DBP regulations.

Along with urbanization, climatic factors may influence reservoir nutrient concentrations. Only one of six ENSO indices was associated with measured TOC data. The small negative correlation between ONI and TOC concentrations may suggest higher TOC associated with lower streamflow of La Niña. Simulated TN and TP were correlated with ENSO phase with El Niño events having higher reservoir concentrations. This relationship was not evident in chlorophyll-a or TOC indicating that a delayed response and other factors such as temperature, light and reservoir flushing may have a larger impact on monthly in-reservoir TOC concentrations than TN and TP concentrations in Converse Reservoir. Converse watershed should be managed to retain forest cover. Water providers can use predictions of ENSO phase to estimate changes to streamflow, stream nutrient loads and in-reservoir TN and TP concentrations, thereby minimizing some uncertainty in the provision of potable water.

Acknowledgments: We thank Jamie Childers (TetraTech, Atlanta, GA), Amy Gill, (Alabama United States Geological Survey), and Tony Fisher (Mobile Area Water and Sewer Systems) for their assistance in this research. We also acknowledge and sincerely thank the Center for Forest Sustainability, Auburn University, for funding this research.

Author Contributions: Emile Elias conducted the watershed and reservoir modeling and primary authorship of this research. Puneet Srivastava and Mark Dougherty provided project guidance, particularly related to watershed modeling and ENSO. Hugo Rodriguez, the expert in EFDC modeling, provided guidance and technical help to support reservoir model simulation. Darren James contributed to the statistical analyses of nutrient concentrations and ENSO phase. Ryann Smith compiled ENSO indices and provided technical and administrative support.

Conflicts of Interest: The authors declare no conflict of interest.

References

1. Elsin, Y.K.; Kramer, R.A.; Jenkins, W.A. Valuing drinking water provision as an ecosystem service in the neuse river basin. *J. Water Resour. Plan. Manag.* **2010**, *136*, 474–482. [CrossRef]
2. Postel, S.L.; Thompson, B.H. Watershed protection: Capturing the benefits of nature's water supply services. *Nat. Resour. Forum* **2005**, *29*, 98–108. [CrossRef]
3. Singer, P.C.; Chang, S.D. Correlations between trihalomethanes and total organic halides formed during water treatment. *Am. Water Works Assoc.* **1989**, *81*, 61–65.
4. American Cancer Society. *Bladder Cancer Overview*; New York, NY, USA, 2010.
5. U.S. Environmental Protection Agency. *Economic Analysis for the Final Stage 2 Disinfectants and Disinfection Byproducts Rule*; EPA 815-R-05-010; Washington, DC, USA, 2005.

6.   Walker, W.W.J. Significance of eutrophication in water supply reservoirs. *Am. Water Works Assoc.* **1983**, *75*, 38–42.

7.   Canale, R.P.; Chapra, S.C.; Amy, G.L.; Edwards, M.A. Trihalomethane precursor model for lake youngs, washington. *J. Water Resour. Plan. Manag.* **1997**, *123*, 259–265. [CrossRef]

8.   Wear, D.N.; Greis, J.G. *Southern Forest Resource Assessment*; Southern Research Station: Asheville, NC, USA, 2002.

9.   Walsh, C.J.; Roy, A.H.; Feminella, J.W.; Cottingham, P.D.; Groffman, P.M.; Morgan, R.P. The urban stream syndrome: Current knowledge and the search for a cure. *J. N. Am. Benthol. Soc.* **2005**, *24*, 706–723. [CrossRef]

10.   Mobile Metropolitan Planning Organization. *2030 Long Range Trasnportation Plan*; South Alabama Regional Planning Commission: Mobile, AL, USA, 2005.

11.   Stein, S.M.; McRoberts, R.E.; Alig, R.J.; Nelson, M.D.; Theobald, D.M.; Eley, M.; Dechter, M.; Carr, M. *Forests on the Edge: Housing Development on America's Private Forests*; General Technical Report PNW-GTR-636; U.S. Department of Agriculture: Washington, DC, USA, 2005.

12.   Mondal, P.; Srivastava, P.; Kalin, L.; Panda, S.N. Ecologically sustainable surface water withdrawal for cropland irrigation through incorporation of climate variability. *J. Soil Water Conserv.* **2011**, *66*, 221–232. [CrossRef]

13.   Sharda, V.; Srivastava, P.; Chelliah, M.; Kalin, L. Quantification of el niño southern oscillation impact on precipitation and streamflows for improved management of water resources in alabama. *J. Soil Water Conserv.* **2012**, *67*, 158–172. [CrossRef]

14.   Sharda, V.; Ortiz, B.; Srivastava, P. *Impact of El Niño Southern Oscillation on Precipitation in Alabama*; Alabama Cooperative Extension System: Auburn, AL, USA, 2010.

15.   Sharma, S.; Srivastava, P.; Kalin, L.; Fang, X.; Elias, E.H. Predicting total organic carbon load with el nino southern oscillation phase using hybrid and fuzzy logic approaches. *Trans. ASABE* **2014**, *57*, 1071–1085.

16.   Murdoch, P.S.; Baron, J.S.; Miller, T.L. Potential effects of climate change on surface-water quality in north america. *J. Am. Water Resour. Assoc.* **2000**, *36*, 347–366. [CrossRef]

17.   Oh, J.; Sankarasubramanian, A. Interannual hydroclimatic variability and its influence on winter nutrient loadings over the southeast united states. *Hydrol. Earth Syst. Sci.* **2012**, *16*, 2285–2298. [CrossRef]

18.   Keener, V.W.; Feyereisen, G.W.; Lall, U.; Jones, J.W.; Bosch, D.D.; Lowrance, R. El-nino/southern oscillation (enso) influences on monthly no3 load and concentration, stream flow and precipitation in the little river watershed, tifton, georgia (ga). *J. Hydrol.* **2010**, *381*, 352–363. [CrossRef]

19.   Sharma, S.; Srivastava, P.; Fang, X.; Kalin, L. Incorporating climate variability for point-source discharge permitting in a complex river system. *Trans. Asabe* **2012**, *55*, 2213–2228. [CrossRef]

20.   Journey, C.A.; Gill, A.C. *Assessment of Water-Quality Conditions in the J.B. Converse Lake Watershed, Mobile County, Alabama, 1990–98*; Water-Resources Investigations Report 01-4225; U.S. Geological Survey: Reston, VA, USA, 2001; p. 131.

21.   Journey, C.A.; Psinakis, W.L.; Atkins, J.B. *Streamflow in and Water Quality and Bottom Material Analyses of the JB Converse Lake Basin, Mobile County, Alabama, 1990–92*; 95-4106; U.S. Geological Survey: Reston, VA, USA, 1995.

22.   Elias, E.H.; Dougherty, M.; Srivastava, P.; Laband, D. The impact of forest to urban land conversion on streamflow, total nitrogen, total phosphorus, and total organic carbon inputs to the converse reservoir, southern alabama, USA. *Urban Ecosyst.* **2011**, *16*, 79–107. [CrossRef]

23.   Gill, A.C.; McPherson, A.K.; Moreland, R.S. *Water Quality and Simulated Effects of Urban Land-Use Change in J.B. Converse Lake Watershed, Mobile County, Alabama, 1990–2003*; 2005-5171; US Geological Survey: Montgomery, AL, USA, 2005; p. 124.

24.   *Loading Simulation Program in C++ (LSPC), version 3.0*; 2010. Software for technical computation; Tetra Tech, Inc.: Fairfax, VA, USA, 2003.

25.   Hamrick, J.M. *A Three-Dimensional Environmental Fluid Dynamics Computer Code: Theoretical and Computational Aspects*; Virginia Institute of Marine Science, College of William and Mary: Gloucester Point, VA, USA, 1992.

26.   Alabama Department of Environmental Management. *Adem Reservoir Water Quality Monitoring Program Report (1990–1995)*; Montgomery, AL, USA, 1996.

27.   Bayne, D.R.; Seesock, W.C.; Reutebuch, E. *Limnological Study of Big Creek Lake*; Auburn University: Auburn, AL, USA, 1998.

28.   Alabama Department of Environmental Management. *Surface Water Quality Screening Assessment of the Escatawpa river, Mobile Bay, and Upper and Lower Tombigbee river Basins—2001*; Montgomery, AL, USA, 2003.

29. Carlson, C.S.; Archfield, S.A. *Hydrogeologic Conditions and a Firm-Yield Assessment for J.B. Converse Lake, Mobile County, Alabama, 1991–2006*; 2008-5005; US Geological Survey: Reston, VA, USA, 2009.

30. U.S. Department of Agriculture Natural Resources Conservation Service. Hydrologic soil groups. In *National Engineering Handbook Part 630*; Washington, DC, USA, 2009.

31. U.S. Bureau of Land Management. *Bureau of Land Management Letter to Permittees in Las Cruces Grazing District*; B.o.L.M., Ed.; U.S. Department of Interior: Las Cruces, NM, USA, 2011; p. 11.

32. Hamrick, J.M. Linking hydrodynamic and biogeochemical transport models for estuarine and coastal waters. In *Estuarine and Coastal Modeling*; ASCE: Oak Brook, IL, USA, 1994.

33. Wool, T.A.; Davie, S.R.; Rodriguez, H.N. Development of three-dimensional hydrodynamic and water quality models to support total maximum daily load decision process for the neuse river estuary, north carolina. *J. Water Resour. Plan. Manag.* **2003**, *129*, 295–306. [CrossRef]

34. Moustafa, M.Z.; Hamrick, J.M. Calibration of the wetland hydrodynamic model to the everglades nutrient removal project. *Water Qual. Ecosyst. Model.* **2000**, *1*, 141–167. [CrossRef]

35. *The Environmental Fluid Dynamics Code User Manual us Epa Version 1.01*; Tetra Tech Inc.: Fairfax, VA, USA, 2007.

36. Ambrose, R.B.; Wool, T.A.; Martin, J.L. *The Water Quality Analysis Simulation Program, Wasp5 Part A: Model Documentation*; Environmental Research Laboratory: Athens, GA, USA, 1993.

37. Cerco, C.F.; Cole, T. *User's Guide to the CE-Qual-ICM Three-Dimensional Eutrophication Model*; Technical Report EL-95-15: Vicksburg, MS, USA; March; 1995.

38. *The environmental Fluid Dynamics Code Theory and Computation Volume 3: Water Quality Module*; Tetra Tech Inc.: Fairfax, VA, USA, 2007.

39. Blumberg, A.F.; Mellor, G.L. A description of a three-dimensional coastal ocean circulation model. In *Three-Dimensional Coastal Ocean Models*; American Geophysical Union: Washington, DC, USA, 1987; pp. 1–16.

40. Stein, S.M.; McRoberts, R.E.; Nelson, M.D.; Theobald, D.M.; Eley, M.; Dechter, M. Forests on the edge: A gis-based approach to projecting housing development on private forests. In *Monitoring Science and Technology Symposium: Unifying Knowledge for Sustainability in the Western Hemisphere Proceedings RMRS-P-42CD*; U.S. Department of Agriculture: Fort Collins, CO, USA, 2006.

41. Elias, E.H. Valuing ecosystem services from forested landscapes: How urbanization influences drinking water treatment cost. Ph.D. Dissertation, Auburn University, Auburn, AL, USA, 2010.

42. *Vogg: A Visual Orthogonal Grid Generation Tool for Hydrodynamic and Water Quality Modeling*; Tetra Tech Inc.: Fairfax, VA, USA, 2002.

43. *Standard Methods for the Examination of Water and Wastewater*, 19th ed.; American Public Health Association: Washington, DC, USA, 1995.

44. Moriasi, D.N.; Arnold, J.G.; van Liew, M.W.; Bingner, R.L.; Harmel, R.D.; Veith, T.L. Model evaluation guidelines for systematic quantification of accuracy in watershed simulations. *Trans. ASABE* **2007**, *50*, 885–900. [CrossRef]

45. Wilcoxon, F. Individual comparisons by ranking methods. *Biometrics Bull.* **1945**, *1*, 80–83. [CrossRef]

46. Bamston, A.G.; Chelliah, M.; Goldenberg, S.B. Documentation of a highly enso-related sst region in the equatorial pacific: Research note. *Atmos. Ocean* **1997**, *35*, 367–383. [CrossRef]

47. National Oceanic and Atmospheric Administration. *Oceanic Niño Index dataset*; Available online: http://www.cpc.ncep.noaa.gov/products/analysis_monitoring/ensostuff/ensoyears.shtml (accessed on 4 November 2015).

48. Trenberth, K.E.; Stepaniak, D.P. Indices of el niño evolution. *J. Clim.* **2001**, *14*, 1697–1701. [CrossRef]

49. Wolter, K.; Timlin, M. Monitoring enso in coads with a seasonally adjusted principal component index. In Proceedings of the 17th Climate Diagnostics Workshop, Norman, OK, USA, 1993; NOAA/NMC/CAC, NSSL, Oklahoma Clim. Survey, CIMMS and the School of Meteor., Univ. of Oklahoma: Norman, OK, USA; pp. 52–57.

50. National Oceanic and Atmospheric Administration. *Niño 3.4 sst Index dataset*; Silver Spring, MD, USA, 2012.

51. Donigian, A.S. Watershed model calibration and validation: The hspf experience. *Proc. Water Environ. Fed.* **2002**, *2002*, 44–73. [CrossRef]

52. Tillman, D.H.; Cerco, C.F.; Noel, M.R.; Martin, J.L.; Hamrick, J.M. *Three-Dimensional Eutrophication Model of the Lower ST. Johns River, Florida*; ERDC/EL TR-04-13; US Army Corps of Engineers Waterways Experiment Station: Vicksburg, MS, USA, 2004.

53. Cerco, C.F.; Linker, L.; Sweeney, J.; Shenk, G.; Butt, A.J. Nutrient and solids controls in virginia's chesapeake bay tributaries. *J. Water Resour. Plan. Manag.* **2002**, *128*, 179–189. [CrossRef]
54. Lind, O.T. *Handbook of Common Methods in Limnology*; Kendall/Hunt Publishing Company: Bubuque, IA, USA, 1985.
55. Nõges, P.; Poikane, S.; Kõiv, T.; Nõges, T. Effect of chlorophyll sampling design on water quality assessment in thermally stratified lakes. *Hydrobiologia* **2010**, *649*, 157–170. [CrossRef]
56. Elias, E.H.; Laband, D.N.; Dougherty, M. Estimating the public water supply protection value of forests. *J. Contemp. Water Resour.* **2013**, *152*, 94–104. [CrossRef]
57. Elias, E.H.; Laband, D.; Dougherty, M. Estimating the public water supply protection value of forests. *J. Contemp. Water Res. Educ.* **2013**, *152*, 94–104. [CrossRef]
58. Marcé, R.; Rodríguez-Arias, M.À.; García, J.C.; Armengol, J. El niño southern oscillation and climate trends impact reservoir water quality. *Glob. Chang. Biol.* **2010**, *16*, 2857–2865. [CrossRef]
59. Mirhosseini, G.; Srivastava, P. Effect of irrigation and climate variability on water quality of coastal watersheds: Case study in alabama. *J. Irrig. Drain. Eng.* **2015**, *142*, 05015010. [CrossRef]

forests

MDPI

Article

Spatial Variations of Soil Moisture under *Caragana korshinskii* Kom. from Different Precipitation Zones: Field Based Analysis in the Loess Plateau, China

Yuanxin Liu [1], Wenwu Zhao [1,2,*], Lixin Wang [2], Xiao Zhang [1], Stefani Daryanto [2] and Xuening Fang [1]

[1] State Key Laboratory of Earth Surface Processes and Resource Ecology, College of Resources Science & Technology, Beijing Normal University, Beijing 100875, China; liuyuanxin2010@163.com (Y.L.); sdtazx@sina.com (X.Z.); summerfxn@126.com (X.F.)

[2] Department of Earth Sciences, Indiana University-Purdue University Indianapolis, Indianapolis 46202, USA; lxwang@iupui.edu (L.W.); stdaryan@iupui.edu (S.D.)

* Correspondence: zhaoww@bnu.edu.cn; Tel./Fax: +86-10-5880-2125

Academic Editors: Ge Sun, James M. Vose and Eric J. Jokela
Received: 29 September 2015; Accepted: 14 January 2016; Published: 29 January 2016

Abstract: Soil moisture scarcity has become the major limiting factor of vegetation restoration in the Loess Plateau of China. The aim of this study is: (i) to compare the spatial distribution of deep (up to 5 m) soil moisture content (SMC) beneath the introduced shrub *Caragana korshinskii* Kom. under different precipitation zones in the Loess Plateau and (ii) to investigate the impacts of environmental factors on soil moisture variability. Soil samples were taken under *C. korshinskii* from three precipitation zones (Semiarid-350, Semiarid-410, Semiarid-470). We found that the highest soil moisture value was in the 0–0.1 m layer with a large coefficient of variation. The soil water storage under different precipitation zones increased following the increase of precipitation (*i.e.*, Semiarid-350 < Semiarid-410 < Semiarid-470), although the degree of SMC variation was different for different precipitation zones. The SMC in the Semiarid-350 zone initially increased with soil depth, and then decreased until it reached the depth of 2.8-m. The SMC in the Semiarid-410 zone showed a decreasing trend from the top soil to 4.2-m depth. The SMC in the Semiarid-470 zone firstly decreased with soil depth, increased, and then decreased until it reached 4.6-m depth. All SMC values then became relatively constant after reaching the 2.8-m, 4.2-m, and 4.6-m depths for Semiarid-350, Semiarid-410, and Semiarid-470, respectively. The low but similar SMC values at the stable layers across the precipitation gradient indicate widespread soil desiccation in this region. Our results suggested that water deficit occurred in all of the three precipitation zones with precipitation, latitude, field capacity, and bulk density as the main environmental variables affecting soil moisture. Considering the correlations between precipitation, SMC and vegetation, appropriate planting density and species selection should be taken into account for introduced vegetation management.

Keywords: soil moisture; precipitation zones; spatial distribution; *Caragana korshinskii* Kom.; redundancy analysis; Loess Plateau; China

1. Introduction

The Loess Plateau of China covers an area of more than 6.2×10^5 km^2, with diverse rainfall, soil, and vegetation patterns. Vegetation restoration is the primary task of ecological rehabilitation here under the "Grain to Green Program" in the Loess Plateau of China [1], aiming to reverse the existing farmlands to their original grassland or woodland condition. Currently, the ecological restoration of the Loess Plateau has led to significant achievements such as increases in vegetation coverage, decreases in soil erosion, and enhancement of ecosystem services [2,3]. Soil moisture shortages, however, commonly occur as a result of limited rainfall and strong evaporation in this semiarid region of China [4]. The continued expansion of the "Grain to Green Program" might instead lead to dry soil layers, negatively affecting the vegetation sustainability in the Loess Plateau [5] as precipitation is the only source of soil moisture in the region [6]. Since soil moisture is critical in regulating plant growth in these semiarid regions [7], it is crucial to identify the spatial variation and factors affecting soil moisture in different areas of the Loess Plateau of China [8].

Extensive studies on soil moisture have been carried out at the plot, watershed, and regional scale in the Loess Plateau, providing important information for vegetation restoration in the region. Due to the large spatial coverage of the Loess Plateau, however, the relationships between soil moisture and environmental factors may be different from one area to another. Various factors, such as land use [9–13], topography [14,15], soil properties [16] and atmosphere dynamics [17], have been recorded to affect soil moisture variability. Most studies on soil moisture have been done during the rainy season (July to September) [8,18,19], and, therefore, the results might be affected by the amount of individual rainfall. Although there were some studies which did not consider the soil moisture in the upper layer (*i.e.*, 0–1 m depth) to avoid the confounding effects of rainfall variation [19], the results might be incomplete for a whole soil profile study. Our study, which examined a complete soil moisture profile (*i.e.*, from 0–5 m deep) across different precipitation gradients was, therefore, conducted before the rainy season to improve our understanding of soil moisture spatial distributions and the contributing factors.

In the Loess Plateau, forest land occupies 16% of the total area [2]. Shrub, an important part of forest land, is mainly distributed north of the 550 mm rainfall isoline. In many parts of semiarid regions, shrubs have exacerbated the desertification process due to their ability to modify soil water characteristics by increasing water infiltration around them [20]. They also have minimal nutrient requirements, wide adaptation ability, and strong stress resistance [21], making them superior in resource-poor environments [22]. *Caragana korshinskii* is an introduced leguminous shrub in the semiarid Loess Plateau that has good economic benefits and high ecological values [21]. The ability of *C. korshinskii* to conserve water and soil has been reported [23], and it quickly became the dominant species with a well-developed root systems (*i.e.*, more than 5 m) in the process of ecological rehabilitation. However, several researchers have reported that *C. korshinskii* would aggravate water scarcity and lead to soil desiccation in the deeper horizons [24]. For example, Wang *et al.* (2010) found that drier soil layers were observed under *C. korshinskii* after a three-year growing period when compared to alfalfa (*Medicago sativa* L.) [18]. Since *C. korshinskii* had a well-developed root system [23,24], over the years, it might generate layers of dried soil at a regional scale [18]. It is therefore necessary to identify the spatial variations of the soil moisture under *C. korshinskii* along different rainfall gradients in the Loess Plateau of China.

Based on the above-mentioned research background, this study aimed to: (1) compare the soil moisture spatial variation beneath *C. korshinskii* grown under different precipitation zones of the Loess Plateau; (2) investigate the impacts of other environmental factors (e.g., mean annual temperature, bulk density, slope gradient) on soil moisture variability and identify the controlling factors in semiarid regions; and (3) provide suggestions for the regional ecological rehabilitation in the Loess Plateau of China.

2. Materials and Methods

2.1. Study Area

The Loess Plateau in China is located in the middle reaches of the Yellow River, extending from a longitude of 100°54' to 114°33' E and a latitude of 33°43' to 41°16' N [25]. The Loess Plateau comprises 6.67% of the territory in China and supports 8.5% of the Chinese population [2]. This study was conducted in a portion of the semiarid climatic region in the Loess Plateau, located in Shaanxi province and Inner Mongolia. The topography of the study area is hilly and gully [26], with an elevation of sampling points ranging from 927 to 1505 m above sea level. The study area is located in a continental monsoon region where the average annual precipitation ranges from 350 mm in the northwest to 500 mm in the southeast, 70% of which falls from June to September [27]. The main soil type in this area is loess and it is vulnerable to erosion [28]. The dominant shrub species are *C. korshinskii*, *Hippophae rhamnoides* L., *Sophora viciifolia* Franch., *Vitex negundo* var. *Heterophylla, Rosa xanthine* Lindl., and *Syringa oblate* Lindl..

2.2. Sampling Design

Precipitation data were collected from 63 weather stations in the Loess Plateau from 1998 to 2012. The locations of weather stations can be found in Figure 1. The Kriging interpolation method in ArcGIS Desktop (version 9.3) was used to obtain average annual precipitation isolines. Previous studies divided the Loess Plateau into three climatic regions: arid, semiarid, and semi-humid [29]. In this study, part of the semiarid regions was selected, and divided into three precipitation zones based on average annual precipitation (P): Semiarid-350 zone (350 mm < P < 410 mm), Semiarid-410 zone (410 mm ⩽ P < 470 mm), and Semiarid-470 zone (470 mm ⩽ P < 500 mm) (Figure 2).

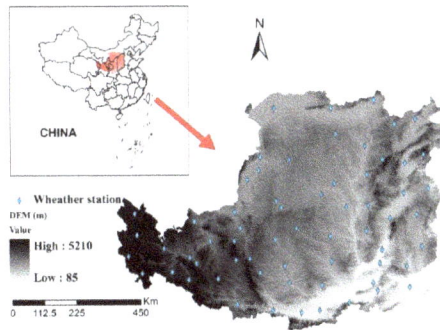

Figure 1. Location of the weather stations in the Loess Plateau of China.

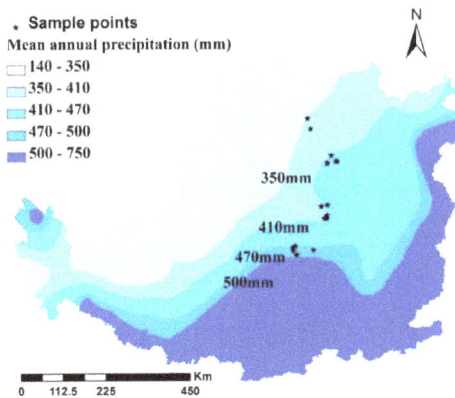

Figure 2. The sampling points and precipitation zones of the study area.

In 2014, 17 5 m × 5 m *C. korshinskii* plots were established. The estimated age of the shrubs according to interviews with local farmers were between 30 and 40 years old. Seven, six, and four typical sampling points were taken from the Semiarid-350, Semiarid-410, and Semiarid-470 precipitation zone, respectively. A preliminary field survey considering the geographic distribution and logistics were conducted during the process of determining those sampling points. The description of each sampling point is shown in Table 1. For comparative analysis, 10 abandoned lands were randomly chosen from the surrounding areas as a control group and the average soil moisture content was calculated for both *C. korshinskii* and control plots. All of the control plots had been abandoned for more than 20 years. Basic topographic information (longitude, latitude, elevation above sea-level, slope gradient, slope aspect, slope position) was collected using the Garmin GPS (version eTrex 30) and the geological compass (DQL-8).

2.3. Data Collection

Soil samples were collected from 27 April to 20 May 2014. Soil moisture measurements were conducted at the beginning of the growing season for two different soil profiles: (i) the 0–1 m profile in 0.1 m increments and (ii) the 2–5 m profile in 0.2 m increments. Soil samples were taken by a drill and stored in sealed aluminum cases, and soil moisture content was calculated using a gravimetric approach (*i.e.*, oven-dry method at 105 °C for 24 h) [30]. Each time three sampling profiles were randomly chosen to calculate the average soil moisture for each site. At each sampling site, six undisturbed soil cores from the surface soil were also collected in metal cylinders (diameter 5 cm, length 5 cm) to measure bulk density and saturated hydraulic conductivity [31]. A total of 1632 soil samples were collected. Similarly, soil compaction was measured for each sampling site with a pocket penetrometer (Eijkelkamp, 0603). Sampling dates were chosen after a period of seven rainless days to minimize the effects of rainfall variability.

In this study, the depth-averaged SMC (SMC_d) of each sampling point was calculated by Equation (1):

$$SMC_d = \frac{1}{k} \sum_{i=1}^{k} SMC_i \qquad (1)$$

where k is the number of measurement layers and SMC_i is the mean soil moisture content in layer *i* calculated by three random sampling profiles. The total number of measurement layers is 30.

Table 1. General information of the sampling points.

Precipitation Zones	Sample points	Lng (°)	Lat (°)	P (mm)	T (°C)	Ele (m)	SG (°)	Abbreviation in RDA					
								SA	SP	SC (kg·cm⁻²)	BD (g·cm⁻³)	FC (%)	SHC (mm·min⁻¹)
	KP1	109.8	39.9	351.8	7.9	1505	11	South	Middle	2.0	1.6	10.5	2.0
	KP2	109.9	39.6	367.1	8.0	1254	10	South	Downhill	2.0	1.8	8.5	0.9
	KP3	110.2	37.5	401.8	10.1	927	5	South	Hilltop	1.6	1.3	22.5	1.1
Semiarid-350	KP4	110.1	37.8	407.2	9.8	970	5	South	Middle	0.6	1.3	16.9	0.8
	KP5	110.3	37.6	408.2	10.1	941	32	South	Upper	1.8	1.2	21.9	1.6
	KP6	110.3	37.5	409.3	10.1	935	28	South	Upper	1.3	1.3	23.0	1.5
	KP7	110.5	39.0	409.9	8.6	1068	5	South	Hilltop	1.2	1.4	23.8	1.1
	KP8	110.4	38.8	413.6	8.8	1259	5	South	Hilltop	1.9	1.5	24.2	0.6
	KP9	110.4	38.8	416.0	8.8	1233	8	North	Upper	1.0	1.4	25.3	1.4
	KP10	110.3	37.8	417.6	9.8	1053	30	West	Upper	1.5	1.3	20.6	1.0
Semiarid-410	KP11	110.6	38.8	420.3	8.7	1197	5	South	Hilltop	1.1	1.4	23.2	1.0
	KP12	110.7	38.8	421.7	8.7	1233	5	South	Hilltop	1.6	1.5	19.4	1.2
	KP13	109.3	36.9	465.8	10.2	1293	22	South	Upper	0.9	1.3	40.4	3.6
	KP14	109.3	36.8	472.8	10.1	1383	5	South	Hilltop	1.0	1.2	25.5	2.0
	KP15	109.9	36.8	478.7	10.6	1079	26	South	Upper	1.1	1.3	27.2	0.9
Semiarid-470	KP16	109.3	36.8	479.1	10.2	1241	5	South	Hilltop	0.7	1.2	30.9	1.7
	KP17	109.4	36.7	490.1	10.3	1290	38	South	Upper	0.5	1.0	24.4	2.6

RDA represents redundancy analysis; Lng represents longitude; Lat represents latitude; P represents annual mean precipitation; T represents annual mean temperature; Ele represents elevation above sea-level; SG represents slope gradient; SA represents slope aspect; SP represents slope position; SC represents soil compaction; BD represents bulk density; FC represents field capacity; SHC represents saturated hydraulic conductivity.

The spatially averaged SMC (SMC$_s$) of each precipitation zone was calculated by Equation (2):

$$SMC_s = \frac{1}{m} \sum_{i=1}^{m} SMC_i \qquad (2)$$

where m is the number of sampling points under each precipitation zone.

The soil water storage (SWS) of each precipitation zone was calculated by Equation (3):

$$SWS = 5000 \times SMC \times BD \qquad (3)$$

where SMC is average soil moisture content and BD is bulk density.

2.4. Statistical Methods

The basic statistical parameters (mean, standard deviation, minimum, maximum, kurtosis, skewness, coefficient of variation) were calculated and reported for each layer (Table 3). One-way ANOVA and least significant difference (LSD) were used to assess the effect of precipitation regime on soil moisture. SPSS (version 18.0) was used for all of the statistical analysis.

Ordination techniques are based on either a linear response model or a unimodal response model. In this study, we employed detrended correspondence analysis (DCA) to determine whether the linear or unimodal model should be used. DCA is a multivariate statistical technique widely used by ecologists to find the main factors or gradients in large, species-rich but usually sparse data matrices [32]. If the largest value of the DCA gradient lengths is shorter than 3.0, soil moisture is best described by the linear method [33]. Table 2 shows all gradient lengths that were shorter than 3.0, and redundancy analysis (RDA) was then applied for identifying the environmental factors that best explained the *C. korshinskii* soil moisture variations [33]. RDA is an alternative to canonical correlation analysis, allowing the relationship between two tables of variables Y and X to be examined. In RDA, the components of X variables are extracted in such a way that they are as much as possible correlated with the variables of Y. Similarly, the components of Y are extracted so that they are as much as possible correlated with the components extracted from X. The SMC was divided into five depths (0–1 m, 1–2 m, 2–3 m, 3–4 m and 4–5 m), and then, the SMC$_d$ at each sampling point was calculated. Monte Carlo permutation test was first applied to reduce the number of unrelated environmental variables. Specifically, each environmental factor was used to reject those with relatively large *p*-values and small eigenvalues. Finally, eight environmental variables (longitude (Lng), latitude (Lat), average annual precipitation (P), average annual temperature (T), soil compaction (SC), bulk density (BD), field capacity (FC), and saturated hydraulic conductivity (SHC)), were selected for further RDA analysis. Lng and Lat can reveal the distribution characters of sampling points, while P and T represent meteorological factors. Four kinds of factors (SC, BD, FC, SHC) reflect soil properties. DCA and RDA were performed using the program CANOCO (version 4.5). The graphs were drawn using SigmaPlot for Windows (version 10.0) and Canodraw for windows (version 4.0).

Table 2. Length of gradient from the detrended correspondence analysis (DCA) and eigenvalues from the redundancy analysis (RDA).

Gradient Analysis Methods		Axis 1	Axis 2	Axis 3	Axis 4
DCA	Lengths of gradient	1.6	0.9	0.7	0.4
RDA	Eigenvalues	0.8	0.0	0.0	0.0

3. Results

3.1. Summary Statistics

The summary statistics of soil moisture at various depths were provided in Table 3. The highest mean value (9.1%) and standard deviation (5.1%) were both observed at the 0.0–0.1 m depth. In general, the mean value of soil moisture showed a decreasing trend with depth. Specifically, soil moisture content decreased slightly at 0.0–2.0 m depth, and then it experienced a dramatic decrease at 2.0–4.4 m depth. The coefficient of variation, however, showed a different pattern where it initially increased with depth (*i.e.,* 0.3–2.6 m) but then decreased below 2.6 m depth. Standard deviation was 5.1% at the surface soil, which indicated that soil moisture experienced a relatively high variability. Soil moisture for different soil depths was positively skewed, except at the depth of 4.8–5.0 m and the highest skewness value was observed at 4.0–4.2 m depth. Negative values of kurtosis occurred at most depths, and the lowest value occurred at the 0.0–0.1 m depth.

Table 3. Summary statistics of the soil moisture at various depths.

Depth (m)	n	Mean (%)	Std. Deviation (%)	Minimum (%)	Maximum (%)	Kurtosis	Skewness	Coefficient of Variation
0.0–0.1	17	9.1	5.1	3.4	17.5	−1.4	0.6	0.6
0.1–0.2	17	8.5	3.9	3.5	16.1	−0.6	0.9	0.5
0.2–0.3	17	8.9	3.8	3.6	16.1	−0.6	0.7	0.4
0.3–0.4	17	8.4	3.6	3.7	15.1	−0.9	0.6	0.4
0.4–0.5	17	8.6	4.0	3.7	15.9	−0.7	0.7	0.5
0.5–0.6	17	8.4	4.1	3.9	15.4	−0.8	0.7	0.5
0.6–0.7	17	8.5	4.1	4.0	16.2	−0.7	0.8	0.5
0.7–0.8	17	8.6	4.1	3.9	16.0	−0.6	0.8	0.5
0.8–0.9	17	8.4	4.0	3.8	15.9	−0.6	0.8	0.5
0.9–1.0	16	8.4	4.0	3.6	15.8	−0.6	0.7	0.5
1.0–1.2	16	8.6	4.2	3.8	16.9	−0.6	0.7	0.5
1.2–1.4	16	8.4	4.1	3.6	15.9	−0.8	0.7	0.5
1.4–1.6	16	8.2	4.2	3.6	15.9	−0.9	0.6	0.5
1.6–1.8	16	8.1	4.4	3.0	15.6	−1.2	0.5	0.5
1.8–2.0	16	8.1	4.8	3.0	16.6	−0.8	0.8	0.6
2.0–2.2	15	7.6	4.7	2.7	15.0	−1.0	0.8	0.6
2.2–2.4	15	7.3	4.6	2.7	17.0	−0.1	1.1	0.6
2.4–2.6	15	7.0	4.6	2.8	16.9	−0.2	1.1	0.7
2.6–2.8	15	6.6	4.2	2.9	15.1	−0.2	1.2	0.6
2.8–3.0	15	6.4	4.0	2.5	13.8	−0.4	1.1	0.6
3.0–3.2	15	6.2	3.5	2.7	13.7	0.2	1.2	0.6
3.2–3.4	15	6.0	3.4	2.7	13.3	0.6	1.3	0.6
3.4–3.6	15	5.9	3.4	2.8	13.1	1.0	1.4	0.6
3.6–3.8	15	5.7	3.1	2.5	13.3	2.0	1.7	0.6
3.8–4.0	15	5.2	2.6	2.7	12.3	4.0	2.1	0.5
4.0–4.2	15	4.9	2.2	2.7	11.6	6.2	2.3	0.4
4.2–4.4	15	4.7	1.6	3.0	9.1	3.8	1.8	0.3
4.4–4.6	15	4.5	1.0	2.6	6.3	0.0	0.5	0.2
4.6–4.8	15	4.6	1.0	2.8	6.3	−0.2	0.2	0.2
4.8–5.0	15	4.6	1.0	2.6	6.2	−0.3	-0.2	0.2

3.2. Variation of SWS under Different Precipitation Zones

Table 4 shows that SWS fits with a normal distribution according to a Kolmogorov-Smirnov test (K-S) under each precipitation zone. The degree of variation for the Semiarid-470 zone was the greatest (SD = 0.6), whereas the Semiarid-350 zone underwent relatively small changes (SD = 0.1). The SWS among precipitation zones increased following the increase in precipitation (Table 4 and Figure 3). Specifically, the SWS in the Semiarid-410 zone increased by 12% comparable with that in the Semiarid-350 zone. The SWS in the Semiarid-470 zone was 630.3, which means that the SWS gap between the Semiarid-470 zone and the Semiarid-410 zone was even greater.

Table 4. Summary statistics of soil water storage within profile under three different precipitation zones.

Precipitation Zone	n	Mean (mm)	SD (m)	Minimum (mm)	Maximum (mm)	K-S
Semiarid-350	7	388.5	0.1	296.5	517.7	N(0.8)
Semiarid-410	6	437.1	0.2	282.5	789.8	N(0.8)
Semiarid-470	4	630.3	0.6	427.7	770.2	N(1.0)

n represents the number of sampling points; SD represents standard deviation; N represents normal distribution (significance level is in parentheses).

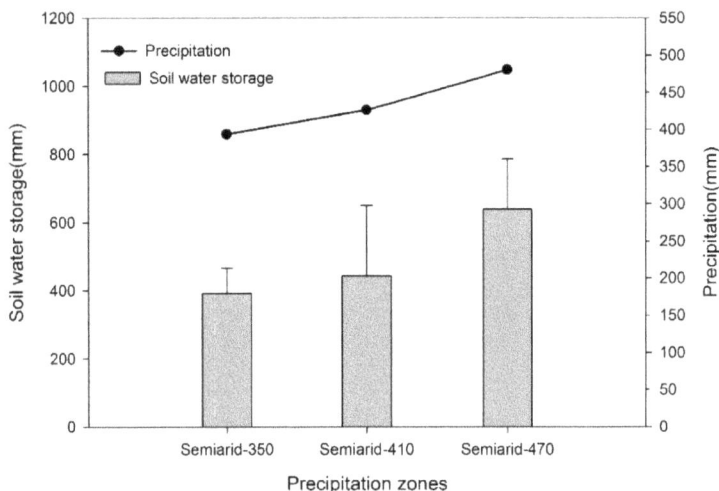

Figure 3. Comparison of the depth averaged soil water storage (0–5 m) under different precipitation zones.

3.3. Variation of the Spatial-Averaged SMC under Different Precipitation Zones

Figure 4 and one-way ANOVA showed that there were significant differences of SMCs among different precipitation zones. Vertical distribution of SMC was different among the three precipitation zones. Specifically, the SMC in the Semiarid-350 zone initially increased with soil depth, and then decreased until the 2.8-m depth where the SMC was relative stable. The SMC in the Semiarid-410 zone showed a decreasing trend from top layer to the 4.2-m layer and then reached stability. The SMC in the Semiarid-470 zone firstly decreased with soil depth, then increased and lastly decreased until 4.6-m layer, which showed a different vertical changing trend from the other two zones. Generally, the SMC under different precipitation zones within the 0–4.6 m profile was in the following order: Semiarid-470 > Semiarid-410 > Semiarid-350 (Figure 4), equating with the SWS shown in Figure 3. Figure 4 also showed the value of SMC in the three precipitation zones was smaller than that in abandoned land at most soil layers. Water deficit, calculated as the difference between control and treatment, occurred in all of the three precipitation zones. Greater surface water deficit, however, was observed in the area with lower rainfall (*i.e.*, Semiarid-350 and Semiarid-410 zones), while deeper soil water deficit was more obvious in the Semiarid-470 zone, particularly from the 3-m layer onwards. The values of SMC at the deeper soil layer (*i.e.*, 4.6–5 m) were almost identical between the three zones.

soil moisture content (g/g)

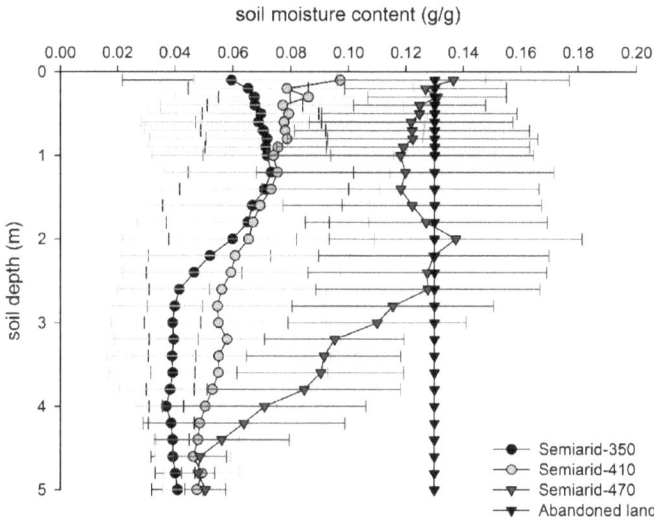

Figure 4. Comparison of the average SMC under different precipitation zones. Note: Semiarid-350 represents the spatially averaged soil moisture content in the 350–410 mm precipitation zone; Semiarid-410 represents the spatially averaged soil moisture content in the 410–470 mm precipitation zone; Semiarid-470 represents the spatially averaged soil moisture content in the 470–500 mm precipitation zone.

3.4. RDA Ordination

Table 2 shows that the two main axes had eigenvalues > 0.01 and accounted for 82% of the total variance. Axis 1 was the most essential, explaining 82% of the total variance with average annual precipitation, latitude, field capacity, and bulk density as the greatest contributors. Table 5 and Figure 5 show that RDA ordination well described the relationship between the soil moisture spatial pattern and the environmental factors. Axis 1 was positively correlated with Lng, Lat, SC, and BD, but negatively correlated with P, T, FC, and SHC. Axis 2 was negatively correlated with P, BD, and FC, but positively correlated with the other environmental variables. A Monte Carlo permutation test for the significance of influence indicated that P exerted the greatest effect on soil moisture variation ($p = 0.002$, $F = 38.55$). The canonical coefficients of SHC and Lng were relatively small (Table 5), indicating weak correlations with soil moisture variation. Specifically, the soil moisture content of *C. korshinskii* increased with precipitation, temperature, field capacity, and saturated hydraulic conductivity but decreased with soil capacity, longitude, latitude, and bulk density.

Table 5. Canonical coefficients of the environmental factors with the first two axes of redundancy analysis (RDA).

Environmental Variables	Axis 1	Axis 2
Lng	0.6	0.0
Lat	0.8	0.0
P	−0.9	−0.2
T	−0.7	0.0
SC	0.6	0.4
BD	0.7	−0.1
FC	−0.8	−0.0
SHC	−0.5	0.0

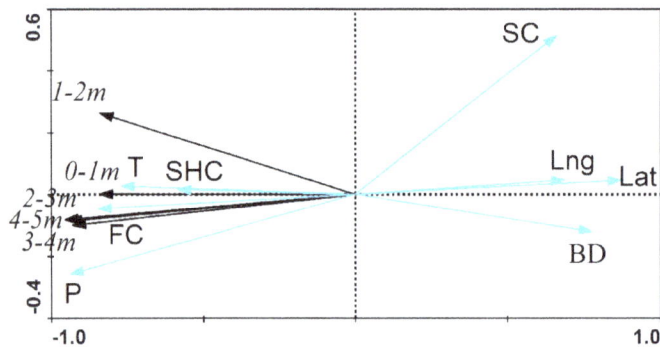

Figure 5. Redundancy analysis ordination biplot showing the relationship between soil moisture content and environmental factors. Note: 0–1 m represents the average soil moisture content in the 0–1 m layers; 1–2 m represents the average soil moisture content in the 1–2 m layers; 2–3 m represents the average soil moisture content in the 2–3 m layers; 3–4 m represents the average soil moisture content in the 3–4 m layers; 4–5 m represents the average soil moisture content in the 4–5 m layers.

4. Discussion

4.1. Spatial Variation of SMC and Relationships between Precipitation, SMC and Vegetation

While the highest soil moisture value of *C. korshinskii* was found in the surface layers, greater coefficients of variation were also observed in these layers (Table 3), similar to several other studies [34,35]. Large variations in SMC occurred on the surface as it was exposed to greater changes in the precipitation, temperature, and aeration [36]. Smaller variation range was found in deeper soils (Table 3) because of the scarcity of precipitation in the semiarid Loess Plateau, limiting rainfall infiltration replenishment only to the shallow soil horizon. The SMC in the semiarid Loess Plateau decreased from the surface soil layer to the deep layer (Table 3), which means that soil became drier with depth.

The SWS and SMC among precipitation zones increased following the increase in precipitation, but there was no linear relationship between SMC and precipitation (Table 4, Figures 3 and 4). We found that there were changes in SMC in the deeper layer such as those from the 2 m layer to the 4.6 m layer in the Semiarid-470 zone (Figure 4). We suggested that other factors than precipitation such as root water uptake might generate such changes. Previous studies indicated that *C. korshinskii* aged over 20 years has deep rooting systems (more than 5 m) [37], enabling them to consume moisture from deep soil layers, below the rainfall infiltration depth [24]. Greater water loss was even observed during growing seasons where water consumption under *C. korshinskii* and some other introduced vegetation types exceeded precipitation in those months [38]. These findings were consistent with our results where SMC underneath *C. korshinskii* was reduced compared with the abandoned land (Figure 4). In this study, the degree of soil desiccation in the 0.0–4.6 m layer followed the order: Semiarid-350 > Semiarid-410 > Semiarid-470. However, the SMC in the 4.6–5.0 m layer remained stable, and the values of SMC were relatively small and almost identical between the three zones (Figure 4). This indicated severe soil desiccation was widespread in the semiarid Loess Plateau. This condition may lead to the formation of a dried soil layer (DSL), a condition where SMC in the soil is lower than the stable field capacity [18,19,39]. DSL usually occurred if soil moisture could not be recharged over a prolonged period of water shortage, causing a severe soil moisture deficit.

DSL is a common phenomenon found in the Loess Plateau [40,41] as a result of imbalanced plant–soil–atmosphere interactions [42]. DSL can prevent the vertical exchange of soil water between upper and lower soil layers, and further negatively affects the water cycle at both local and regional scales [29]. Studies have suggested that DSLs were worsened in areas covered by shrubs compared to areas covered by grasses because of the higher evapotranspiration rate of the former [43]. In *C. korshinskii* lands with heavy DSL, secondary seedling has been difficult to find and natural renewal was almost impossible [24]. Our results therefore suggested that more attention should be paid to the planning and management of introduced vegetation growth in semiarid regions. The planting densities should take into account the water resources and the effects plant growth will have on them [18,44]. In semiarid regions, the densities of shrub should be controlled to about 4950–6600 plants/hm^2 [45]. When the re-introduced shrub matures, the density should be further reduced according to soil water conditions [24]. Previous studies showed that 2490 plants/hm^2 was an optimum density for mature *C. korshinskii* in sandy land of Yanchi [46].

4.2. The Effects of Environmental Factors on the SMC

While our results suggested that vegetation had a significant effect on the SMC (Figure 4), other factors such as precipitation, latitude, and soil characteristics (field capacity and bulk density) also contributed to the variability (Figure 5). Average annual precipitation, field capacity, average annual temperature, and saturated hydraulic conductivity displayed positive correlations with soil moisture, whereas other factors (soil capacity, longitude, latitude, and bulk density) showed negative correlations. Average annual precipitation was the most significant factor affecting soil moisture, consistent with previous studies [47]. Since we used rainfall gradient across different latitudes, it is unsurprising that latitude played a significant role in determining soil moisture.

Although precipitation was the most significant factor affecting soil moisture under *C. korshinskii*, other environmental factors had different effects on different layers. Even on the surface soils (0–1 m), SMC was influenced by various factors other than precipitation (*i.e.*, P, Lat, FC, BD, T) (Table 5), indicated by the overlapping soil moisture in 0–1 m layer and Axis 1 (Figure 5). These results were similar to another study in the Pernambuco semiarid region that also proved that soil properties had significant effects on soil moisture variability [48]. Bulk density most significantly affected SMC in the 1–2 m layer compared to the other soil layers, while field capacity had more effect on soil moisture of deep layers (2–5 m) than the 1–2 m layer.

4.3. Implications on Vegetation Restoration under Climate Change

The implementation of the "Grain to Green Program" is challenging since success depends on the water consumption characteristics and local soil moisture conditions. Yet, we found that vegetation restoration using *C. korshinskii* did not always correspond with improved soil conditions. Although it has successfully decreased soil erosion [49,50], the introduced vegetation including *C. korshinskii* consumed more soil moisture in the deep layers, decreasing potential water yield and changing the spatial pattern of soil moisture. Our study thus confirmed other finding which indicated that vegetation restoration might result in soil desiccation in the Loess Plateau [29]. Understanding the driving mechanism of soil moisture deficit is therefore one of the most important factors to be considered for vegetation restoration and sustainable development in the Loess Plateau [51].

Studies have indicated that drought has occurred more frequently in recent years, causing more damage to the degraded semiarid areas [24]. Although *C. korshinskii* has good economic benefits and high drought tolerance [23], it also consumed a large amount of water. As precipitation was found to decrease annually by an average of 0.97 mm [2], planting *C. korshinskii* in large quantities for restoration purposes is questionable as it might worsen the already dry conditions. While soil moisture profiles differed across different precipitation zones (Table 4 and Figure 4), they became identical at deep soil layers (4.6–5.0 m) under *C. korshinskii* compared to control (abandoned land). So far, there have been no guidelines on plant species' selection and their corresponding density for restoration purposes under climate change. High planting density over years of planting, however, is not recommended as it could lead to DSL [38]. Instead of planting water-consuming shrubs, planting xerophytes and mesophytes would be more suitable in the regions with annual rainfall less than 400 mm. In the regions with annual rainfall of 400–500 mm, shrub was preferable but intermediate cuttings and density adjustment should be carried out in time during the luxuriant growing period [24]. For future research, the interaction between vegetation, SMC, and climate change should be further detailed to identify the appropriate planting density for specific areas without jeopardizing soil water resources.

5. Conclusions

In this study, we found that precipitation was the key factor dominating the spatial variations in soil moisture under *C. korshinskii* shrubs, particularly in the top 5 m of the soils. The highest soil moisture value was found at the surface layers (0–0.1 m), but with a large coefficient of variation. Although soil water storage increased with precipitation, the degree of SMC variation varied with different precipitation zones. The SMC became relatively stable at the 2.8 m layer, 4.2 m layer, and 4.6 m layer for Semiarid-350, Semiarid-410, and Semiarid-470, respectively. Water deficit occurred in all three precipitation zones, especially in the Semiarid-350 and Semiarid-410 due to the introduced vegetation species (*i.e.*, *C. korshinskii*).

Using redundancy analysis to clarify the controlling factors of soil moisture, it was shown that the soil moisture content increased with precipitation, temperature, field capacity, and saturated hydraulic conductivity but decreased with soil capacity, longitude, latitude, and bulk density. Among those variables, precipitation is the determining factor of soil moisture conditions in semiarid regions, followed by latitude, field capacity, and bulk density. Considering the relationships between precipitation, SMC and vegetation, appropriate planting density and species selection should be taken into account for introduced vegetation management. In the semiarid Loess Plateau, planting density should be adjusted according to different growth stages.

Acknowledgments: This study was supported by the National Natural Science Foundation of China (No. 41390462) and the Program for Changjing Scholars and Innovative Research Team in University (No. IRT_15R06).

Author Contributions: Yuanxin Liu and Wenwu Zhao designed the research; Yuanxin Liu, Xiao Zhang and Xuening Fang performed the field works; Lixin Wang supervised the research; Yuanxin Liu analyzed the data; Yuanxin Liu, Wenwu Zhao and Lixin Wang wrote the paper; Stefani Daryanto edited and contributed to the paper writing.

Conflicts of Interest: The authors declare no conflict of interest.

References

1. Lü, Y.H.; Ma, Z.M.; Zhang, L.W.; Fu, B.J.; Gao, G.Y. Redlines for the greening of China. *Environ. Sci. Policy* **2013**, *33*, 346–353. [CrossRef]
2. Lü, Y.H.; Fu, B.J.; Feng, X.M.; Zeng, Y.; Liu, Y.; Chang, R.Y.; Sun, G.; Wu, B.F. A policy-driven large scale ecological restoration: Quantifying ecosystem services changes in the loess plateau of China. *PLoS ONE* **2012**, *7*, e31782. [CrossRef] [PubMed]
3. Feng, X.; Fu, B.; Lu, N.; Zeng, Y.; Wu, B. How ecological restoration alters ecosystem services: An analysis of carbon sequestration in China's loess plateau. *Sci. Rep.* **2013**, *3*, 2846. [CrossRef] [PubMed]
4. Wang, Y.; Shao, M.A.; Zhang, C.; Han, X.; Mao, T.; Jia, X. Choosing an optimal land-use pattern for restoring eco-environments in a semiarid region of the Chinese loess plateau. *Ecol. Eng.* **2015**, *74*, 213–222. [CrossRef]
5. Chen, Y.; Wang, K.; Lin, Y.; Shi, W.; Song, Y.; He, X. Balancing green and grain trade. *Nat. Geosci.* **2015**, *8*, 739–741. [CrossRef]
6. Yang, L.; Chen, L.; Wei, W.; Yu, Y.; Zhang, H. Comparison of deep soil moisture in two re-vegetation watersheds in semi-arid regions. *J. Hydrol.* **2014**, *513*, 314–321. [CrossRef]
7. Ferreira, J.N.; Bustamante, M.; Garcia-Montiel, D.C.; Caylor, K.K.; Davidson, E.A. Spatial variation in vegetation structure coupled to plant available water determined by two-dimensional soil resistivity profiling in a Brazilian savanna. *Oecologia* **2007**, *153*, 417–430. [CrossRef] [PubMed]
8. Yao, X.L.; Fu, B.J.; Lü, Y.H.; Chang, R.Y.; Wang, S.; Wang, Y.F.; Su, C.H. The multi-scale spatial variance of soil moisture in the semi-arid loess plateau of China. *J. Soils Sediments* **2012**, *12*, 694–703. [CrossRef]
9. Fu, B.J.; Wang, J.; Chen, L.D.; Qiu, Y. The effects of land use on soil moisture variation in the danangou catchment of the loess plateau, China. *Catena* **2003**, *54*, 197–213. [CrossRef]

10. Montenegro, S.; Ragab, R. Impact of possible climate and land use changes in the semi arid regions: A case study from north eastern brazil. *J. Hydrol.* **2012**, *434–435*, 55–68. [CrossRef]

11. Yang, L.; Wei, W.; Chen, L.D.; Mo, B.R. Response of deep soil moisture to land use and afforestation in the semi-arid loess plateau, China. *J. Hydrol.* **2012**, *475*, 111–122. [CrossRef]

12. Gao, X.; Wu, P.; Zhao, X.; Wang, J.; Shi, Y.; Zhang, B.; Tian, L.; Li, H. Estimation of spatial soil moisture averages in a large gully of the loess plateau of China through statistical and modeling solutions. *J. Hydrol.* **2013**, *486*, 466–478. [CrossRef]

13. Zhao, J.; Yan, X.; Guo, J.; Jia, G. Evaluating spatial-temporal dynamics of net primary productivity of different forest types in northeastern China based on improved forcchn. *PLoS ONE* **2012**, *7*, e48131. [CrossRef] [PubMed]

14. Burt, T.P.; Butcher, D.P. Topographic controls of soil moisture distributions. *J. Soil Sci.* **1985**, *36*, 469–486. [CrossRef]

15. Shi, Y.G.; Wu, P.T.; Zhao, X.N.; Li, H.C.; Wang, J.W.; Zhang, B.Q. Statistical analyses and controls of root-zone soil moisture in a large gully of the loess plateau. *Environ. Earth Sci.* **2013**, *71*, 4801–4809. [CrossRef]

16. Hawley, M.E.; Jackson, T.J.; McCuen, R.H. Surface soil-moisture variation on small agricultural watersheds. *J. Hydrol.* **1983**, *62*, 179–200. [CrossRef]

17. Ramos, M.C.; Mulligan, M. Spatial modelling of the impact of climate variability on the annual soil moisture regime in a mechanized mediterranean vineyard. *J. Hydrol.* **2005**, *306*, 287–301. [CrossRef]

18. Wang, Y.Q.; Shao, M.A.; Shao, H.B. A preliminary investigation of the dynamic characteristics of dried soil layers on the loess plateau of China. *J. Hydrol.* **2010**, *381*, 9–17. [CrossRef]

19. Wang, Y.Q.; Shao, M.A.; Liu, Z.P. Large-scale spatial variability of dried soil layers and related factors across the entire loess plateau of China. *Geoderma* **2010**, *159*, 99–108. [CrossRef]

20. Daryanto, S.; Eldridge, D.J.; Wang, L. Spatial patterns of infiltration vary with disturbance in a shrub-encroached woodland. *Geomorphology* **2013**, *194*, 57–64. [CrossRef]

21. He, X.L.; Zhao, L.L.; Yang, H.Y. Diversity and spatial distribution of arbuscular mycorrhizal fungi of caragana korshinskii in the loess plateau. *Acta Ecol. Sin.* **2006**, *26*, 3835–3840.

22. Yang, X.M. Study on the characteristics of water environment in shrubbery of loess plateau. *Arid Zone Res.* **2001**, *18*, 8–13.

23. Cheng, X.; Huang, M.; Shao, M.; Warrington, D.N. A comparison of fine root distribution and water consumption of mature caragana korshinkii kom grown in two soils in a semiarid region, China. *Plant Soil* **2008**, *315*, 149–161. [CrossRef]

24. Chen, H.S.; Shao, M.A.; Li, Y.Y. Soil desiccation in the loess plateau of China. *Geoderma* **2008**, *143*, 91–100. [CrossRef]

25. Tasumi, M.; Kimura, R. Estimation of volumetric soil water content over the liudaogou river basin of the loess plateau using the swest method with spatial and temporal variability. *Agric. Water Manag.* **2013**, *118*, 22–28. [CrossRef]

26. Zhao, W.W.; Fu, B.J.; Qiu, Y. An upscaling method for cover-management factor and its application in the loess plateau of China. *Int. J. Environ. Res. Public Health* **2013**, *10*, 4752–4766. [CrossRef] [PubMed]

27. Kimura, R.; Kamichika, M.; Takayama, N.; Matsuoka, N.; Zhang, X. Heat balance and soil moisture in the loess plateau, China. *J. Agric. Meteorol.* **2004**, *60*, 103–113. [CrossRef]

28. Zhao, W.W.; Fu, B.J.; Chen, L.D. A comparison between soil loss evaluation index and the c-factor of rusle: A case study in the loess plateau of China. *Hydrol. Earth Syst. Sci.* **2012**, *16*, 2739–2748. [CrossRef]

29. Wang, Y.Q.; Shao, M.A.; Zhu, Y.J.; Liu, Z.P. Impacts of land use and plant characteristics on dried soil layers in different climatic regions on the loess plateau of China. *Agric. For. Meteorol.* **2011**, *151*, 437–448. [CrossRef]

30. Dobriyal, P.; Qureshi, A.; Badola, R.; Hussain, S.A. A review of the methods available for estimating soil moisture and its implications for water resource management. *J. Hydrol.* **2012**, *458–459*, 110–117. [CrossRef]

31. Li, W.; Wang, Q.J.; Wei, S.P.; Shao, M.A.; Yi, L. Soil desiccation for loess soils on natural and regrown areas. *For. Ecol. Manag.* **2008**, *255*, 2467–2477.

32. Hill, M.O.; Gauch, H.G. Detrended correspondence analysis: An improved ordination technique. *Vegetatio* **1980**, *42*, 47–58. [CrossRef]

33. Zhu, H.D.; Shi, Z.H.; Fang, N.F.; Wu, G.L.; Guo, Z.L.; Zhang, Y. Soil moisture response to environmental factors following precipitation events in a small catchment. *Catena* **2014**, *120*, 73–80. [CrossRef]

34. Penna, D.; Borga, M.; Norbiato, D.; Fontana, G.D. Hillslope scale soil moisture variability in a steep alpine terrain. *J. Hydrol.* **2009**, *364*, 311–327. [CrossRef]

35. Hu, W.; Shao, M.A.; Han, F.P.; Reichardt, K. Spatio-temporal variability behavior of land surface soil water content in shrub- and grass-land. *Geoderma* **2011**, *162*, 260–272. [CrossRef]

36. Gao, X.D.; Wu, P.T.; Zhao, X.N.; Shi, Y.G.; Wang, J.W.; Zhang, B.Q. Soil moisture variability along transects over a well-developed gully in the loess plateau, China. *Catena* **2011**, *87*, 357–367. [CrossRef]

37. Wang, Z.Q.; Liu, B.Y.; Liu, G.; Zhang, Y.X. Soil water depletion depth by planted vegetation on the loess plateau. *Sci. China Ser. D Earth Sci.* **2009**, *52*, 835–842. [CrossRef]

38. Jian, S.; Zhao, C.; Fang, S.; Yu, K. Effects of different vegetation restoration on soil water storage and water balance in the Chinese loess plateau. *Agric. For. Meteorol.* **2015**, *206*, 85–96. [CrossRef]

39. Wang, Y.Q.; Shao, M.A.; Liu, Z.P.; Zhang, C.C. Characteristics of dried soil layers under apple orchards of different ages and their applications in soil water managements on the loess plateau of China. *Pedosphere* **2015**, *25*, 546–554. [CrossRef]

40. Li, Y.S. The properties of water cycle in soil and their effect on water cycle for land in the loess plateau. *Acta Ecol. Sinica* **1983**, *3*, 91–101.

41. Hou, Q.C.; Han, R.L.; Li, H.P. On problems of vegetation reconstruction in Yan'an experimental area: III significance of native trees in plantation. *Res. Soil Water Conserv.* **2000**, *7*, 119–123.

42. Yan, W.M.; Deng, L.; Zhong, Y.Q.W.; Shangguan, Z.P. The characters of dry soil layer on the loess plateau in China and their influencing factors. *PLoS ONE* **2015**, *10*, e0134902. [CrossRef] [PubMed]

43. Shangguan, Z.P. Soil desiccation occurrence and its impact on forest vegetation in the loess plateau of China. *Int. J. Sustain. Dev. World Ecol.* **2007**, *14*, 299–306. [CrossRef]

44. Mendham, D.S.; White, D.A.; Battaglia, M.; McGrath, J.F.; Short, T.M.; Ogden, G.N.; Kinal, J. Soil water depletion and replenishment during first- and early second-rotation eucalyptus globulus plantations with deep soil profiles. *Agric. For. Meteorol.* **2011**, *151*, 1568–1579. [CrossRef]

45. Yang, W.Z.; Shao, M.A. *Study on Soil Water on the Loess Plateau of China*; Science Press: Beijing, China, 2000.

46. Shu, W.H.; Jiang, Q.; Wang, Z.J.; He, J.L. The temporal and spatial changes of soil moisture in different density of caragana korshinskii in sandy land of Yanchi, Ningxia. *J. Arid Land Resour. Environ.* **2012**, *26*, 172–176.

47. He, Q.H.; He, Y.H.; Bao, W.K. Research on dynamics of soil moisture in arid and semiarid mountainous areas. *J. Mt. Sci.* **2003**, *21*, 149–156.

48. Dos Santos, T.E.M.; Montenegro, A.A.A.; Silva, D.D. Soil moisture in pernambuco semiarid using time domain reflectometry (tdr). *Revista Brasileira de Engenharia Agricola e Ambiental* **2011**, *15*, 670–679.

49. Chen, L.D.; Wang, J.P.; Wei, W.; Fu, B.J.; Wu, D.P. Effects of landscape restoration on soil water storage and water use in the loess plateau region, China. *For. Ecol. Manag.* **2010**, *259*, 1291–1298. [CrossRef]

50. Lü, Y.H.; Feng, X.M.; Chen, L.D.; Fu, B.J. Scaling effects of landscape metrics: A comparison of two methods. *Phys. Goegr.* **2013**, *34*, 4–49.

51. Lü, Y.H.; Fu, B.J.; Wei, W.; Yu, X.B.; Sun, R.H. Major ecosystems in China: Dynamics and challenges for sustainable management. *Environ. Manag.* **2011**, *48*, 13. [CrossRef] [PubMed]

forests

MDPI

Article

Long-Term Forest Paired Catchment Studies: What Do They Tell Us That Landscape-Level Monitoring Does Not?

Daniel G. Neary

USDA Forest Service, Rocky Mountain Research Station, 2500 South Pine Knoll Drive, Flagstaff, AZ 86001, USA; dneary@fs.fed.us; Tel.: +1-928-853-1861; Fax: +1-928-556-2130

Academic Editors: Ge Sun and James M. Vose
Received: 15 December 2015; Accepted: 22 July 2016; Published: 29 July 2016

Abstract: Forested catchments throughout the world are known for producing high quality water for human use. In the 20th Century, experimental forest catchment studies played a key role in studying the processes contributing to high water quality. The hydrologic processes investigated on these paired catchments have provided the science base for examining water quality responses to natural disturbances such as wildfire, insect outbreaks, and extreme hydrologic events, and human-induced disturbances such as timber harvesting, site preparation, prescribed fires, fertilizer applications, pesticide usage, rainfall acidification, and mining. This paper compares and contrasts the paired catchment approach with landscape-level water resource monitoring to highlight the information on hydrologic processes provided by the paired catchment approach that is not provided by the broad-brush landscape monitoring.

Keywords: forest catchments; long-term studies; monitoring; water quantity; water quality

1. Introduction

The most sustainable and best quality freshwater sources in the world originate in forested watersheds [1–5]. The biological, chemical, and physical characteristics of forest soils are particularly well suited to delivering high quality water to streams (e.g., low in sediment content and nutrient load, and contain low amounts of bacteria and other microorganisms). They are also excellent in moderating the climatic extremes that affect stream hydrology and water quality [6]. Forest soils are usually characterized by high porosities, low bulk density, and high saturated hydraulic conductivities and infiltration rates [7]. Consequently, surface runoff is rare in forest environments, and most rainfall moves to streams by subsurface flow pathways where nutrient uptake, cycling, and contaminant sorption processes are rapid. Because of the dominance of subsurface flow processes, peak flows are moderated and baseflows with high water quality are prolonged [8,9].

In many parts of the world, municipalities ultimately rely on forested watersheds to provide adequate quantities of high quality water for continually growing demand [1]. This is particularly true in semi-arid regions where water supplies are limited, water quality is affected by high mineral content, and human populations are large or growing rapidly. Forest soils provide the perfect conditions for creating high quality water supplies [6]. Research using paired catchments provides the scientific basis for understanding disturbance effects in forests and led to development of Best Management Practices (BMPs) for sustaining water quality [10].

The early 20th century was unique in that it had the beginnings of paired catchment research in several parts of the world. The Sperbelgraben and Rappengraben experimental catchments were established in 1903 near Emmental, Switzerland [11]. This was followed by establishment of the Ota watershed study in Japan in 1908 and the Wagon Wheel Gap study in Colorado, USA, in 1910 [12,13].

Paired catchment experiments have been reviewed by a number of authors [14–22]. Most of these reviews have dealt with the topic of water yield. However, many of the paired catchment experiments initially designed for water yield research have been expanded to include water quality.

Landscape-level hydrologic monitoring is being carried out by a number of agencies throughout the world. These include the U.S. Geological Survey (USGS) in the United States, the National Institute of Water and Atmospheric Research in New Zealand, CSIRO and the Bureau of Meteorology in Australia, Environment Canada in Canada, municipal and state water authorities in Germany, Federal Service for Hydrometeorology and Environmental Monitoring in Russia, and the State Environmental Protection Agency and the Ministry of Water Resources in China, to mention a few.

This paper provides a historical perspective of the many accomplishments of water quantity and quality research over the past century, made possible by using the paired catchment methodology. It examines the paired catchment approach versus landscape level monitoring to describe what each approach provides in terms of hydrological science and what type of information is needed for watershed management in the 21st Century.

2. U.S. Geological Survey Landscape-Level Monitoring

2.1. Background

The U.S. Geological Survey (USGS) has been gathering hydrologic and climatic data for more than 100 years at some of its monitoring stations. Long-term streamflow data generated at more than 7200 sites create environmental baseline data sets that can be used to assess important parameters and significant changes [23]. For example, gathering long-term water data helps answer questions like:

- What is the height of stream rise in 100-year floods?
- How effective are stream restoration and streamside management practices?
- What are current stream levels in respect to historic highs and lows?
- What are the trends in streamflows with respect to current climate and variations?
- What are the characteristics of streamflows in different biogeographical provinces?

Disadvantages of landscape level time-trend monitoring include hydrograph time resolution, sampling frequency for chemical analysis, climate variability, stream gauge accuracy, and a mixture of land uses. This approach provides a "snapshot" of hydrological conditions but is way too coarse for teasing out hydrological processes and their causes. Climate variability between sites is a major problem particularly when convective thunderstorms are a main source of rainfall input. Some USGS gauges have proper weirs but others do not and utilize natural control sections. This is understandable for large catchments with a wide range of flows. However, this method does not produce records that are as accurate as those derived from standard weirs. The mixture of land uses and conditions common with the landscape-level gauges makes it difficult to sort out causes and effects attributable to specific uses and conditions. Chemical analyses may be limited and spaced out over different time frames, making it difficult to make inter-basin comparisons. Metadata availability is often limited by different gauge histories compared to paired catchments.

As indicated above, streamflow records can provide an important history of climatic variation over a hydrologic basin [24]. This ability is a function of the collection of water data in the absence of confounding factors such as land use change and management impacts that override climate signals. National streamflow records that are relatively free of confounding anthropogenic influences are important for studying and understanding of the variation in surface-water conditions throughout the United States. Confounding effects are difficult to avoid, especially if large basins are used for study. The smaller catchments used for paired catchment research are usually better at avoiding these effects but the method is not "foolproof" [1,3].

Providing users with the history of climatic and hydrologic variation over a catchment is a primary objective of the national hydrologic records generated by the landscape-level USGS streamflow recording system [24]. The USGS National Water Storage and Retrieval System (WATSTORE) gauging station data are reviewed jointly with hydrology and climate data specialists in each USGS District office. The resulting assemblage of stations, each with its respective period of record, is called the Hydro-Climatic Data Network, or HCDN. The HCDN is composed of 1,659 sites throughout the country and its territories. This produces a network of 73,231 water years of daily mean discharge values for evaluating water resource conditions across the many diverse landscapes of the United States. For each station in the HCDN, the appropriate daily mean discharge values are compiled by month and year, and statistical characteristics, including monthly mean discharges and annual mean, minimum and maximum discharges, are tabulated. The stream discharge data are assessed and compared in a companion report on national water resources. This process provides an understanding of the variation in national surface-water conditions but does not evaluate the impacts of anthropogenic disturbances such as agriculture, forestry, urbanization, vegetation conversion, and wildfires.

Currently, the USGS collects streamflow and other data on variable time intervals that range from 15 min to yearly at more than 7200 sites that are gauging stations for streamflow. Most of the stations are funded and operated in cooperation with other federal agencies, such as the U.S. Army Corps of Engineers, the U.S. Forest Service, the Bureau of Land Management, the Bureau of Reclamation, and the U.S. Fish and Wildlife Service, and with state, Tribal, county, and municipal agencies. These cooperators use the USGS-derived data for making decisions such as when to withdraw water from rivers or reservoirs for agricultural and municipal use, and whether or not to permit discharge of treated wastewater into surface waters. Provisional data from most of the gauging sites are available on-line in within hours of recording (http://waterdata.usgs.gov/nwis). The USGS water resources system provides access to its and cooperator water-resources data collected at approximately 1.5 million sites in all 50 States, the District of Columbia, Puerto Rico, the Virgin Islands, Guam, American Samoa and the Commonwealth of the Northern Mariana Islands. These sites include estuaries, lakes, streams, springs, wells, caves, wetlands, and industrial and municipal facilities.

2.2. Monitoring Scales and Settings

USGS water resource monitoring aims to investigate local problems and trends in a specific stream, county, state, or large catchment systems such as the Columbia River or the Mississippi River Basin. Uniform methods of sampling and analysis are selected to provide consistent information across and within landscapes. Monitoring is conducted at sites that are representative of national watersheds so that comprehensive comparisons and assessments can be made at larger scales. This multi-scale approach helps with determining if certain types of water yield or water quality issues are isolated, biogeographical region dependent, or wide-spread nationally. This approach allows streams, rivers, and lakes to be compared to those in other geographic and environmental settings. Therefore, the data can help answer comparative questions including the following:

- Is the water quality of a particular stream typical of streams in the Atlantic Coastal Plain?
- Are streams in the arid west experiencing reduced flows and elevated salinity?
- Are cation and anion concentrations exceeding water quality standards?
- Are stream baseflows diminishing, stabilizing, or increasing across specific hydrologic regions or nationally?

2.3. A Monitoring Protocol

Landscape-level monitoring is necessary to ensure that water resources can continue to support the many different ways water resources are used [25]. This level of large scale monitoring is also used to determine the effectiveness of protection and restoration measures. The information obtained from monitoring helps with state and national prioritizing of water quantity and quality the issues to be addressed by state and Federal programs, and for selecting the geographic areas in which to focus water research and restoration efforts. This approach helps to ensure cost-effective water resource management.

Effective landscape-level monitoring has the attributes of being is regular, long-term, and inclusive of biological, physical, and chemical parameters. It should be "regular" to detect changes in water resource conditions. In many instances, changes are more important in determining water quantity and quality problems. Regular monitoring at consistent time intervals allows identification of changes in the noisy background of water parameter fluctuations. Allied to "regular", is the monitoring characteristic of "long-term". Collection of water resource data in the "long-term", using consistent and comparable methodology, is necessary for identification of trends or patterns that indicate there are significant changes in water resource parameters. Water quality is constantly changing on a diurnal, seasonal, and annual basis. To separate real trends from short-term changes, consistent and systematic data are required over the long term. However, without the comparative data generated by a "paired watershed" approach, it might be difficult to determine "cause and effect" from observed water resource changes or the potential magnitude of those changes. Even then the effort might be intractable and detailed study and focused monitoring may be required to solve problems.

Water quantity (streamflow) is an important companion parameter to water quality in that the quantity of streamflow is a critical in determining water quality and interpreting water-quality trends. The potential effects of contaminant concentrations and loadings on drinking-water supplies and aquatic habitats depend largely on the amount of water flowing in streams. Higher flows usually mean that rivers and streams have the capacity to carry a greater load of chemical contaminants and sediment. High flows result in increased bedload scour and suspended sediment transport, in part because of greater overland runoff relative to baseflows. On the other hand, greater streamflows may result in a reduction of concentrations and an apparent improvement in water quality. This could include concentrations of nonpoint source pollutants, loading of pollutants, biological content, and thermal conditions. All are components of water quality but the former is usually measured the most.

Access to streamflow data at the appropriate temporal resolution allows for more accurate evaluation of water-quality data. An observed trend in water quality (for example, increasing concentrations of a chemical contaminant over a six-month period) may indicate an actual water-quality change or may be the indirect result of differences in flow volumes when the water samples were collected. Long intervals (monthly, yearly, and biennial) between water sampling aggravates the problem of separating management-related water quality changes from volume-seasonal effects.

The USGS collects samples from streams across the United States and its territories, and analyzes these samples for chemical, physical, and biological properties [25]. Data are collected for studies that range from national in scale, such as the National Water-Quality Assessment Program (NAWQA), to studies in small watersheds.

Through its landscape level monitoring program, the USGS has no regulatory responsibilities, but the agency focuses on evaluating the entire national water resource. Important uses that motivate USGS landscape-level monitoring include drinking water sources, water used for irrigation, livestock water supply, industrial water supplies, and recreation. The USGS water resources data thereby complement the data collected by the States and by EPA, which focus on monitoring for compliance with regulations, and land management agencies, such as the U.S. Forest Service, that are concerned about management activity impacts.

3. Paired Catchment Studies

3.1. Rationale and Criticism

As mentioned in the Introduction, paired catchment studies began in the early 20th Century and expanded considerably from the 1930s through the 1970s [15]. The rationale for the use of this methodology in hydrologic studies was providing solid data for predicting the effects of forest cover on water yield. Hibbert [14] reviewed 39 paired catchment studies across the world and came to the conclusion that these studies supported several generalizations:

1. Reduction of forest cover increases water yield.

2. Establishment of forests on sparsely vegetated land in low rainfall areas reduces water yield.
3. Responses to vegetation management are highly variable due to climate regime, vegetation type, geology, soils, area treated, and aspect.

Many more paired catchment studies since 1967 reinforced Hibbert's conclusions [14]. Indeed, at that time and still today, much of the knowledge about forest vegetation effects on the hydrologic cycle and man's influences came from paired catchment studies.

At about the same time a number of criticisms arose about the use of paired catchment studies in hydrological science. The main criticisms were that paired catchment experiments were too costly, unrepresentative, used leaky watersheds, had questionable application of results, and did not contribute to scientific progress on hydrological processes [26,27]. A rebuttal by Hewlett [28] titled *In Defense of Experimental Watersheds* clearly pointed out that the long-term time-trend studies proposed as an alternative to paired catchment research were weaker because there are usually no climate controls (calibration period). These studies also lacked a control catchment needed to separate vegetation cover effects from climate effects. Hewlett and his co-authors [28] believed strongly that time-trend studies are circumstantial and that paired catchment studies are strong evidence of forest vegetation effects on the water cycle. Hence, they concluded that the paired catchment methodology was scientifically sound and had a secure future in hydrological science.

3.2. Disturbance Effects

Most forest catchment water quality studies reported in the literature deal with tree harvesting and post-harvest site preparation since much of the early interest in paired catchment science related to vegetation management to increase water yield. In addition, harvesting practices were considered to produce the most disruptions to ecological processes and therefore the most influence on water quality. Other disturbances include wildfire, prescribed fire, pesticide application, recreation activities, wildland–urban development, sewage discharges, landslides, grazing, mining, and invasive species spread.

Since forest fertilization has been a basic feature of intensive forest management throughout the world, the impact of fertilizers on water quality has been an issue easily addressed by paired catchment research [29]. Paired catchments provided a sound basis for acid deposition research in the 1980s and 1990s [30], and continue to support scientific endeavors on climate change in the 21st century [31].

A number of water parameters are affected by disturbances, but only streamflow and nutrients will be discussed in the limited space available for this paper. Other papers present a much more detailed discussion of these topics [9,16,20,32,33].

3.3. Water Yield

Most paired catchment studies were established to determine the impact of forest management on water yield (Tables 1 and 2). These studies have allowed the comparison of forest harvesting in a number of forest ecosystems and across a range of precipitation regimes and evapotranspiration gradients. Measured first year increases in streamflow volumes have ranged from none (with 457 mm annual precipitation [34]) to 280% (with 1,020 mm annual precipitation [35]). In absolute amounts, the range is from 0 mm [34] to 650 mm [36]. Paired watershed studies allow this comparison of undisturbed and disturbed because of the nature and designs of the studies. These watershed studies also facilitate the comparisons and evaluations of the effects of forest types on water yield (conifer vs. deciduous). In general, there is a significant increase in streamflow with 100% forest cutting.

Increases in annual streamflow volumes in area-depths in forested catchments caused by vegetation removal or manipulation begin at around 500 mm annual precipitation and increase as precipitation input increases (Figure 1, Table 1). These data were developed from paired watershed studies in a range of forest ecosystems in North America, Europe, Asia, Africa, Australia, and New Zealand (Tables 1 and 2). Most are from the USA due to substantial investments by government agencies such as the U.S. Forest Service.

Table 1. First year streamflow responses to forest harvesting by precipitation amount, 450 to 1200 mm precipitation, forest ecosystems in Europe, North America, Australia, and Japan. Adapted from [20].

Forest type	Location	Ppt.	Mean Annual Flow	Cut	1st Year Inc.	Percent Increase	Reference
		mm	mm	%	mm	%	
Pinyon-juniper	Arizona USA	457	20	100	0	0	[34]
Spruce-fir	Alberta Canada	513	147	100	84	57	[37]
Aspen-conifer	Colorado USA	536	157	100	34	22	[38]
Eucalyptus spp.	Victoria Australia	596	86	100	20	23	[39]
Ponderosa pine	Arizona USA	570	153	100	96	63	[40]
Oak woodland	California USA	635	144	99	33	23	[41]
Pine-spruce	Sweden	732	271	100	371	119	[42]
Spruce-fir-pine	Colorado USA	770	340	40	84	25	[43]
Aspen-birch	Minnesota USA	775	107	100	45	42	[44]
Spruce-fir	Alberta Canada	840	310	100	79	25	[45]
Slash pine	Florida USA	1020	48	74	134	280	[35]
Hardwood	Japan	1153	293	100	209	18	[46]

Table 2. First year streamflow responses to forest harvesting by precipitation amount, 1200 to 2600 mm precipitation forest ecosystems in North America, Africa, Australia, and New Zealand. Adapted from [20].

Forest type	Location	Ppt.	Mean Annual Flow	Cut	1st Year Inc.	Percent Increase	Reference
		mm	mm	%	mm	%	
Coastal redwoods	California	1200	67	100	34	51	[47]
Mixed Hardwoods	Georgia USA	1219	467	100	254	54	[48]
Northern hardwoods	New Hampshire	1230	710	100	343	48	[49]
Loblolly pine	Arkansas	1317	214	100	101	47	[50]
Dry Eucalpytus	Victoria Australia	1520	330	95	350	106	[51]
Mixed hardwoods	North Carolina	1900	880	100	362	41	[52]
Montane forest	Kenya Africa	2014	568	100	457	80	[53]
Cascade Douglas-fir	Oregon USA	2388	1376	100	462	34	[54]
Coastal Douglas-fir	Oregon USA	2483	1885	82	370	20	[55,56]
Beech and podocarps	New Zealand	2600	1500	100	650	43	[36]

The largest and most consistent increases in streamflow with vegetation removal occur between 2000 and 2750 mm (Figure 1, Table 2). Although landscape-level gauging has been conducted in virtually every region and country around the world, the best data in terms of quality and length of record come from forest paired watershed studies [15]. Projects that incorporated controlled, human interventions such as logging have been able to develop the best understanding of hydrologic processes [17]. Landscape-level monitoring that minimized or avoided disturbances would not have achieved the same of understanding [21].

A considerable amount of research has been conducted in the past on the hydrologic effects of forest disturbances, primarily harvesting, on over 105+ individual paired catchments. The results have been summarized in a number of syntheses [15–17,20,57,58]. These studies have been very expensive to install, maintain, and monitor. Their existence is a tribute to the substantial dedication to their continuity by hydrologic scientists. The earliest catchment experiments were installed in Switzerland, Japan, and the United States in the first ten years of the twentieth century when the continuity of water supplies was a big issue. Some have been in existence since the 1930s. Scientists and watershed managers have studied harvesting intensities, configurations, and timing with a view to optimizing water yield and quality. With a 100% clearcut harvest, first-year water yield increases reported in the literature generally range from 0% to 280% over a range of forest vegetation from juniper (dry) to tropical (wet) (Table 1). The absolute amount of water yield is strongly related to a number of factors at the time of harvesting such as the annual rainfall, vegetation type, ET regime, aspect and slope, leaf area reduction, geology, soil type, soil moisture, and soil depth [6,17,59]. Although the water yields increase the first year after harvesting and increase with total precipitation, the percentage increase is poorly correlated to precipitation amount (Figure 1). Although tropical forests have higher rainfall, increases after harvesting are reduced by high year-round ET. Indeed, the greatest variation occurs at 100% harvest because other factors in the hydrologic equation override transpiration reduction. Vegetation type is strongly correlated to streamflow increases after forest harvesting [60]. Broadleaved forests have the highest mean increase in water quantity after harvesting (237 mm) compared to coniferous forests (161 mm) or mixed conifer-broadleaved forests (170 mm) [58].

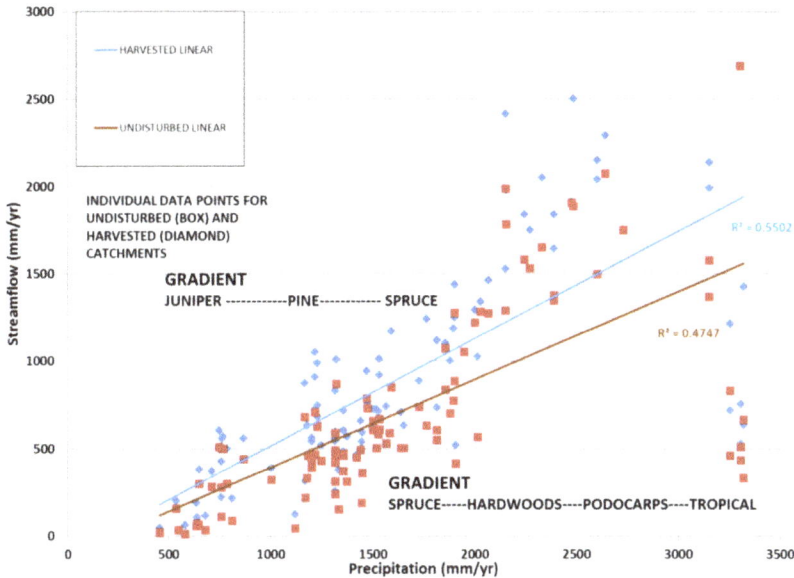

Figure 1. Streamflow increases produced by harvesting paired catchment studies. Adapted from [15–17,20,57,58].

Harvesting of forests has been used to augment municipal water supplies because of the resulting increases in water yield [15]. The duration of the response depends on a number of factors. Generally, the increase in total water yield after harvesting is considered to be a benefit, and not of sufficient magnitude to produce adverse hydrologic or ecosystem effects (e.g., flooding). However, vigorously growing young forest stands provide and opposite response. They can cause subsequent water yield declines after initial increases due to rapid resprouting. Short-rotation *Eucalyptus* spp. plantations in Australia and South Africa are good examples [61,62]. *E. regnans* and *E. delegatensis* are the main culprits but not all *Eucalyptus* species produce the same effect.

3.4. Water Quality

Although the initial focus of early catchment research was water yield, the adoption of the paired catchment approach set the stage for examining physical, chemical, and biological processes that controlled nutrient cycling and other water quality related functions of forest catchments [63]. The untreated half of catchment study pairs provides the opportunity to study natural processes that controlled water quality. However, the disturbances to these processes produced by practices such as harvesting, site preparation, road construction, fire, fertilization, herbicide use and insect outbreaks provide the real insight into natural catchment processes that affect water quality.

Nutrients such as nitrate nitrogen (NO_3–N) in streamflow from forested watersheds have been an issue for 50 years or more because of the release of NO_3–N after harvesting or other disturbances and the low water quality standard. Water quality is a justified concern of watershed management since many municipalities depend on high quality water coming from forested and other non-urbanized lands for their water supplies.

However, there have been many misperceptions about the impacts of forest management practices on water quality. Paired catchments provide the ideal locations for examining the real management effects on the important water quality parameters such as NO_3–N. Of the 30 paired watershed studies listed in Tables 3 and 4 that examined NO_3–N concentrations after partial or complete clearcutting, only one showed an alarming increase (0.3 to 11.9 mg·L^{-1}) that exceeded the international water quality standard (10 mg·L^{-1}) [59].

Table 3. Paired catchment comparison of the effects of forest harvesting on mean NO_3–N concentrations in streamflow in North America the year after cutting. Adapted from [20,57,64].

Forest Type	Location	NO_3–N		Reference
		Uncut	Cut	
		mg·L^{-1}		
Lodgepole Pine	Alberta, Canada	0.2	0.7	[65]
Spruce, Fir	British Columbia, Canada	0.1	0.2	[66]
Spruce, Fir	British Columbia, Canada	<0.1	0.5	[67]
Northern Hardwoods	New Brunswick, Canada	0.1	0.6	[68]
Spruce, Fir, Pine, Birch	Quebec. Canada	<0.1	<0.1	[69]
Spruce, Fir, Pine	Nova Scotia, Canada	<0.1	0.3	[70]
Mixed Conifer	Montana, USA	0.1	0.2	[71]
Spruce, Fir	Colorado, USA	<0.1	<0.1	[72]
Mixed Conifer	Idaho, USA	0.2	0.2	[73]
Douglas-fir	Oregon, USA	<0.1	0.2	[74]
Mixed Conifers	Oregon, USA	<0.1	0.2	[74]
Loblolly Pine	Georgia, USA	0.1	0.1	[48]
Loblolly Pine	South Carolina, USA	<0.1	<0.1	[75]
Mixed Hardwoods	North Carolina, USA	<0.1	0.1	[76]
Aspen, Birch, Spruce	Minnesota, USA	0.1	0.2	[44]
Mixed Hardwoods	West Virginia, USA	0.1	0.5	[77]
Northern Hardwoods	New Hampshire, USA	0.3	11.9	[59]

Table 4. Paired catchment comparison of the effects of forest harvesting on mean NO_3–N concentrations in streamflow in Europe, Africa, Asia, and the South Pacific the year after cutting. Adapted from [20,64].

Forest Type	Location	NO_3–N		Reference
		Uncut	Cut	
		mg·L^{-1}	mg·L^{-1}	
Native Beech-Podocarp	Chile	<0.1	<0.1	[78]
Spruce, Fir, Peat	Finland	<0.1	0.1	[79]
Spruce, Fir, Beech	Germany	0.7	1.0	[80]
Native Hardwoods[#]	Japan	0.7	1.6	[81]
Radiata Pine	New Zealand	<0.1	0.5	[82]
Beech-Podocarp	New Zealand	<0.1	<0.1	[61]
Radiata Pine	New Zealand	<0.1	0.2	[83]
Evergreen Forest/Scrub	South Africa	<0.1	0.1	[61]
Pine, Spruce, Hardwood	Sweden	0.1	0.2	[84]
Spruce, Moor	United Kingdom	0.2	0.3	[85]
Eucalyptus spp.	Victoria, Australia	<0.1	<0.1	[86]

[#] 4 years after cutting

Pierce et al. [59] raised concerns about water quality and forestry practices 45 years ago but was shown to be an anomaly [87]. All of the studies listed in Tables 3 and 4 post-dated the Pierce et al. [59] Hubbard Brook study and came to the same conclusion that there would be increases in NO_3–N but they would be minor and not anywhere close to the 10 mg L^{-1} standard that the Hubbard

Brook study violated. The side-by-side comparison of disturbed watersheds with undisturbed controls highlighted an analysis in 1977 that this case is an outlier in the literature and not the general ecosystem trend [87]. Hubbard Brook was unique in that vegetation regrowth was prevented by herbicides. Lacking plants to take up nitrogen liberated by harvesting an old-growth forest, NO_3–N concentrations in streamflow soared. Paired watershed studies like those listed in Tables 3 and 4 have been able to improve understanding of nutrient cycling and the changes in water quality which occur after harvesting. Landscape-level monitoring may have picked up the rise in NO_3–N, but then been unable to clearly demonstrate the source of the extra nitrogen.

4. Method Comparisons

A comparison of the characteristics of landscape-level monitoring and paired catchment water studies is presented in Table 5. This highlights the question raised by the title of this paper, "Long-term forest paired catchment studies: What do they tell us that landscape-level monitoring does not?"

Table 5. Comparison of characteristics of landscape-level monitoring and paired watershed research.

Watershed Characteristic	Landscape-Level Monitoring	Paired Watershed Approach
Short-term Studies	Yes	Yes
Long-term Studies	Yes	Yes
Large Scale Basins	Yes	Usually Not
Small Scale Basins	Some	Yes
Research Primary Objective	No	Yes
Water Yield Studies	Yes, but Limited	Yes
Water Quality Studies	Yes, but Limited	Yes
Process Research Capable	Usually Not	Yes
Individual Watershed Expense	Moderate	Moderate to High
Program Operating Expense	High	Moderate to Low
National Assessment Capable	Yes	Limited
Program Commitment	National	Regional to Local
Trend Detection	Moderate	High to Very High
Focus on Disturbance Effects	No	Yes
Disturbance Assessment	Moderate	High to Very High
Disturbance Comparisons	No	Yes
Cooperators Used	Yes	Yes
Web-Available Information	Yes	Yes

In their Preface to the 2012 publication "Revisiting Experimental Catchment Studies in Forest Hydrology", the editors clearly point out that much of what is known about the hydrological role of forests has derived from paired catchment experiments [88]. Paired catchment studies are designed for research into hydrologic processes whereas landscape-level monitoring is not (Table 5). They also focus on management related disturbances (e.g., harvesting, site preparation, fertilization, herbicide application, road construction and use, prescribed fire etc.) while landscape-level monitoring seeks to gather hydrologic information in the absence of most anthropogenic disturbances. Paired catchment studies are able to do this efficiently, while landscape-level monitoring does not. Most paired catchment studies involve process research that is aimed at understanding the hydrologic and ecological processes that control water flow and nutrient cycling [89]. Because of their design as before-after-control-impact experiments (BACI), paired catchment studies are more accurate in elucidating the water yield and quality impacts of forest disturbances. Landscape-level monitoring is more focused on broad scale trends. However, paired catchment studies are better suited to detecting trends amidst the "noise" that is common with water studies. Disturbance comparisons can be made with paired catchments studies, but rarely so with landscape-level monitoring due to confounding factors with the latter methodology.

5. Summary and Conclusions

This paper compared two different approaches to collect information on water resources in the United States, although other countries have similar approaches. The USGS uses a landscape monitoring approach to acquire data on water resources from over 7200 gauging stations to report on the status and trends of water resources in the country. It also utilizes data from cooperators to assemble information on 1.5 million sites in the USA. The other approach is the paired catchment method. It involves the BACI method of comparing side-by-side catchments to determine the impact of various disturbances. A variety of research organizations utilize the paired catchment approach because of the type of information they are interested in. While the landscape-level monitoring is important for discerning national water resources trends, most of what is known about the hydrological role of forests comes from paired catchment studies using the BACI method.

The hydrologic and ecological impacts of specific land management practices and the functioning of the hydrologic cycle in forest ecosystems have been developed from studies using the paired catchment approach over the past century. Hewlett [28] clearly pointed out that the long-term time-trend studies proposed as an alternative to paired catchment research were weaker because there are no climate controls (calibration period). These studies also lack a control catchment needed to separate vegetation cover effects from climate effects. Hewlett and his co-authors stated strongly that time-trend studies are circumstantial, and that paired catchment studies are strong evidence of forest vegetation effects on the water cycle [28]. Hence, they concluded that the paired catchment methodology was scientifically sound and had a secure future in hydrological science.

Both methods need to be maintained in the light of climate changes going on in the beginning of the 21st Century, but paired catchment studies are absolutely essential and are more likely to identify changes in hydrologic processes. Some of the water relationships determined by research in the 20th Century could be altered by different dynamics in the atmosphere with climate change. The legacy of 20th century paired catchment studies provides a solid and more accurate framework for evaluating and predicting 21st century changes.

Both approaches must be carried forward into the 20th Century. Landscape-level monitoring covers a greater extent of the USA and other nations as well as their forests. It would be cost-prohibitive for all the USGS sites to function as paired catchments (doubling or tripling the funding commitment). Paired catchments provide the venue for detailed research on a limited number of forest types and an attraction for national programs such as the USA Long Term Ecological Research network and the National Ecological Observatory Network [89]. There will need to be solid commitments from scientific organizations, government agencies, and private organizations and enterprises to achieve this goal.

Acknowledgments: The author would like to acknowledge the USDA Forest Service Research and Development division for providing support and training during his 38-year career in order to develop insights and experience in conducting paired watershed science. He would also like to thank SCION Forest Research Institute, Rotorua, New Zealand, for getting him into this aspect of the hydrological sciences.

Conflicts of Interest: The author declares no conflict of interest.

References

1. Lee, R. *Forest Hydrology*; Columbia University Press: New York, NY, USA, 1980; p. 349.
2. Dissmeyer, G.E., Ed.; Drinking water from forests and grasslands: A synthesis of the scientific literature. In *USDA Forest Service, General Technical Report SRS-39*; Southern Research Station: Asheville, NC, USA, 2000; p. 246.
3. Brooks, K.N.; Ffolliott, P.F.; Gregersen, H.M.; DeBano, L.F. *Hydrology and the Management of Watersheds*; Iowa State Press: Ames, IA, USA, 2003; p. 574.
4. Barten, P.K.; Ernst, C.E. Land conservation and watershed management for source protection. *J. Am. Water Works Assoc.* **2004**, *96*, 121–135.

5. Emelko, M.B.; Silins, U.; Bladon, K.D.; Stone, M. Implications of land disturbance on drinking water treatability in a changing climate: Demonstrating the need for "source water supply and protection" strategies. *Water Res.* **2011**, *45*, 461–472. [CrossRef] [PubMed]

6. Neary, D.G.; Ice, G.G.; Jackson, C.R. Linkages between forest soils and water quantity and quality. *Forest Ecol. Manag.* **2009**, *258*, 2269–2281. [CrossRef]

7. Neary, D.G. Impacts of wildfire severity on hydraulic conductivity in forest, woodland, and grassland soils. In *Hydraulic Conductivity—Issues, Determination and Applications*; Elango, L., Ed.; INTECH: Rijeka, Croatia, 2011; pp. 123–142.

8. Vertessy, R.A. The impacts of forestry on streamflows: A review. In *Forest Management for the Protection of Water Quality and Quantity*, Proceedings of the Second Erosion in Forests Meeting, Warburton, Australia, 4–6 May 1999; Croke, J., Lane, P., Eds.; Cooperative Research Centre for Catchment Hydrology: Canberra, Australia; pp. 93–109.

9. Ice, G.G.; Stednick, J.D. *A Century of Forest and Wildland Watershed Lessons*; Society of American Foresters: Bethesda, MD, USA, 2004; p. 287.

10. Ice, G. History of innovative Best Management Practice development and its role in addressing water quality limited waterbodies. *J. Environ. Eng.* **2004**, *130*, 684–689. [CrossRef]

11. Penman, H.L. *Vegetation and Hydrology: Technical Communication No. 53, Commonwealth Bureau of Soils*; Commonwealth Agricultural Bureau: Wallingford, UK, 1963.

12. Steen, H.K. *The US Forest Service, a History*; University of Washington Press: Seattle, WA, USA, 1976.

13. Neary, D.G. Changing perceptions of watershed management from a retrospective viewpoint. In Proceedings of Land Stewardship in the 21st Century: The Contributions of Watershed Management, Tucson, Arizona, USA, 13–16 March 2000; USDA Forest Service Proceedings RMRS-P-13, Rocky Mountain Research Station: Fort Collins, CO, USA, 2000; pp. 167–176.

14. Hibbert, A.R. Forest treatment effects on water yield. In *International Symposium on Forest Hydrology*; Sopper, W.W., Lull, H.W., Eds.; Pergamon Press: Oxford, UK, 1967; pp. 527–543.

15. Bosch, J.M.; Hewlett, J.D. A review of catchment experiments to determine the effect of vegetation changes on water yield and evapotranspiration. *J. Hydrol.* **1982**, *55*, 3–23. [CrossRef]

16. Binkley, D.; Brown, T.C. Forest practices as nonpoint sources of pollution in North America. *Water Res. Bull.* **1993**, *29*, 729–740. [CrossRef]

17. Neary, D.G.; Hornbeck, J.W. Impacts of harvesting practices on off-site environmental quality. In *Impacts of Harvesting on Long-Term Site Productivity*; Dyck, W.J., Cole, D.W., Comerford, N.B., Eds.; Chapman and Hall: London, UK, 1994; pp. 81–118.

18. Sahin, V.; Hall, M.J. The effects of afforestation and deforestation on water yields. *J. Hydrol.* **1996**, *178*, 293–309. [CrossRef]

19. Stednick, J.D. Monitoring the effects of timber harvest on annual water yield. *J. Hydrol.* **1996**, *176*, 79–95. [CrossRef]

20. Neary, D.G. Environmental sustainability of forest energy production, 6.3 Hydrologic values. In *Bioenergy from Sustainable Forestry: Guiding Principles and Practices*; Richardson, J., Smith, T., Hakkila, P., Eds.; Elsevier: Amsterdam, The Netherlands, 2002; Chapter 6; pp. 36–67.

21. Andréassian, V. Water and forests: From historical controversy to scientific debate. *J. Hydrol.* **2004**, *291*, 1–27. [CrossRef]

22. Brown, A.E.; Zhang, L.; McMahon, T.A.; Western, A.W.; Vertessy, R.A. A review of paired catchment studies for determining changes in water yield resulting from alterations in vegetation. *J. Hydrol.* **2005**, *310*, 28–61. [CrossRef]

23. Maupin, M.A.; Kenny, J.F.; Hutson, S.S.; Lovelace, J.K.; Barber, N.L.; Linsey, K.S. *Estimated Use of Water in the United States in 2010*; U.S. Geological Survey: Reston, VA, USA, 2014; p. 64.

24. Slack, J.R.; Landwehr, J. Hydro-climatic data network (HCDN); a U.S. Geological Survey streamflow data set for the United States for the study of climate variations, 1874–1988. *U.S. Geological Survey Open-File Report 92–129*; U.S. Geological Survey: Reston, VA, USA, 1992; p. 193.

25. Horowitz, A.J.; Demas, C.R.; Fitzgerald, K.K.; Miller, T.L.; Rickert, D.A. U.S. Geological Survey protocol for the collection and processing of surface-water samples for the subsequent determination of inorganic constituents in filtered water. *U.S. Geological Survey Open-File Report 94–539*; U.S. Geological Survey: Reston, VA, USA, 1994; p. 57.

26. Ackermann, W.C. *Guidelines for Research on the Hydrology of Small Watersheds*; U.S. Department of the Interior, Office of Water Resources Research: Washington, DC, USA, 1966; p. 52.

27. Reynolds, E.C.R.; Layton, L. Research data for forest policy: The purpose, methods, and progress of forest hydrology. In Proceedings of the 9th British Commonwealth Forestry Conference, New Delhi, India; University of Oxford, Oxford, United Kingdom, 6–8 January 1968; pp. 1–16.

28. Hewlett, J.D.; Lull, H.W.; Reinhart, K.G. In defense of experimental watersheds. *Water Resour. Res.* **1969**, *5*, 306–316. [CrossRef]

29. Binkley, D.; Burnham, H.; Allen, H.L. Water quality impacts of forest fertilization. *Forest Ecol. Manag.* **1999**, *121*, 191–213. [CrossRef]

30. Likens, G.E.; Driscoll, C.T.; Buso, D.C. Long-term effects of acid rain: Response and recovery of a forest ecosystem. *Science* **1996**, *272*, 244–246. [CrossRef]

31. Bouraoui, F.; Grizzetti, B.; Granlund, K.; Rekolainen, S.; Bidoglio, G. Impact of climate change on the water cycle and nutrient losses in a Finnish catchment. *Clim. Chang.* **2004**, *66*, 109–126. [CrossRef]

32. Scatena, F.N. Goals of the report. In *Drinking Water from Forests and Grasslands: A Synthesis of the Scientific Literature, 7–25*. USDA Forest Service General Technical Report SRS-39; Dissmeyer, G.E., Ed.; Southern Research Station: Asheville, NC, USA, 2000; Chapter 2; p. 250.

33. Swanson, F.J.; Scatena, F.N.; Dissmeyer, G.E.; Fenn, M.E.; Verry, E.S.; Lynch, J.A. Watershed processes—Fluxes of water, dissolved constituents, and sediment. In *Drinking Water from Forests and Grasslands: A Synthesis of the Scientific Literature, 7–25*. USDA Forest Service General Technical Report SRS-39; Dissmeyer, G.E., Ed.; Southern Research Station: Asheville, NC, USA, 2000; Chapter 3, p. 250.

34. Clary, W.P.; Baker, M.B., Jr.; O'Connell, P.F.; Johnsen, T.N., Jr.; Campbell, R.E. Effects of pinyon-juniper removal on natural resource products and uses in Arizona. In *USDA Forest Service Research Paper RM-128*; Rocky Mountain Forest and Range Experiment Station: Fort Collins, CO, USA, 1974; p. 28.

35. Neary, D.G.; Lassiter, C.J.; Swindel, B.F. Hydrologic responses to silvicultural operations in southern coastal plain flatwoods. In *Impacts of Intensive Forest Management Practices*; Coleman, S.S., Mace, A.C., Jr., Swindel, B.F., Eds.; School of Forest Resources and Conservation, University of Florida: Gainesville, FL, USA, 1982; p. 110.

36. Pearce, A.J.; Rowe, L.K.; O'Loughlin, C.L. Effects of clearfelling and slash burning on water yield and storm hydrographs in evergreen mixed forests, western New Zealand. In Proceedings of the Influence of Man on the Hydrological Regime with Special Reference to Representative and Experimental Basins, Helsinki, Finland, June 1980; pp. 119–127.

37. Swanson, R.H.; Hillman, G.R. Predicted Increased Water Yield after Clear-Cutting Verified in West Central Alberta. In *Information Report NOR-X-198*; Canadian Department of Fisheries and Environment, Canadian Forestry Service, Northern Forestry Centre: Edmonton, AB, Canada, 1977.

38. Reinhart, K.G.; Eschner, A.R.; Trimble, G.R., Jr. Effect on streamflow of four forest practices in the mountains of West Virginia. In *USDA Forest Service Research Paper NE-1*; Northeastern Forest Experiment Station: Broomall, PA, USA, 1974; p. 59.

39. Burch, G.J.; Bath, R.K.; Moore, I.D.; O'Loughlin, E.M. Comparative hydrological behavior of forested and cleared catchments in southeastern Australia. *J. Hydrol.* **1987**, *90*, 12–42. [CrossRef]

40. Brown, H.E.; Baker, M.B., Jr.; Rogers, J.J.; Clary, W.C.; Kovner, J.L.; Larson, F.R.; Avery, C.C.; Campbell, R.E. Opportunities for increasing water yields and other multiple use values on ponderosa pine forest lands. In *USDA Forest Service Research Paper RM-129*; Rocky Mountain Forest and Range Experiment Station: Fort Collins, CO, USA, 1974; p. 36.

41. Lewis, D.C. Annual hydrologic response to watershed conversion from oak woodland to annual grassland. *Water Resour. Res.* **1968**, *4*, 59–72. [CrossRef]

42. Rosen, K. Effect of clear-felling on runoff in two small watersheds in central Sweden. *Forest Ecol. Manag.* **1984**, *9*, 267–281. [CrossRef]

43. Leaf, C.F. Watershed management in the central and southern Rocky Mountains: A summary of the status of our knowledge by vegetation type. In *USDA Forest Service Research Paper RM-142*; Rocky Mountain Forest and Range Experiment Station: Fort Collins, CO, USA, 1975; p. 28.

44. Verry, E.S. Effect of aspen clearcutting on water yield and quality in northern Minnesota. In *Watersheds in Transition*; Proceedings of a Symposium, Colorado State University, Fort Collins, CO, USA, 19–22 June 1972; Csallany, S.C., McLaughlin, T.G., Striffler, W.D., Eds.; American Water Resources Association: Middleburg, VA, USA, 1972; pp. 276–284.

45. Swanson, R.H.; Golding, D.L.; Rothwell, R.L.; Bernier, P.Y. Hydrologic Effects of Clear-Cutting at Marmot Creek and Streeter Watersheds, Alberta. In *Information Report NOR-X-278*; Northern Forestry Centre, Canadian Forestry Service: Edmonton, AB, Canada, 1986; p. 27.

46. Nakano, H. *Effect on Streamflow of Forest Cutting and Change in Regrowth on Cutover Area*; Bulletin of the Japanese Government Forest Experiment Station: Tokyo, Japan, 1971; pp. 1–125.

47. Keppler, E.T.; Ziemer, R.R. Logging effects on streamflow: Water yield and summer low flows at Caspar Creek in northwestern California. *Water Resour. Res.* **1990**, *26*, 1669–1679. [CrossRef]

48. Hewlett, J.D.; Doss, R. Forests, floods, and erosion: A watershed experiment in the Southeastern Piedmont. *Forest Sci.* **1984**, *30*, 424–434.

49. Hornbeck, J.W.; Martin, C.W.; Pierce, R.S.; Bormann, F.H.; Likens, G.E.; Eaton, J.S. The northern hardwood forest ecosystem: 10 years of recovery from clearcuttting. In *USDA Forest Service Research Paper NE-596*; Northeastern Forest Experiment Station: Broomall, PA, USA, 1987; p. 30.

50. Miller, E.L.; Beasley, R.S.; Lawson, E.R. Forest harvest and site preparation effects on stormflow and peakflow of ephemeral streams in the Ouachita Mountains. *J. Environ. Qual.* **1988**, *17*, 212–218. [CrossRef]

51. Bren, L.J.; Papworth, M. Water yield effects of conversion of slopes of a eucalypt forest catchment to radiata pine plantation. *Water Resour. Res.* **1991**, *27*, 2421–2428. [CrossRef]

52. Swift, L.W., Jr.; Swank, W.T. Long-term responses of streamflow following clearcutting and regrowth. In *International Association of Hydrological Sciences Publication No. 130 1980*, Proceedings on the Influence of Man on the Hydrological Regime with Special Reference to Representative and Experimental Basins, Helsinki, Finland, June 1980; pp. 245–256.

53. Pererira, H.C. Research into the effects of land use on streamflow. *Trans. Rhod. Sci. Assoc. Proc.* **1964**, *1*, 119–124.

54. Rothacher, J. Increases in water yield following clear-cut logging in the Pacific Northwest. *Water Resour. Res.* **1970**, *6*, 653–658. [CrossRef]

55. Harr, R.D. Forest practices and streamflow in western Oregon. In *USDA Forest Service General Technical Report PNW-49*; Pacific Northwest Forest and Range Experiment Station: Portland, OR, USA, 1976; p. 18.

56. Harris, D.D. Hydrologic changes after clearcut logging in a small Oregon coastal watershed. *J. Res. U.S. Geol. Survey* **1973**, *1*, 487–491.

57. Neary, D.G. Experimental forest catchment studies contributions to the understanding of the effects of disturbances on water quality: Past, present, and future. In *International Association of Hydrological Sciences Book*, Proceedings of the Workshop "Revisiting Experimental Catchment Studies in Forest Hydrology", 2011 International Union of Geodesy and Geophysics XXV General Assembly, Melbourne, Australia, 6–8 July 2011; Webb, A.A., Bonell, M., Bren, L., Lane, P.N.J., McGuire, D., Neary, D.G., Nettles, J., Scott, D.F., Stednick, J.D., Wang, Y., Eds.; pp. 169–184.

58. Neary, D.G.; Koestner, K.A. Forest bioenergy feedstock harvesting effects on water supply. Wiley 5-Interdisciplinary Reviews in Energy and Environment. *WIRES Energy Environ.* **2012**, *1*, 270–284. [CrossRef]

59. Pierce, R.S.; Hornbeck, J.W.; Likens, G.E.; Bormann, F.H. Effect of elimination of vegetation on stream water quality and quantity. *Int. Assoc. Hydrol. Sci.* **1970**, *96*, 311–328.

60. Swindel, B.F.; Lassiter, C.J.; Riekerk, H. Effects of clearcutting and site preparation on water yields from slash pine forests. *Forest Ecol. Manag.* **1982**, *4*, 101–113. [CrossRef]

61. O'Loughlin, C.L.; Rowe, L.K.; Pearce, A.J. Sediment yield and water quality responses to clearfelling of evergreen mixed forests in western New Zealand. In *PIAHS-AISH Publication No. 130*, Proceedings of the Helsinki Symposium on the Influence of Man on the Hydrological Regime with Special Reference to Representative and Experimental Basins, Helsinki, Finland, 23–26 June 1980; pp. 285–292.

62. Hopmans, P.; Bren, L.J. Long-term changes in water quality and solute exports in headwater streams of intensely managed radiate pine and natural eucalypt forest catchments in south-eastern Australia. *Forest Ecol. Manag.* **2007**, *253*, 244–261. [CrossRef]

63. Bormann, F.H.; Likens, G.E. Nutrient cycling. *Science* **1967**, *155*, 424–429. [CrossRef] [PubMed]

64. Webb, A.A.; Bonell, M.; Bren, L.; Lane, P.N.J.; McGuire, D.; Neary, D.G.; Nettles, J.; Scott, D.F.; Stednick, J.D.; Wang, Y. *International Association of Hydrological Sciences Book*, Proceedings of the Workshop "Revisiting Experimental Catchment Studies in Forest Hydrology", 2011 International Union of Geodesy and Geophysics XXV General Assembly, Melbourne, Australia, 6–8 July 2011; p. 234.

65. Singh, T.; Kalra, Y.P. *Changes in Chemical Composition of Natural Waters Resulting from Progressive Clearcutting of Forest Catchments in West Central Alberta, Canada*; International Association of Scientific Hydrology Symposium Proceedings: Tokyo, Japan, 1975; pp. 435–449.

66. Hetherington, E.D. *Dennis Creek: A look at water quality following logging in the Okanagan Basin*; Environment Canada, Canadian Forestry Service: Ottawa, Canada, 1976; pp. 1–28.

67. Feller, M.C.; Kimmins, J.P. Effects of clearcutting and slash burning on streamwater chemistry and watershed nutrient budgets in southwestern British Columbia. *Water Resour. Res.* **1984**, *20*, 29–40. [CrossRef]

68. Krause, H.H. Nitrate formation and movement before and after clear-cutting of a monitored watershed in central New Brunswick, Canada. *Can. J. Forest Res.* **1982**, *12*, 922–930. [CrossRef]

69. Carignan, R.; D'Arcy, P.; Lemontagne, S. Comparative impacts of fire and forest harvesting on water quality in Boreal Shield lakes. *Can. J. Fish. Aquat. Sci.* **2000**, *57* (Suppl. S2), S105–S117. [CrossRef]

70. Vaidya, O.C.; Smith, T.P.; Fernand, H.; McInnis, N.R. Best Management Practices: Evaluation of alternate streamside management zones on stream water quality in Pockwock Lake and Five Mile Lake Watersheds in Central Nova Scotia, Canada. *Environ. Monit. Assess.* **2008**, *137*, 1–14. [CrossRef] [PubMed]

71. Bateridge, T. Effects of clearcutting on water discharge and nutrient loss. Bitterroot National Forest, Montana. Master's Thesis, Office of Water Resources Research, University of Montana, Missoula, MT, USA, 1974.

72. Stottlemyer, R. Nitrogen mineralization and streamwater chemistry, Rock Creek Watershed, Denali National Park, Alaska, USA. *Arch. Alp. Res.* **1992**, *24*, 291–303. [CrossRef]

73. Snyder, G.G.; Haupt, H.F.; Belt, G.H., Jr. Clearcutting and burning slash alter quality of stream water in Northern Idaho. In *USDA Forest Service Research Paper INT-1698*; Intermountain Forest and Range Experiment Station: Ogden, UT, USA, 1975; p. 34.

74. Fredriksen, R.L.; Moore, D.G.; Norris, L.A. Impact of timber harvest, fertilization, and herbicide treatment on stream water quality in the Douglas-fir regions. In *Forest Soils and Forest Land Management*, Proceedings of the Fourth North American Forest Soils Conference, Laval University, Quebec City, QC, Canada, August 1973; Bernier, B., Winget, C.H., Eds.; 1975; pp. 283–313.

75. Van Lear, D.H.; Douglass, J.E.; Fox, S.K.; Augsberger, M.K. Sediments and nutrient export in runoff from burned and harvested pine watersheds in the South Carolina Piedmont. *J. Environ. Qual.* **1985**, *14*, 169–174. [CrossRef]

76. Swank, W.T. Stream chemistry responses to disturbance. In *Forest Hydrology and Ecology at Coweeta*; Swank, W.T., Crossley, D.A., Eds.; Springer-Verlag: New York, NY, USA, 1988; Chapter 25; pp. 339–357.

77. Aubertin, G.M.; Patric, J.H. Water quality water after clearcutting a small watershed in West Virginia. *J. Environ. Qual.* **1974**, *3*, 243–249. [CrossRef]

78. Oyarzun, C.; Aracena, C.; Rutherford, P.; Godoy, R.; Deschrijver, A. Effects of land use conversion from native forests to exotic plantations on nitrogen and phosphorus retention in catchments of southern Chile. *Water Air Soil Pollut.* **2007**, *179*, 341–350. [CrossRef]

79. Ahtiainen, M.; Huttunen, P. Long-term effects of forestry managements on water quality and loading in brooks. *Boreal Environ. Res.* **1999**, *4*, 101–114.

80. Bäumler, R.; Zech, W. Effects of forest thinning on the streamwater chemistry of two forest watersheds in the Bavarian Alps. *Forest Ecol. Manag.* **1999**, *116*, 119–128. [CrossRef]

81. Ohrui, K.; Mitchell, M.J. Stream water chemistry in Japanese forested watersheds and its variability on a small regional scale. *Water Resour. Res.* **1998**, *34*, 1553–1561. [CrossRef]

82. Graynoth, E. Effects of logging on stream environments and faunas in Nelson. *N. Z. J. Mar. Freshw.* **1979**, *13*, 79–109. [CrossRef]

83. O'Loughlin, C.L. The forest and water quality relationship. *N. Z. For.* **1994**, *39*, 26–30.

84. Scott, D.F.; Lesch, W. Streamflow responses to afforestation with *Eucalyptus grandis* and *Pinus. patula* and to felling in the Mokobulaan experimental catchments. *J. Hydrol.* **1997**, *199*, 360–377. [CrossRef]

85. Rosen, K. Effect of clear-felling on streamwater quality in forest catchments in central Sweden. *Forest Ecol. Manag.* **1996**, *83*, 237–244. [CrossRef]

86. Neal, C.; Fisher, R.; Smith, C.J.; Hill, S.; Neal, M.; Conway, T.; Ryland, G.P.; Jeffrey, H.A. The effects of tree harvesting on stream-water quality at an acidic and acid-sensitive spruce forested area: Plynlimon, mid-Wales. *J. Hydrol.* **1992**, *135*, 305–319. [CrossRef]

87. Neary, D.G. Impact of timber harvesting on nutrient losses in streamflow. *N. Z. J. For.* **1977**, *22*, 53–63.

88. Webb, A.A.; Bonell, M.; Bren, L.; Lane, P.N.J.; McGuire, D.; Neary, D.G.; Nettles, J.; Scott, D.F.; Stednick, J.D.; Wang, Y. *Revisiting Experimental Catchment Studies in Forest Hydrology*; IAHS Press: Wallingford, UK, 2012; p. 235.

89. Swank, W.T.; Crossley, D.A. *Forest Hydrology and Ecology at Coweeta*; Springer-Verlag: New York, NY, USA, 1988; p. 469.

Article

Mapping Temporal Dynamics in a Forest Stream Network—Implications for Riparian Forest Management

Anneli M. Ågren [1,†,*], **William Lidberg** [1] and **Eva Ring** [2,†]

[1] Department of Forest Ecology and Management, Swedish University of Agricultural Science, Umeå 901 83, Sweden; william.lidberg@slu.se

[2] Skogforsk, The Forestry Research Institute of Sweden, Uppsala Science Park, Uppsala 751 83, Sweden; eva.ring@skogforsk.se

* Author to whom correspondence should be addressed; anneli.agren@slu.se; Tel.: +46-72-714-4792.

† These authors contributed equally to this work.

Academic Editor: Ge Sun

Received: 1 June 2015; Accepted: 25 August 2015; Published: 28 August 2015

Abstract: This study focuses on avoiding negative effects on surface waters using new techniques for identifying wet areas near surface waters. This would aid planning and designing of forest buffer zones and off-road forestry traffic. The temporal variability in the geographical distribution of the stream network renders this type of planning difficult. A field study was performed in the 68 km² Krycklan Catchment to illustrate the variability of a boreal stream network. The perennial stream length was 140 km while the stream length during high-flow conditions was 630 km. Comparing the field-measured stream network to the network presented on current maps showed that 58% of the perennial and 76% of the fully expanded network was missing on current maps. Similarly, cartographic depth-to-water maps showed that associated wet soils constituted 5% of the productive forest land during baseflow and 25% during high flow. Using a new technique, maps can be generated that indicate full stream networks, as well as seasonally active streams and associated wet soils, thus, forestry planning can be performed more efficiently and impacts on surface waters can be reduced.

Keywords: Bearing capacity; rutting; trafficability; buffer zone; streams; riparian management; forestry; soil

1. Introduction

Today, forestry is often performed using various forest machinery and forest soils can be subjected to traffic several times during a rotation period. Because of the increasing need for forest bioenergy to meet green energy targets including the EU Renewable Energy Directive, harvest intensity is expected to increase in many countries [1,2]. This will place additional pressure on boreal water quality [3,4], for instance by increased off-road forestry traffic. Driving with heavy machinery on forest soils can cause rutting and soil compaction [5]. This can affect soil biology and change the microbial community [6,7], gas emission rates [8,9], root development [10] and thereby tree growth [11]. Here, we focus on the effects on surface water, caused by changing the natural flow-paths and erosion of mineral soil exposed in wheel tracks which can lead to increased sediment transports in discharging streams. In forestry, primary sediment sources are road crossings [12], logging roads and skidder trails [13] and ditching activities [14]. Sediment transport can cause siltation in downstream gravelly stream beds [15], thereby decreasing reproductive success of fresh-water fish by reducing permeability of spawning gravels and reduce oxygen supply to ova [16]. It can also affect the benthic macroinvertebrate communities by particle accumulation on body surfaces, respiratory structures or disrupt the feeding system of filterers [17]. Rutting along slopes and wet soils can create new channels for runoff and change the natural course of a stream by providing alternative pathways in wheel tracks. Moreover, rutting can lead to increased leakage of mercury to surface waters. Munthe and Hultberg [18] reported a six-fold increase in the stream concentration of methyl-mercury over a period of at least three years after a tractor had crossed a stream and created a temporary dam upstream.

Since the 1950s, forestry has become heavily mechanized in many parts of the world. Cut-to-length logging is common in the northern boreal zone [19,20]. This system includes a harvester and a forwarder, of which the latter usually exerts the highest total pressure on the soil. A large laden forwarder can weigh 40 Mg. Forest machinery may also be used at thinning, fertilization, site preparation and harvest of logging residues for energy production. The machinery used for these operations are generally more light weight compared with a large forwarder. However, site preparation and harvest of logging residues after final felling (for energy production) are typically performed at more sensitive ground conditions, *i.e.*, on regeneration areas where the groundwater level has risen due to harvesting and enlarged the discharge areas.

Forest buffer zones along surface water have been recognized as a means to mitigate negative effects of forestry on aquatic ecosystems [21]. As the interface between upland areas and surface water, the riparian forests (RF) provide many ecosystem functions that are important for biodiversity and biogeochemistry of both terrestrial and aquatic ecosystems [22,23]. Hence, riparian forests require special attention in forestry planning. Their filtering function protects aquatic ecosystems against excessive loading of nutrients, pollutants and sediments [12,24] and RFs have an important role in soil biochemical cycles [3]. RFs also provide inputs of nutrients and dead wood for aquatic organisms and control water temperature and insolation by shading [25]. In most of the major temperate and boreal timber-producing regions (e.g., Fennoscandia, North America, and Russia), forest buffer zones comprising parts of or the entire RF are left around lakes and streams [26–28]. Because it is convenient and easy to implement, fixed-width forest buffers have become a standard practice [29]. Buffer strips can range from 2–3 m to 300 m and depending on the aim of the buffer, for example to protect water quality or the habitat and species, studies have shown that the buffers need to have different widths to be effective [28,30].

While small streams (first and second order streams) have been in focus for hydrological and biogeochemical research for decades, small or intermittent streams have not been given the same attention in ecological research [31], in mandated monitoring [32] or by commercial forestry. Forest buffer zones are often missing along small streams in North America and Fennoscandia [29]. The legal protection of intermittent streams and how they are incorporated into policy and management vary widely depending on how temporary waters are defined by authorities, as well as the kind of protection given [33]. However, due to the organization of stream networks and thus the large total length of small streams [34], increasing the protection for small, temporary streams could affect substantial areas of forest land, which may decrease overall timber production. So, while environmental advocates argue that intermittent streams are essential to the integrity of entire stream networks, developers argue that full protection will be too costly [33]. Another issue for management is that many small streams are missing on hydrological or topographic maps [35].

Logging residues, also known as slash or brash, *i.e.*, tops, branches and needles, are an important resource and many countries use logging residues as a biofuel source. However, these logging residues are also used as ground protection to prevent rut formation in sensitive areas. This leads to a possible conflict regarding the use of logging residues, as an energy source or for ground protection. However, this potential conflict could be partly offset by improving the forestry planning. With more detailed information on the location of sensitive areas, the need for logging residues as ground protection can be better optimized. Detailed maps of stream networks and wet areas provide crucial information when planning forestry operations to avoid serious impacts on surface water. With this type of information, the use of logging residues can also be better optimized between energy production and soil and water protection. This study aims to improve the planning tools to be used in operational forestry.

The forest soil trafficability changes temporally and spatially over time with the seasons and current weather. Such temporal and spatial changes have implications for forestry planning and operation performance. In the study region, where seasonal dynamics in forest hydrology are pronounced, stands are often divided into two categories to avoid soil damage; stands growing on dry soils are assigned for summer harvest, while stands on wetter soils are assigned for harvest on frozen soils. However, with climate change, winters in Scandinavia are predicted to be warmer [35] and wetter, and runoff during winter is predicted to increase [36]. The risk for soil damage during off-road operations is therefore likely to increase in the future; hence, new planning systems which address the trafficability of forest soils in more detail are needed.

The aim of this study was to develop a framework of how high-resolution maps calculated from digital elevation models, taking into account seasonal variability in forest hydrology, could be used as planning tools in operational forestry. We used empirical data from the boreal 68 km^2 Krycklan Catchment to determine how the stream network changes throughout the year to develop map models showing the seasonal dynamics in the stream network and discuss the implications from a perspective of improving the protection of surface waters. We also show empirical data of the consequences of driving on forest soil, by presenting results from a forestry traffic experiment and discuss the challenges of expanding discharge areas. We believe that the arguments and tools presented here represent a significant step forward and should bring many benefits to modern forestry, as well as increasing the surface water protection by including seasonal variability in stream networks into forestry planning.

2. Experimental Section

2.1. Stream Network Variability

2.1.1. Site Description

The spatial variability of the stream network was analyzed by a combination of field mapping and GIS modelling for the boreal 68 km^2 Krycklan Catchment in Northern Sweden [37]. Forest and mires cover most of the landscape (87% and 9%, respectively). Agricultural land covers only 3% and lakes 1%. Forestry is the main land use and most of the area is second growth forest, however 25% of the catchment lies within the Svartberget Reserch Park and has been protected from forestry since 1922. The forests are dominated by Scots pine (*Pinus sylvestris* L.) and Norway spruce (*Picea abies* (L.) H. Karst). The mineral soils are dominated by till in which well-developed iron podzols have developed. The catchment has been further described in Laudon *et al.* [37].

2.1.2. Field Survey of Stream Heads

Stream heads were defined from the point in the landscape from which water was running on top of the soil down to the stream network (Figure 1A,B). Stream heads were located upstream of recognizable stream channels during high flow but inside distinct channels or on peat soils (Figure 1C) during baseflow. Local puddles were excluded as they were not connected to the streams through surface runoff. During high flow many of these intermittent streams are only active during a couple of days and do not have a clear stream channel, however, running water on top of the soil indicate saturated conditions and a high groundwater level, so for the purpose of mapping flow initiation thresholds as a basis for modelling groundwater levels (DTW, see below), we argue that this is a better definition of stream heads than the use of channel initiation. One hundred and twenty-one stream heads were located in the field and the geographical positions for each head were determined using hand-held GPS, with an accuracy of <10 m for 95% of the measurements. For this study, all stream heads were mapped on till soils and mires. The stream heads were mapped nine times during different hydrological conditions in 2013–2014. The mapping during the highest discharge was conducted on the 14 May 2013, only three days after the peak of snowmelt, when specific discharge was 4.13 mm·day^{-1}. Discharge measurements were conducted using a pressure transducer connected to a Campbell Scientific datalogger at the monitored V-notch weir using established rating-curves in the Krycklan Catchment, Kallkällsbäcken, C7, a.k.a. Svartberget catchment, which lies in the middle of the surveyed area [38]. Mapping during the lowest base flow conditions, when the specific discharge was 0.06 mm·day^{-1}, was conducted on 30 October 2013 after a long drought period. During this occasion, another monitored stream in the Krycklan Catchment, Västrabäcken, C2, dried out, which has only happened three times in the 30 years since measurements started. This drought can therefore be considered a 10-year event.

Figure 1. (**A,B**) Example of stream heads (trickles) during snowmelt; (**C**) Example of a stream head during base flow.

2.1.3. GIS Modelling of Stream Network

The hydrological modelling was conducted from a bare-ground digital elevation model (DEM), generated for all of Sweden by the Swedish Mapping, Cadastral and Land Registration Authority. The DEM is based on high-resolution elevation scans using LiDAR technology (Light Detection and Ranging) with a point density of 0.5–1 points per m^2, an average *xy* point error of 0.4 m (SWEREF 99 ™), and a vertical accuracy of 0.1 m (RH 2000). A 2 m × 2 m bare-ground DEM, with an average elevation error of 0.5 m, was generated from the ground elevation returns of the LiDAR signals using triangulated irregular network (TIN) interpolation. The resulting DEM was hydrographically corrected by automatically breaching roadside impoundments and by removing DEM-wide depression artifacts [39].

The coordinates of the stream heads were mapped in ArcMap 10.2 and superimposed on the DEM. The area draining to each stream head was calculated using the D8 algorithm [40,41]. This gives the field mapped "stream initiation thresholds", sometimes also referred to as "channelization threshold" or "source areas", *i.e.*, how much drainage area is needed to initiate a stream. The stream initiations thresholds were plotted against daily average discharge and the curve-estimation procedure in IBM SPSS Statistics 22 was used to fit curves to the data. All methods were tested and the best fitted curve (the inverse curve) is displayed in Figure 2.

By varying the flow initiation threshold according to the results from the field study of stream heads (ranging from 1 ha during spring flood to 15 ha during baseflow), different stream networks were generated, showing the expansion and shrinkage of the stream network over time (Figure 3A,B). The stream network length was calculated for several flow initiation thresholds ranging from 1–15 ha (Figure 4). The resulting modelled stream networks were compared to the stream network on the most detailed map currently available, the Property map (1: 12,500), Lantmäteriet, Gävle.

191

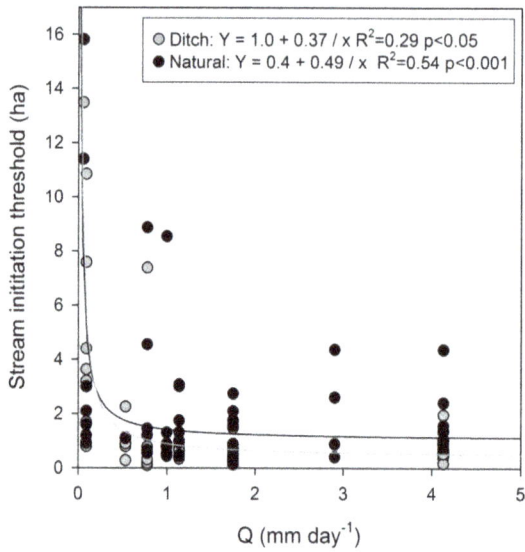

Figure 2. Stream initiation threshold area (ha), also known as channelization threshold or source area, for the stream heads of natural streams and ditches, respectively. The dots denote field measurements on till soils during different flow situations (Q), *i.e.*, how much land area (ha) is needed before a stream develops.

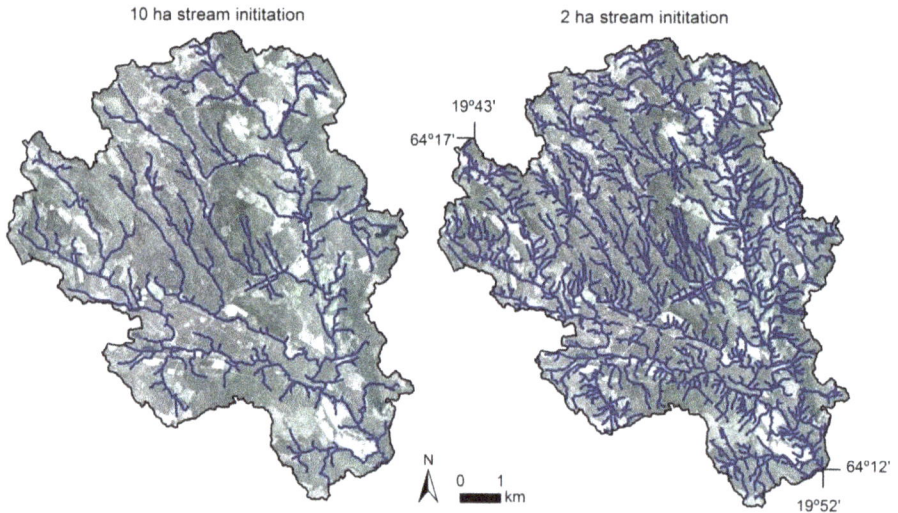

Figure 3. The stream network in the Krycklan Catchment during baseflow (**left**) (using 10 ha stream initiation threshold) and spring flood (**right**) (using 2 ha stream initiation threshold).

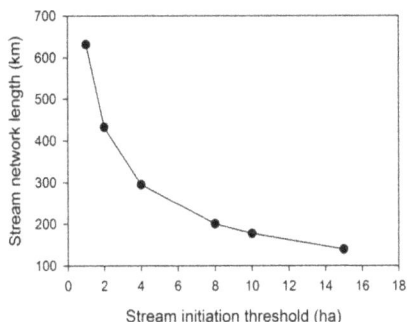

Figure 4. The stream network length for the Krycklan Catchment as a function of the stream initiation threshold area.

2.2. Wet Areas Mapping

The distribution of wet areas, the discharge areas was modelled throughout the landscape from the DEM. A discharge area is an area where groundwater emerges at the surface; an area where upward pressure or hydraulic head moves groundwater towards the surface. Ågren *et al.* [42] tested several methods of calculating wet areas from digital terrain indices and found that cartographic Depth-to-water index (DTW) was a robust method with high predictive power for soil wetness. The DTW index [43,44] is the least-cost elevation difference (in meters) to the nearest open water body (in our case the field-mapped stream network). The cells in the stream network were set to be 0. DTW was then determined for each of the resulting flow networks according to Equation (1).

$$\left[DTW\ (m) = \left[\sum \frac{dz_i}{dx_i} a \right] x_c \right] \tag{1}$$

where dz/dx is the slope of a cell along the least-elevation path, i is a cell along the path, a is 1 when the path crosses the cell parallel to the cell boundaries and 1.414214 when it crosses diagonally; x_c represents the grid cell size (m) [43].

The area of the landscape that was classified as a discharge area (DTW < 1 m) was calculated (Figure 5). In the lower lying part of the catchment there is a sedimentary area including patches of agriculture land, and large low-productive mires are common in the upper parts of the catchment. Because the focus of this study is on forest land, anything outside productive forest land (defined as land with a potential mean yield capacity of at least 1 m³ for total stem volume over bark per ha and year over one rotation period) was excluded from the calculations.

2.3. A Case Study: Rutting Caused by Forwarder Traffic in Relation to Generated DTW-Maps

Data from a study-plot experiment situated in Northern Sweden (Figure 6) on 64°32.5′ N, 20°4.3′ E and 64°19.4′ N, 20°35.5′ E were used to compare the results of the DTW-maps against field measurements of rutting. DTW-maps were generated for the study sites as described in Section 2.2 and compared with the rutting caused by repeated passes with a laden forwarder. The treatments, applied to study plots established along four harvested hillslopes, consisted of no forwarder traffic and forwarder traffic without soil protection, on logging residues and on logging mats, respectively. The study plots were clear-cut, without driving on the plots, about half a year and one and a half year, respectively, before applying the treatments. Here, we only present results from the treatment without soil protection (Figures 6 and 7).

Figure 5. The black and white background map shows the sunlit elevation model of a subsection of the Krycklan catchment. Superimposed are the depth-to-water index maps which mark the wet areas along the stream network. Blue areas indicate wet areas during spring flood and green areas indicate areas that remain wet during baseflow. The darker colors (blue or green) indicate that the modelled groundwater level is closer to the soil surface and hence wetter.

The forwarder was a John Deere 1410D with eight wheels mounted on four axles. It was equipped with 700 mm wide tires and bogie tracks on both front and rear wheel pairs. The total weight (obtained from measurements) of the laden forwarder was approx. 35 Mg at site 294 Rotflaka Myran and 33 Mg at site 296 Trågalidberget. The forwarder drove up and down the harvested slopes two to three times, a total of four to six passes. Due to severe rutting, some passes had to be shortened at the downslope end. The rut depth from the original soil surface was measured with a ruler at 1 m interval along the study plots.

2.4. Expansion of Discharge Areas Following Final Felling

After final felling, the water balance changes because evapotranspiration is reduced after removal of the trees. This in turn leads to an increase in storage of water, *i.e.*, increasing groundwater levels which in turn increase runoff but also expand the discharge area. Using Darcy's law and Dupuit assumptions that the flow on each level is horizontal, the expansion of discharge area up along the hillside can be calculated. Site 294 Rotflaka Myran was used as an example because the till at 296 Trågalidberget was more heterogeneous.

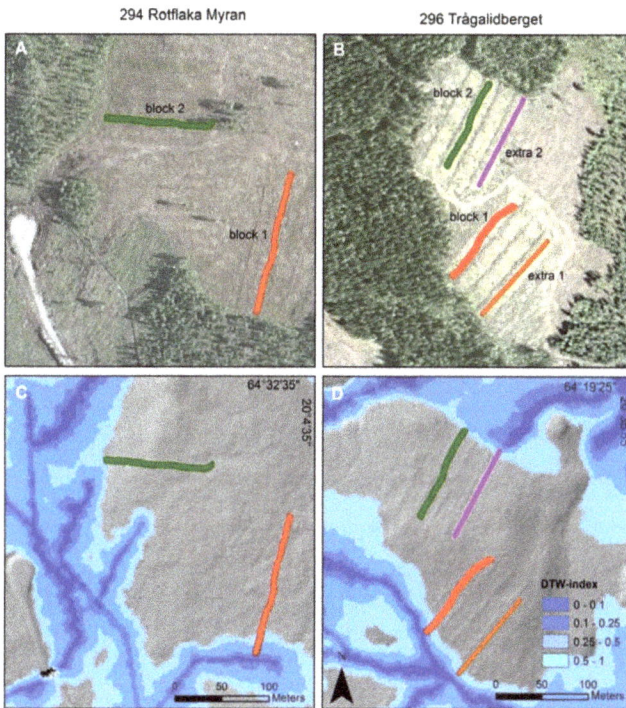

Figure 6. Field experiment in northern Sweden, using study plots in a randomized block design, to study forwarder traffic on harvested slopes. (**A,B**) show the aerial photos of the study sites and the location of the wheel tracks in the study plots subjected to the treatment forwarder traffic without soil protection (red lines for the wheel tracks in block 1, green lines for block 2, and purple and orange lines for two additional plots which were not part of the original study); (**C,D**) show the sunlit elevation model (in greyscale) with a high flow DTW-index map superimposed (1 ha stream initiation). The location of the green baseflow DTW model as seen in Figure 5 is not visible in these areas, but starts just outside the displayed maps.

The saturated discharge area starts at a distance from the water divide where the recharge to the groundwater above equals the maximum possible groundwater discharge (when the groundwater reaches the soil surface). Mathematically,

$$\left[R \cdot x \cdot w = -K \cdot t \cdot w \cdot \frac{dh}{dx} \right] \tag{2}$$

where:

R = recharge to the groundwater (m·s^{-1})
x = distance to the water divide (m)
w = width of the slope (m)
K = saturated hydraulic conductivity of the soil layer (m·s^{-1})
t = thickness of the soil layer (m)
$\frac{dh}{dx}$ = slope of the groundwater surface (assumed to be the same as the soil surface)

The K-value was calculated using *SOILPAR 2.0*, a program that estimates soil physical and hydrological parameters. The Puckett method [45] was selected and the K-value was calculated from the average particle size distribution of four soil samples sampled at 20 cm depth along the plots (Figure 6). We also calculated the *K*-value by solving the equation for *K* based on the following assumptions; The recharge to groundwater (*R*) on till soils in the study region is 375 mm·yr^{-1} [46]. *x* was measured to 175 m based on the distance from the top of the hill down to a mire below the plots that was defined as the border of the discharge area prior to felling. *w* was the same before and after final felling and can therefore be deleted on both sides of the equation. In till soils, hydraulic conductivity typically decreases more or less exponentially with depth. Here, we approximated that all lateral water movements along the slope occurred in the upper 1 m of the soil (*t*), which is a good approximation for many Fennoscandian till soils [47,48]. *dh/dx* was measured on the digital elevation model to 0.06 m·m^{-1}. The expansion of the discharge area was calculated by solving the equation for *x* assuming that clear cutting the area increased the recharge to the groundwater by 200 mm·yr^{-1} [49]. Assuming that all of the recharge to groundwater becomes runoff, 200 mm·yr^{-1} seems to be a fair approximation since six catchments in Scandinavia showed increases in runoff, up to 10 years following clear-cut, by on average 193 mm·yr^{-1} (SD = 90) [50].

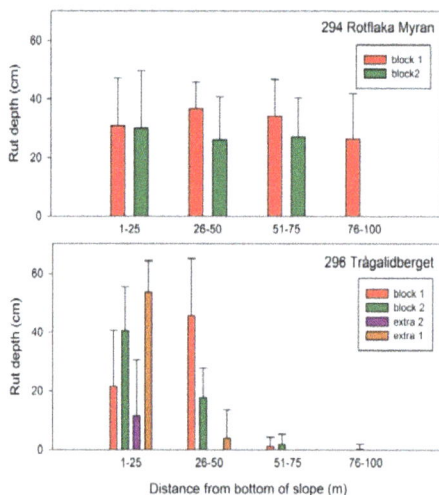

Figure 7. Rut depth in study plots subjected to repeated passes by a laden forwarder in the study-plot experiments (means for the left and right wheel tracks). The rut depth was not measured in case the mineral soil was unexposed in the track. The colors of the bars correspond to the plots in the map (Figure 6) and the error bars represents the standard deviation.

2.5. Measurements of Soil Bearing Capacity and Soil Moisture

Soil bearing capacity and soil moisture was measured at 160 locations in the Krycklan by Edlund [51]. The soil bearing capacity, here measured as Rammsonde Pressure (RP), was measured using a modified Swiss Rammsonde [52]. In short, a cone penetrometer sits mounted on a hollow shaft with a drop hammer mounted on top. The cone is placed on the soil and the penetration into the soil was measured after dropping the hammer 40 cm above the shaft five times. The RP was calculated according to [52]. The RP is the force per m^2 needed to penetrate the probe in the soil. Soil moisture was measured with TDR technique using a ThetaProbe ML2x.

3. Results and Discussion

3.1. Spatial and Temporal Variability in Stream Drainage Network and Associated Wet Soils

In this study, we found that there was a large temporal variability in the drainage area needed before a stream head was found, *i.e.*, in stream initiation threshold area. During the two snowmelt events (Q = 4.13 and 2.9 mm·day^{-1}) the stream heads corresponded to threshold areas between 0.4 and 4.4 ha (Figure 2).

The re-inventory during the lowest base flow event showed that only three streams were still actively transporting water and the stream heads were found after 11.4–15.8 ha. The smallest stream initiation areas were often associated with ditches that were activated during times of high flow, while natural trickles occurred on top of the forest floor (Figure 1A,B). During baseflow, the trickles were associated with peat soil in small valley bottoms (Figure 1C) or in the main channels. The stream initiation threshold was inversely related to specific discharge (Figure 2). At times with high specific discharge (Q > 0.5 mm·day^{-1}), the stream initiation threshold was approximately 2 ha (and 1 ha if the land was drained by ditches). During baseflow situations (Q < 0.5 mm·day^{-1}), the stream initiation threshold increased rapidly to about 10–15 ha. Because of the larger variability during baseflow and the fact that the threshold changed rapidly with Q during baseflow situations (Figure 2), it is difficult to identify one threshold value representative of baseflow situations. The long term discharge records for the monitored site C7 (Svartberget) in the Krycklan Catchment, from 1981 and onwards [37], show that the specific discharge is below 0.5 mm·day^{-1} during 50% of the snow-free period (May–November). Hence, the stream network using the 2 ha flow initiation is active during 50% of the bare ground-period.

By varying the stream initiation threshold in the GIS calculations, the stream network during different flow conditions can be mapped (Figure 3). Figure 4 illustrates how the total length of the stream network changes with stream initiation threshold, which reflects changes with the hydrological situation. According to our calculations, the Krycklan stream network expands from 177 km during baseflow (using a conservative threshold of 10 ha which can be seen to represent a normal year) to 432 km during spring flood (using a conservative threshold of 2 ha) (Figures 3 and 4).

Thus, on an annual basis, the length of the stream network at high-flow conditions is 2.4 times the length at baseflow conditions. On the national map of Sweden with the highest resolution, the Property map (1:12,500, Lantmäteriet, Gävle), the stream network in the study catchment is 102 km. Consequently, only 58% of the estimated 177 km perennial stream network was present on the Property map. When taking into consideration that the entire stream network (using 2 ha flow initiation) was active during 50% of the snow free-period, this corresponds to a situation where 76% of the stream network is lacking on the most detailed map (1: 12,500). These numbers are similar to the findings from a study conducted in the Chattooga River catchment in southern US [53], where 50%–75% of the perennial streams were identified on topographic maps, depending on scale (1:24,000 and 1:100,000). In the same study, only 14%–21% of the fully expanded stream network was mapped on topographic maps. The main explanation to this is that the current maps have been drawn from aerial photos where the smaller streams in the forest landscape are invisible under tree canopies. Obviously, if more than half of the streams are missing on the maps, this renders forestry planning with respect to surface water difficult.

The depth-to-water map illustrates how different stream networks can be used to model discharge areas during different flow situations. During low flow, 8% of the forest land was classified as being wet (following the DTW < 1) while during high flow the corresponding share was 31%. This number includes the mires which are integral parts of the forest landscape, but they are often low-productivity sites and are therefore often not subjected to forest management. Of the productive forest land ($\geq$1 m^3·ha^{-1}·yr^{-1} for total stem volume over bark), the discharge area covered 5% and 25% during low and high flow, respectively. This illustrates the dynamics of forest hydrology and the challenges this poses in planning forestry activities for which the variability in trafficability needs to be taken into account. However, from the field survey of the stream heads, we can capture the expansion and shrinkage of the stream-network in a GIS-model and map the discharge areas during dry and wet conditions (Figure 5).

The map shows the modelled wet areas around the perennial stream network (green area, Figure 5) and the expansion during high flows (blue). Best management practices for riparian buffer zones vary throughout the world [21]. A general trend though is that, due to their large length in the landscape [34], small headwater streams receive less protection [29,54]. The new maps (as the map in Figure 5) can be used to create hydrologically adapted buffer zones as suggested by Kuglerova *et al.* [55,56] and improve protection for surface water quality by identifying wet areas where for instance off-road forestry traffic and fertilization should be avoided. The main advantages with these new maps are that: (1) the entire perennial stream network is present on the maps; (2) the maps can be made available on computers of forest machinery, thus, providing machine operators with detailed site information. Furthermore, areas sensitive to physical soil disturbance [57] can be identified, since the blue areas on the maps (Figure 5) indicate areas with high hydrological connectivity. Because of this connectivity, any exposed mineral soil in these areas is likely to be transported to the stream network at high-flow situations, increasing erosion and sediment transport in the draining stream with deleterious effects on downstream aquatic habitats [58]. By identifying areas that could be operated during dry conditions but should be avoided during wet conditions, more rutting and soil scarification can be avoided and one major concern for water quality due to forestry can be addressed. While field verification (using hydric soils, the hydrophytic vegetation or the presence of subsurface or surface water to detect the wet soils) is the most reliable way [53] to properly plan management of riparian forests, we propose that the time for this can be reduced by using DEM derived stream networks and associated wet soils. The maps can also be used in snowy conditions when the snow hinders field verifications and unfrozen wet soils underneath the snow can be sensitive for trafficking. To take into account temporal variability in the stream network, in operational forestry is a challenge for the future, but one that can be addressed with these kinds of LiDAR derived maps (Figure 5).

3.2. Soil Bearing Capacity as a Function of Soil Moisture and Soil Type

The DTW maps model the depth down to a supposed groundwater surface, from that it follows that the closer the groundwater level is to the ground surface the wetter the soil should be. However, for forest soil trafficking, it is not so much soil moisture *per se* that is of interest, but the effect the moisture has on the bearing capacity on the soil. A field study measuring soil bearing capacity in the Krycklan catchment using a modified Swiss Rammsonde [52] showed that there was a significant negative relationship between Rammsonde Pressure and soil moisture (Figure 8). The organic soils had the lowest bearing capacity with RPs less than 500 kPa, independent of the soil moisture. From a surface water protection perspective, this has implications as riparian soils both are wet (which decrease the bearing capacity of mineral soils) and it is common with formation of riparian peats along stream channels [59] due to elevated groundwater levels during much of the year. On dryer soils, ruts are shallow and are mainly formed by compaction of the soil, while on wetter soils rutting causes soil deformation and displacement [60]. This means that the soils along streams are more sensitive to deformation because of both high water content and higher organic content (Figure 8). The large variability in the scatterplot could partly be attributed to the fact that local soil bearing capacity of forest soils also depend on stoniness and root systems, which was observed during the field inventory (Edlund, [61]).

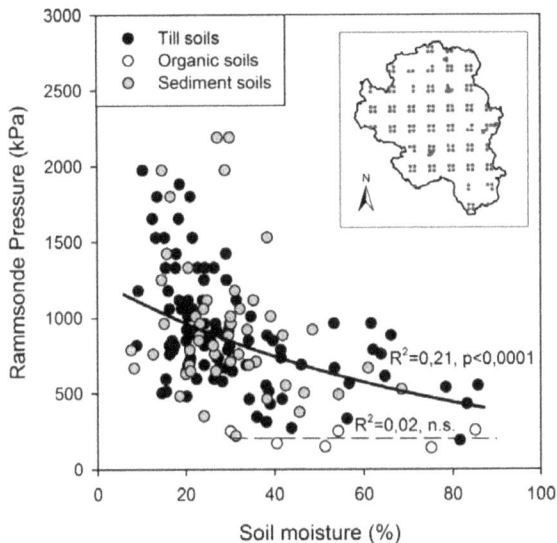

Figure 8. Rammsonde Pressure (RP) and soil moisture measured at 160 locations in the Krycklan Catchment (inset figure). Results are divided into mineral soils (grey and black dots) and organic soils (white dots). Modified from Edlund [52].

3.3. Expansion of Discharge Areas Following Final Felling

When tree stands are harvested the water balance changes, evapotranspiration is reduced until the tree cover has re-established and during this period water storage in soils and runoff increases [62,63]. This means that discharge areas expand uphill following final felling hence, ruts or other soil disturbances within this area may be connected to surface water and cause deleterious sediment transport. Predicting and mapping this expansion would give forestry planning a way to better manage the quality of surface waters. Using the K-value estimated from SOILPAR, the distance from the water divide to the discharge area changed from 1003 m to 654 m following clear-cutting, meaning that the discharge area would expand 349 m upslope following clear-cutting. When solving the equation for the K-value, the distance from the water divide to the discharge area changed from 175 m to 114 m following clear-cutting, meaning that the discharge area would expand 61 m upslope. This shows how sensitive the calculations of the expansions are to the K-value and how uncertain the K-values are. In our study, the K-value for the soil calculated from soil texture was 1.9×10^{-4} m·s^{-1}, while the K-value by solving the equation for K was 3.3×10^{-5} m·s^{-1}. Another investigation comparing different measurement techniques on a till soil gave K-values ranging from 5.7×10^{-6} to 1.9×10^{-2} mm·s^{-1} [64]. This illustrates how K-values are notoriously difficult to measure and development of maps that can predict the expansion of the discharge areas with any kind of accuracy seems unlikely because of the (1) sensitivity of the calculations to the K-value; (2) large uncertainties in measured K-values; (3) general lack of K-values for different parts of the landscape and also (4) large spatial variation in K-values within till soils (the dominating quaternary deposits in northern boreal zone).

Despite this, we can still put these results in the perspective of the study-plot experiment. The expansion of the discharge area, based on the K-value measured at 20 cm depth, gave unreasonable numbers. K-values have been found to decrease with soil depth in Scandinavia [48,65–68] and elsewhere [69,70], and using a K-value from 20 cm depth (1.9×10^{-4} m·s^{-1}) therefore overestimates the overall groundwater-flow in the slope.

The saturated hydraulic conductivity calculated by solving the equation for K (3.3×10^{-5} m·s^{-1}) was close to measured values of saturated hydraulic conductivity in a soil profile in till at Gårdsjön, southern Sweden, where average K was 3×10^{-5} m·s^{-1} [66]. Based on this K-value, the discharge area would expand in the order of 60 m upslope following clear-cutting at Rotflaka Myran. In the rutting experiment ruts were formed up along the hillslope of roughly that order (Figure 7), indicating wet conditions of up to 100 m uphill.

3.4. Preventing Rutting

The soil bearing capacity at a given time and space is determined by several interacting factors like soil type, stoniness, root systems and weather situation in combination with the wetting up of soils following clear-cut [71–73]. The DTW maps for the study-plot experiment (Figure 6) predicted that only the area at the very bottom of the hillslopes acted as discharge areas. Yet, ruts ($\geq$20 cm deep wheel tracks) were formed some 75–100 m uphill at 294 Rotflaka Myran (Figure 7), and 26–50 m at 296 Trågalidberget, indicating that the DTW maps cannot be used for predicting rutting. However, they can be used to identify the areas where rutting can lead to deleterious sediment transports in adjacent streams and ditches. Ruts in the grey areas on the map in Figure 5 pose a smaller risk for increased sediment transport than ruts in the blue and green areas where the connectivity to the stream is high, and the soils are wetter and richer in organic matter which makes them more susceptible to soil disturbance (Section 3.2). The DTW maps provide the foresters with information on where off-road traffic should be avoided or soil reinforcement must be made, for instance by applying slash or logging mats. Since logging residues constitutes a significant source for forest biofuel, we further suggest that the maps can be used to balance the use of slash for soil and surface water protection and bioenergy harvest. From a surface-water perspective aiming at protecting the near-stream zone from soil disturbance, harvest of slash can be conducted on the soils that are indicated to be dry on the DTW maps which in our case corresponded to 75% of the productive forest area (Figure 5). Note, however, that extra consideration to avoid soil disturbance might be needed also within the grey areas on the maps for example to protect cultural heritage or recreational values.

Apart from protecting the blue and green areas from soil disturbance, it would be useful to also include the area which temporarily will act as discharge area after final felling. However, today we find it difficult to use the DTW maps for predicting the expansion of the discharge areas following final felling, mainly due to the difficulty in finding or estimating accurate K-values for forest soils. The large variability in the length of the ruts at 296 Trågalidberget probably mirrors the variation in soil types within the site, and consequently the variation in K-values.

4. Conclusions

The field survey showed that there was a large temporal and spatial variability in the stream network. It is important to consider this variability when planning forestry operations. Wet area maps (DTW maps) using different flow initiation thresholds can be used to map discharge areas around stream networks for different flow situations representative of different seasons. Our calculations show that due to the lack of, and the poor quality of K-values, it is not possible today to model the expansion of discharge areas following clear-cutting. Thus, the DTW maps cannot be used to predict rutting in general but they can target those areas in need of most protection from a surface-water perspective. The maps can be used in forestry planning to: identify zones sensitive to traffic and soil disturbance, suggest site-specific forest buffer zones around the perennial stream network, and plan routes for the forestry machinery. We argue that the DTW map for the base-flow stream network (green in Figure 5) can be used to design hydrologically adapted forest buffer zones, variable in width, along perennial streams as suggested by Kuglerova [56]. We further argue that the area within the DTW maps for high-flow situations (Blue in Figure 5) can be used to indicate areas sensitive to soil disturbance, for instance, that caused by off-road forestry traffic and soil scarification. Thus, the transport of deleterious sediment to adjacent streams may be avoided.

Acknowledgments: This project was financed by the Swedish Energy Agency, Mistra's Future Forest program, The Swedish Research Council Formas, Formas' ForWater, Stiftelsen fonden för skogsvetenskaplig forskning, the Kempe foundation and VINNOVA.

Author Contributions: Anneli Ågren planned the field investigation in the Krycklan catchment, performed all GIS analysis and calculations, analyzed the data, reanalyzed the data from Edlund [51], and led the writing of the article. William Lidberg performed the field survey of the stream heads and contributed to the writing. Eva Ring lead the study-plot experiment at 294 Rotflaka Myran and 296 Trågalidberget and contributed to the writing.

Conflicts of Interest: The authors declare no conflict of interest.

References

1. Egnell, G.; Laudon, H.; Rosvall, O. Perspectives on the Potential Contribution of Swedish Forests to Renewable Energy Targets in Europe. *Forests* **2011**, *2*, 578–589. [CrossRef]
2. Stephenson, A.L.; FRS, D.J.M. Life Cycle Impacts of Biomass Electricity in 2020. Available online: https://www.gov.uk/government/uploads/system/uploads/attachment_data/file/336038/beac_report.png (accessed on 1 June 2015).
3. Kreutzweiser, D.P.; Hazlett, P.W.; Gunn, J.M. Logging impacts on the biogeochemistry of boreal forest soils and nutrient export to aquatic systems: A review. *Environ. Rev.* **2008**, *16*, 157–179. [CrossRef]
4. Laudon, H.; Tetzlaff, D.; Soulsby, C.; Carey, S.; Seibert, J.; Buttle, J.; Shanley, J.; McDonnell, J.J.; McGuire, K. Change in winter climate will affect dissolved organic carbon and water fluxes in mid-to-high latitude catchments. *Hydrol. Process.* **2013**, *27*, 700–709. [CrossRef]
5. Naghdi, R.; Solgi, A. Effects of Skidder Passes and Slope on Soil Disturbance in Two Soil Water Contents. *Croat. J. For. Eng.* **2014**, *35*, 73–80.
6. Frey, B.; Kremer, J.; Rudt, A.; Sciacca, S.; Matthies, D.; Luscher, P. Compaction of forest soils with heavy logging machinery affects soil bacterial community structure. *Eur. J. Soil Biol.* **2009**, *45*, 312–320. [CrossRef]
7. Schnurr-Putz, S.; Baath, E.; Guggenberger, G.; Drake, H.L.; Kusel, K. Compaction of forest soil by logging machinery favours occurrence of prokaryotes. *Fems Microbiol. Ecol.* **2006**, *58*, 503–516. [CrossRef] [PubMed]
8. Frey, B.; Kremer, J.; Rudt, A.; Sciacca, S.; Matthies, D.; Luscher, P. Heavy-Machinery Traffic Impacts Methane Emissions as Well as Methanogen Abundance and Community Structure in Oxic Forest Soils. *Appl. Environ. Microbiol.* **2011**, *77*, 6060–6068. [CrossRef] [PubMed]
9. Teepe, R.; Brumme, R.; Beese, F.; Ludwig, B. Nitrous oxide emission and methane consumption following compaction of forest soils. *Soil Sci. Soc. Am. J.* **2004**, *68*, 605–611. [CrossRef]
10. Schaffer, J.; Wilpert, K.V. *In situ* observation of root growth behind rhizotron windows—A pilot study. *Allg. Forst Und Jagdztg.* **2012**, *183*, 1–15.
11. Curzon, M.T.; D'Amato, A.W.; Palik, B.J. Harvest residue removal and soil compaction impact forest productivity and recovery: Potential implications for bioenergy harvests. *For. Ecol. Manag.* **2014**, *329*, 99–107. [CrossRef]
12. Kreutzweiser, D.P.; Capell, S.S. Fine sediment deposition in streams after selective forest harvesting without riparian buffers. *Can. J. For. Res.* **2001**, *31*, 2134–2142. [CrossRef]
13. Sidle, R.C.; Ziegler, A.D.; Negishi, J.N.; Nik, A.R.; Siew, R.; Turkelboom, F. Erosion processes in steep terrain—Truths, myths, and uncertainties related to forest management in Southeast Asia. *For. Ecol. Manag.* **2006**, *224*, 199–225. [CrossRef]
14. Prevost, M.; Plamondon, A.P.; Belleau, P. Effects of drainage of a forested peatland on water quality and quantity. *J. Hydrol.* **1999**, *214*, 130–143. [CrossRef]
15. Lisle, T.E. Sediment Transport and Resulting Deposition in Spawning Gravels, North Coastal California. *Water Resour. Res.* **1989**, *25*, 1303–1319. [CrossRef]
16. Soulsby, C.; Youngson, A.F.; Moir, H.J.; Malcolm, I.A. Fine sediment influence on salmonid spawning habitat in a lowland agricultural stream: a preliminary assessment. *Sci. Total Environ.* **2001**, *265*, 295–307. [CrossRef]
17. Lemly, A.D. Modification of benthic insect communities in polluted streams: Combined effects of sedimentation and nutrient enrichment. *Hydrobiologia* **1982**, *87*, 229–245. [CrossRef]
18. Munthe, J.; Hultberg, H. Mercury and Methylmercury in Runoff from a Forested Catchment—Concentrations, Fluxes, and Their Response to Manipulations. *Water Air Soil Pollut. Focus* **2004**, *4*, 607–618. [CrossRef]

19. Gerasimov, Y.; Sokolov, A.; Fjeld, D. Improving Cut-to-length Operations Management in Russian Logging Companies Using a New Decision Support System. *Balt. For.* **2013**, *19*, 89–105.

20. Hiesl, P.; Benjamin, J.G. Applicability of International Harvesting Equipment Productivity Studies in Maine, USA: A Literature Review. *Forests* **2013**, *4*, 898–921. [CrossRef]

21. Broadmeadow, S.; Nisbet, T.R. The effects of riparian forest management on the freshwater environment: A literature review of best management practice. *Hydrol. Earth Syst. Sci.* **2004**, *8*, 286–305. [CrossRef]

22. Gundersen, P.; Lauren, A.; Finer, L.; Ring, E.; Koivusalo, H.; Saetersdal, M.; Weslien, J.O.; Sigurdsson, B.D.; Hogbom, L.; Laine, J.; *et al.* Environmental Services Provided from Riparian Forests in the Nordic Countries. *Ambio* **2010**, *39*, 555–566. [CrossRef] [PubMed]

23. Luke, S.H.; Luckai, N.J.; Burke, J.M.; Prepas, E.E. Riparian areas in the Canadian boreal forest and linkages with water quality in streams. *Environ. Rev.* **2007**, *15*, 79–97. [CrossRef]

24. Vidon, P.; Allan, C.; Burns, D.; Duval, T.P.; Gurwick, N.; Inamdar, S.; Lowrance, R.; Okay, J.; Scott, D.; Sebestyen, S. Hot Spots and Hot Moments in Riparian Zones: Potential for Improved Water Quality Management. *J. Am. Water Resour. Assoc.* **2010**, *46*, 278–298. [CrossRef]

25. Wilkerson, E.; Hagan, J.M.; Siegel, D.; Whitman, A.A. The effectiveness of different buffer widths for protecting headwater stream temperature in Maine. *For. Sci.* **2006**, *52*, 221–231.

26. Blinn, C.R.; Kilgore, M.A. Riparian management practices—A summary of state guidelines. *J. For.* **2001**, *99*, 11–17.

27. Lee, P.; Smyth, C.; Boutin, S. Quantitative review of riparian buffer width guidelines from Canada and the United States. *J. Environ. Manag.* **2004**, *70*, 165–180. [CrossRef]

28. Sweeney, B.W.; Newbold, J.D. Streamside forest buffer width needed to protect stream water quality, habitat, and organisms: A literature review. *J. Am. Water Resour. Assoc.* **2014**, *50*, 560–584. [CrossRef]

29. Richardson, J.S.; Naiman, R.J.; Bisson, P.A. How did fixed-width buffers become standard practice for protecting freshwaters and their riparian areas from forest harvest practices? *Freshw. Sci.* **2012**, *31*, 232–238. [CrossRef]

30. Richardson, J.S.; Danehy, R.J. A synthesis of the ecology of headwater streams and their riparian zones in temperate forests. *For. Sci.* **2007**, *53*, 131–147.

31. Mazor, R.D.; Stein, E.D.; Ode, P.R.; Schiff, K. Integrating intermittent streams into watershed assessments: Applicability of an index of biotic integrity. *Freshw. Sci.* **2014**, *33*, 459–474. [CrossRef]

32. Bishop, K.; Buffam, I.; Erlandsson, M.; Folster, J.; Laudon, H.; Seibert, J.; Temnerud, J. Aqua Incognita: The unknown headwaters. *Hydrol. Process.* **2008**, *22*, 1239–1242. [CrossRef]

33. Acuna, V.; Datry, T.; Marshall, J.; Barcelo, D.; Dahm, C.N.; Ginebreda, A.; McGregor, G.; Sabater, S.; Tockner, K.; Palmer, M.A. Why Should We Care About Temporary Waterways? *Science* **2014**, *343*, 1080–1081. [CrossRef] [PubMed]

34. Blyth, K.; Rodda, J.C. Stream Length Study. *Water Resour. Res.* **1973**, *9*, 1454–1461. [CrossRef]

35. Rummukainen, M.; Bergstrom, S.; Persson, G.; Rodhe, J.; Tjernstrom, M. The Swedish Regional Climate Modelling Programme, SWECLIM: A review. *Ambio* **2004**, *33*, 176–182. [CrossRef] [PubMed]

36. Andreasson, J.; Bergstrom, S.; Carlsson, B.; Graham, L.P.; Lindstrom, G. Hydrological change—Climate change impact simulations for Sweden. *Ambio* **2004**, *33*, 228–234. [CrossRef] [PubMed]

37. Laudon, H.; Taberman, I.; Ågren, A.; Futter, M.; Ottosson-Löfvenius, M.; Bishop, K. The Krycklan Catchment Study—A flagship infrastructure for hydrology, biogeochemistry, and climate research in the boreal landscape. *Water Resour. Res.* **2013**, *49*, 7154–7158. [CrossRef]

38. Laudon, H.; Berggren, M.; Agren, A.; Buffam, I.; Bishop, K.; Grabs, T.; Jansson, M.; Kohler, S. Patterns and Dynamics of Dissolved Organic Carbon (DOC) in Boreal Streams: The Role of Processes, Connectivity, and Scaling. *Ecosystems* **2011**, *14*, 880–893. [CrossRef]

39. Lindsay, J.B.; Dhun, K. Modelling surface drainage patterns in altered landscapes using LiDAR. *Int. J. Geogr. Inf. Sci.* **2015**, *29*, 397–411. [CrossRef]

40. Jenson, S.K.; Domingue, J.O. Extracting Topographic Structure from Digital Elevation Data for Geographic Information-System Analysis. *Photogramm. Eng. Remote Sens.* **1988**, *54*, 1593–1600.

41. Ocallaghan, J.F.; Mark, D.M. The Extraction of Drainage Networks from Digital Elevation Data. *Comput. Vis. Graph. Image Process.* **1984**, *28*, 323–344. [CrossRef]

42. Ågren, A.M.; Lidberg, W.; Strömgren, M.; Ogilvie, J.; Arp, P.A. Evaluating digital terrain indices for soil wetness mapping—A Swedish case study. *Hydrol. Earth Syst. Sci.* **2014**, *18*, 1–12. [CrossRef]

43. Murphy, P.N.C.; Ogilvie, J.; Arp, P. Topographic modelling of soil moisture conditions: A comparison and verification of two models. *Eur. J. Soil Sci.* **2009**, *60*, 94–109. [CrossRef]

44. Murphy, P.N.C.; Ogilvie, J.; Meng, F.R.; White, B.; Bhatti, J.S.; Arp, P.A. Modelling and mapping topographic variations in forest soils at high resolution: A case study. *Ecol. Model.* **2011**, *222*, 2314–2332. [CrossRef]

45. Puckett, W.E.; Dane, J.H.; Hajek, B.F. Physical and Mineralogical Data to Determine Soil Hydraulic-Properties. *Soil Sci. Soc. Am. J.* **1985**, *49*, 831–836. [CrossRef]

46. Rodhe, A.; Lindström, G.; Rosberg, J.; Pers, C. *Grundvattenbildning i svenska Typjordar - Översiktlig Beräkning med en Vattenbalansmodell*; Report Series A2006; Institutionen för geovetenskaper, Uppsala Universitet: Uppsala, Sweden; p. 27. (In Swedish)

47. Seibert, J.; Grabs, T.; Kohler, S.; Laudon, H.; Winterdahl, M.; Bishop, K. Linking soil- and stream-water chemistry based on a Riparian Flow-Concentration Integration Model. *Hydrol. Earth Syst. Sci.* **2009**, *13*, 2287–2297. [CrossRef]

48. Bishop, K.; Seibert, J.; Nyberg, L.; Rodhe, A. Water storage in a till catchment. II: Implications of transmissivity feedback for flow paths and turnover times. *Hydrol. Process.* **2011**, *25*, 3950–3959. [CrossRef]

49. Grip, H.; Rodhe, A. *Vattnets väg från regn till bäck*, 3rd ed.; Hallgren & Fallgren: Uppsala, Sweden, 1994. (In Swedish)

50. Sorensen, R.; Ring, E.; Meili, M.; Hogbom, L.; Seibert, J.; Grabs, T.; Laudon, H.; Bishop, K. Forest Harvest Increases Runoff Most during Low Flows in Two Boreal Streams. *Ambio* **2009**, *38*, 357–363. [CrossRef] [PubMed]

51. Edlund, J. Harvesting in the Boreal Forest on Soft Ground—Ways to Reduce Ground Damage. Ph. D. Thesis, Department of Forest Rescource Management, Swedish University of Agricultural Science, Arkiteketkopia, Umeå, 2012.

52. Bodin, A. Development of a tracked vehicle to study the influence of vehicle parameters on tractive performance in soft terrain. *J. Terramechanics* **1999**, *36*, 167–181. [CrossRef]

53. Hansen, W.F. Identifying stream types and management implications. *For. Ecol. Manag.* **2001**, *143*, 39–46. [CrossRef]

54. Fries, C.; Carlsson, M.; Dahlin, B.; Lämås, T.; Sallnäs, O. A review of conceptual landscape planning models for multiobjective forestry in Sweden. *Can. J. For. Res.* **1998**, *28*, 159–167. [CrossRef]

55. Kuglerová, L.; Jansson, R.; Ågren, A.; Laudon, H.; Malm-Renöfält, B. Groundwater discharge creates hotspots of riparian plant species richness in a boreal forest stream network. *Ecology* **2013**, *95*, 715–725. [CrossRef]

56. Kuglerová, L.; Ågren, A.; Jansson, R.; Laudon, H. Towards optimizing riparian buffer zones: Ecological and biogeochemical implications for forest management. *For. Ecol. Manag.* **2014**, *334*, 74–84. [CrossRef]

57. Miwa, M.; Aust, W.M.; Burger, J.A.; Patterson, S.C.; Carter, E.A. Wet-weather timber harvesting and site preparation effects on coastal plain sites: A review. *South. J. Appl. For.* **2004**, *28*, 137–151.

58. Wood, P.J.; Armitage, P.D. Biological effects of fine sediment in the lotic environment. *Environ. Manag.* **1997**, *21*, 203–217. [CrossRef]

59. Grabs, T.; Bishop, K.; Laudon, H.; Lyon, S.W.; Seibert, J. Riparian zone hydrology and soil water total organic carbon (TOC): Implications for spatial variability and upscaling of lateral riparian TOC exports. *Biogeosciences* **2012**, *9*, 3901–3916. [CrossRef]

60. Williamson, J.R.; Neilsen, W.A. The influence of forest site on rate and extent of soil compaction and profile disturbance of skid trails during ground-based harvesting. *Can. J. For. Res. Rev. Can. Rech. For.* **2000**, *30*, 1196–1205. [CrossRef]

61. Edlund, J.; (Department of Forest Resource and Management, Swedish University of Agricultural Science, Umeå, Sweden). Personal Communication, 2012.

62. Lundin, L. Effects on hydrology and surface water chemistry of regeneration cuttings in peatland forests. *Int. Peat J.* **1999**, *9*, 118–126.

63. Brown, A.E.; Zhang, L.; McMahon, T.A.; Western, A.W.; Vertessy, R.A. A review of paired catchment studies for determining changes in water yield resulting from alterations in vegetation. *J. Hydrol.* **2005**, *310*, 28–61. [CrossRef]

64. Mohanty, B.P.; Kanwar, R.S.; Everts, C.J. Comparison of Saturated Hydraulic Conductivity Measurement Methods for a Glacial-Till Soil. *Soil Sci. Soc. Am. J.* **1994**, *58*, 672–677. [CrossRef]

65. Bishop, K.H.; Grip, H.; Oneill, A. The Origins of Acid Runoff in a Hillslope During Storm Events. *J. Hydrol.* **1990**, *116*, 35–61. [CrossRef]

66. Nyberg, L. Water-Flow Path Interactions with Soil Hydraulic-Properties in Till Soil at Gardsjon, Sweden. *J. Hydrol.* **1995**, *170*, 255–275. [CrossRef]

67. Laudon, H.; Seibert, J.; Köhler, S.; Bishop, K. Hydrological flow paths during snowmelt: Congruence between hydrometric measurements and oxygen 18 in meltwater, soil water, and runoff. *Water Resour. Res.* **2004**, *40*, W03102. [CrossRef]

68. Beldring, S. Runoff generating processes in boreal forest environments with glacial tills. *Nord. Hydrol.* **2002**, *33*, 347–372.

69. Kendall, K.A.; Shanley, J.B.; McDonnell, J.J. A hydrometric and geochemical approach to test the transmissivity feedback hypothesis during snowmelt. *J. Hydrol.* **1999**, *219*, 188–205. [CrossRef]

70. Soulsby, C.; Reynolds, B. Influence of Soil Hydrological Pathways on Stream Aluminum Chemistry at Llyn-Brianne, Mid-Wales. *Environ. Pollut.* **1993**, *81*, 51–60. [CrossRef]

71. Uusitalo, J.; Ala-Ilomaki, J. The significance of above-ground biomass, moisture content and mechanical properties of peat layer on the bearing capacity of ditched pine bogs. *Silva Fenn.* **2013**, *47*. article ID 993. [CrossRef]

72. Vega-Nieva, D.J.; Murphy, P.N.C.; Castonguay, M.; Ogilvie, J.; Arp, P.A. A modular terrain model for daily variations in machine-specific forest soil trafficability. *Can. J. Soil Sci.* **2009**, *89*, 93–109. [CrossRef]

73. Saarilahti, M. Soil interaction model. Available online: http://ethesis.helsinki.fi/julkaisut/maa/mvaro/publications/31/soilinte.png (accessed on 1 June 2015).

forests

MDPI

Article

A Global Index for Mapping the Exposure of Water Resources to Wildfire

François-Nicolas Robinne [1,*], Carol Miller [2], Marc-André Parisien [3], Monica B. Emelko [4], Kevin D. Bladon [5], Uldis Silins [6] and Mike Flannigan [7]

1   Western Partnership for Wildland Fire Science, Department of Renewable Resources, University of Alberta, Edmonton, AB T6G 2H1, Canada
2   Aldo Leopold Wilderness Research Institute, Missoula, MT 59801, USA; cmiller04@fs.fed.us
3   Natural Resources Canada, Canadian Forest Service, Northern Forestry Centre, Edmonton, AB T6H 3S5, Canada; marc-andre.parisien@canada.ca
4   Department of Civil and Environmental Engineering, University of Waterloo, Waterloo, ON N2L 3G1, Canada; mbemelko@uwaterloo.ca
5   Department of Forest Engineering, Resources, and Management, Oregon State University, Corvallis, OR 97331, USA; bladonk@oregonstate.edu
6   Department of Renewable Resources, University of Alberta, Edmonton, AB T6G 2H1, Canada; uldis.silins@ualberta.ca
7   Western Partnership for Wildland Fire Science, Department of Renewable Resources, University of Alberta, Edmonton, AB T6G 2H1, Canada; mike.flannigan@ualberta.ca
*   Correspondence: robinne@ualberta.ca; Tel.: +1-587-589-6449

Academic Editors: Ge Sun and James M. Vose
Received: 2 October 2015; Accepted: 5 January 2016; Published: 13 January 2016

Abstract: Wildfires are keystone components of natural disturbance regimes that maintain ecosystem structure and functions, such as the hydrological cycle, in many parts of the world. Consequently, critical surface freshwater resources can be exposed to post-fire effects disrupting their quantity, quality and regularity. Although well studied at the local scale, the potential extent of these effects has not been examined at the global scale. We take the first step toward a global assessment of the wildfire water risk (WWR) by presenting a spatially explicit index of exposure. Several variables related to fire activity and water availability were identified and normalized for use as exposure indicators. Additive aggregation of those indicators was then carried out according to their individual weight. The resulting index shows the greatest exposure risk in the tropical wet and dry forests. Intermediate exposure is indicated in mountain ranges and dry shrublands, whereas the lowest index scores are mostly associated with high latitudes. We believe that such an approach can provide important insights for water security by guiding global freshwater resource preservation.

Keywords: wildfire water risk; global index; wildfire hazard; water security; water resources exposure

1. Introduction

Wildfires are essential to ecosystem function across the globe [1], influencing a wide spectrum of ecosystem components and natural processes [2], among which is the hydrological cycle. Accordingly, an abundant literature has described the effects of vegetation burning and post-fire recovery on local hydrology in different biogeographic areas [3–6]. Vegetation cover, litter and soil organic matter can be dramatically reduced by large fires and can lead to higher surface runoff and soil erosion, increasing water quantity, but decreasing water quality. The water requirements of rapidly growing post-fire vegetation can subsequently limit water quantity [4], even though water quality may improve [7].

Although a significant number of studies have examined such second-order fire effects on surface freshwater resources [8], most have been conducted at a local or regional scale [8–12], whereas global-scale studies do not exist. Despite the ubiquitous nature of fire and the potential for adverse consequences on ecosystems and populations [13], large-scale assessments of the risks that fire can pose to water resources are lacking. However, several important advancements in natural resources global mapping [14] and the development of innovative methods and global databases now make it possible to better understand the intersection of wildfire activity [15,16] and water resource availability [17,18] at the scale of the planet.

The large diversity of data types and derived metrics in these global databases creates a challenge for conducting global assessments, particularly when combining data from two fields, pyrogeography and hydrogeography. Often, resource or risk indices are created by aggregating proxy variables, called indicators, that are known to play a role in the occurrence of the studied phenomenon [19–22]. In such an approach, raster datasets representing indicators are selected and normalized to assign each pixel a score. Each indicator is then assigned a weight according to its assumed importance to the phenomenon of interest. Numerous indicators can then be aggregated to create a final raster index, whereby pixel values reflect the degree of risk or resource availability. Finally, the index can be tested for its sensitivity to each indicator and assigned weight. Several key global studies used this approach to underline issues in water security and riverine biodiversity [20], ocean vulnerability to human impact [22] and to identify natural areas of great importance for ecosystem functioning [19].

Inspired by this effective approach, we introduce here the concept of the wildfire water risk (WWR), which we define as the potential for wildfires to adversely affect water resources important for downstream ecosystems and human water needs for adequate water quantity and quality. We present a spatial framework as a foundation for assessing this underappreciated risk and introduce the global wildfire water exposure index (GWWEI) as a first step toward an integrated global assessment of the WWR. We then evaluate the sensitivity of the GWWEI to seven indicators relevant to fire and to water resources. Finally, we discuss how inclusion or variation in individual exposure indicators affects the interpretation of the index.

2. Materials and Methods

We detail below the procedure of the GWWEI concept, starting with a precise description of the data selected to be used as indicators in our framework (Figure 1). We then explain how those data were transformed to obtain normalized indicators, resulting in pixel values ranging from 0 to 100. We follow with an explanation of the weighted aggregation process of indicators' scores, known as indexation, and finally, we perform a thorough sensitivity analysis of the resulting index to test its stability.

2.1. Data Selection and Indicators' Definition

We selected a parsimonious set of global indicators that described the potential for wildfire activity and the availability of surface freshwater resources (Table 1). A total of seven indicators were selected based on their availability at the global scale, their relevance to the GWWEI and the nature of the information (*i.e.*, yearly to multi-decadal averages). All data used in this study are "off-the-shelf" and freely available on the Internet or by request from the authors. Although our data have some discrepancies in their time period, they are the product of large-scale long-term monitoring, which substantially smooths spatial and temporal variability, making them suitable for use in a global model. Although slight temporal mismatches may be responsible for some inaccuracies, there is reason to believe that these would be relatively minor.

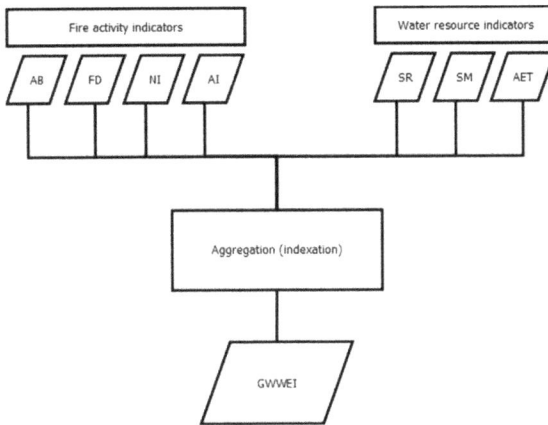

Figure 1. Schematic of the global wildfire water exposure index (GWWEI) framework. AB, area burned; FD, fire danger; NI, natural ignitions; AI, anthropogenic influence; SR, surface runoff; SM, soil moisture; AET, actual evapotranspiration.

Table 1. Summary of datasets used to develop the GWWEI indicators. NASA: National Aeronautic and Space Administration, SEDAC: Socioeconomic Data and Applications Center, GWSP: Global Water System Project, CGIAR-CSI: Consortium of International Agricultural Research Centers-Consortium for Spatial Information.

Indicator	Data Source	Units	Native Resolution	Coverage Years
Area Burned (AB)	Giglio *et al.*	Ha/month	0.25°	1997–2013
Fire Danger (FD)	NASA	unitless	0.5° × 2/3°	1980–2014
Natural Ignitions (NI)	NASA	Flashes/km^2/year	0.5°	1995–2010
Anthropogenic Influence (AI)	SEDAC	Unitless (0–100)	0.08°	1960–2004
Surface Runoff (SR)	GWSP	mm/year	0.5°	1950–2000
Soil Moisture (SM)	Terrestrial water budget; data archive	mm/m	0.5°	1950–1999
Actual Evapotranspiration (AET)	CGIAR-CSI	mm/year	0.08°	1960–1990

Area burned (AB) has been found to be a good global proxy for fire activity [23], especially as fire size is an important factor of post-fire impact to water resources [3]. Mean monthly area burned (hectares) for large fires (>120 ha) was extracted from the Global Fire Emission Database (GFED) V4, a database derived from remote-sensing imagery acquired with several sensors. Data span 1995–2014, and are spatially aggregated at a 0.25° pixel resolution [24,25]. Our AB indicator, as an average of the monthly area burned for the past 20 years, provides a view of areas experiencing most of the fire activity across the planet.

Fire danger (FD) is a measure of the potential for a fire to ignite and spread across the landscape and therefore is critical to assess water resources exposure. The most common fire danger metrics are calculated using the Canadian Fire Weather Index (FWI) System [26], which estimates existing fire danger across an area as derived from observations of four fire-weather elements (*i.e.*, temperature, relative humidity, wind speed, and precipitation). An increasing index value means lower fuel moisture, higher wind speed and, consequently, a greater fire danger. Data come from the Global Fire Weather Database (GFWED), a global database of the FWI system and its components. Data are derived from the Modern Era-Retrospective Analysis for Research and Applications (MERRA) climate product provided by NASA and ground weather stations, compiled for 1980–2012 at a resolution of 0.5° latitude × 2/3° longitude [27,

28]. Our FD indicator, based on the final FWI, provides information about the potential for fire activity, but does not account for actual area burned, vegetation composition or human influence on fire activity.

In many places of the world, lightning activity is an important factor of fire ignition [23] that can lead to a large area burned when it occurs in remote areas [29–31]. We used the mean annual lightning flash rate as an indicator of natural ignitions (NI), expressed as the number of flashes per km^2 and per year. Data come from the High Resolution Flash Climatology, a sub-product of the Gridded Lightning Climatology dataset produced by the Lightning and Atmospheric Electricity Research Team at NASA using LIS/OTD remote-sensing observations. It is the result of flash counts per area scaled by the detection efficiency of sensors and gridded at a resolution of 0.5° for 1995–2010 [32]. We build our NI indicator considering that a higher lightning flash rate is associated with a higher chance for lightning to reach the ground, potentially starting a fire when the strike occurs in a vegetated area. As it does not account for individual strikes, lightning activity should not be considered as an actual fire ignition product.

The anthropogenic influence (AI) on fire activity is well known, but is still a matter of debate, as the nature of this influence is complicated [33–35]. Nonetheless, a recent study argues that human influence tends to decrease fire activity at the global scale [16] and, consequently, the area burned. We thus consider higher levels of AI as an indicator of lower fire activity. As a proxy for AI, we used the Human Footprint Index (HFP) V2 data from the Socioeconomic Data and Applications Center from NASA, computed from 1995 to 2004 at a one-kilometer pixel resolution. This data depicts the extent and density of human features, conveying higher levels of disturbances to natural areas, with lower values showing a lower footprint, on a 0–100 score scale [36]. However, scores are scaled per biome and, thus, encompass different socio-environmental configurations, which, in turn, have different effects on fire activity across the globe [35].

Surface runoff (SR) is excess precipitation contributing to surface river-stream networks after evaporative and drainage losses. It can be greatly increased due to changes in water interception by vegetation and alteration of soil properties caused by wildfires. SR data is available as long-term average runoff, derived from a global water-balance model and river gauging stations, computed in mm/year at a 0.5° pixel resolution over the 1950–2000 period [37,38]. For this study, our indicator assumes that areas showing higher levels of SR play a prominent role in the amount of available water resources and are thus more vulnerable to disturbances. We thus considered them as preferential areas of post-fire runoff increases. That said, if natural SR increases when vegetation cover is reduced, it becomes more difficult to predict and can lead to greater erosion levels and floods.

Soil moisture (SM) reserves are critical to sustain surface runoff and dry season river-stream baseflows. Although high levels of SM favor runoff and water availability, it is also sensitive to post-fire changes in vegetation cover [39]. SM data were compiled from the Atlas of the Biosphere [40] and based on the Terrestrial Water Budget Data Archive produced by the Center for Climatic Research at the University of Delaware [40–42]. Data were derived from several thousands of weather stations records from 1950 to 1999 and interpolated at a 0.5° pixel resolution. Our indicator assumes that a drop in soil moisture content after a fire is caused by greater inputs of radiative energy [43], which, in turn, negatively impact SR levels and amounts of water during the dry season.

The reduction of the vegetation cover after a fire might impact actual evapotranspiration (AET) levels [44], which is the effective quantity of water released by vegetation transpiration and water evaporation from the soil. AET data come from the Consortium of International Agricultural Research Centers-Consortium for Spatial Information (CGIAR-CSI) [45] and show the average of AET in mm/year at a 0.08° pixel resolution, from 1950 to 2000, based on WorldClim inputs. Our indicator is used as a proxy for post-fire water-balance change, based on the reasonable assumption that without vegetation interception and respiration, AET will mainly be converted to runoff. This process would be limited, however, by expected increases in post-fire soil-water evaporation.

2.2. Data Processing and Aggregation

All data were rasterized, reprojected to the WGS84 geographic coordinate system and resampled to a 0.5° pixel resolution. We used the FWI layer, which does not account for desert areas, as an extraction mask for other layers. Therefore, we avoided result biases by including arid areas where climatic conditions restrain water availability, as well as vegetation growth and, consequently, wildfire activity. We also processed the grids in order to match the spatial coverage of FD. Finally, small islands without consistent coverage through the different layers were removed, as well as Greenland and Antarctica (28% of global land surface). Data were processed with ArcGIS 10.1 [46] and exported as GeoTIFF images for post-processing.

Prior to the indexation process, data were normalized between 0 and 100 scores and then considered as actual indicators of the GWWEI (Figure 2). Normalization, in this context, makes indicators comparable to each other by replacing initial values (e.g., mm or ha) according to a common and standard scale, here 0–100. Our raw exposure index is then a simple pixel-wise additive aggregation process of the selected indicators, based on their respective attributed weight:

$$I = \sum_{i=1}^{n} w_i x_{n,i}$$

where I is our final risk index; n is the number of indicators (*i.e.*, 7); w_i is the relative weight of each indicator; $x_{n,i}$ is the normalized value of each indicator [47].

Our weighting scheme assigns 50% to fire indicators and 50% to water indicators and equally partitions the weights within each of these groups. Therefore, we assigned a 16.6% weight to each water indicator (3) and a 12.5% weight to each fire indicator (4). As a result, one pixel's final score in the index theoretically ranges from 0 to 100, a higher score meaning a higher concentration of exposure factors. This method is inspired by the work of Freudenberger *et al.* [19]. Data normalization and index calculation were carried out using Insensa-GIS (0.2.0.1), 64-bit version [47].

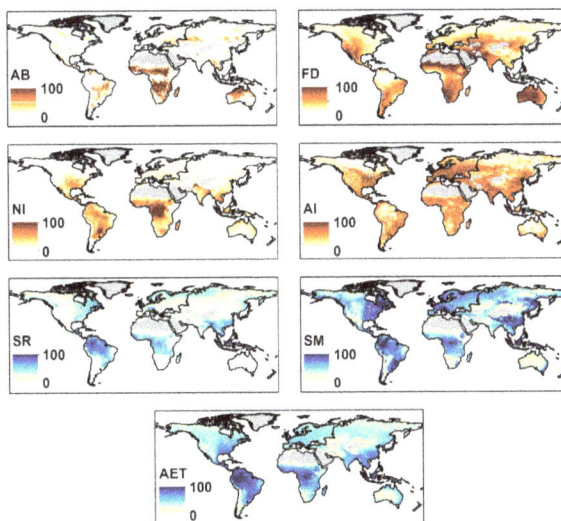

Figure 2. Map series of selected spatial indicators. Wildfire indicators are shown in orange tones; water indicators are shown in blue tones.

2.3. Sensitivity Analysis

It is critical in indexation models to test the robustness of the aggregated index to evaluate the level of confidence in the final score [48]. We thoroughly evaluated the sensitivity of the raw index to the seven indicators using one non-spatial approach and six spatial approaches (Table 2). The main product of this analysis is a measure of score variability expressed as a coefficient of variation that was computed from the re-weighting of the indicators and by omitting some indicators from the calculation in order to assess their relative weight to the final score.

Table 2. Details pertaining to each sensitivity analysis method.

Sensitivity Analysis Method	Procedure Detail	Weight Variation Scheme	# of Modified Indices
Spearman/Pearson correlation	Calculus of correlation coefficients between index and indicators	-	-
Stepwise	One-by-one addition of each indicator until final index	-	-
Jackknifing	Iterative exclusion of each indicator in the aggregation process	-	7
Low/high case scenario	Bounded weight variation based on indicator distribution	Within 6.5% and 18.5% for fire indicators; Within 10.6% and 22.6% for fire indicators	2
Random variation	Bounded random weight variation	Within 6.5% and 18.5% for fire indicators; Within 10.6% and 22.6% for fire indicators	14
Systematic variation	Incremental bounded weight variation	Within 6.5% and 18.5% for fire indicators; Within 10.6% and 22.6% for fire indicators	28

The first common technique we applied was to non-spatially analyze index sensitivity by measuring the level of correlation between the GWWEI and each indicator separately, as well as among indicators (Table 3). The Spearman correlation coefficient table was generated as a measure of dependency, such that indicators highly correlated with the final index have an overall higher influence on final index scores.

Table 3. Spearman correlation coefficients between the GWWEI and source indicators, as well as between indicators.

		GWWEI	Fire				Water		
			AB	FD	NI	AI	AET	SM	SR
GWWEI		1.00	0.21	−0.11	0.55	−0.06	0.76	0.74	0.66
Fire	AB	0.21	1.00	0.36	0.35	−0.06	0.20	−0.13	−0.04
	FD	−0.11	0.36	1.00	0.41	−0.31	−0.14	−0.58	−0.57
	NI	0.55	0.35	0.41	1.00	−0.41	0.65	0.15	0.15
	AI	−0.06	−0.06	−0.31	−0.41	1.00	−0.40	−0.16	−0.02
Water	AET	0.76	0.20	−0.14	0.65	−0.40	1.00	0.68	0.63
	SM	0.74	−0.13	−0.58	0.15	−0.16	0.68	1.00	0.76
	SR	0.66	−0.04	−0.57	0.15	−0.02	0.63	0.76	1.00

The simplest spatial approach we used for our sensitivity analysis was the "stepwise" method. We reprocessed GWWEI adding one indicator at a time. We started with the weighted aggregation of only AB and SR, as the former is the recorded fire activity and the latter is the recorded natural water availability; together, these indicators logically provide the simplest possible index. Then, we added the other indicators individually, alternating fire and water indicators until all were included (*i.e.*, the GWWEI itself). This simple stepwise approach to sensitivity analysis allowed us to monitor the spatial changes caused by the addition of each new variable included and to assess variation in the spatial distribution of risk scores.

Insensa-GIS [47] also implements several modes allowing for a thorough spatial sensitivity analysis. We used jackknifing; low-high case scenario weighting; random weighting; and systematic weighting of indicators. These four methods captured the variability in indicator aggregation, giving information about their intrinsic influence when compared to the original index results (Table 2). For all weight variation modes, we computed a pixel-wise mean and coefficient of variation and averaged them into one final map of the index's overall coefficient of variation.

The jackknifing mode involves the iterative exclusion of each indicator from the aggregation procedure. As this process removes our seven indicators successively to create a new index each time, jackknifing produced eight modified indices; in other words, one for each missing indicator.

Lower and higher case scenarios modify the weight of indicators according to a predefined range of variation, which is based on their influence on the aggregation result. As such, if an indicator favors high index scores, its weight will be depreciated, yet not below the predefined minimum. The opposite is true for a higher case scenario, whereby an indicator lowering the final index scores will be over-weighted, below or equal to the upper bound of the range of variation. We set the lower case weight boundary to 6.5% and the higher case weight boundary to 18.5% for fireindicators and 10.6%–22.6% for water indicators, a range we consider wide enough to capture index variability. This process produced two modified indices, one for each scenario.

Random weight variation involves the randomization of each indicator's weight during the aggregation procedure, according to a predefined variation range. We set the same variation range as for the previous mode, which means that an indicator can randomly be assigned any weight in this range during indexation. We applied this procedure several times to increase the detection of variations in index scores, which resulted in 14 new modified indices.

Finally, we created a rule set to apply the systematic weighting variation mode. We kept the same range of variation that we used for previous modes with a 3% step increment. The process is repeated for each indicator, resulting in 28 new modified indices. In total, the sensitivity analysis created 51 modified versions of the index (not shown), with the coefficient of variation computed for each of the four modes. We averaged those to produce a map of the per-pixel mean variability of the GWWEI scores, where areas showing higher variability are thus more sensitive to changes in the indicators' values.

3. Results and Discussion

3.1. Geography of the GWWEI

Our GWWEI (Figure 3a) shows the distribution of the exposure of water resources to wildfires across the globe. Highest scores are concentrated in the tropical latitudes, more specifically in the forests of the Amazon basin, the Congo basin and Indonesia. Moderately high scores are mostly located in the subtropical humid forests of southeastern Asia, southeastern North America, Central America and in fire-prone dry forested savannas of Africa, southeastern South America and southeastern Oceania. A large part of northeastern North America, as well as many mountain ranges across the globe, also show moderately high scores. Intermediate scores are shown in dry savannas, dry steppes and dry shrublands on all continents, as well as in the Mediterranean, the northwest of the Eurasian boreal forest and the southern range of the North American boreal forest. The lowest scores are seen in the temperate prairies of North America, South America and Eurasia, as well as in the northern boreal and the tundra (Figure 3b).

At this stage of our framework development, it is important to recall that the GWWEI does not describe a quantitative likelihood or probability of impacts on water resources. It rather depicts the geographic overlay of important drivers of the WWR and identifies areas where such quantitative assessments must be carried out. Working at the global scale usually smooths regional differences, and in this regard, the scores should be interpreted according to specific environmental, socio-cultural and economic factors. For instance, high scores in African savannas are mostly driven by the AB, as those ecosystems experience most of fire activity on Earth [24], whereas high scores in mountain ranges are mostly driven by intermediate to high scores of SM. It is important to note that indicators are global-scale proxies that may not be suitable when estimating fire risk or water discharge across small areas.

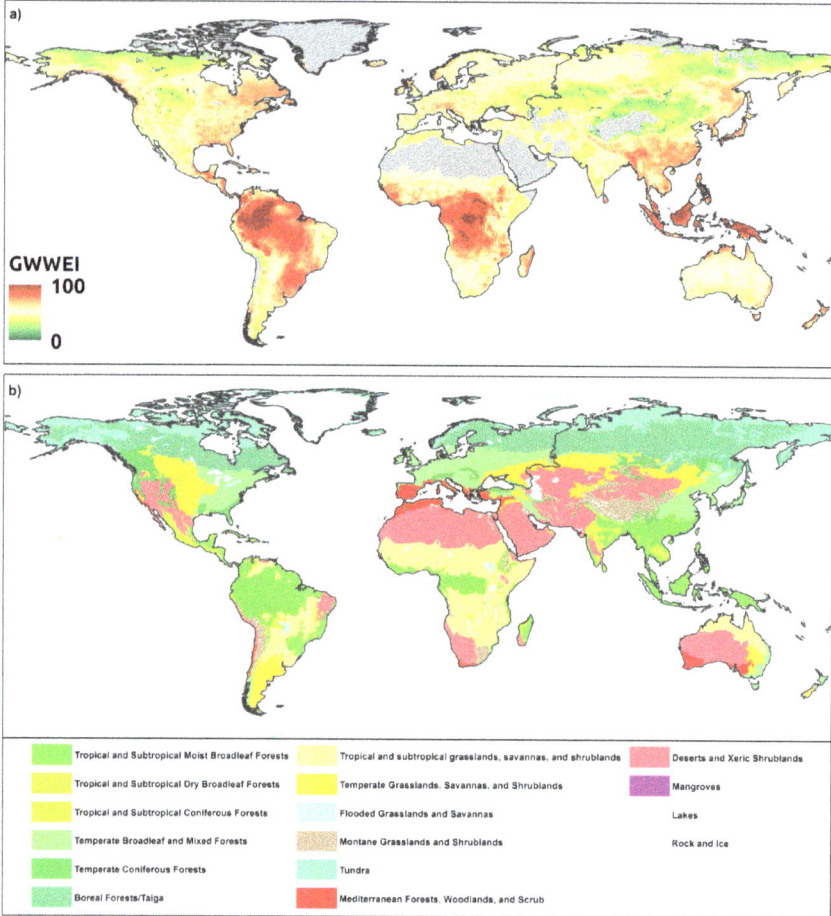

Figure 3. (**a**) Map of the global GWWEI as provided by additive aggregation. The index is dimensionless; scores stretched to 0–100. Higher values (100, dark red) mean a higher concentration of risk factors; (**b**) A map of terrestrial biomes [49] is also provided for comparison purposes (see Section 3.1).

3.2. Sensitivity of the GWWEI

The Spearman correlation coefficients (Table 3) between the GWWEI and indicators show that the most influential water indicators are AET (0.76), SM (0.74) and SR (0.66), whereas the most influential fire indicators are NI (0.55) and AB (0.21). The correlation between the index and water indicators explains the pattern of high values in tropical areas, which naturally concentrate a very dynamic hydrological cycle. This influence of water resource indicators is confirmed by the stepwise approach, where the inclusion of AET in the simplest version of the index (Figure 4a) sets a pattern that is conserved and enforced through all steps (Figure 4b–f), with SM being critical in setting the pattern for mountain ranges, such as the Himalayas or Southern Alaska, as well as increasing scores for the southern fringe of the boreal forest (Figure 4c). NI and AB are the fire indicators that add the most to the pattern of the final index, whereas FD and AI show surprisingly low influence. We assume that the strong pattern shown by water indicators may mask information contained in fire indicators, thus showing lower levels of correlation in them.

Although several nonlinear relationships and interactions might exist, they are not explored with these simple correlation coefficients.

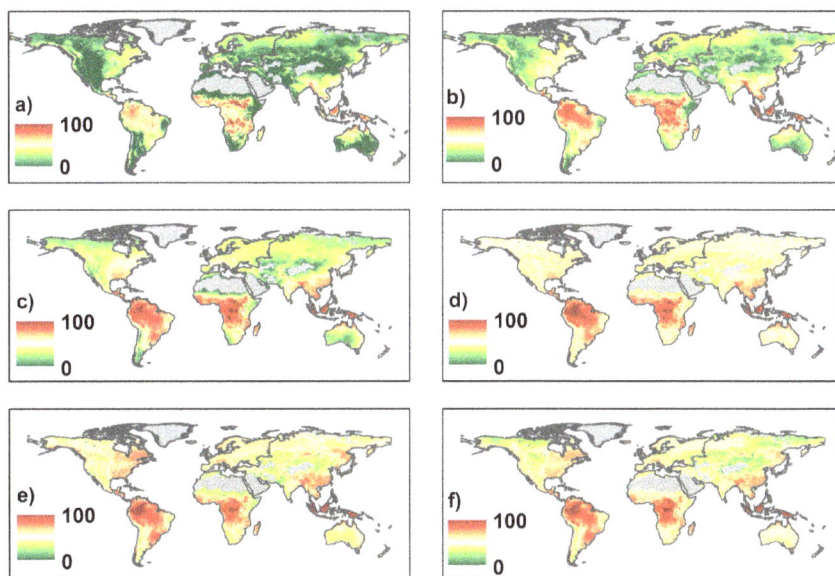

Figure 4. Map of the stepwise sensitivity analysis as provided by additive aggregation. (**a**) AB + SR; (**b**) AB + SR + NI; (**c**) AB + SR + NI + AET; (**d**) AB + SR + NI + AET + AI; (**e**) AB + SR + NI + AET + AI + SM; (**f**) AB + AET + NI + SM + AI + SR + FD, *i.e.*, the GWWEI (see Figure 1). The index is unitless; scores stretched to 0–100. Higher values (100, dark red) mean a higher concentration of risk factors.

The highest values of the coefficient of variation (Figure 5) (*i.e.*, where the index is less robust) are mostly concentrated at northern latitudes (*i.e.*, the tundra and northern fringe of the circumboreal forest), where water indicators have the most influence on the wildfire water risk exposure pattern (Figure 6). Moderately high to high variability in index scores is also shown in areas of dense human pressure, like Japan, Western Europe and eastern North America. That said, this pattern is clearly localized, giving clusters of spotted areas on the map. Several mountain ranges, such the Andes, the Rocky Mountains, the European and New-Zealand Alps, also show this range of moderately high values. Moderately low levels of variability cover most of circumboreal, temperate, tropical, and sub-tropical forests and dry shrublands in both hemispheres. Robust estimates of the GWWEI, *i.e.*, the lowest coefficient of variation values, are concentrated in the tropical savannas and the dry temperate steppes, except for the North American prairies, which show a wide range of variability, and for northern Australia, which shows a constant high level in all individual indicator scores.

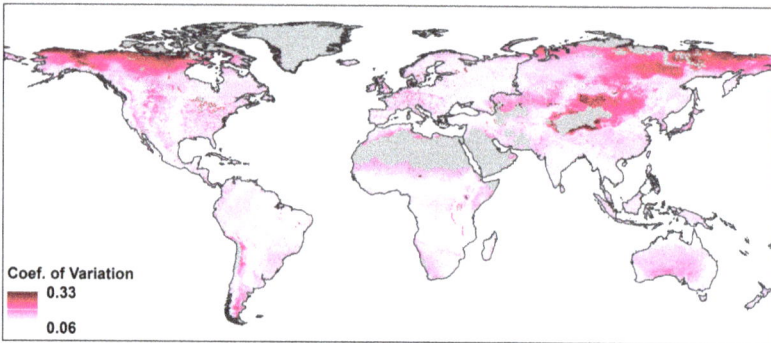

Figure 5. Map of the average coefficient (Coef.) of variation derived from modified indices. Higher values (dark purple) show higher sensitivity to the weighting scheme used.

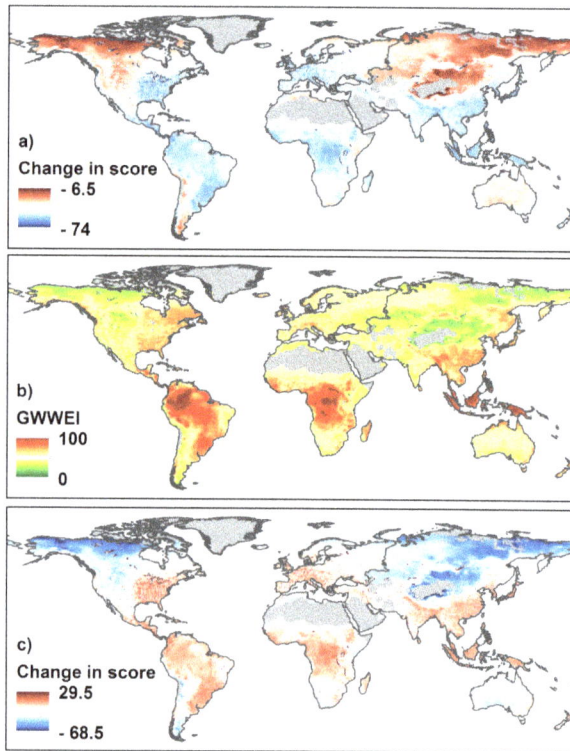

Figure 6. Map set of the relative change (%) in final GWWEI scores using the low case (**a**) and high case (**c**) scenario mode in the sensitivity analyses. The role of water resource indicators is made clear by the pattern of change when compared with the GWWEI (**b**).

3.3. The GWWEI and Its Implications for Water Resource Protection

Water security was originally defined as the guarantee of a safe, affordable and sustainable amount of water to fulfill one's basic daily needs [50]. This definition has been subsequently extended to include the amount of water resources necessary to secure ecological functions, as well as agricultural or industrial activities [51]. Knowing the potential exposure of water resources to wildfire activity, as provided by this study, as well as the current pressure on the water supply worldwide [20,52,53], we argue that a high level of GWWEI can have potential implications for water security. This is especially true in areas that are dependent on surface water coming from a highly fire-prone river basin. Regional studies from Thompson *et al.* [12], Santos *et al.* [54] and Moody and Martin [11], as well as reports from the U.S. Forest Service [9] and the Water Research Foundation [55] showed that wildfire risk in source watersheds raises concerns for water treatment and supply. The global information provided by our index might be a good way to identify regions across the planet showing higher levels of exposure, potentially requiring more detailed wildfire water risk analysis for regional water planning and management.

Surprisingly, wildfires are rarely considered as a critical threat to water resources by international authorities. This lack of recognition, despite major worldwide concerns about water sustainability and scarcity, is underlined by the absence of dedicated mentions in most of the global reports and mapping initiatives focusing on water security, water management issues or forested water basin monitoring; in contrast, the role of forests for water resource preservation is widely aknowledged. The GWWEI, as a part of a larger WWR framework, can contribute to knowledge improvement, especially in mountainous areas, known as "water towers", across the globe. Viviroli *et al.* [56] indeed showed that several mountainous regions provide at least a "supportive" amount of water for downstream supply needs, and Nogués-Bravo *et al.* [57] pointed out the extreme sensitivity of headwaters to natural hazards in the context of climate change, though wildfire was not considered. Mori and Johnson [58], for instance, demonstrated that mountains might experience significant changes in their fire regime because of climate change, whereas Moody and Martin [11] showed the critical exposure of mountainous reservoirs to wildfire impacts, although limited to the western U.S. In this respect, our framework can be used to identify and prioritize sensitive areas and initiate the creation or improvement of resource management plans or mitigation actions.

A recent study by Green *et al.* [59] shows global population dependence on upstream freshwater sources. According to our index, water resources' exposure to fire activity potentially threatens the water supply of a large portion of the human population, as underlined by several localized events. For example, the 2013 Rim Fire raised concerns with California State authorities when it threatened the Hetch Hetchy reservoir, which provides most of the water supplied to the San Francisco Bay Area, *i.e.*, 2.6 million people. This recent event brought to light the threat induced by large and severe wildfires to communities dependent on surface freshwater to ensure daily potable water needs, as is the case with 78% of large cities on the planet [60]. Other major blazes that occurred in the past decade had significant impacts on several cities' water supply, such as Melbourne in Australia and Denver, Boulder and Santa Fe in the United States [61], as well as numerous large cities across the world, such as San Salvador, Caracas and Istanbul, all of which are considered exposed to potential water provision issues in case of a major fire in their watershed [62].

Although fire activity can increase the net quantity of water downstream, potentially severe impacts on water quality and timing/magnitude of event flows (*i.e.*, floods) can impact a wide range of ecological and human water resource uses (*i.e.*, drinking water). This aspect will be explored in further versions of the index. We argue that the WWR should be viewed primarily as a source of cumulative effects on water resources whose watersheds are exposed, if not already impacted, by forest degradation and human activities [63].

3.4. Limitations and Improvements

The sensitivity analysis showed that water resource indicators tend to overwhelm fire-related indicators in the pattern of the GWWEI. This raises a question about the assumption of equal weight used in the aggregation process. While we considered this assumption acceptable to create our framework, the variability in the spatial pattern of the index shows that different weighting schemes could improve its robustness. The following versions will integrate an intermediate step based on a survey of scientists, in order to obtain a robust rating of the score we should assign to each indicator. This step has been previously used in several studies describing the creation of risk and resource indices [20,22,59].

Our initial pool of data is a collection of common variables that are known to affect wildfire activity and freshwater availability. Our indicator list is intentionally simple, though we expect to extend it to explore the effect of alternative variables in future versions of the index. For instance, area burned could be replaced by adding different variables that contribute to fire probability, such as ecosystems' net primary productivity or drought proneness [64]. Similarly, the Build-Up Index of the FWI System may be a better proxy to fire impacts than FWI, because it better reflects burn severity, a critical determinant of post-fire hydrological effects. The correlation in water resource indicators must also be addressed by the inclusion of innovative information on surface freshwater availability, such as lake density or stream network connectivity. Moreover, resulting estimates of GWWEI could be improved if indicator data were averaged for biome-specific fire seasons, rather than annually. It is important to underline that we were dependent on data availability; the improvement of our index will therefore depend on the creation of and enhancements to global datasets, especially regarding water-related indicators, given that several wildfire indicators already exist.

Our current version of the framework only considers overlapping additive effects mostly based on long-term indicator averages. Further versions will address downstream cumulative effects in space and time and explicitly consider existing connectivity in water systems that could potentially lead to adverse effects on the water supply [65]. Extending the WWR framework to take into account the induced risk to the downstream water supply implies the integration of a "spatial transmission" process, in other words the capacity of a hazardous process to impact geographically-distant values at risk [66]. This process has been translated in the "downstream routing" method recently used in several studies related to the impact of human activities on water security at the global and continental scale [20,59,67] and may be considered in future versions of the GWWEI.

4. Conclusions

A unique global view of the potential exposure of water resources to wildfire activity and a valuable approach complementary to recent worldwide assessments of global exposure towards natural hazards was presented herein [68,69]. The highest exposure scores were mostly clustered in the tropical wet forests, whereas intermediate scores tended to be localized in tropical dry forest and shrublands, as well as in several mountain ranges and boreal forests. The lowest levels were found in the tundra, temperate forests and temperate prairies. These results represent an important source of information that can be considered in the international governance of forested areas and freshwater resources.

Notably, the sensitivity analysis showed an overwhelming influence of water resource indicators on the final index scores, which indicates the need for several modifications in the weighting scheme, such as incorporating expert opinion or including a larger set of variables. Future improvements to the WWR framework should also explore restricting indicators' score range to worldwide fire seasons and develop new complementary indices that allow for the assessment of downstream water supply vulnerability and the subsequent risk to dependent populations and ecosystems.

The global index presented in this study can help us pinpoint regions of potential concern that may require a more detailed assessment of wildfire-induced risk to water resources. Indeed, high exposure levels may reveal the potential for deleterious impacts on water quality and downstream cumulative effects that might in turn affect local to regional water security, especially in river basins serving large populations. Although wildfires can impair water provision services from ecosystems, they are a natural and essential ecosystem process. Therefore, a trade-off has to be found between the preservation of natural fire regimes and the need for risk mitigation and source water protection. In this regard, the definition of a WWR opens new perspectives in the understanding of the global water and land systems. This framework adds an important component to the global water security paradigm in the context of climate change that do not presently encompass global wildfire water risk.

Acknowledgments: We want to thank the Canadian Water Network for funding this research. We are also grateful to the following people for providing advice and data: Enric Batllori from InForest Joint Research Unit CSIC-CTFC-CREAF, Alan Cantin from the Great Lake Forestry Centre of the Canadian Forest Service, Tom Gleeson from the Civil Engineering Department at McGill University, Victoria Naipal from the Max Plank Institute for Meteorology and Arnout van Soesbergen from the UNEP World Conservation Monitoring Centre.

Author Contributions: F-N Robinne designed the study and ran the analysis. All the authors assisted with the interpretation of results and the manuscript writing.

Conflicts of Interest: The authors declare no conflict of interest.

References

1. Bond, W.J.; Woodward, F.I.; Midgley, G.F. The global distribution of ecosystems in a world without fire. *New Phytol.* **2005**, *165*, 525–537. [CrossRef] [PubMed]
2. Lavorel, S.; Flannigan, M.D.; Lambin, E.F.; Scholes, M.C. Vulnerability of land systems to fire: Interactions among humans, climate, the atmosphere, and ecosystems. *Mitig. Adapt. Strateg. Glob. Chang.* **2007**, *12*, 33–53. [CrossRef]
3. USDA. *Wildland Fire in Ecosystems: Effects of Fire on Soil and Water*; Gen. Tech. Rep. RMRS-GTR-42-vol.4. Ogden; U.S Department of Agriculture, Forest Service: Ogden UT, USA, 2005; Volume 4.
4. Kuczera, G. Prediction of water yield reductions following a bushfire in ash-mixed species eucalypt forest. *J. Hydrol.* **1987**, *94*, 215–236. [CrossRef]
5. DeBano, L.F. The role of fire and soil heating on water repellency in wildland environments: A review. *J. Hydrol.* **2000**, *231–232*, 195–206. [CrossRef]
6. Seibert, J.; McDonnell, J.J.; Woodsmith, R.D. Effects of wildfire on catchment runoff response: A modelling approach to detect changes in snow-dominated forested catchments. *Hydrol. Res.* **2010**, *41*, 378–390. [CrossRef]
7. Dunnette, P.V.; Higuera, P.E.; Mclauchlan, K.K.; Derr, K.M.; Briles, C.E.; Keefe, M.H. Biogeochemical impacts of wildfires over four millennia in a Rocky Mountain subalpine watershed. *New Phytol.* **2014**, *203*, 900–912. [CrossRef] [PubMed]
8. Scott, J.H.; Helmbrecht, D.J.; Thompson, M.P.; Calkin, D.E.; Marcille, K. Probabilistic assessment of wildfire hazard and municipal watershed exposure. *Nat. Hazards* **2012**, *64*, 707–728. [CrossRef]
9. Weidner, E.; Todd, A.H. *From the Forest to the Faucet Methods Paper*; U.S Department of Agriculture, Forest Service: Ogden, UT, USA, 2011.
10. Boerner, C.; Coday, B.; Noble, J.; Roa, P.; Roux, V. *Impacts of Wildfire in Clear Creek Watershed on the City of Golden's Drinking Water Supply*; Colorado School of Mines: Golden, CO, USA, 2012.
11. Moody, J.A.; Martin, D.A. Wildfire impacts on reservoir sedimentation in the western United States. In Proceedings of the Ninth International Symposium on River Sedimentation, Yichang, China, 18–21 October 2004; pp. 1095–1102.
12. Thompson, M.P.; Scott, J.H.; Langowski, P.; Gilbertson-Day, J.W.; Haas, J.; Bowne, E. Assessing Watershed-Wildfire Risks on National Forest System Lands in the Rocky Mountain Region of the United States. *Water* **2013**, *5*, 945–971. [CrossRef]
13. Emelko, M.B.; Silins, U.; Bladon, K.D.; Stone, M. Implications of land disturbance on drinking water treatability in a changing climate: Demonstrating the need for "source water supply and protection" strategies. *Water Res.* **2011**, *45*, 461–472. [CrossRef] [PubMed]
14. Shi, P.; Kasperson, R. *World Atlas of Natural Disaster Risk*; Springer: Berlin, Germany, 2015.
15. Bowman, D.M.J.S.; Balch, J.K.; Artaxo, P.; Bond, W.J.; Carlson, J.M.; Cochrane, M.A.; Antonio, C.M.D.; Defries, R.S.; Doyle, J.C.; Harrison, S.P.; *et al.* Fire in the Earth System. *Science* **2009**, *324*, 481–484. [CrossRef] [PubMed]
16. Knorr, W.; Kaminski, T.; Arneth, A.; Weber, U. Impact of human population density on fire frequency at the global scale. *Biogeosciences* **2014**, *11*, 1085–1102. [CrossRef]
17. Oki, T.; Kanae, S. Global hydrological cycles and world water resources. *Science* **2006**, *313*, 1068–1072. [CrossRef] [PubMed]

18. Davies, E.G.R.; Simonovic, S.P. Global water resources modeling with an integrated model of the social-economic-environmental system. *Adv. Water Resour.* **2011**, *34*, 684–700. [CrossRef]
19. Freudenberger, L.; Hobson, P.R.; Schluck, M.; Ibisch, P.L. A global map of the functionality of terrestrial ecosystems. *Ecol. Complex.* **2012**, *12*, 13–22. [CrossRef]
20. Vörösmarty, C.J.; McIntyre, P.B.; Gessner, M.O.; Dudgeon, D.; Prusevich, A.; Green, P.A.; Glidden, S.; Bunn, S.E.; Sullivan, C.A.; Liermann, C.R.; *et al.* Global threats to human water security and river biodiversity. *Nature* **2010**, *467*, 555–561. [CrossRef] [PubMed]
21. Dickson, B.; Blaney, R.; Miles, L.; Regan, E.; van Soesbergen, A.; Väänänen, E.; Blyth, S.; Harfoot, M.; Martin, C.S.; McOwen, C.; *et al. Towards a Global Map of Natural Capital: KEY Ecosystem Assets*; United Nations Environment Program: Nairobi, Kenya, 2014.
22. Halpern, B.S.; Walbridge, S.; Selkoe, K.A.; Kappel, C.V.; Micheli, F.; D'Agrosa, C.; Bruno, J.F.; Casey, K.S.; Ebert, C.; Fox, H.E.; *et al.* A global map of human impact on marine ecosystems. *Science* **2008**, *319*, 948–952. [CrossRef] [PubMed]
23. Krawchuk, M.A.; Moritz, M.A.; Parisien, M.-A.; van Dorn, J.; Hayhoe, K. Global pyrogeography: The current and future distribution of wildfire. *PLoS ONE* **2009**, *4*, e5102. [CrossRef] [PubMed]
24. Giglio, L.; Randerson, J.T.; van der Werf, G.R. Analysis of daily, monthly, and annual burned area using the fourth-generation global fire emissions database (GFED4). *J. Geophys. Res. Biogeosci.* **2013**, *118*, 317–328. [CrossRef]
25. Giglio, L.; Loboda, T.; Roy, D.P.; Quayle, B.; Justice, C.O. An active-fire based burned area mapping algorithm for the MODIS sensor. *Remote Sens. Environ.* **2009**, *113*, 408–420. [CrossRef]
26. Van Wagner, C. *Development and Structure of the Canadian Forest Fire Weather Index System*; Canadian Forestry Servic, Ed.; Government of Canada: Ottawa, ON, Canada, 1987.
27. Field, R.D.; Spessa, A.C.; Aziz, N.A.; Camia, A.; Cantin, A.; Carr, R.; de Groot, W.J.; Dowdy, A.J.; Flannigan, M.D.; Manomaiphiboon, K.; *et al.* Development of a Global Fire Weather Database. *Nat. Hazards Earth Syst. Sci.* **2015**, *15*, 1407–1423. [CrossRef]
28. Chen, M.; Shi, W.; Xie, P.; Silva, V.B.S.; Kousky, V.E.; Higgins, R.W.; Janowiak, J.E. Assessing objective techniques for gauge-based analyses of global daily precipitation. *J. Geophys. Res. Atmos.* **2008**, *113*, 1–13. [CrossRef]
29. Stocks, B.J.; Mason, J.A.; Todd, J.B.; Bosch, E.M.; Wotton, M.B.; Amiro, B.D.; Flannigan, M.D.; Hirsch, K.G.; Logan, K.A.; Martell, D.L.; *et al.* Large forest fires in Canada, 1959–1997. *J. Geophys. Res.* **2002**, *108*, 8149. [CrossRef]
30. Bond, W.J.; Keeley, J.E. Fire as a global "herbivore": The ecology and evolution of flammable ecosystems. *Trends Ecol. Evol.* **2005**, *20*, 387–394. [CrossRef] [PubMed]
31. Ramos-Neto, M.B.; Pivello, V.R. Lightning fires in a Brazilian Savanna National Park: Rethinking management strategies. *Environ. Manag.* **2000**, *26*, 675–684. [CrossRef] [PubMed]
32. Cecil, D.J.; Buechler, D.E.; Blakeslee, R.J. Gridded lightning climatology from TRMM-LIS and OTD: Dataset description. *Atmos. Res.* **2014**, *135–136*, 404–414. [CrossRef]
33. Aldersley, A.; Murray, S.J.; Cornell, S.E. Global and regional analysis of climate and human drivers of wildfire. *Sci. Total Environ.* **2011**, *409*, 3472–3481. [CrossRef] [PubMed]
34. Bistinas, I.; Oom, D.; Sá, A.C.L.; Harrison, S.P.; Prentice, C.I.; Pereira, J.M.C. Relationships between human population density and burned area at continental and global scales. *PLoS ONE* **2013**, *8*, e81188. [CrossRef] [PubMed]
35. Archibald, S.; Lehmann, C.E. R.; Gómez-dans, J.L.; Bradstock, R.A. Defining pyromes and global syndromes of fire regimes. *Proc. Natl. Acad. Sci. USA* **2013**, *110*, 6442–6447. [CrossRef] [PubMed]
36. Sanderson, E.W.; Jaiteh, M.; Levy, M.A.; Redford, K.H.; Wannebo, A.V.; Woolmer, G. The Human Footprint and the Last of the Wild. *Bioscience* **2002**, *52*, 891–904. [CrossRef]
37. Fekete, B.M. High-resolution fields of global runoff combining observed river discharge and simulated water balances. *Glob. Biogeochem. Cycles* **2002**, *16*, 15-1–15-10. [CrossRef]
38. GWSP. *Digital Water Atlas Map 38: Mean Annual Surface Runoff 1950–2000 (V1.0)*; GWSP International Project Office: Bonn, Germany, 2008.
39. Kasischke, E.S.; Bourgeau-Chavez, L.L.; Johnstone, J.F. Assessing spatial and temporal variations in surface soil moisture in fire-disturbed black spruce forests in Interior Alaska using spaceborne synthetic aperture radar imagery—Implications for post-fire tree recruitment. *Remote Sens. Environ.* **2007**, *108*, 42–58. [CrossRef]

40. Willmott, C.J.; Matsuura, K. *Terrestrial Water Budget Data Archive: Monthly Time Series (1950–1999)*; University of Delaware: Newark, DE, USA, 2001.

41. Legates, D.R.; Willmott, C.J. Mean seasonal and spatial variability in gauge-corrected, global precipitation. *Int. J. Climatol.* **1990**, *10*, 111–127. [CrossRef]

42. Legates, D.R.; Willmott, C.J. Mean seasonal and spatial variability in global surface air temperature. *Theor. Appl. Climatol.* **1990**, *41*, 11–21. [CrossRef]

43. Moody, J.A.; Ebel, B.A.; Nyman, P.; Martin, D.A.; Stoof, C.; McKinley, R. Relations between soil hydraulic properties and burn severity. *Int. J. Wildland Fire* **2016**. in press. [CrossRef]

44. Nolan, R.H.; Lane, P.N.J.; Benyon, R.G.; Bradstock, R.A.; Mitchell, P.J. Changes in evapotranspiration following wildfire in resprouting eucalypt forests. *Ecohydrology* **2014**, *7*, 1363–1377. [CrossRef]

45. Zomer, R.J.; Trabucco, A.; van Straaten, O.; Bossio, D.A. *Carbon, Land and Water:A Global Analysis of the Hydrologic Dimensions of Climate Change Mitigation through Afforestation/Reforestation*; International Water Management Institute: Colombo, Sri Lanka, 2006; Volume 101.

46. Environmental Systems Research Institute. *ArcGIS: Release 10.1 SP1 for Desktop*; Environmental Systems Research Institute: Redlands, CA, USA, 2012.

47. Biber, D.; Freudenberger, L.; Ibisch, P.L. *Insensa-GIS: An Open-Source Software Tool for GIS Data Processing and Statistical Analysis*; Eberswalde University for Sustainable Development: Eberswalde, Germany, 2011.

48. OECD. *Handbook on Constructing Composite Indicators*; European Comission: Bruxelles, Belgium, 2008.

49. Olson, D.M.; Dinerstein, E.; Wikramanayake, E.D.; Burgess, N.D.; Powell, G.V.N.; Underwood, E.C.; D'amico, J.A.; Itoua, I.; Strand, H.E.; Morrison, J.C.; *et al.* Terrestrial Ecoregions of the World: A New Map of Life on Earth. *Bioscience* **2001**, *51*, 933–938. [CrossRef]

50. Falkenmark, M. The Greatest Water Problem: The Inability to Link Environmental Security, Water Security and Food Security. *Int. J. Water Resour. Dev.* **2001**, *17*, 539–554. [CrossRef]

51. Norman, E.; Cook, C.; Dunn, G.; Allen, D. *Water Security: A Primer*; University of British Columbia: Vancouver, BC, Canada, 2010.

52. Postel, S.L.; Daily, G.C.; Ehrlich, P.R. Human Appropriation Of Renewable Fresh Water. *Science* **1996**, *271*, 785–788. [CrossRef]

53. Falkenmark, M.; Rockström, J.; Karlberg, L. Present and future water requirements for feeding humanity. *Food Secur.* **2009**, *1*, 59–69. [CrossRef]

54. Santos, R.M.B.; Sanches Fernandes, L.F.; Pereira, M.G.; Cortes, R.M.V.; Pacheco, F.A.L. Water resources planning for a river basin with recurrent wildfires. *Sci. Total Environ.* **2015**, *526*, 1–13. [CrossRef] [PubMed]

55. Ho Sham, C.; Tuccillo, M.E.; Rooke, J. *Effects of Wildfire on Drinking Water Utilities and Best Practices for Wildfire Risk Reduction and Mitigation*; Water Research Foundation: Denver, CO, USA, 2013.

56. Viviroli, D.; Dürr, H.H.; Messerli, B.; Meybeck, M.; Weingartner, R. Mountains of the world, water towers for humanity: Typology, mapping, and global significance. *Water Resour. Res.* **2007**, *43*, 1–13.

57. Nogués-Bravo, D.; Araújo, M.B.; Errea, M.P.; Martínez-Rica, J.P. Exposure of global mountain systems to climate warming during the 21st Century. *Glob. Environ. Chang.* **2007**, *17*, 420–428. [CrossRef]

58. Mori, A.S.; Johnson, E.A. Assessing possible shifts in wildfire regimes under a changing climate in mountainous landscapes. *For. Ecol. Manag.* **2013**, *310*, 875–886. [CrossRef]

59. Green, P.A.; Vörösmarty, C.J.; Harrison, I.; Farrell, T.; Sáenz, L.; Fekete, B.M. Freshwater ecosystem services supporting humans: Pivoting from water crisis to water solutions. *Glob. Environ. Chang.* **2015**, *34*, 108–118. [CrossRef]

60. McDonald, R.I.; Weber, K.; Padowski, J.; Flörke, M.; Schneider, C.; Green, P.A.; Gleeson, T.; Eckman, S.; Lehner, B.; Balk, D.; *et al.* Water on an urban planet: Urbanization and the reach of urban water infrastructure. *Glob. Environ. Chang.* **2014**, *27*, 96–105. [CrossRef]

61. Bladon, K.D.; Emelko, M.B.; Silins, U.; Stone, M. Wildfire and the Future of Water Supply. *Environ. Sci. Technol.* **2014**, *48*, 8936–8943. [CrossRef] [PubMed]

62. Dudley, N.; Stolton, S. *Running Pure*; World Bank/WWF Alliance for Forest Conservation and Sustainable Use: Washington, DC, USA, 2003.

63. Millar, C.I.; Stephenson, N.L. Temperate forest health in an era of emerging megadisturbance. *Science* **2015**, *349*, 823–826. [CrossRef] [PubMed]

64. Moritz, M.A.; Parisien, M.-A.; Batllori, E. Climate change and disruptions to global fire activity. *Ecosphere* **2012**, *3*, 1–22. [CrossRef]

65. Alcamo, J.M.; Flörke, M.; Märker, M. Future long-term changes in global water resources driven by socio-economic and climatic changes. *Hydrol. Sci. J.* **2007**, *52*, 247–275. [CrossRef]

66. Miller, C.; Ager, A.A. A review of recent advances in risk analysis for wildfire management. *Int. J. Wildland Fire* **2013**, *22*, 1–14. [CrossRef]

67. Vörösmarty, C.J.; Douglas, E.M.; Green, P.A.; Revenga, C. Geospatial indicators of emerging water stress: An application to Africa. *Ambio* **2005**, *34*, 230–236. [CrossRef] [PubMed]

68. Lerner-Lam, A. Assessing global exposure to natural hazards: Progress and future trends. *Environ. Hazards* **2007**, *7*, 10–19. [CrossRef]

69. Peduzzi, P.; Dao, H.; Herold, C.; Mouton, F. Assessing global exposure and vulnerability towards natural hazards: the Disaster Risk Index. *Nat. Hazards Earth Syst. Sci.* **2009**, *9*, 1149–1159. [CrossRef]

MDPI AG

St. Alban-Anlage 66

4052 Basel, Switzerland

Tel. +41 61 683 77 34

Fax +41 61 302 89 18

http://www.mdpi.com

Forests Editorial Office

E-mail: forests@mdpi.com

http://www.mdpi.com/journal/forests

www.ingramcontent.com/pod-product-compliance
Lightning Source LLC
Chambersburg PA
CBHW051314020426
42333CB00028B/3329